Butoh and Suzuki Performance in Australia

Australian Playwrights

AND AUSTRALIAN DRAMA, THEATRE AND PERFORMANCE

Series editor

Jonathan Bollen (*National Taiwan Normal University*)

Founded by

Ortrun Zuber-Skerritt

Developed by

Veronica Kelly, Peta Tait and Denise Varney

VOLUME 20

The titles published in this series are listed at *brill.com/ap*

Butoh and Suzuki Performance in Australia

Bent Legs on Strange Grounds, 1982–2023

By

Jonathan W. Marshall

BRILL

LEIDEN | BOSTON

Cover illustration: Yumi Umiumare (left) & Ben Rogan (right) in DasSHOKU Hora!! (Malthouse: 2006). Photograph Jeff Busby. Reproduction courtesy of Busby.

Library of Congress Cataloging-in-Publication Data

Names: Marshall, Jonathan W., author.
Title: Butoh and Suzuki performance in Australia : bent legs on strange grounds, 1982-2023 / by Jonathan W. Marshall.
Description: Leiden ; Boston : Brill, 2025. | Series: Australian playwrights, 0921-2531 ; vol.20 | Includes bibliographical references and index.
Identifiers: LCCN 2024050182 (print) | LCCN 2024050183 (ebook) | ISBN 9789004712300 (paperback) | ISBN 9789004712317 (ebook)
Subjects: LCSH: Butō–Australia. | Modern dance–Australia. | Suzuki, Tadashi, 1939—Influence. | Dance–Australia–Japanese influences.
Classification: LCC GV1783.2.B87 M37 2025 (print) | LCC GV1783.2.B87 (ebook) | DDC 792.80994–dc23/eng/20241112
LC record available at https://lccn.loc.gov/2024050182
LC ebook record available at https://lccn.loc.gov/2024050183

Typeface for the Latin, Greek, and Cyrillic scripts: "Brill". See and download: brill.com/brill-typeface.

ISSN 0921-2531
ISBN 978-90-04-71230-0 (paperback)
ISBN 978-90-04-71231-7 (e-book)
DOI 10.1163/9789004712317

Copyright 2025 by Koninklijke Brill BV, Plantijnstraat 2, 2321 JC Leiden, The Netherlands.
Koninklijke Brill BV incorporates the imprints Brill, Brill Nijhoff, Brill Schöningh, Brill Fink, Brill mentis, Brill Wageningen Academic, Vandenhoeck & Ruprecht, Böhlau and V&R unipress.
All rights reserved. No part of this publication may be reproduced, translated, stored in a retrieval system, or transmitted in any form or by any means, electronic, mechanical, photocopying, recording or otherwise, without prior written permission from the publisher. Requests for re-use and/or translations must be addressed to Koninklijke Brill BV via brill.com or copyright.com.
For more information: info@brill.com.

This book is printed on acid-free paper and produced in a sustainable manner.

[*Maro said*] "The Butoh virus is spreading now. You've got the Butoh virus already!" Maro felt happy about making people "sick" with the Butoh virus. He knew they would then go back to their countries and spread it to other people ... Butoh ... makes some people crazy ... I'm very happy when I think about that.

—*Yuyama Daiichiro of Dairakudakan (Bradley 2017: 248)*

Contents

Acknowledgements XI
List of Figures XII

1   Bodies Possessed by History: An Introduction to Butoh and Suzuki 1
    1   Introduction 1
    2   Butoh, Suzuki and the Move to Australia 3
    3   Primal Scenes of Butoh Encounter 4
    4   What is Butoh? 8
    5   Suzuki Technique and the Way of Stomping 11
    6   Lineages of Descent Ancient and Modern in Butoh and Suzuki 14
    7   Butoh and Suzuki Technique in Other National Contexts 19
    8   Criticism and Reception of Japanese Performance in Australia 21
    9   Emptiness and Possession 24
    10   Primary Sources and Thick Description 25
    11   Overview and Book Structure 27

2   Butoh and the Australian Context: Dancing the Landscape while Dancing Global Relations 30
    1   Introduction 30
    2   Consolidation in Japan and Movement to Australia 31
    3   Tanaka's "Map of History through Dancing" in the Contested Lands of Australia 33
    4   Corpus Nullius: Moving beyond the Emptiness of the Butoh Body 34
    5   Expressive Japanese Performance as a Counter to the Postmodern "Performance of Absence" 36
    6   Bodies in Opposition to the Australian Legend: Butoh, Suzuki and Grotowski 39
    7   Troubled Relations between Australia and Asia Prior to the Japan Theatre Boom 43
    8   The Japanese Theatrical Boom in Australia, 1982–1994 48

3   De Quincey Takes Body Weather Inland: Lake Mungo and Alice Springs 50
    1   Introduction 50
    2   De Quincey's Butoh Encounter and Position within Australian Dance 50

    3   Tanaka Min and Body Weather   52
    4   De Quincey's Development from Postwar Britain to Australia   56
    5   De Quincey's First Solos in Australia   61
    6   Body Weather as an Uncanny Project: Tracing an "Interactive History of the Senses" on Australia's Colonised Lands   63
    7   De Quincey's Lake Mungo Workshops, 1991–92, and beyond   65
    8   Lake Mungo Performance Works and on to Alice Springs   73
    9   Triple Alice, 1999–2001   79
    10   Triple Alice Performances and *Dictionary of Atmospheres* (2005)   98

4   **Body Weather Comes Back from the Desert: De Quincey's Urban Works, the Hysterical Body, and Other Body Weather Performers in Australia**   105
    1   Introduction   105
    2   De Quincey's Urban and Industrial Site-Specific Works: *Compression 100* (1996), *City to City* (2000), *The Stirring* (2007), *Run* (2009)   105
    3   A Masterpiece of Hysterio-Choreography: *Nerve 9* (2001–05)   114
    4   Other Body Weather Artists in Australia   119
    5   Heywood and Humanimal Body Weather   119
    6   European Tanztheater Meets Australian Body Weather: Martin Del Amo   121
    7   Post-Colonial Butoh and Rejecting the Empty Body: Gretel Taylor   124
    8   Evidence of Bodily Emergences   128
    9   Fragmented and Dialectical Bodies   129

5   **Diasporic Austral-Asian Fusions 1: Early Works by Umiumare and Yap**   131
    1   Introduction   131
    2   Umiumare's and Yap's Butoh Encounters   131
    3   Umiumare and Yap within the Context Butoh   133
    4   Maro and Dairakudakan   135
    5   Umiumare: From Regional Japan to Urban Australia   141
    5   Tony Ding Chai Yap: From Melakan Trance to Australian Physical Theatre   146
    6   Theatre of Sacrifice and Redemption: Yap in IRAA, 1988–94   150
    7   Mixed Company and Tony Yap Company, 1993-Present   153
    8   Umiumare and Yap in *Love Suicides* (1998), *Miss Tanaka* (2001), and *Meat Party* (2000)   154
    9   *Kagome* (1996–98)   158
    10   *Sunrise at Midnight* (2001): A Sequel to De Quincey's Mungo Workshops   162

CONTENTS   IX

    11   Duets by Umiumare and Yap: *How Could You Even Begin to Understand?* (1996–2007), *In-Compatibility* (2003) and *Zero Zero* (2010–14)   166
    12   Umiumare's *Fleeting Moments* (1998)   170
    13   Yap's *Decay of the Angel* (1999)   172
    14   Conclusion   174

6   Diasporic Austral-Asian Fusions 2: Yap's Trance Dance and Umiumare's Butoh Cabaret, Character Dances and First Nations Collaborations   176
    1   Introduction   176
    2   Butoh Cabaret and Hystericised Character Dances: Umiumare's *DasSHOKU* Series (1999–2015) and *EnTrance* (2009–12)   177
    3   Umiumare's First Nations Collaborations: Marrugeku's *Burning Daylight* (2006–09) and Big hArt's *Ngapartji Ngapartji* (2007–12)   188
    4   Yap and Trance Dance; Umiumare and Jujutsu   199
    5   Yap's *Eulogy for the Living* (2009–17), *Rasa Sayang* (2010), and *Liminal City* (2021–22)   204
    6   A Trance Dance Masterpiece: Yap's *Animal/God: The Great Square* (2021)   207
    7   Conclusion: Yap's MAP Fest (2008-Present) and Umiumare's ButohOUT! (2017-Present)   209

7   Stomping Downunder: Suzuki and Frank Theatre   211
    1   Introduction   211
    2   Carroll's and Nobbs' Encounters with Suzuki   212
    3   Suzuki Tadashi in Japan and Australia   214
    4   The Australian Production of *Chronicle of Macbeth* (1992)   228
    5   Foundation of Frank Theatre   233
    6   Larrikin Orientalism: Frank Theatre's Early Works   235
    7   Universalism, Localism and Racial Hierarchies   241
    8   Nobbs Suzuki Praxis (NSP)   243
    9   Butoh Incursions, the Hysterical Body, and Emptiness   246
    10   Frank's *Doll Seventeen* (2002–03)   248
    11   Conclusion: The Way Forward is Mixed   253

8   Butoh in the Southern Tropics: Zen Zen Zo and Associates   255
    1   Introduction   255
    2   Bradley's and Woods' Encounters with Japanese Performance   255
    3   Zen Zen Zo's Foundation and the Development of Its Aesthetic, 1992–98   257

    4   Zen Zen Zo's Early Work and Brisbane Physical Theatre   259
    5   Zen Zen Zo, Frank and Reworking Japanese Aesthetics   263
    6   Zen Zen Zo's Early Butoh Productions and Butoh Choruses   272
    7   Fusing Butoh with Suzuki: Zen Zen Zo's *Cult of Dionysus* (1994–96)   278
    8   Frances Barbe's Tōhoku Australis   282
    9   Butoh Diffusions   285

9   Conclusion: Two Closing Scenes from Australian Adaptations of Butoh and Suzuki   288
    1   NYID's *the Dispossessed* (2008) and Hunt's *Copper Promises* (2016)   288

Bibliography   295
Index   325

Acknowledgements

The genesis of this book is, like that of butoh itself, multiple and braided. It was Peter Eckersall who first suggested the idea of writing a historical survey of butoh in Australia, but the seeds of this book were sown earlier. In 1992, as an undergraduate at the University of Melbourne, I was in the unusual position of being invited by Norman Price and Glenn D'Cruz to act as dramaturg on Price's adaptation of Mishima Yukio's *Madame de Sade*—a choice of play undoubtedly inspired by Suzuki Tadashi's initial suggestion for what he wanted to stage for Playbox. I delivered to my peers four of my own lectures on Japanese history, performance, and Mishima. In order to do this, I was given access to Price's collection of documents on butoh and Suzuki. I still have photocopies of many of these items, and some are cited in this book. I was subsequently fortunate to be generously accepted as a critic and commentator by many of the artists cited in this book, who not only staged performances discussed below, but also in many instances shared with me their perspectives as well as documents and videos. Tony Yap deserves my special thanks for acting as one of two research assistants on my contribution to the Australian Research Council Linkage Infrastructure, Equipment and Facilities project AusStage LIEF 7: The International Breakthrough, together with Sean Weatherly. I have, at one time or another, received generous support, advice and/or information from Tess de Quincey, Anne Norman, Yumi Umiumare, Darren Jorgenson, Ian Maxwell, Frances Barbe, Jeremy Neideck, Jacqui Carroll, Lynne Bradley, Simon Woods, David Pledger, Peter Eckersall, Rosemary Candelario, Marnie Kee née Orr, Ben Rogan, Matthew Crosby, Nareeporn Vachananda, Robert Reid, Martin Del Amo, Gretel Taylor, Paul Monaghan, Rachael Swain, Nourit Masson-Sékiné, Michael Sakamoto, Jim Denley, Darrin Verhagen, Amanda Stewart, Peta Tait, Rosa van Hensbergen, and others. In addition, I would particularly like to thank those who helped source images for this book and in many cases generously supplied reproductions at little or no charge. I am grateful to you all. While influenced by the many individuals whose ideas and materials I have drawn upon, I take responsibility for the opinions, arguments, and any errors in this book.

Finally, no book is possible without editorial help and guidance, and I would like to thank Jonathan Bollen for his support of this project, as well as my partner Sharon Matthews, who has listened to and read much of this work several times.

Figures

1   Members of Dairakudakan in *Natsu no Inori* (*A Summer's Prayer*) (Hakuba: 2015). Photo: Simon Woods. Reproduction courtesy of Woods.   3

2   Director Suzuki Tadashi's *Chronicle of Macbeth* (Playbox: 1992). Left to right: Oliver Sidore (Chorus / Witch #2), John Nobbs (Banquo's Ghost) and Peter Curtin (Macbeth). Photo: Reimund Zunde. Reproduction courtesy of Zunde.   12

3   Frances Barbe's *Fine Bone China* (Brisbane tour, programmed by Frank at the Woodward Theatre: 2008). Photo: Phil Hargreaves. Reproduction courtesy of Barbe and Hargreaves.   38

4   Direct engagement with the national landscape: Lynne Santos in *Golden Circle* installation by Keith Armstrong and Richard Manner, one in a series of performance installations as part of De Quincey Co's *Triple Alice 1* (Hamilton Downs, Arrernte Country, Central Desert, 1999). Archival video-still courtesy of Armstrong.   47

5   Tess de Quincey in *IS* (The Performance Space: 1994). Installation and projections Stuart Lynch. Photo: Robyn Murphy. Image courtesy of De Quincey Co.   76

6   De Quincey Co's *Dictionary of Atmospheres* (Lhere Mparntwe/Todd Riverbed, Alice Springs Festival, Arrernte Country, Central Australia: 2005). Performers left to right: Linda Luke, Kristina Harrison, Victoria Hunt, Tom Davies, Peter Fraser. Photo: Mayu Kanamori. Courtesy of Kanamori.   102

7   De Quincey Co's *Run – A Performance Engine* (The Performance Space: 2009). Performers: Tom Davies (left) and Victoria Hunt (right). Photo: Heidrun Löhr. Image courtesy of Löhr and De Quincey Co.   112

8   Tess de Quincey in *Nerve 9* (The Performance Space: 2002). Projections and photo Russell Emerson. Courtesy of Theatre and Performance Studies, University of Sydney, and De Quincey Co.   116

9   Yumi Umiumare (left) and Tony Yap (right) in *Sunrise at Midnight* (writer/dir. Sean O'Brien: 2001). Archival video still courtesy of O'Brien.   163

10   Tony Yap (left) and Yumi Umiumare (right) in *Zero Zero* (2010), from Yap (2011). Courtesy Of Yap.   167

11   Tony Yap in *Decay of the Angel* (Chapel of Change: 1999). Photo: Rainsford (Paul Towner). Reproduction courtesy of Yap.   173

12   Trevor Jamieson (left) and Yumi Umiumare (right) in *Ngapartji Ngapartji* (Belvoir Street Theatre: 2008). Photo: Heidrun Löhr. Reproduction courtesy of Löhr.   196

13   Tony Yap in *Animal/God: The Great Square* (2021). Courtesy of Yap.   208

FIGURES	XIII

14 Frank Theatre's *Romance of Orpheus* (Princess Theatre: 1994; dir. Jacqui Carroll). Image left shows John Nobbs (Orpheus, at the left) and Irena Haze (Euridice, right). Image right shows Nobbs (forward) with chorus of (left to right): Lisa O'Neill, Frances Barbe, Christina Koch, Sonia Davies. Images courtesy of Carroll and Nobbs.   237

15 Frank Theatre's *Doll Seventeen,* by Ray Lawler (Visy Theatre, Brisbane Powerhouse: 2002; dir. Jacqui Carroll). Left to right: Lisa O'Neill (The Doll), Conan Dunning (Barney), Leah Shelton (Pearl), Caroline Dunphy (Olive), John Nobbs (Roo). Image courtesy of Carroll and Nobbs.   250

16 Mark Hill (left) and Dale Thorburn (right) in Zen Zen Zo Physical Theatre's *Zeitgeist* (dir. and choreog. Lynne Bradley; Old Museum: 2008). Photo: Simon Woods. Reproduction courtesy of Woods.   273

17 Zen Zen Zo Physical Theatre's *Cult of Dionysus* (dir. Simon Woods; movement dir. Lynne Bradley; Princess Theatre: 1996). Image at left shows the Chorus of (left to right): Stacey Callaghan, Rebecca Murray, Lynne Bradley, Helen Cassidy. Image at right shows Christopher Beckey as Dionysus (left) and Peter Lamb as Pentheus (right). Stills from archival video by Woods.   279

18 *The Dispossessed* (Seoul Arts Centre: 2008), presented by Seoul Performing Arts Festival and co-produced by NYID with Wuturi Theatre; concept/direction David Pledger. Photos: Guiman Shin. Reproduction courtesy of NYID.   289

19 Victoria Hunt in *Copper Promises: Hinemihi Haka* (Sydney: The Performance Space, 2016). Photo: Heidrun Löhr. Reproduction courtesy of Victoria Hunt.   290

CHAPTER 1

Bodies Possessed by History: An Introduction to Butoh and Suzuki

1   Introduction

Butoh dance and Suzuki technique are physical theatre forms that aim to harness energies and forces from outside of the body to move and dance. Butoh and Suzuki technique originated in Japan during the 1960s, achieving global recognition in the 1980s and 1990s. They involve the performer undertaking intensive physical training in methods distinctive to each. There are however overlaps in terms of physical regimen and the rhetoric which surrounds them. A number of individual performers brought these methods to Australia in the 1990s and these techniques have been widely used as well as taught at Australia's leading arts academies, theatres, and elsewhere. This book traces the evolution of butoh and Suzuki in Australia through a close analysis of key artists active in Australia since the 1990s. I argue that the Japanese origins of the two forms were both a boon and a hinderance to their adoption in Australia, and it has taken many years for anything akin to a naturalisation process to have been achieved. This transition is the focus of my discussion.

I sketch an overarching historical portrait of Australian butoh and Suzuki practitioners by surveying central pioneering figures and companies in Australia, specifically Tess de Quincey, Tanaka Min, Yumi Umiumare, Tony Ding Chai Yap, Maro Akaji, John Nobbs, Jacqui Carroll, Suzuki Tadashi, Lynne Bradley, Simon Woods and Frances Barbe. The lineage for these techniques derives principally from Tanaka, Maro and Suzuki, while butoh's founder Hijikata Tatsumi has also been a significant influence in Australia, his approach being communicated indirectly via former students Tanaka and Maro, as well as through Hijikata's published writings and photographic documentation. Hijikata's association with author Mishima Yukio also meant that where butoh was invoked, allusions to Mishima's life and novels were often drawn upon, as was the case for Yap. I situate my analyses of the Australian artists in relation to the work of Hijikata, Tanaka, Maro and Suzuki.

In 1982, Tanaka Min became the first butoh artist to visit Australia (Cermak 1982; Molloy 1982: 1). Billed as gallery performance rather than dance, this event had little immediate impact, but it heralded the forthcoming introduction of Japanese physical theatre into the Australian context during the 1990s. Several of Tanaka's former students produced influential projects in Australia, as well as training others. Tess de Quincey in particular pioneered Tanaka's sub-genre of Body Weather, subjecting the reactive body of herself and her dancers to the harsh landscapes of the interior of the continent, as well as exploring hysterical, abject and industrialised bodies. Ten years after Tanaka's first visit, the Japanese butoh company Dairakudakan toured Australia with their signature piece *Kaiin no Uma* (*Tale of the Sea-Dappled Horse*), featuring director Maro Akaji. Yumi Umiumare, a member of Dairakudakan, moved to Australia after 1992, offering workshops and performances (Umiumare and Eckersall 2012). Several other Australians came to draw on Maro's approach, notably Lynne Bradley of Zen Zen Zo Physical Theatre company, founded in Brisbane by Bradley and Simon Woods in 1992 (Woods 2006: 7). Umiumare, Bradley and Woods would all produce their own butoh-esque works in Australia and train others. Japanese theatre maker Suzuki Tadashi directed Playbox Theatre's 1992 production *Chronicle of Macbeth*, converting many Australians to his related if distinct model of physical theatre. Bradley and Woods synthesised elements of his approach with that of butoh, while Jacqui Carroll and John Nobbs were more faithful to Suzuki's method. Carroll and Nobbs founded Frank Theatre at the end of 1992, staging works and developing a local variant of Suzuki training (Carroll 1998: 35). Umiumare, Zen Zen Zo and Frank shared a spectacular, often comedic style of episodic performance derived from the exuberant tableaux of Suzuki and Maro (Figure 1), and, in the case of Zen Zen Zo and Frank, often featured butoh-like choruses. Tony Yap was originally associated with Grotowski style physical performance produced by IRAA theatre in Melbourne, but he became identified with butoh during the 1990s, partly through his collaborations with Umiumare, but also because Yap developed his own form of trance dance, inspired both by butoh and by ritual practices of the Indo-Pacific region (Yap and Eckersall 2012). Yap too has trained and influenced many others.

My contention is that the discursive construction of butoh and Suzuki technique caused the pathways followed by their adherents in Australia to move beyond being simply derivative of Japanese practices, and hence the story of butoh and Suzuki in Australia puts key elements of the two forms into relief, acting to rewrite history by developing new lineages and ancestors in Australia and elsewhere. This is characteristic of butoh globally (see Marshall 2013). Suzuki and butoh offered an emotional expressivity at a time when Expressionist dance and theatre was under challenge. Butoh and Suzuki technique were seen as offering an alternative to Naturalistic psychological acting and formalistic postmodern dance. Appeals to the body have provided the main strategies for localised acculturation, as well as subtle shifts of rhetoric, or in the case of Yap's diasporic work, and Umiumare's collaborations with First Nations artists, shifts and movements which disrupt ethnic positioning itself.

FIGURE 1 Members of Dairakudakan in *Natsu no Inori* (*A Summer's Prayer*) (Hakuba: 2015)
PHOTO: SIMON WOODS. REPRODUCTION COURTESY OF WOODS

Despite this, the Japanese heritage of both forms has proven hard to shake, and still resonates today.

Butoh and Suzuki activate historical, political and racial forces within bodies and cultures, offering an explicitly material response to the past and the present, which is manifest—first and foremost—through the body of the performer and its responses to sensory and discursive inputs. Bodies become porous and shake with histories real and fantasmatic. The body constructed out of the engagement with these techniques has a transhistorical character, serving to bridge spaces and times in ways which can be unsettling, particularly in colonialist and imperialist contexts of Australia and Japan. Butoh and Suzuki technique work to critically estrange rather than to comfortably emplace; to render expression as Uncanny and haunted, rather than render it as unified or grounded. As Hijikata observed, butoh presents a vision of a "corpse standing straight up in a desperate bid for life" (Hijikata et al. 1993: 58).

2 Butoh, Suzuki and the Move to Australia

This first chapter of the book introduces the Japanese postwar dance of butoh, and the allied theatre work of Suzuki Tadashi, both often being described as centred around low to the ground movement and acts of possession. I examine the concept of stomping and the use of language as generative of movement as factors which link Suzuki's approach to butoh dance. Body Weather is a third related dance form, which was developed by Tanaka, with some input by butoh dancers from Dairakudakan and other groups (Baird 2022: 214). Tanaka would later affiliate himself with Hijikata, and continued to teach Hijikata's choreographies after the latter's death in 1986. I analyse the key features of Japanese butoh, referring to Hijikata's *Kinjiki* (1959), *Nikutai no Hanran* (1968), and the growth of "white butoh" companies which developed out of Dairakudakan.

I note the widespread interest of butoh artists, Suzuki, and those modernists who influenced them, in primal, premodern and/or folk cultures. Nearly all of the Australian artists, as well as the Japanese, saw butoh and Suzuki technique as excavating something primal and premodern in the human subject, which needed to be reworked to reform modernity. This interest led some artists in Australia to evoke a relation with First Nations cultural practice.

In this chapter I briefly survey key scholarship around butoh and Suzuki in Australia, and identify my approach as a national-cultural analysis in which I focus on the formal elements, mise en scène and the discourse surrounding these arts, aligning my work with historical applications of Clifford Geertz's semiological model of "thick description" and Robert Darnton's cultural history. The Australian context into which butoh and Suzuki technique emerged from the 1980s onwards is further developed in chapter two.

3 Primal Scenes of Butoh Encounter

In the early 1990s, I switched on the television to see what was showing on the Australian Broadcasting Corporation's *Arts on Sunday* program. I was awestruck. This screening introduced me personally—and many of my peers—to the worlds of butoh, Suzuki and Body Weather.

The ABC was showing the ground-breaking Franco-Japanese butoh company, Sankai Juku, specifically video documentation of *Unetsu* (*Eggs Standing Out of Curiosity*), which had toured the Adelaide Festival in 1988. These and other productions from Sankai Juku helped establish the international profile of what butoh looked like—although many butoh artists did not perform quite what Sankai Juku offered. The ensemble featured four bald, visibly Asian performers in white makeup. Although presumably men, their svelte form, earrings, and dress-like costumes established a sense of gender ambiguity or crossing. Hand movements were intricate and involved, mouths often agape, the performers either emoting outwards in extreme poses, or intensely focussed inward. Asymmetrical, crooked limbs and bent poses arose in climactic scenes as Amagatsu Ushio first exploded into frenetic action, and then stood recovering, his chest and intercostal muscles heaving even as the rest of his body remained motionless. The music ranged from meditative to extremely loud. I could not remember seeing anything like it before and I was hooked.

Many artists from Australia and elsewhere relate a similar moment of encounter, where the speaker witnessed a disorientating yet mesmerising example of butoh dance or Suzuki's theatre. One is tempted to relate these encounters to the childhood primal scene described by the founder of psychoanalysis Sigmund Freud in that, at least for those who experienced them, many of these encounters would become sketchy in memory, but nevertheless key features, intensities, and responses remained burned into the viewer's psychophysical consciousness. Upon later recollection, they would summon up something at once familiar and elusive. US dancer Michael Sakamoto (2020: 21–2, 61–79) states that while watching Ohno Kazuo's 1993 performance of *Admiring La Argentina* in Los Angeles, his eyes "welled up with tears ... for the first time I saw myself in another human being". This inspired him to souvenir a poster, which he would periodically gaze at for years to come. Peter Snow, who would collaborate with Australian butoh dancers Tess de Quincey and Gretel Taylor, reported that after seeing Sankai Juku in Sydney, 1988, he "left the theatre in such a state of heightened awareness I could hear the snapping of twigs on trees across the road" (2002: 2). Rachael Swain (2024), who would go on to form intercultural performance company Marrugeku and work with Australian butoh artist Yumi Umiumare, describes seeing Sankai Juku as one of her "most impressive theatrical experiences", because "the visuals of butoh were so powerful" particularly in terms of expressing what she identifies as "postwar histories of shame".[1]

Even those whose work shows little overt influence of butoh relate such encounters with butoh and Suzuki. Former member of Pina Bausch's company and later director of Australian Dance Theatre, Meryl Tankard—likely recognising a common thread of Expressionistic influence upon both her mentor Bausch as well as upon butoh itself—attributed witnessing *Unetsu* to making "me aware of space, the universe ... of nature", including the Australian landscape, as "part of a much bigger world" (McKinnon 2020: 68). Australian postdramatic director Benedict Andrews claimed the performance allowed him access to an "otherness which lodged in my imagination and opened a door, a tunnel, which I have followed ever since" (ibid: 42). Even the founder of butoh himself, Hijikata Tatsumi, claimed that when he first witnessed his elder

---

1 This is briefly touched upon in Swain (2020: 83). See "Umiumare's First Nations Collaborations" in chapter six.

collaborator Ohno Kazuo dance that it was like being infected with a "deadly poison [geki yaku]" which changed his life forever (Vangeline 2020: xxvii). Novelist Mishima Yukio missed the premiere of Hijikata's *Kinjiki* (1959)—a performance the title for which was taken from Mishima's work—but witnessing an impromptu studio reenactment of *Kinjiki* produced in him a "profound interest in this most avant-garde experiment" (Mishima 2019: 52) leading him later to "become a dancer himself" through a project with Hijikata's collaborator Hosoe (Hosoe and Mishima 1985).

My argument in what follows is that part of what rendered these encounters primal is their Uncanny nature.[2] Butoh was and remains able to startle and surprise, even as most of its promoters insist it taps into a deep wellspring of chthonic emotional and embodied potentialities lodged within our shared histories. Butoh dance does not simply manifest for us in the present. It is transhistorical; a "tunnel", as Andrews would have it, which links diverse spatiotemporal realms. Butoh artists typically purport to harness now and into the future forces which come from the past, from memory, or from the body itself, developing possessive energies which return to the viewer like spectres from a forgotten past (Marshall 2013 and below). Hijikata's own production of *Nikutai no Hanran* (*Rebellion of the Body*; 1968) was attended by such later butoh pioneers as Tanaka Min, Maro Akaji, and Amagatsu Ushio (Vangeline 2020: XXXII), as well as theatre maker Suzuki Tadashi (Akihiko 2000: 62), all of whom would cite Hijikata's performance in years to come.

What is also so striking about these encounters is how frequently a career-spanning interest in butoh and related forms developed from one initiating event (Robertson 2017: 121–135). Although the original exposure was soon mediated by further experiences and information, many artists place importance on a singular catalysing meeting with something radically different yet affectively resonant within butoh and Suzuki, which generated ideas and questions. I can attest to the effect of such encounters on dancers and audiences because it also happened to me.

These encounters are also indicative of the status of butoh dance and Suzuki technique at the time they began to move out of Japan and become global phenomena. These responses show that while these styles were was not unknown, familiarity with them was not great, and so many individuals who saw butoh were ignorant of the form and its history prior to their first exposure. Butoh was therefore encountered first and foremost as estranging. This explains in part why many non-Japanese critics and viewers initially fell

---

2 See "Body Weather as an Uncanny Project" in chapter three.

back on a limited repertoire of Japanese references in an attempt to understand butoh: it was apparently Oriental, mysterious, similar to noh theatre and presumably related to Buddhism or other forms of Japanese spirituality (see Sykes 1989). Less obvious parallels with say twentieth century Euro-American modern dance, Surrealism, French mime, kabuki, Japanese Shintoism and folk beliefs, let alone Japanese Christianity (the last a strong influence on Ohno Kazuo if not butoh as a whole) were less likely to be noted, at least at first. Nevertheless, one of the reasons butoh was so gripping was its Uncanny familiarity. Butoh presented aesthetic tropes well established within international culture which viewers, not always well versed in their own cultural histories, responded to. Certainly butoh's proximity to Euro-American Expressionist dance theatre and interwar German ausdruckstanz struck a chord with many. Butoh helped licence a return to expressivity and emotion within an otherwise often formalistic dance scene. Sylviane Pagès (2017: 243) argues that the "expressionist gesture" pioneered by those German interwar choreographers who had influenced butoh itself had become a "veritable taboo" within dance after the 1970s, and so could "only reappear" via an "exotic … detour" through Japanese butoh or via the German Pina Bausch's more opaque task based choreographies.[3] Although rarely recognised at the time, butoh was also closely related to gallery performance and performance art more generally. Sankai Juku's use of set and design was more precise and restricted than many companies, but the bumpy rear wall of their production *Shijima* (1988) featured impressions of backs, hands and buttocks in a way that harks back to Japanese performance artist Shiraga Kazuo's *Challenging Mud* (1955), where he pressed his body into wet soil. One might also trace links with the highly muscular, corporeal gestures of action painting captured in films and photographs of US Abstract Expressionist Jackson Pollock. Butoh was not the same as these, and yes, it was certainly Japanese, but it was not quite as other to Western traditions as some naively felt. Butoh was a riddle of influences and approaches. In this book, I sketch the trajectory of these interpretative acts as reflected in the work and careers of the principal butoh performers based in Australia. I also include discussion of Australian interactions with the work of theatre artist Suzuki Tadashi because butoh and Suzuki have many close links, not least in their Australian uptake. Both have yet to break free of their association with Japanese cultural conventions, and seem unlikely to entirely do so. Australian artists must therefore interrogate their own national position with regard to these practices. I argue that it is precisely through these ongoing dialectical

---

3   All translations from French by the author.

acts of puzzling that butoh and Suzuki technique have become important elements within Australian and global performance practice, unsettling the local, even as they draw links to Japan and beyond.

4 What is Butoh?

Butoh was developed by Hijikata during the late 1950s and early 1960s, when he was a young dancer from northern Japan, eking out an existence in the Tokyo underground. Hijikata worked closely with mature artist Ohno Kazuo. Influenced by German ausdruckstanz, Hijikata contributed significantly to several of Ohno's solo productions, notably *Admiring La Argentina* (1977), which included sections reworked from Ohno's contribution to Hijikata's butoh premiere, *Kinjiki* (1959; Baird 2022: 120). The title of this first butoh work was derived from Mishima Yukio's account of a conflicted queer young man, though Hijikata distilled the novel into a violent sexual encounter between himself, the young dancer Ohno Yoshito (Ohno Kazuo's son), and a live chicken. Mishima praised Hijikata's *Kinjiki* for its "Discontinuous continuity", which the novelist claimed allied butoh with both venerable "religious ceremonies" as well as the "fearful nightmare of the modern" (1961: 53)—identifying butoh as a dance sketching a dialectic between the past and modernity. The performance of *Kinjiki* (1959), together with Hijikata's later work *Nikutai no Hanran* (*Rebellion of the Body*; 1968), established butoh as a force to be reckoned with, first in Japan, and later across the globe. Hijikata's photographic collaboration with Hosoe Eiko entitled *Kamaitachi* (Hosoe and Hijikata 1969/2005)—meaning "sickle demon"—also proved influential in the transmission of butoh, and acted as a touchstone for the consideration of issues of homeland in Australian butoh and elsewhere.

Butoh is an approach to dance and performance, rather than a set of clearly defined physical positions or a specific choreographic vocabulary. Its choreographic tendencies are recognisable through the tensions which the body moves between, or as Sakamoto puts it (2022: 7), the butoh "body in crisis" is constructed through a series of "oppositional binaries … and dialectic frameworks". "White butoh", as epitomised by Sankai Juku, is the best known and most easily identifiable variant of butoh. Its gestural consistency arises in part from the fact that Amagatsu, building on the work of Hijikata, strove to develop a repeatable choreographic form after he relocated from Japan to Paris, in the heart of the world of modern neoclassical ballet. Sankai Juku's style of butoh therefore owes something to ballet and its concept of an elegant, standardised repertoire of gestural vocabulary. Hijikata's own approach was more fungible.

Late in his career he developed what was known as butoh-fu or butoh notation. Dancers would be presented with a range of poetic and/or visual stimuli, which were recorded in notebooks and pasted assemblages. Ohno's method was less systematised, but also depended on visual, poetic, narrative or musical stimuli which were then translated into performance works. Hijikata's butoh-fu was used not only to devise, but to recall positions, their order, and especially to retain the all-important *quality* of the movement—beyond its disposition in space. As Basile Doganis puts it, the images used in butoh and other modern dance processes can be considered "internal fictions, decompositions, [or] imaginary and organic reconstructions" which are used to generate an internal "sensation" or "creation" of sorts, functioning as an idiosyncratic yet intuitively transmissible "territory" out of which the dance arises (Pagès 2017: 199). The same is true of Body Weather, which includes within its repertoire a series of images gifted to Tanaka by Hijikata.[4] One of Hijikata's most poetic provocations was the "ash pillar walk" (Baird 2012: 178), where the dancer imagines their body to consist of stacked, cremated ash which falls apart with every movement. This produced a body felt to be "composed of tactile sensations and particles" (Hijikata in Nanako 2000: 17), or as de Quincey put it (2002), a "swarm body", as if made up of millions of nominally independent particles moving chaotically in and out of a shaking, shimmering mass, always on the verge of orgiastic dissipation. Other images offered by Hijikata (2000b: 46) included the final spark of life contained in the walk of a condemned man on death row, or of the peasant children he encountered in the winters of Tōhoku, whose legs had become numb, twisted and tingling because of protracted periods of being bound in a basket (Hijikata 2000d: 77–79).

All butoh dance is to some extent "improvisational" in that the precise location of the body in space and time has variations and is generated semi-impulsively in the moment. Butoh is in this sense quite different from classical Japanese dance and buyō, which are structured around a series of kata which dictate bodily position so as to encourage an inner flowering (yūgen). Butoh is nevertheless explicitly choreographic in that the poses which are eventually adopted remain guided by preestablished aims and limits. A range of similar approaches have existed ever since "free" or "modern" dance was proposed by the likes of Isadora Duncan in the late nineteenth century.

Butoh's specific focus on abstract visual texts and/or images (poetry, text, paintings, sketches, photographs, reproductions) to generate movement is particular to the form. There is also a typology of poses that butoh instructions

---

4 See "Tanaka Min & Body Weather" in chapter three.

tend to generate. As I have previously observed, at its most forceful, butoh presents a damaged or debilitated body on the verge of collapse. Recurrent motifs in butoh include those of the dying or dead body, the diseased body, the aborted body, the foetal body, and so on; a body which strives for a divine or beautiful state and whose failed incompleteness gives butoh much of its lyricism. Gestures include:
- tremor such as would normally indicate uncertain neuromuscular control and/or debilitated physical stamina;
- optical convulsion leading to the eyes rolling upwards;
- facial grimaces, often including the protrusion and contortion of the tongue, or a wide, open-mouthed gape;
- closed, cramped, or clawed movements of the hands, limbs, feet, and extremities recalling paralytic poses such as balled feet or hands;
- the rapid alternation of near stasis (paralysis, catalepsy, laboured or very slow movement) with almost seizure-like frenzy and speed;
- relatively few transitional poses between these various stochastic, convulsive physical expressions;
- a body that moves from hypersensitivity to hysterical aesthesia and numbness;
- asymmetric, jagged, multidirectional, and hence often zigzag or electrical-like neuromuscular action; and
- gesture at the limits of human capacities, sometimes suggestive of non-human movement or action, evoking mammals, reptiles, insects, mineral bodies, etcetera.

Bruce Baird (2022: 6) adds to this a focus on:
- shocking content, such as homoerotics, criminality, movement derived from people with disabilities, illness, or geriatric decrepitude;
- rigidity and stillness, contrasted with athletic movement;
- pedestrian or everyday movement; non-dancerly events or actions;
- de-emphasizing the dancer as human and their physiognomy, by facing away from the audience, and drawing attention to the back.

These corporeal expressions generally derive in the first instance from the poetic stimuli drawn upon by the dancer, and are only rarely developed through corporeal mimeticism or copying, as is more commonly the case for other dances. As we see in chapter eight, the artists of Zen Zen Zo demur slightly regarding this interpretation of butoh principles, employing mimeticism to develop internal states, and vice versa. Mirrors are certainly used in butoh studios, but they are there largely to assist self reflection.

Butoh is not however an inherently dour form, nor is it limited in its repertoire. Butoh often functions as a kind of non-choreography, in that bodily postures are so twisted, fleeting, and constantly metamorphosing that they process without necessarily condensing into clear images or structures. The butoh body remains highly fungible, and while Suzuki's performers are typically more disciplined and controlled, they too sometimes explode into chaotic disharmony and spasm. Both Suzuki's theatre and butoh can also be truly zany, funny and joyous. Some indication of these opposing trends in butoh is offered by the interest Hijikata and Ohno had in flamenco dance, a form whose stochastic and percussive tendencies both dancers celebrated, and which is echoed in much of Tony Yap's work (chapters four and five). The joyously thumping, leaping and pounding body is also a sign of butoh's vital but threatened energies. In *Nikutai no Hanran* (1968), Hijikata danced an extensive flamenco burlesque in which he intermittently turned to the audience to lift his billowing dress and flash his underwear.[5] In 2004, I attended a performance in which Kamata Makiko inverted a plastic bucket over her head before solemnly moving forward, naked, on the stage of DanceBox, Kyoto (Marshall 2004: 4–5). The combination of embodied contradictions with absurdity, of a carnal flirtatiousness, alongside powerful yet contained bodily energies, recur throughout butoh.

5 Suzuki Technique and the Way of Stomping

Both butoh and the work of Suzuki Tadashi were products of the general vibrancy of the postwar Japanese avant-garde, which extended into photography, installation, performance art, sculpture, cinema, literature and other forms (Munroe 1994; Eckersall 2006). There was considerable cross fertilization between the worlds of theatre and those of dance, most notably in the acting engagements of Maro Akaji, Tanaka Min, and Hijikata himself. There were also strong conceptual links and affinities in terms of practice. Nevertheless, within Japan itself, Suzuki's theatre training, butoh, and even Tanaka's sub-genre of Body Weather, were often seen as distinct from butoh proper. It was typically outside of Japan, and especially in Australia, that the three would be brought together. Hijikata did however argue in a panel discussion which he and Suzuki participated that the separation between theatre and dance was not a "matter of words" versus "the body. After all, dance and theatre were joined in one-act [noh] plays for a very long time". Rather, "still sleeping intact"

---

5 The documentation of *Nikutai no Hanran* is extensive if not complete, and includes cinematic fragments, as well as the wonderful photographs of Nakatani Tadao; see Nakatani (2003); Asbestos-kan (1987); Morishita (2004).

FIGURE 2   Director Suzuki Tadashi's *Chronicle of Macbeth* (Playbox: 1992)
Left to right: Oliver Sidore (Chorus / Witch #2), John Nobbs (Banquo's Ghost) and Peter Curtin (Macbeth)
PHOTO: REIMUND ZUNDE. REPRODUCTION COURTESY OF ZUNDE

within the body there are "various mythic things", both from the theatre and from the world in general. The challenge was "how to excavate them" so that in some sense one dances "with your own body—without any intermediary", to which Suzuki responded "I agree" (Akihiko 2000: 68).

Hijikata's unremitting emphasis on nikutai and the body certainly placed his own work in the realm of dance. Even so, his intense interest in linguistic signs and speech as generative of movement allied his work to theatre and interdisciplinary performance. Butoh is, properly speaking, a dance theatre form, like the work of the German interwar tanztheater practitioners to whom Hijikata and Ohno were heirs. Suzuki's approach to theatre, particularly as rendered by the Australian trainer and performer John Nobbs of Frank Theatre, is no less tied to language. Nobbs, building on Suzuki, uses a range of metaphors and linguistic prompts in association with guided exercises and tasks to develop within the actor a disciplined responsiveness. Although choreographically very different from most butoh, the slightly hypnotised look of Suzuki's actors has parallels with the butoh dancer's entranced modality (Figure 2).

The bent legged stance has particular importance for both Suzuki and butoh. Bent legs tie the performer metaphorically to the ground and all that may be drawn from it: stamps, thuds, noises, power, dark urges, chthonic themes. Indeed, Suzuki (1986: 15) himself would note some kinship between the stamping movements which he developed with those techniques applied in much Australian First Nations dance. Certainly the entanglement of butoh's and Suzuki's lineage with Euro-American modernism is part of what made butoh resonate so strongly for Australian artists and audiences.

Butoh commentators and Suzuki have articulated the significance of their own models of groundedness in similar ways to each other. As Suzuki explains:

> A basic part of my method of training involves actors stomping on the floor ... or ... walking around fiercely beating the floor with the feet in a semi-squatting posture. Then, the moment the music stops, the actors relax their bodies totally, falling on the floor ... [before again] they slowly rise to their feet.
> SUZUKI 1984: 31

Briefly known as ankoku buyō and then later ankoku butō (暗黒舞踏), the word butoh itself is formed from the Japanese pronunciation of the Chinese characters for "dance" (bu or 舞) and "tread" or "stomp" (toh or 踏). Generally translated in English as the "dance of utter darkness", the French term "danse des ténèbres" or "dance of the shadows" helps further convey the nuances of the Japanese expression. As Bruce Baird explains, in the 1950s, "butoh" also referred to "Western-style dances" performed at Taisho era balls, including "flamenco, waltz, and ballet. So ankoku butō originally meant something like 'dark black waltz'", though it is now more commonly translated as "stomping dance" (Baird 2022: 6). Many critics and butoh artists have related the act of stamping to the percussive force employed in noh temple dance to summon or placate the gods (Moore 1991; Marshall 1995: 55). The term therefore allies butoh with both historic Japanese practices as well as the more unruly fusions arising out of Japan's conflicted relationship with Euro-American culture. Suzuki (1984: 33) himself sees the act of stomping as a para-religious act, noting that "in traditional Japanese theatrical forms, such as noh and kabuki" there is an "affinity with the earth" in which "performers invariably stomp ... and ... appearing on the stage in itself signifies the treading down of evil spirits under the ground" together with a "sanctifying" of the performance space. While Suzuki's work is typically much more measured than Hijikata's, it also includes allusions to the modern condition and the chaos that may be left in its wake, as well as intense music whose high volume approaches even that of a Dairakudakan performance.

The most significant linkages between butoh and Suzuki technique lie not in any formal affinities though, and even less in their ideological make up. Rather the yoking together of the two methods in Australian practice has largely been historical and pragmatic. Suzuki and Hijikata emerged out of the same context as part of a new generation of complex, assertive and broadly counter-cultural Japanese art. Australians have been described as approaching performance training as "collectors" or "bricoleurs, building a place for themselves" and their work in Australia with "what[ever] they can scrounge and appropriate" (Maxwell 2017: 326)—be this Japanese performance, modernist dance, or even First Nations cultural inspirations. Suzuki and butoh both offered a physical approach to performance at a time in which Australian artists were still negotiating how to develop a national tradition of physical theatre. Butoh and Suzuki presented interesting, poetic and physically disciplined ways to do this, which shared a basic cultural heritage and context of generation. Each moreover carried with it what seemed to be a self-contained ethos and set of values within which non-Japanese students could immerse themselves, or as Steven Durland said, what those who sought out Tanaka during the 1980s "were looking for [was] a discipline and a teacher to turn their lives over to" (1990: 49). This is not to say the distinction between SMAT, Body Weather and butoh was entirely ignored in Australia, but a tendency towards eclectic fusion certainly dominated.

6   Lineages of Descent Ancient and Modern in Butoh and Suzuki

Much of what drove butoh first in Japan and later in Australia was Hijikata's aim to dramatize the jarring interactions of modernity with older local and global traditions, reaching back into history, or as Tanaka put it, "I intend to be a legitimate child of dance initiated in ancient time" (in Snow 2002: 80)—even as Tanaka danced across cityscapes, industrial sites, and other modern environments (Fuller 2016: 77). Part of my aim in this book is to not only show how artists in Australia engaged with national tropes, but to argue that global butoh might be considered to exceed such national concepts. The trajectory taken by butoh and Suzuki technique in Australia shows how conventional mappings of the historical centres of gravity and authority in art, empire, and even butoh, are thrown into question when one considers the multi-temporal, corporeal exchanges between Europe, the UK, the USA, Australia and Japan.

The paradigmatic example of these kinds of dramatic encounters between localised premodern histories and contemporary forces was Hijikata's 1968 solo work *Nikutai no Hanran*. The full title of the piece was *Tatsumi Hijikata to Nihonjin: Nikutai no Hanran*, or *Hijikata and the Japanese: Rebellion of the Body*. The name itself establishes a tense space between its author, Hijikata, and—or perhaps more accurately versus—"the Japanese", producing a "rebellion of the body" across time and space. *Nikutai no Hanran* drew on research he and Hosoe had conducted in the under-developed northern region of Tōhoku for the photobook *Kamaitachi* (1968–69). The kamaitachi, or "sickle weasel" is a Japanese "yōkai" or "strange apparition" which includes oni (demons), spirits, and mischievous beings which cannot be fully accounted for (Foster 2015). Most are regionally specific, kamaitachi being most prevalent in the snowbound north in Tōhoku and Honshu. Yōkai themselves are also paradoxical temporal figures, being closely connected to premodern Japanese folk beliefs, as well as later mediatised cultural forms, and were widely represented in illustrated compendia from the seventeenth century, through to contemporary cinema.

The harsh traditional lifestyle of Tōhoku served as a touchstone for *Nikutai no Hanran* and several other of Hijikata's works, the dancer referring to his upbringing there in several essays (see especially Hijikata 2000d: 71–81). *Nikutai no Hanran* began with Hijikata reprising an image from *Kamaitachi,* by entering carried on a catafalque beneath a sunshade, evoking both premodern Japanese rural festivals, and the description of the crowning of the emperor Heliogabalus from a novel by Artaud (Hosoe and Hijikata 2005; Asbestos-kan 1987; Baird 2012: 123–125; Nakatani 2003; Morishita 2004). Later in *Nikutai no Hanran,* Hijikata gyrated madly, crashing into sharp, shining, swinging metal plates that reflected shafts of light and distorted images of the dancer in all directions (Asbestos-kan 1987; Nakatani 2003; Morishita 2004). In *Nikutai no Hanran,* Hijikata's body was framed in the opening as proximate to peasant traditions, only to be literally smashed against harsh modern steel panels. The butoh body may be read here confronted incompatible shards of history, alluding to the past as well as the present; or as Sakamoto argues, Hijikata "situated the ambivalence of Japanese postwar identity between a late capitalist Western body and a premodern Japanese body" (2022: 7).

Reconnecting with the history of humanity and of the world prior to modernism has been a recurrent theme across butoh and its discourse ever since. Amagatsu of Sankai Juku argued that it was not until he was reminded of the prehistoric "primitive wall paintings of [the] Lascaux" caves or "megalithic structures [found] across Europe" such as such as dolmens, tombs and stone circles that he felt it was appropriate for him to practice butoh in France (Watanabe 2013). Sankai Juku's production of *Jōmon-sho* (1982) was explicitly framed in terms of a return to primal origins. The title refers to the Jōmon peoples of Japan, whose archaeological remains are concentrated in Tōhoku and northern Japan. Jōmon culture represents the earliest examples of artefacts and practices indigenous to Japan which can be distinguished from those of Korea or China. In Amagatsu's account of *Jōmon-sho,* he further links the human antiquity alluded to in the title to Ernst Haeckel's theory of evolutionary recapitulation. Over the course of *Jōmon-sho,* dancers evolve from pendulous lumps of flesh, to grub-like forms, to groping humans, recalling how, according to Haeckel, the developing embryo:

> transforms from fish to amphibian, then from reptile to mammal ... it replays the majestic drama, which lasted tens of millions of years during the second half of the Palaeozoic era, the landing of vertebrates on the banks of the continent, beaten by the waves of the ocean. Ontogeny [embryonic development] recapitulates phylogeny [evolution].
> AMAGATSU in BAIRD 2022: 199

Irrespective of the accuracy of these conceptions (now rejected by most embryologists), it shows that Amagatsu, Hijikata and many of their peers worked to project a corporeal past behind themselves and dance it into the present, developing novel and disruptive fantasmic histories of descent and ascent.

This fascination with ancient lineages of descent is not however unique to butoh, and derives in no small part from trends within global modernism as a whole. The composer Igor Stravinsky, for example, claimed that for his landmark modernist ballet *Rite of Spring,* he "dreamed a scene of pagan ritual in which a chosen sacrificial virgin danced herself to death" (1962: 159). Choreographed by Vaslav Nijinsky, Christopher Innes explains that the piece was:

> Set in prehistoric Russia and depicting a pagan ritual of mating and human sacrifice, in which a virgin possessed by ancestral spirits dances in an ecstasy to music of increasing violence and volume until she falls lifeless to the ground, this ballet brings together all the primitive and mythic tendencies we have noted in expressionism.
> 1993: 47

German Expressionist dancer Mary Wigman—a major influence on butoh (Elswit et al. 2019: 126–136)—was likewise seen by her contemporaries as representative of a "pagan" model of premodern embodiment (Odom 1980: 84). The 1930s critic of German Expressionist art and associate of Wigman, Ernst Scheyer, noted that she consulted European anthropological literature and museum collections to research her productions (1970: 20), much as like designer Nicholas Roerich had for *Rite of Spring.* The mask Wigman used in *Hexentanz (Witch Dance)* (1926) was even modelled on a Japanese noh mask (Scheyer 1970: 20).

A key work of dance in Australia was the modern ballet *Corroboree,* scored by John Anthill, depicting an Aboriginal initiation ritual rising to a frenzy, based on the model of Stravinsky's and Nijinsky's *Rite of Spring*. Choreographed by Rex Reid in 1950 and then by Beth Dean in 1954, both productions drew on anthropological sources. Dean, an American dancer, visited several Australian Aboriginal communities, including Yuendumu in Central Australia, and appears to have had good relations with members of the Napangardi family (Spunner 2005: 143–164; Dean and Carell 1955: 111–138), kin of whom Australian butoh artists Tess de Quincey and Gretel Taylor would later encounter as part of their own research during the 1990s and 2000s. Dean described her version of *Corroboree* as "based on the drama human of trail-by-ordeal as enacted in the initiation ceremony we witnessed [in the] outback" (Dean and Carell 1983: 145).[6]

Australia occupies a crucial, if problematic, place within global discourses around accessing ancient knowledge. Early anthropological descriptions of Australia's native peoples by Charles Darwin and others postulated that their culture and possibly their biology represented a uniquely early point in the development of humanity as a whole (Jones 1989: 2–13). Consequently while Euro-American and Japanese modernists interacted more extensively with those groups geographically proximate to them or their own colonies—principally the peoples of Africa and the "Near East" for Europeans, or the indigenous northern Ainu for the Japanese (S. Tanaka 1993)—Australian Aborigines held a particular fascination for artists and scholars internationally. The founder of the interwar European Dadaist movement, Tristan Tzara, sampled Australian Aboriginal words and sounds for his primal, nonsensical poetry recitals (Ross and Lindgren 2017: 292). The German Expressionist Emil Nolde, a close friend of Wigman and Scheyer, visited the German protectorate of New Guinea just across the Torres Straits from Australia in 1912 (A. Carroll 2017: 58–63), drawing on the arts of Australasia, Oceania, Japan and Africa to develop his own style of painting, inspired by what Ernst Scheyer described as "primitive masks and masked dancers" which, in Scheyer's opinion, "anticipated an important trend in Mary Wigman's art" (1970: 16). In 1947, the modernist dance luminary Ted Shawn took advantage of a tour to Australia to see Aboriginal dance in person, attempting to learn some of their movements, and in turn dancing for the locals (Harris 2023: 45–46; Ewers 1947: 31–36). Jiří Kylian of Netherlands Dance Theatre followed suit in 1983, attending an Indigenous dance festival in northern Australia, which informed a pair of Kylian's own choreographies (Webb 1987: 178–189).

---

6 Dean was also choreographer on the problematic but significant Australian film on Aboriginal identity, *Jedda* (1955; Dean & Carell 1983: 150–1).

The interest of Japanese artists was also piqued by Aboriginal precedents. Suzuki Tadashi quoted an account of Australian Aboriginal dance published in a gestalt study of ballet by the Jungian theorist Gerhard Zacharias (Jackson et al. 2021: 325), which was in turn derived by Zacharias from interwar German ethnology. Suzuki's aim in doing so, like that of other twentieth century commentators, was to find precedents for his own practice—in this case Suzuki's linking of the actor's energy to the ground through stomping. Suzuki contended that his own work enabled the actor to "discover the primal sensibility of the character" (in Nobbs and Brokering 2016: 84), entering a "precognitive, preverbal" state close to premodern shamanic possession (ibid.: 78). Indeed, Stefan Tanaka (1993) has argued that Tōhoku and some of the other islands of Japan served as modern Japan's "own Orient", or site of primal otherness, in that Japanese constructed Tōhoku and the north as a resource for the recovery of their nation's premodern cultural expressions. Ōsuka Isamu of Byakkosha similarly argued that dance emerges out of a "primitive reminiscence in the cells of the body, and a mythical archetype" (Viala and Masson-Sékiné 1988: 195). As Gretel Taylor observes, the rhetoric of Suzuki, Ōsuka, and others often suggests a "belief in (and valuing of) the potential to erase or undo the (social [and historical]) experiences of the body in a return to an idealised 'purity' or untainted state" (Taylor 2010: 78), bridging Japan with Australia, or Germany with northern Japan.

In both Australia and Japan, the description of contemporary Indigenous peoples and their cultures as "ancient" justified the imposition of allegedly more sophisticated yet repressive colonial regimes (see Morris-Suzuki 1994: 597–612). It also created a space where a revaluing of the so-called "primitive" or premodern could serve as a rhetorical critique of modernism, and perhaps more importantly, produced historiographic and cultural linkages between peoples and practices which scrambled linear models of historical and cultural development.[7] Ruth Phillips argues that this discourse of "Aesthetic primitivism" helps account for the "global adaptability" of modernism as a wider movement, which she describes as "dedicated to the appropriation of new ancestors" in order to justify and explore new aesthetic, cultural and political formulations (2015: 6). Peter Snow—who worked closely with Australian Body Weather pioneer Tess de Quincey—argued that while it would be an exaggeration

---

[7] I am here influenced by McClintock's study of the duality of sexual and colonial power relations (1995), as well as Marianna Torgovnick's recognition that Western definitions of primitivism were based on an ambivalent interaction of attraction and repulsion which was central to the construction of that which it was presumed not to be—that is to say modernist Western culture (1990).

"to claim that the Mungo project" or the other workshops which de Quincey and her dancers conducted in the Australian outback were "an attempt to reclaim a primitive body through some sort of approach to aboriginality", their experiences in these and other activities were "deeply spiritual" for the largely settler-descent artists "in ways that are hard to explicate" (2002: 97). Snow ambiguously concludes that "Perhaps it is better to leave some things unsaid".

What I am proposing is that just as the work of *Rite*'s choreographer Nijinsky has been shown to be an ancestor of sorts to butoh in light of the quotation of Nijinsky's choreography in Hijikata's work (Morant 2004: 268–277), the staging of works like *Corroboree* in Australia—works which explicitly drew on and evoked non-Western and/or First Nations dances—created the preconditions which butoh has since been able to reclaim as part of its own decentred history. As a result of these filiations, contemporary Japanese physical performance opens up the possibility for an estranged re-routing of otherness in different contexts, allowing for the sensual and ultimately fantasmatic but still deeply felt grounding of non-Indigenous artists within the Australian context. Such acts of gestural estrangement and emplacement move beyond, or at least confuse, normative colonial categories of race and/or belonging. Here, as in Australian history more generally, we see what must be considered a history which is at least double (MacLean 2023), wherein First Nations cultural practices and politics have remained in ever present dialogue with dominant national and settler-descent ideologies—often in a repressed, opaque or indirect form, but present nevertheless, inflecting or haunting cultural practices, and in this case, Australian dance and performance.

7 Butoh and Suzuki Technique in Other National Contexts

In her excellent study of butoh in the Americas, Tanja Calamoneri traces the history of artists and productions, but leaves largely untouched the complex issues of what might be the national, ethnic and racial implications of the transplantation of Japanese butoh to the US and South America which the formulations of Tanaka and others create. Calamoneri argues that butoh is "part of the American performance commons" (2022: 3). Magdalena Zamorska (2018: 38–40) makes much the same claim in her account of Polish butoh, characterising it as a form whose mixed origins and Euro-American influences render it "transculturally effective" and hence available to be adopted outside of Japan. Butoh's Euro-American elements certainly rendered it suitable for critiques of modernism in many contexts, but local disputes over land, race and national character, amongst other issues, mark its regional emplacement in Australia.

The diffusion of butoh first into, and later out of, France has been more critically analysed. Sylviane Pagès stresses the initially Orientalist reception of butoh in France, followed by a period after the 1980s when the dance was often perceived as a belated homecoming for Europe's own modernist traditions (Pagès 2017; Pavis 1998; Marshall 2013). As French dancer Catherine Diverrès put it, "Meeting Ohno in 1982" it seemed as if she had encountered the deceased 1930s dance stars from interwar Germany such as Harald Kreutzberg, or South America's Antonia Merce (whose stage name gave Ohno the title to his solo *Admiring La Argentina*, 1977), thus enabling Diverrès and her peers "to travel backwards" in history and beyond France's geographic limits (Pagès 2017: 216). Pagès argues that this was a consequence of the relatively weak uptake of German, Austrian and American Expressionist choreography in France, where neoclassicism had historically been more accepted, while Germanic and US forms were often viewed as dubious foreign imports. Pagès concludes that the "transfer of butoh cannot be grasped" as the product of a "binary relationship" between France and Japan, but should rather be seen as a multi-directional "dynamic" involving the "third pole" of Germany, together with France and Japan themselves (Pagès 2017: 169, 244–259). Cécile Iwahara and others have moreover argued that butoh benefited from a "reverse importation (gyaku yūnyū)" (Pagès 2017: 169), whereby the success of butoh outside of Japan lifted the institutional status of butoh in Japan itself.

The uptake of butoh in France and elsewhere was moreover partly facilitated by the coincident global diffusion of the German Pina Bausch's neo-Expressionist work during the 1980s, seen as exemplary of new trends in European tanztheater, all of which occurred in tandem with not simply the rise of Japan as an economic power, but also the return of Germany to the global stage as a major geopolitical force. Prior to this in France, as in Australia, there had been an implicit assumption that it was all but impossible for those not of Japanese descent to perform butoh or Suzuki technique because of the styles' socio-cultural and racial origins, especially in light of Japan's unique proximity to the traumas of atomic warfare. As one French critic declared: "It is always extremely difficult for occidental artists to acquire the sense of presence, interiority and the expressive intensity of Japanese dancers because they are neither … nourished nor … impregnated" within the same "culture" as their Oriental counterparts (Pagès 2017: 142). Scholar-dancer Vangeline points out that some critics have even suggested that changes to the physical stature of Japanese populations arising from improved diet after World War Two now means that the Japanese themselves are today unable to perform butoh's low to the ground movements (2020: 199–204). Vangeline, who is ethnically French, has been interrogated by audience members as to if she is "half-Japanese" given she performs butoh. Tamano Hiroko, a former student of Hijikata offering butoh training in the US, has opted to at least teach "Japanese lifestyle classes" alongside dance to ensure Western students are better able to fully respond to the demands of the art (Vangeline 2020: 199). As we shall see, de Quincey, Zen Zen Zo and others have retained select Japanese rituals within their training regimes to help set these exercises apart from the everyday and impart the right mindset. Readings of butoh and Suzuki as modalities necessarily born of the Japanese's unique experience of atomic warfare have moreover helped licence a return to those emotional, Expressionistic and psychological forms of dance pioneered in Germany, Austria and Switzerland, but which had fallen out of favour following the rise Merce Cunningham's impersonal geometric approach, as well as postmodern pedestrianism, and new outgrowths of neo-classicism in dance.[8] In short, butoh's and Suzuki's status as part of a transcultural global commons remains complex and contested, while racial, national and regional factors continue to inflect its meaning, status and execution.

8 Criticism and Reception of Japanese Performance in Australia

Butoh and Suzuki have attracted interest in Australia too regarding their racial and cultural positioning. Is butoh an interloper in the Australian context? Is it really Japanese? Can white Australians really "do" butoh, or do they tend to exoticize it, presenting something closer to a kitsch fantasy of Oriental cosmopolitanism? Helen Gilbert and Jacqueline Lo (2009) considered some of these questions in the context of cosmopolitanism as it applies to the programming of performing arts in Australia. They conclude that cosmopolitanism in the contemporary global art market is a relatively shallow concept, principally facilitating cultural and economic consumption over critical analysis. The syncretic cultural and racial utopias promised by global cultural exchange post World War Two have not always eventuated. Gilbert and Lo however say relatively little about the aesthetic qualities of Australian butoh and Suzuki-based performances. These aesthetic markers, inflected as they are by global and national socio-political forces, are my own focus.

There has been some sensationalistic coverage following the arrival of contemporary Japanese performance in Australia, starting with outraged responses

---

8 As recently as 2012, a French journalist remarked: "From Hiroshima to Fukushima, the trauma continues for Japan. No other country has been so farcefully bruised, right through to the flesh, by nuclear power. The bomb [was] a nightmare that gave birth to butoh" (Pagès 2017: 140).

to a billboard featuring the near naked dancers of Dairakudakan erected alongside Punt Road for the 1991 Melbourne Festival. Many Australian critics have, moreover, naively assumed butoh and related works such as Suzuki's performances principally followed "traditional oriental theatre forms" (Neill 1992: 10). By and large though, accounts have been considered, if not always supportive or fully informed. Helen Thompson in 1987 for *The Australian,* for example, confessed that while her own feelings about Byakkosha were "mostly negative", she nevertheless recognised that the sketches offered were "not traditional theatre forms, but [ones] of revolt" and that the production presented a vision of "man as a lower animal. Sometimes he is only a belly-crawling insect ... androgynous, or suggesting a perverted sexuality" (10).

Pagès notes that Occidental readings of Japanese performance have often been "marked by its dichotomous dimension: any positive image is likely to be to be accompanied by a negative counterpart" such that "fascination" is always "on the verge of repulsion", offering the Western viewer various forms of "Frightening beauty" (Pagès 2017: 149). Neil Jillett of *The Age* newspaper in Melbourne went even further, his loathing for the avant-garde already well established. He trounced Byakkosha's 1987 Melbourne performance, claiming it took its "governing principle" from:

> traditional Japanese theatre: [that] a thing may not be worth doing, but since we are going to do it, let's do it as slowly as possible; let's test the audience's boredom threshold or ... their capacity for deluding themselves that they are being given a dose of Serious Oriental Culture.
> 1987: 15

He went on to unfavourably compare the performance to everything from Balinese dance to "Hare Krishna street parades ... Lindsay Kemp's malodorous campery ... old Hollywood horror movies", Pina Bausch and more. Of Dairakudakan's landmark Australian premiere in 1991, he concluded that it was no more than "an exhibition of bad manners and ... Japanese theatrical traditions", concluding "There is no theatrical magic, no sense of mystery and wonder ... It just plods around in a succession of ... nightmarish images" (Jillett 1991: 12). Butoh may not have won over Australian conservatives like Jillett, but its renown amongst the more liberal arts community itself did in fact grow rapidly, as the success of the Australian artists discussed below shows—despite some of these early critical drubbings from Jillett and his peers.

Peter Eckersall is a central author-practitioner in the field of Australian butoh and Suzuki, who in the late 1990s and early 2000s made the case that imports of performance into Australia should be based on a considered engagement with Japanese cultural politics and the philosophical and textual documents which surround this. Eckersall's own role as dramaturg for the physical theatre company, Not Yet It's Difficult, served as a model for such engagements, and Eckersall detailed this work in his own publications. In addition to Pagès, Robertson, Lo and Gilbert, Eckersall has been a central guide in the materials I examine.

Tess de Quincey is Australia's leading expert on the subvariant of butoh entitled Body Weather. De Quincey was the first to present workshops in butoh and Body Weather in Australia, and she has also had an extensive engagement with academia. She was an artist in residence at the University of Sydney. Staff and students from the Universities of Sydney and Western Sydney—notably Gay McAuley, Ian Maxwell and Jane Goodall—joined de Quincey at the Triple Alice laboratories in the Central Dessert of Australia, authoring a range of critical analyses. Frank Theatre and especially Zen Zen Zo had close relations with the University and Queensland and the Queensland University of Technology (UQ and QUT), both institutions fostering the companies' work and publications. There are therefore a number of close study academic articles about de Quincey, Zen Zen Zo and Frank, as well as published analyses of Umiumare's cabaret performances. All of these sources are drawn upon below.

Commentators have tended to be ambivalent regarding attempts by de Quincey, Zen Zen Zo and Frank to move beyond importing an Oriental otherness to the Australian context, especially in light of Australia's ongoing vexed debates around race, colonialism and culture (Gilbert and Lo 2009: 165). The relationship of white and/or settler-descent individuals with a landscape which literally and metaphorically bears the scars of colonial violence and land theft is often deemed too complex, too riven, to be overcome through dance alone.

I accept the logic of these criticisms, but my aim below is largely to critically expand on the positions which the artists themselves have offered in the face of these and other challenges, and then place these ideas in context with other instances of colonial encounter in Australian dance, literature and iconographic histories. My conclusion is that *these very debates* have enabled Australian butoh and Suzuki to become considered, critically rich and politically informed practices. Even in Australia, butoh dancers "seem to be performing acrobatic feats on oil", as Hijikata would have it (in Viala and Masson-Sékiné 1988: 188), such that the lack of corporeal rigidity in the support of the body upon the ground becomes an embodied metaphor of socio-political uncertainty and displacement. The artists surveyed below by and large insist that *bodies themselves* can think, and while that may not always fully resolve the philosophical or pragmatic implications of the political context, artists have deployed explicitly *material*—that is to say *bodily*—approaches in the face of the realpolitik of colonialism and other issues (Figure 4). In these and related methods, the carnal body (nikutai) of butoh and Suzuki meets the Australian context in a literal fashion. This does not mean butoh might not itself act as a tool of colonialism, but the tendency of butoh and Body Weather to celebrate bodily self-division, complexity, even generating a sense of aporia and hysterical abjection—all this makes butoh and Suzuki technique more suited to complexifying relationships, rather than erasing, denying or transcending pre-existing colonial histories.

9   Emptiness and Possession

The butoh performer is one who is often moved by something outside of, or beyond, themselves. The body is divided, and different types of movement or sensations may occur simultaneously in different parts of the body. Former Dairakudakan member Yumi Umiumare offered a simple demonstration of this in a 2014 documentary, where she shifted from the classic uplifting pose of Euro-American modern dance such as that developed by Martha Graham, with the arms held wide in a V above the head, to cross her limbs jaggedly over her chest, the left hand pointing past the right side of the body, and vice versa. "This finger [the left] and this finger [right] are going to go in different directions", Umiumare explained, pulling the body apart and around, and so there is "constant movement happening that way" and in oppositional directions (A. Carroll 2014). The term "omnicentral" is often used to convey this: a body which has no singular or unified core from which movement or volition would proceed—as would be the case in Euro-American modern dance. Butoh artists talk about making the body feel "empty" or "hollow" so that other things may come into the dancer and take them over. Butoh performance therefore often resembles possession or a state of trance. Tony Yap and Yumi Umiumare in particular have built on butoh to explore altered states and ritual, Yap now calling his practice "trance dance" while Umiumare terms her own exploration of possession and altered states "jujutsu" or "magic".[9] John Nobbs insists that Suzuki technique acts as a kind of "shamanism", with extra-normal or even otherworldly forces stilling the performer and filling them with a potent energetic presence.

This engagement with an otherness drawn into and out of the performer's body and psyche is central to butoh, and it is visible in Suzuki technique too.

---

9 See "Umiumare & Jujutsu" in chapter six.

Both performance styles are based on psychocorporeal self-reflection which is directed both inward and outward in search of a dynamic exchange. It is this that gives butoh its tremulous, fungible character.

Australian Body Weather artist Gretel Taylor (2010: 72–87) and others have challenged the frequent invocation of corporeal "emptiness" within butoh, noting that the emptying out or erasing of that which lodges within an inevitably racialized body is problematic in the context of colonial and imperial histories. It is ultimately a Caucasian fantasy—and a Japanese one too—to think that one might "empty" the body of qualities so that one could simply take on those that surround oneself, particularly if the land upon which one operates was acquired through war, conquest and dispossession, as is the case for Australia as a settler-colonial state, as well as for Japan, as a group of semi-independent kingdoms whose amalgamation represented the beginnings of the wider Japanese Imperial project. I return to Taylor's challenge in chapter two.

What is at stake is not so much the *term* "empty", but what is *meant* by it. "Emptiness" is a metaphor, and while the butoh body may be a "hollow" body within which other things may be lodged, woven throughout its porous structures are the particular experiences and histories of the dancer, including national and fantasmatic ones. Hijikata (2000c: 58; 2000d: 77) spoke of having his deceased sister moving within him, as did other butoh artists such as Carlotta Ikeda (Vangeline 2020: 117). This corporeal haunting tied Hijikata to the specifics of his upbringing in northern Tōhoku and to the traumas which he and others claimed to have endured there. The access of deeply buried corporeal memories has indeed been shown to be a side-effect of butoh "emptying" out. This is something I return to below, particularly in my discussion of Body Weather and trance dance.

10   Primary Sources and Thick Description

In my discussion, while I include details of who did what when, I am less concerned with these matters per se than with affiliations between forms, aesthetic trends, and the poetic and fantasmatic justifications which artists have offered for their own practice. Since the late 2000s, many mature artists have sought affirmation and/or a space of personal reflection by completing a postgraduate degree at one of Australia's universities, producing a rich array of practitioner theses. These documents provide reflective artist biographies, often submitted in association with late career performance works. I have gained enormous insight into rehearsal processes and the ways artists have thought about their work by consulting these texts, but only the thesis by Jo Robertson provides a critical survey which extends beyond the author themselves. Robertson offers the fullest history of Australian butoh to date.

Because so much of this scholarship is structured around artists' first-person accounts, I include my own selected first-person reminiscences from attending or viewing works, such as that regarding viewing Sankai Juku on television above. From 1992 to 2004, I was a critic and reviewer of performance for the Melbourne street magazine *IN Press,* and the national publication *RealTime Australia*, first in Melbourne from 2000, and then Perth, 2004–09. I witnessed much early butoh and Suzuki in Australia, and spoke with or interviewed artists throughout this time, as well as for this book. I draw on reviews that I wrote for *IN Press*, particularly in my discussion of Umiumare, Yap, and de Quincey's *Nerve 9*.[10] My perspective is that of a non-practicing critic. My personal recollections are compared with published sources, including reviews, critical accounts and videos, some of which I obtained directly from artists and their companies. There are notable interviews with three of Australia's leading butoh artists—Tess de Quincey, Yumi Umiumare, and Tony Yap—available from the National Library of Australia. Most artists have their own webpages with posted resources. Many artist statements and similar documents have been published in different forms and under multiple titles. I preferentially cite formal chapters and articles over most of these earlier versions, except where significant differences exist. Rare and archival materials, including videos, are also cited below.

Although mine is a cultural and political analysis of the problematics of combining Japanese theatrical modes with Australian performance traditions, I place considerable emphasis on the *formal* elements of the productions and training. This book is a work of what Clifford Geertz christened "thick description" (1973: 3–32), using such thickened or detailed and expansive descriptions to identify "core symbols", gestures and dramaturgical configurations through which one might unpack the meanings, implications, corporeal rhythms, sonic qualities, and other elements, which cast light on the nature of the work. Although influenced by Geertz's methods, mine is an art historical (not an anthropological) survey. Like Robert Darnton in his own semiological approach to the past, I have attempted a historically informed reading of key events and what Darnton calls their "appended texts" (1999: 5)—be these iconographic sources, histories of site and cultural geography, artist biographies, generic parallels in other media, or literary forms. This serves to thicken and explode my readings, building on the artists' own interpretations. As Darnton puts it, "The

---

10   *IN Press* is available in unindexed hardcopy at the State Library of Victoria.

mode of exegesis may vary, but in each case one reads" in the first instance for "the meaning inscribed by contemporaries" (5).

My aim has also been to descriptively enhance and enliven my critical analysis by attempting to convey some sense of what it must have been like to *attend or participate* in these events, and so make accessible some of this detail both for readers and future scholars. I combine the attention to detail of a reviewer with the analytic focus of the scholar.

11 Overview and Book Structure

Chapters one and two introduce the theatrical, cultural and political context of butoh's spread in Australia. Building on developments which began with Australian New Wave theatre of the 1970s, many artists were seeking to identify new physical techniques to support non-Naturalistic, expressive theatre and performance. These developments emerged during the Prime Ministership of Paul Keating, who helped position Australia as a key state in the Asia-Pacific. Coinciding with Western recognition of Japan's significance in Cold War logistics, economics and culture, this marked a shift in emphasis of Australian policy. Organisations to promote intercultural exchanges between Japan and Australia followed, leading to Suzuki directing the Melbourne production of *Chronicle of Macbeth* (1993). The major butoh companies of Sankai Juku, Dairakudakan, Hakutōbō, Byakkosha and Suzuki Company Of Toga all toured Australia. This was also when the first performances of butoh and Suzuki technique by non-Japanese as well as by Japanese and Asian immigrants occurred. Tess de Quincey, Yumi Umiumare, Tony Yap, Lynne Bradley, Simon Woods, Frances Barbe, Jacqui Carroll and John Nobbs were all active in Sydney, Melbourne or Brisbane by 1992–93.

De Quincey's two workshop series in the Australian outback remain the most sustained outdoor Body Weather explorations other than Tanaka's farm work (chapter three). De Quincey's oeuvre represents, in the title of her 2008 essay, an attempt to determine "How to Stand in Australia?" (Grant and de Quincey 2008), and her answer is that it involves a melancholic embedding of landscapes and histories within highly disciplined and sensitive bodies. Chapters three and four look at Tanaka and de Quincey and her peers. Their work has been crucial in introducing butoh and related forms into conversations around Australia performance and identity, where the divided body and First Nations histories now occupy an important place. It is clear from participant accounts that de Quincey and her associates found the landscape productively "Uncanny" In the terms of Jane Jacobs and Ken Gelder (1995), the unhomeliness of the space becoming a necessary precondition for their sympathetic, haunted response. These themes, together with the problematics of home, the urgency of engaging with First Nations subjects, and Australia's national iconography, recur in the work of other Australian artists. De Quincey's pieces were not restricted to the desert, and in chapter four I examine her urban site-specific productions, as well as those by her associates. I end chapter four with de Quincey's *Nerve 9* (2001–05), a masterful realisation of the hysterical potentialities embedded within butoh practice.

Chapters five and six move to the work of Asian descent artists in Australia, specifically Yumi Umiumare and Tony Yap. Umiumare occupies a preeminent position in Australian butoh, being of both Japanese descent and a former member of Dairakudakan. Both artists have worked extensively with individuals who have little or no dance training. Umiumare has also engaged with Australian First Nation communities and artists. The careers of Umiumare and Yap exemplify the productively unsettling and ambivalent status of butoh in Australia even as it is to some degree naturalized. Chapter five also surveys the work of Dairakudakan as one of the greatest influences upon Australian butoh, identifying Maro's methods and aesthetics in light of how these resurface in the work of Umiumare, Bradley and others.

Yap developed what he describes as "trance dance", echoing the interest in tropes of possession and the Dionysian which date back to butoh's origins. Umiumare was to develop what she calls "butoh cabaret", premiering this model in *Tokyo DasSHOKU Girl* (1999). This cabaretic style harks back to early Japanese butoh. From 1996 Umiumare and Yap collaborated on a series entitled *How Could You Even Begin to Understand?* a study of the opacity of Asian Australian identity and the corporeal challenges it presents. Chapters five and six survey their careers, key productions, theatre roles, Umiumare's collaborations with First Nations artists, as well as touching on the work of Umiumare and Yap as the directors of the ButohOUT! (2017-present) and the Melaka Arts and Performance festivals (2010-present).

In chapters seven and eight, I turn to the coexistence of butoh and Suzuki in the work of two companies in Brisbane: Australia's leading Suzuki ensemble Frank Theatre (founded by Jacqui Carroll and John Nobbs) and butoh-Suzuki fusion group Zen Zen Zo Physical Theatre (founded by Lynne Bradley and Simon Woods, featuring choreography by Frances Barbe). In the same year that Bradley travelled Japan, John Nobbs was recruited as the only dance-trained artist to participate in Playbox's *Chronicle of Macbeth*. Dancer choreographer Jacqui Carroll was Nobbs' partner. Nobbs now calls their work Nobbs Suzuki Praxis, or NSP, and regularly offers workshops. Although Frank and Zen Zen Zo see each other as distinct in style, the presence of both in Brisbane has

INTRODUCTION

generated a vibrant physical theatre scene in which butoh and Suzuki are often combined. Chapter seven begins with an examination of Suzuki's work first in Japan and then Australia, before moving to a synoptic comparative analysis of Frank's training and a close examination of the company's adaptation of *Summer of the Seventeenth Doll* as *Doll Seventeen* (2002). This production serves as a case study of the compatibility of Japanese physical performance with Australian national tropes such as what Russell Ward called the Australian Legend.[11]

In chapter eight, I survey Zen Zen Zo's butoh programs, the development of their signature butoh choruses, and the landmark butoh-Suzuki fusion piece *Cult of Dionysus* (1994–96). Zen Zen Zo's and Frank's productions show little overt sign of its butoh origins today. Bradley's and Frank's works, like Umiumare's productions, drew on popular culture and frequently had a garish aesthetic, often taking the form of episodic sketches.

I conclude by observing that while relatively few Australian institutions offer regular butoh training—Viewpoints and Suzuki are more common—most Australian undergraduates who train in physical theatre or devising will encounter butoh as part of a mixed program. This has consolidated butoh's influence within both Australian and global performance. The history of Australian butoh shows that butoh and related forms like Suzuki technique continue to inform issues of Country, landscape and corporeal oppression in settler colonial and global contexts. Butoh and Body Weather posit corporeal ways to come at the conflicted nature of our relationships with landscape and national identities. Artists in other global contexts would do well to consider the implications of land ownership, politics, race and identity, and how butoh might help us corporeally engage with pressing issues for our times. These are moreover not issues solely particular to Australia. They are global ones.

---

[11] See "Bodies in Opposition to the Australian Legend" in chapter two.

CHAPTER 2

Butoh and the Australian Context: Dancing the Landscape while Dancing Global Relations

1   Introduction

In this chapter, I trace the consolidation of butoh as a recognised form in Japan and some of the early butoh performances in Australia from the 1980s. A key concept which butoh artists adopted in Australia was Tanaka Min's claim to not simply dance in the landscape, but to dance the landscape itself. In many Australian First Nations cultures, moreover, it is a ceremonial practice to dance the ancestral landscape, or Country.[1] In discussing the relationship between these two concepts, I consider the rhetoric of terra nullius, or empty lands, which legal experts deployed in the twentieth century in an attempt to justify white theft of Indigenous lands. As Australian butoh artist and critic Gretel Taylor has observed, the concept of terra nullius is rhetorically akin to the concept of the butoh body as an "empty" space within which forces might lodge. But neither Australian jurisprudence, nor most butoh artists, have ever accepted that lands or bodies were entirely empty. Rather, as Taylor argues, the rhetoric of butoh forces artists and critics to wrestle with the histories of colonisation in Australia, Japan and globally. Following from this, I consider the inter-race relations and performance in Australia in the context of post World War Two Australian dance, theatre, and the growth of physical theatre during the 1980s-90s, which coincided with the uptake of butoh and Suzuki in Australia. The emergence of the term and practice of physical theatre helped lay the groundwork for the spread of Japanese physical performance, as did a state-endorsed geopolitical shift in diplomatic and economic attention from Europe and America towards the Asia Pacific. Issues of dancing Country, of the history of Chinese and Japanese in Australia, as well as of colonialism and race more generally, had renewed currency. I invoke Russell Ward's analysis of the Australian Legend as a dominant trope of national identity, forged in the violence of settling the land and "taming" the landscape and its inhabitants

1   Smith argues that in Australian First Nations "ceremonial performance", the "space/place [of the performance] itself is transformed into the Ancestral landscape" leading to an "Identification with land" and therefore the dancing "body *creates* this intensified space" of the ancestral landscape (2000: 57–67).

to produce a productive environment, as continuing to inform conceptualisations of Australian dance and theatre—both of which have often been seen to emerge out of a conflicted relationship with local landscapes and conflicts. The physicality of the Australian Legend has at times legitimised Suzuki technique in Australia, even as Suzuki and butoh have tended to undermine images of the healthy, undivided national body.

2 Consolidation in Japan and Movement to Australia

Butoh and Suzuki initially acquired a strong following among avant garde artists in Japan. By the 1980s, both forms were attracting international interest. Hijikata himself never left Japan, and he died in 1986, leaving it to others to spread his legacy, including members of his largely female company Hakutōbō led by Ashikawa Yoko.[2] By now, a number of companies led by Hijikata's and Ohno's former dancers had emerged, the first of which in 1972 was Dairakudakan, founded by artistic director Maro Akaji in association with Yamada Bishop.[3] Maro and many of the later butoh-ka did not have the same level of formal dance training as their predecessors. Maro had in fact been an actor in Kara Jūrō's radical group Jōkyō Gekijo (Situation Theatre) before working with Hijikata, 1964–71. Maro's central role in the subsequent history of butoh and its spread overseas facilitated the crossover of butoh from dance to theatre—a matter of some controversy within butoh itself, but which made the later fusing of elements of Suzuki technique with butoh in Australia more likely. Hijikata broadly endorsed these developments. It was ex-members of Dairakudakan who established many of the subsequent groups, most notably Ariadone (Carlotta Ikeda and Murobushi Kō) and Sankai Juku (founded by Amagatsu Ushio), and these two companies moved to France in 1979 and 1981 respectively. France was to become butoh's second home, from there spreading across Europe and elsewhere. Both Ohno and Sankai Juku appeared at the 1980 Nancy International Theatre Festival and later at the Avignon Festival before moving on to Europe and Britain. Ohno went to the USA in 1981, followed by Sankai Juku in 1984—though Tanaka had preceded them both by performing in New York as early as 1970.

---

2 Ashikawa failed to garner widespread support as Hijikata's successor not only because she was a woman, though this played a role, but because the aesthetic sensibility she helped to establish at Hakutōbō was not always seen as consistent with Hijikata's earlier, more aggressive work; see Vangeline 2020; Blackwood 1990.
3 On Maro, see chapter five.

While Ohno and the newer companies reached out to audiences in Western Europe and the USA, it was Tanaka who first toured many of the places butoh was otherwise slow to reach. So it was Tanaka became the first butoh artist to visit Australia, appearing at the 1982 Sydney Biennale of Art. The performance is interesting because Tanaka was not billed as a dance artist per se, but as a gallery performer staging a durational, time based work of physical sculpture. Photographic documentation shows Tanaka in a classic butoh pose, head shaved, bent in on himself, his hands clawed, as he lay almost naked on the hard ground near the Art Gallery of New South Wales (Cermak 1982; Molloy 1982: 1). Alan Schacher, one of the few Australian performers who was alerted to Tanaka's presence, described Tanaka as a "naked body painted black ... with eyes firmly closed", moving extremely "slowly" (Schacher 2000: 22). Presumably because of its framing as a live gallery work rather than dance, Tanaka's premiering of butoh-derived work in Australia had little direct other impact on local performance practice, but it did signal the beginning of bigger things to come.

While few performing artists attended Tanaka's 1982 demonstration, its depiction in the media revealed how forcefully butoh and its ideas could be communicated through photographic distribution. As Rosemary Candelario observes:

> Hosoe Eikoh's 1969 *Kamaitachi*, featuring photos of Hijikata in northern Japan, has become a legendary text of not only butoh but also twentieth century Japanese photography. Later books such as *Butoh: Dance of the Dark Soul* (Holborn and Hoffman 1987) and *Butoh: Shades of Darkness* (Viala and Masson-Sékiné 1988) became important sources of ... inspiration for dancers around the world, along with other media such as the 1989 [filmic] documentary by Edin Velez, *Butoh: Dance of Darkness*.
> 2019: 250

Dance of the Dark Soul and *Shades of Darkness* included translated statements from Tanaka, Maro, Hijikata, Isamu, and Amagatsu, as well as large numbers of photographs which gave an excellent impression of butoh. Masson-Sékiné's work was particularly significant because it included historic images by Hosoe Eikoh, Hanaga Mitsutoshi, Nakatani Tadao, and others, as well as her own prints. To this list should be added the early Australian documentary *Butoh: Piercing the Mask* (1991), by Richard Moore (who in 1990 performed in Suzuki Tadashi's *King Lear*) which, along with Velez's film, was screened on Australian television. Moore's film featured short excerpts of Suzuki's work, thereby helping to establish the correspondence of butoh and Suzuki.

Suzuki's essay "Culture is the Body!" (1984) also began to circulate in Australia, as did teachers and former students of Suzuki's methods. Many of those who now make up a "transnational" butoh community (as Rosemary Candelario would have it) have since reported their own encounters with photographic representations of butoh—particularly stills from the *Kamaitachi* series—as helping to generate a life long interest in the form (Candelario 2019: 244–253; Sakamoto 2020: 71–72, 122–7). Through these and other developments, butoh and SMAT became international phenomena. By the 1990s, artists working in butoh and related styles were based in France, Germany, Netherlands, UK, USA, Mexico, Argentina, Poland, Russia, and Aotearoa New Zealand, as well as Australia.

3 Tanaka's "Map of History through Dancing" in the Contested Lands of Australia

As noted in the previous chapter, the ancient history of human settlement, art and ritual in Australia since ancient times has been of interest to many modern artists globally, including butoh practitioners and Suzuki.

The dates for first human settlement of the Australian continent have been shown to be over 50,000 years, and are likely upwards of 65,000 years (David et al. 2017). Finds from Lake Mungo in what is currently southern New South Wales, provided some of the earliest human evidence of post-mortem rituals in the world which involve cremation and the application of ochre (dated at 42,000 years).[4] The First Nations peoples of the Australian mainland, as well as of the southern island of Tasmania, and of the Torres Strait region which separates northern Australia from New Guinea, are often described as having the oldest continuously maintained culture in the world, with many instances of rock art galleries in regular use from the ancient past through to the present. These cultures are extremely diverse, representing at least 250 different language groups.

Australia's First Peoples have deep and enduring links to the lands they dwell upon, which is today often referred to as Country, meaning nourishing terrain (Rose 1996). Both rights of usage, and obligations of maintenance, are inherited, as well as being acquired through marriage and adoption (Rose 1992). Different Countries have different histories of their formation. Today these creation narratives and lessons regarding Country are usually referred to as

---

4 See "De Quincey's Lake Mungo Workshops" in chapter three.

Dreamings. The term translates imperfectly between First Nations groups. Also problematic is the implication in English that Indigenous beliefs are a kind of "dream" from which they might one day awake (Wolf 1991: 197–224). The phrase persists however, and while Dreamings vary, the idea of an ever present cosmological period of creation continuing to unfold in the landscape is found across mainland Australia. Dreamings are moreover learned, taught, activated, shared and made present through dance, song, the act of painting, and by walking on Country itself. The diverse forms of First Australian dance represent a range of disciplined physical practices, generally learned from an early age, and are rarely accessible to, or taught to, performers of settler descent.

The Aboriginal concept of dancing Country has parallels with the conceptualisations offered by butoh artist Tanaka Min, who claimed "I dance not in the place, I dance the place" (Goldberg 2004: 161). First Australians have however actively danced the places where they dwell and through which they have traversed for millennia (Tamisari 2000: 31–43; Smith 2000: 57–73). Tanaka does not explicitly cite Australian First Nations practice, but he has argued that, at least in Japan and much of Europe, there is "a kind of hierarchy of the art" of theatre, where "all of those moments" from history—peasants performing beside the fields they work in, early indoor performances in hamlets, and fully rendered urban performances—"still exist in Japan" (in Marshall 2006). For Tanaka, what distinguishes Japan is how various degrees of modern and premodern bodily sensibilities can be found across the islands. Tanaka therefore asserts that he can produce a kind of "map of history through dancing" (in Snow 2002: 80). Tanaka claimed that his own practice provided a way of rediscovering the "original form or the primitive form" of embodiment (in Marshall 2006); he claimed to be "a legitimate child of dance initiated in ancient time" (in Snow 2002: 80). Australian butoh artists such as de Quincey, Snow, Umiumare, the members of Zen Zen Zo and others have rarely explicitly addressed the implication that Tanaka's work and that of First Nations Australians traverse a related "map of history through dancing", but each of these Australian artists has responded—generally indirectly—to the challenges which such a formulation implies, often by seeking out Indigenous peoples to collaborate or learn from, or alternatively to construct some other form of "ancient", primal, or shamanic performance.

4   Corpus Nullius: Moving beyond the Emptiness of the Butoh Body

The British annexation of Indigenous lands in Australia is often said to have been justified on the basis of the legal precept of "terra nullius", meaning a null or void space, empty of long-term inhabitants, or any signs of human labour having worked the landscape. The term was however not formally invoked until 1992 for the legal defence against the challenge launched by First Australian Eddie Mabo against the Queensland government's position that the native rights and entitlements of Mabo and his countrymen had been extinguished when the first British colony in Australian was founded in 1788. The state's defence of terra nullius was rejected by the High Court not on the basis that terra nullius should be considered an illegitimate legal concept, but rather that it had never been formally instituted on Australian lands in the years following 1788. Drawing on First Nations' testimony and the evidence of historian Henry Reynolds (2003), the court found that since the time of British explorer James Cook, the colonial office had in fact recognised and charged its officers to protect Indigenous rights to land and other resources. As Gretel Taylor notes (2008: 70), the colonial government disallowed any putative agreements between white private citizens and First Nations peoples because governors saw themselves as guardians of these lands under British Common Law. Governors had done a very bad job at protecting Indigenous entitlements, and false assertions that the First Australians were itinerant had helped colonial officers maintain the illusion that First Nations landowners could be pushed from one area to another. But at no point did the British colonial office or its successors extinguish Indigenous rights on unallocated lands wholesale, nor enact any other legal fiat through which native rights were extinguished. In short, the court showed that terra nullius had *never been* the overarching legal basis for Australian settlement, and that Indigenous rights had always continued and in many cases coincided with or overlay other more recent designations of land title. Australian state and national governments viewed this revelation with alarm, and new laws were rushed into place to formally extinguish or curtail native title to crown lands as a whole. This remains the situation today, with First Nations Australians retaining limited rights to lands and resources. Even where native title exists, it is not comparable to freehold title.

Gretel Taylor points to a rhetorical parallel between the neo-colonial concept of terra nullius and butoh's suggestion of corporeal emptiness. As Yana Taylor observed in another context, the claim by Peter Brook in *The Empty Space* (1968) and others that "give me an undecided ... unclaimed, and uninhabited place and I can make theatre" has "decidedly terra nullius connotations" which elide the racial and situational privilege which makes it easier for some performers to make such a claim than others (Y. Taylor 1996, 15–18). The recognition that terra nullius does not provide the legal basis for Australian colonial settlement and was only retrospectively invoked as a historically unjustified legal defence complicates matters. It has long been clear that it is false to argue that Australian Indigenes were either itinerant or did not work the land. The use of so-called firestick farming or the firing of the landscape to promote herbage for game and crops is known to have been employed across the continent for perhaps upwards of 30,000 years. Movements of Aborigines and Torres Straits Islanders were seasonal, with many constructing long term housing and permanent settlements, as well as edifices such as fish traps, farming structures, irrigation systems, and so on (Gamage 2012; Pascoe 2014; Cane 2013).

Butoh cannot therefore truly function as a new form of terra nullius in this context. The corporealizations fostered by butoh and Suzuki are intended to be sensitive and porous, open to flows from both inside and outside. While the relationship of the butoh or Suzuki body to Country is clearly different from the interlinked, spiritually infused body of the Indigenous Australia dancer, this potential parallelism between Japanese performance and First Nations concepts was to influence the trajectory of butoh and Suzuki in Australia, where they have tended to act in a dialectical fashion, both grounding yet unsettling the performer.

5 Expressive Japanese Performance as a Counter to the Postmodern "Performance of Absence"

With the exception of First Nations choreographies, most of the dance practiced here originated outside of Australia, was imported, and then naturalised or rendered Australian over time (see Brissenden and Glennon 2010). Australia was a major destination for international artists in dance, vaudeville, circus and theatre even before the colonies became a federation in 1901, with luminaries such as Sarah Bernhardt, Anna Pavlova, and the Ballets Russes de Monte Carlo touring in late nineteenth and early twentieth centuries. Non-white performers also toured, often as part of circus ensembles or related acts, including Japanese artists who entertained their fellows in Broome, Queensland and other locations. Umiumare would later perform as one of these artists in the film *Sunrise at Midnight* (2001).[5]

By the 1960s, Australia had a diverse concert dance scene, with close links to not only the UK and Europe, but also the USA. European expatriates fleeing persecution in Europe made a particularly significant contribution from the 1930s onwards, including Edouard Borovansky, Gertrud Bodenwieser, as well as Margaret Lasica. In addition to ballet, relatively restrained Expressionist and contemporary forms tended to dominate.

---

5 See *"Sunrise at Midnight"* in chapter five.

Attempts to render these Euro-American styles distinctively Australian typically took the form of dramatizing elements of the colonial encounter with either First Nations peoples or the landscape. Bodenwieser, for example, rendered the folk-song which celebrated a defiant nineteenth century Australian "swagman", or rural drifter, into a balletic short named after the ballad *Waltzing Matilda* (1946). In addition to Anthill's *Corroboree* choreographed by Reid and Dean (chapter one), Australian artists produced a steady stream of works inspired by, or set in, the Central Desert or Australia's far north, including Bodenwieser's *Central Australian Suite* (1956), Cheryl Stock's *Ochre Dust* (1987), and others (Burridge 2012: 40–51; Burridge 1997; Harris 2022; Brissenden and Glennon 2010; Dunlop McTavish 1987). Choreographic interpretations of the Australian white athletic body, sometimes facing the challenges of the wilderness and its first inhabitants, had been choreographic subjects from at least the 1940s. As dance educator Shirley McKechnie put it in 1991, Australian dance was seen to be "shaped by the fact of living in this land" wherein the "vastness" of the Australian sunlight and landscape was felt in the very "bones and nerves and muscles" of the dancers.

When choreographer Coraline Hinkley returned to Australia in 1960, however, she claimed that her experience overseas had demonstrated to her how interwar versions of German and American dance theatre, and the Australian and American works derived from them, had been "entirely left behind", leaving a "contemporary dance ... stripped of everything, no exaggerated or extra movements and no movements without a reason. Nothing is wasted" (Card 1999: 92). It was then perhaps to the "bones and nerves and muscles" deep within the national body which McKechnie had invoked to which Australian choreography should perhaps return. This departure from the styles previously pioneered by Martha Graham, Mary Wigman and others was spearheaded by Russell Dumas, Nanette Hassall, Elizabeth Demster and Eva Karczag, who founded Dance Exchange in 1976. They helped establish postmodernism as an innovative force in Australian dance, drawing on the work of Merce Cunningham as well as Trisha Brown, Sara Rudner, Twyla Tharp, Deborah Hay, Mary Fulkerston, and Steve Paxton. Rhetorically combative and supported by their journal *Writings on Dance*, Dumas and his fellow postmodernists attacked both ballet and what they perceived as weak derivations of Anglo-European dance theatre in favour of what has since been characterised as a "sensuous, non-decorative, pedestrian classicism" which "privileges the kinaesthetic aspect of dance" (Le Moal 1999: 22).

Despite a growing interest in formalistic dance, pedestrian movement and postmodernism in Australia, Pina Bausch's revision of German Expressionism attracted considerable attention when Wuppertal Tanztheater performed at

FIGURE 3   Frances Barbe's *Fine Bone China* (Brisbane tour, programmed by Frank at the Woodward Theatre: 2008)
PHOTO: PHIL HARGREAVES. REPRODUCTION COURTESY OF BARBE AND HARGREAVES

the Adelaide Festival in 1980 and 1982. Meryl Tankard, who toured with the company, was originally from Australia. She moved to the national capital of Canberra in 1989, and then in 1992 became artistic director of Australian Dance Theatre in Adelaide. Tankard was one of the many Australians who was deeply struck by butoh when it premiered in Australia (McKinnon 2020: 68), indicating the sympathy between Bausch's aesthetic and that of butoh. Although Australia had a long tradition of expressive, often quite grounded dance styles, these types of dance were under challenge from postmodernism and other innovations throughout the 1980s and 1990s. The link between butoh and Bausch's work was not as strong in Australia as it was in France (see Pagès 2017: 244–259), but butoh and Bausch were nevertheless attracting attention in Australia for similar reasons. As Australian butoh dancer Frances Barbe put it, butoh goes beyond conventional actorly models of direct "emotional expressionism" and instead allows the performer to "experience the quality of *'being moved'*" by either emotions or emotional images (2011: 23, 122; my emphasis; Figure 3). This was largely in opposition to Hinkley's dance "stripped of everything", or what Dumas described as the "performance of absence" (Heywood and Gallasch 2001), in which overt signs of emotion gripping the body were rejected. Butoh and Suzuki therefore offered new alternatives to create affectively rich and conflicted bodies on stage and this would be particularly important for the Queensland based companies of Frank Theatre and Zen Zen Zo (chapters seven and eight).

6 Bodies in Opposition to the Australian Legend: Butoh, Suzuki and Grotowski

As Australia entered the 1980s, the recently established practices of New Wave and performance largely worked to situate butoh dancers—and to a lesser extent Suzuki actors—as oppositional bodies. More so than in dance, plays from the 1970s and 1980s often featured fond but critical depictions of the nation's masculine Anglophone heritage. Margaret Williams argued in 1972 that her contemporaries in New Wave theatre "make imaginative use of the social ritual and verbal cliches of Australian society to explore insecurity and inadequacy behind their defensive [and frequently white masculine social] facades" (310). The stereotype functioned dramatically as both a "mask" which characters put on, and a "cage" which bound them, with playwrights offering variants on "the 'butch' Australian male, legendary womaniser, tower of brute strength, [who] dominates ... bringing the women running ... forcing the men into a sycophantic mateship, and crushing" rivals (310). New Wave theatre offered critical perspectives on these national stereotypes—notably in the plays of John Romeril, which I discuss in chapter five—but many plays nevertheless revolved around ambivalent or sympathetic depictions of this Australian type.

Williams' stereotype was first sketched by Russell Ward in *The Australian Legend* (1958), where he contended that accounts of white Australian pioneers struggling to build a life in the face of a harsh, unforgiving landscape had crystalised into a romanticised ideal of the Australian as represented in theatre, literature, journalism, and the visual arts. Male, white, heterosexual, and employed in manual labour within a bush or rural settling, this mythic type was constructed as being:

> a practical man, rough and ready in his manners and quick to decry any appearance of affectation in others. He is a great improviser, ever willing 'to have a go' at anything, but willing too to be content with a task done in a way that is 'near enough'. Though capable of great exertion in an emergency, he normally feels no impulse to work hard without good cause. He swears hard and consistently, gambles heavily and often, and drinks deeply on occasion. Though he is 'the world's best confidence man', he is

usually taciturn rather than talkative, one who endures stoically rather than one who acts busily. He is a 'hard case', sceptical about the value of religion and of intellectual and cultural pursuits generally. He believes that Jack is not only as good as his master but, at least in principle, probably a good deal better, and so he is a great 'knocker' of eminent people unless, as in the case of his sporting heroes, they are distinguished by physical prowess. He is a fiercely independent person who hates officiousness and authority ... Yet he is very hospitable and, above all, will stick to his mates through thick and thin.

1958: 1–2

Although the Australian Legend brings together sometimes contradictory characteristics (at times "taciturn", yet elsewhere a verbally adept "confidence man"), the crucial element of the stereotype is its grounding in corporeal mastery. As Ward put, representatives of the Legend are true "sons of 'nature', whose physical and moral excellence is held up to the admiration of readers" and audiences, and whose nearest counterparts were their dark skinned counterparts or "noble savage[s]" (sic), found in the Pacific and Australia (1958: 230; Cahir et al 2017: 4–12).

Despite shifts and attenuations in the popular uptake of the Australian Legend, the corporeal ideal which Ward described has remained remarkably persistent. As late as 2008, a journalist for one of Australia's major newspapers reflected that while "Not all Australians are calm and competent and tough and generous, as the myth tells us they must be", it is nevertheless:

easy to end up, as I did, believing that despite a life of high heels and takeaway food and traffic fumes, you are, deep down, the sort of person who can winch a truck out of a river, or break a wild horse, or bring a thousand head of cattle safely home. If Australians have a cultural cliché that is uniquely ours, this is it: that even here, in the dusty dirty city, we all secretly believe we are [fictional pioneering figure] Clancy of the Overflow.

qtd in WARD 2009: 94–95

This model of corporeal mastery in the landscape has found ready expression in popular Australian sports. As Isobel Crombie argues, there has been a persistent image of the Australian national body "in contact with primal forces. These are elemental, regenerating forces, and the body on the beach gains sustenance from the earth, the sun and water" (Artlark 2020), particularly in those beachside leisure activities which proliferated following World War Two (Crombie 2004: 177–190). The persistence of the Australian Legend in dance for the period which is the focus of this book is demonstrated by the runaway success of the dance-percussion work *Tap Dogs* (1994)—in some ways a homegrown version of the UK's *Stomp* (1991)—which offered a cast of highly muscular, male performers in visibly working class garb (tank tops, jeans, work boots) whose ease in the body and with each other was said to be derived from the choreographer's working class upbringing and his family's experience of physically demanding factory work within the now defunct steel industry of Newcastle, north of Sydney (Card 1999: 300–303).

The typical embodiment represented by butoh sits in opposition to such models, often approaching a state of hysteria or spasmodic seizure. Suzuki's work has a more dualistic relationship, but nevertheless might be seen as oppositional to tropes of mastery given Suzuki's tendency to stage grotesque tragedies. Several Australian artists have however likened Suzuki's physical discipline to elite sports, David Pledger for example ascribed the "originating contexts" of his own model of *"body listening"* and expression in theatre as coming from Pledger's experience of "team sports [particularly Australian rules football], contemporary performance practice, architecture, landscape, [and] the Suzuki Acting Method" (2017: 44). Australian Suzuki trainer Simon Woods would even work with the Brisbane Lions Football Club "developing programs in flexibility, core strength and mental skills from 2001–2008" (Lawler 2015). Woods' senior peer John Nobbs of Frank Theatre drew on Australian surfing culture to indigenise his own version of Japanese physical theatre, likening Suzuki stomping to the dances one might perform on the beach to 1960s surf music (2006: 99). Nobbs would go on to perform in Jacqui Carroll's adaptation of that quintessential theatrical study of Australian mateship and rural masculine workers, *Summer of the Seventeenth Doll,* originally produced in 1955, and staged by Carroll and Nobbs as *Doll Seventeen* in 2002.[6]

Lloyd Newson, who danced with Kai Tai Chan's One Extra Company in Australia, was himself more inspired by the narrative and expressive qualities of Bausch's work and European dance theatre. After relocating to London in 1986, the Australian expatriate founded DV8 Physical Theatre, thereby popularising the term "physical theatre". In Australia, the phrase was most commonly applied to acrodance drawing on circus and athletics (Gallasch and Baxter 2012). Members of the Australian Performing Group (APG) had taught themselves juggling and circus arts, and this became the core membership of Circus Oz, founded in 1977, and from 1983–86 a scheme brought Chinese acrobats to Australia to teach locals. The groups in Australia which tended to be described

---

6 See *"Doll Seventeen"* in chapter seven.

as physical theatre such as Sidetrack, Stalker (founded 1985), the Sydney Front, Entr'acte, Strange Fruit, and Legs on the Wall (1984) proliferated just at the time that butoh and Suzuki began to reach Australia. In some cases—notably the Sydney Front and Stalker—members of these acrodance and physical theatre companies would add elements of butoh and Suzuki to their idiosyncratic practice.[7] Virtually paraphrasing Ward, the circus artist Ollie Black mused that part of what made these companies "identifiably Australian" was:

> to do with our weather and space—the freedom to be out in the open, to breathe in the energy of the outdoors, to make our presence felt, to be big, bold and fantastic. And not to take ourselves too seriously.
> in GALLASCH AND BAXTER 2012: 41

In short, the Australian Legend was alive and well within 1990s Australian performance, causing butoh and Suzuki technique to function to some degree as disruptive if not always oppositional traditions.

Many New Wave dramatists of the 1970s had nevertheless been looking to less gymnastically proficient international precedents in their search for new forms. New Wave acting itself tended to depart from English derivations of Stanislavskian acting to adopt a bolder and more presentational style (Meyrick 2002: 65), consistent with the Australian Legend. Jacques Lecoq's model of carnivalesque clown and physical expression was also spreading to Australia, and this influence which would prove decisive on Queensland butoh. The most significant development however was the introduction of the work of Polish director Jerzy Grotowski to Australia.

As Ian Maxwell observes, Grotowski's *Towards a Poor Theatre* (1968) began circulating within Australia within a few years of its publication, and these writings were:

> received as missives from the avant-garde future, and taken up by theatre-makers seeking an alternative to the vernacular Naturalism of the emerging Australian New Wave.
> MAXWELL FORTHCOMING

Do-it-yourself experiments in Grotowski's highly physical, ritualised études and plastiques were mounted by members of the APG at the Pram Factory in Melbourne, La Mama theatre as well as by self-professed radicals like Rex

---

7   See "Umiumare's First Nation Collaborations" in chapter six.

Cramphorn associated with NIDA, the Jane Street theatre, and Nimrod in Sydney (Maxwell 2008: 17–41). Through the intervention of his supporters (notably Mike Mullins), Grotowski was contracted to stage *Apocalypsis cum Figuris* in the crypt of St Mary's Cathedral, Sydney, in 1974. Grotowski also ran a wonderfully weird and challenging workshop on a farm beyond the city, where young Australian performers were asked to "climb into wine kegs full of cold water, lined at the bottom with bristling pineapple heads" or to be "dragged through that earth like a human plough ... it was a forceful and immediate confrontation. The sacred earth!" (Waites 1999: 7). French expatriate Igor Persan was so taken by Grotowski's visit that he founded the Theatre Research Group (TRG), eventually settling in rural New South Wales where the company conducted self-devised workshops and productions in the style of Grotowski, 1974–79. Nikki (or Nicola) Heywood, who later joined a Suzuki class before electing to train with both de Quincey and Tanaka, participated in TRG s early devising practices, including rushing blindfolded through the bush and across riverine flats, practicing kendo, activating one's inner animal being, and other exercises, conducted in bucolic surrounds (Heywood 2017: esp. 43–44, 62–66). Methods like theirs would not have been out of place in the training of butoh or Body Weather, hence it is not surprising that the widespread interest in Grotowski within Australian avant-garde performance laid the ground for the reception of butoh and Suzuki.

7 Troubled Relations between Australia and Asia Prior to the Japan Theatre Boom

The First Australians had relatively little contact with Europeans until the seventeenth century, when Dutch ships travelling to Indonesia began to make sporadically landfalls. Cultural exchange between First Nations peoples and those living north of them, however, predates the beginning of British colonisation in 1788. Various peoples from Asia and the Pacific were linked to First Nations Australians through cultural, economic and social exchanges since at least the eighteenth century, setting indirect precedents for the work of several Australian butoh artists—notably Yap and Umiumare. Traders from the Makassan islands of Indonesia made annual trips to the north of Australia since at least the eighteenth century, harvesting sea cucumber or trepang to trade with the Chinese further north.

After 1788, the next significant influx of Asian peoples to Australia were the Chinese, who began arriving in large numbers during the gold rushes of the 1850s—although their presence was often resented by Anglo-Europeans. The

Chinese also worked in agriculture and other industries, the name of "the Walls of China" being assigned to what was to become a famous line of irregular cracked ridges and worn mounds that bordered Lake Mungo, New South Wales, in allusion to those workers who built the nearby Mungo woodshed (NSW NPWS). The historic woodshed stands today, and would be used by Australian butoh artist de Quincey during her experimental workshop at the lake, 1994–95. De Quincey made no overt reference to these precedents in publications issuing from the Mungo workshops, but the very name of the Walls of China provides a suggestive extra layer to her own importation of a Japanese technique to the site. These multicultural precedents were picked up in Umiumare's and Yap's dance film *Sunrise at Midnight* (2001), later recorded at the same location.[8]

During the 1880s, the Japanese established themselves in the pearling industries of northern Australia and the coast of Western Australia, together with Malays, Timorese and others (Lo 2021: 90–92). They had friendly relations with the local Aborigines, contributing to a kriol culture around Broome and other coastal centres. This would become the subject of two works in which Yap and/or Umiumare were involved. Japanese were also contracted in Queensland to work the cane fields, making up a multiracial labour force there which included Pacific Islanders. As noted above, in 2002 Nobbs and Carroll of Frank Theatre would adapt the landmark Australian play dealing with the lives and loves of a pair of cane cutters, *Summer of the Seventeenth Doll* (1955), inflecting what many see as a quintessentially white Australian story with Japanese theatrical form.

As the federation of the Australian colonies approached, governments moved to curtail non-white populations in Australia, and one of the first acts of the national parliament was the 1901 Immigration Restriction Act. Australia's second Prime Minister, Alfred Deakin explained that the aim was the "prohibition of all alien coloured immigration, and … the deportation or reduction of the number of aliens now in our midst" thereby "securing a 'white Australia'" (NMA). Australian governments would however later see the need for increased immigration to build the economy, leading to the abandonment of the white Australia policy. These longstanding racial tensions initially made the country an unlikely location for the important of Japanese performance. Significant geopolitical developments in the region during the 1990s changed this, however.

A shift in attitudes and demographics in the Asia Pacific and Australasia followed the fall of Saigon in 1975. Australian troops had been deployed against North Vietnamese forces from 1962, including Australian draftees. Following the takeover of South Vietnam and Cambodia by communist forces, many in

---

8 See *"Sunrise at Midnight"* in chapter five.

the region fled by boat. The first ship reached Australian shores in 1976 and within three years, fifty-four vessels had arrived. Although this stimulated heated debate regarding Australia's racial and ethnic character, the consensus was that the USA and its allies had a moral responsibility to take on refugees, with over 50,000 immigrants being settled in Australia (Stevens 2012: 526–541). This coincided with the establishment of multiculturalism as national policy, whereby cultural diversity was formally promoted provided cultural practices did not conflict with core beliefs in citizenship and the law. As a 1977 government report put it:

> what ... Australia should be working towards is not a oneness, but a unity, not a similarity, but a composite, not a melting pot but a voluntary bond of dissimilar people sharing a common political and institutional structure.
> KOLETH 2010

Discourse in Australia is still largely framed by these principles, whereby superficial customs of food, dress, leisure and the arts are embraced, but more fundamental values around ethics and religion are less negotiable and can be seen as threatening to national identity. Pauline Hanson reminded Australians how fragile the apparent multicultural consensus was when she claimed in her 1996 parliamentary speech that Anglo-Australians were "in danger of being swamped by Asians". Hanson later added that she was "fed up with being told" by First Nations Australians that "'This is our land.' Well, where the hell do I go? I was born here, and so were my parents" (Curthoys 1999: 18). Butoh and Suzuki artists have rarely addressed these debates overtly, but the very presence of radical Japanese performance within Australia acts as an irritant to Hanson's exclusionary model of cultural and racial identity.

Other geopolitical developments contributed to making the idealised Australian "composite" somewhat more syncretic and less clearly centred around Anglo-European descent than earlier statements of intent had implied. World War Two had demonstrated that Australia could not depend on Britain for military support. Japanese and Australian forces had fought a bitter campaign in the then Australian protectorate of New Guinea, just across the Torres Straits north of Australia, while the Australian mainland was hit by a number of bombing raids and submarine attacks. The antipathies developed during the war persisted for well over a generation. My parents were children during the 1940s, and despite glowing accounts of my travels to Japan, bluntly told me that they could not countenance a visit to the homeland of their former Asian enemies—though they felt no such qualms about visiting the lands of ex-Axis powers in Europe such as Germany. My uncle bore a bayonet scar sustained in the New Guinea campaign, though he in fact worked closely with many Japanese through the Royal Automobile Club of Victoria. The Victorian state president of the Returned Serviceman's League, Bruce Ruxton, joined then Prime Minister John Howard at denouncing the organisers of the Melbourne Festival for proposing to open the 1999 festival with a homage to Australian war dead performed by Japanese taiko drummers at Melbourne's military Shrine of Remembrance (Eckersall 2000: 41). Another critic dismissed the program of the 1994 Adelaide Festival featuring Hakutōbō and other Japanese acts as having "too much soy sauce" (McKinnon 2020: 177).

The attenuation of British influence, fears of Communist incursions in the region, and the rise of capitalist trading partners in the Asia Pacific such as Japan, Korea, Singapore, Hong Kong and Taiwan (Smith et al. 2005) nevertheless forced Australian economists, culture makers and politicians to survey the local area with increasing sympathy. Paul Keating was to declare in 1995 that: "Australia's relationship with Asia has to lie at the very centre of our external interests" and that consequently "Asian culture and Asian values will … begin to work their impact on mainstream Australian culture just as earlier waves of European migration have done" (1995).

In line with these developments, in 1972, the Japan Foundation (Kokusai Bunka Kaikan) was established as a government body under the auspices of the Japanese foreign ministry to facilitate "people-to-people and institutional exchange in arts and culture, sport, science, media and education" (Chapman and Hayes 2020: 18–20). After 1972, the Japan Foundation was highly active in Australia, and links between the two countries intensified over the next two decades. Japanese became the "most widely studied foreign language in Australia" (Chapman and Hayes 2020: 18–20). Japanese media and goods were also widely distributed. Under Keating, Australia became a key member of the Asia-Pacific Economic Cooperation forum (APEC), and the Association of Southeast Asian Nations (ASEAN). By 1991, the Australia Council for the Arts ruled that half of its international budget be earmarked for art from the Asia Pacific region (Alison Broinowski 1996: 204). The period of the 1980s through to the early 2000s was therefore the beginning of what some were starting to call the "Asian century", and interest in Japan from Australia was at its peak—though attention would move to China in the late 2000s as that nation's economy skyrocketed. Major corporations were involved, with the Australian branch of international oil giant Shell claiming that its support of bringing Japanese director Suzuki Tadashi to Australia reflected the company's "longstanding links with Japan, and forges a new bond between two of the Pacific rim's most vibrant cultures" (Playbox 1992).

Race relations more broadly were also shifting. First Nations Australians became highly visible in culture and politics, coinciding with the emergence

FIGURE 4   Direct engagement with the national landscape: Lynne Santos in *Golden Circle* installation by Keith Armstrong and Richard Manner, one in a series of performance installations as part of De Quincey Co's TRIPLE ALICE 1 (Hamilton Downs, Arrernte Country, Central Desert, 1999).
ARCHIVAL VIDEO-STILL COURTESY OF ARMSTRONG.

of a distinctive form of socially critical Aboriginal realism in the theatre of Jack Davis and others (Maufort 2000: 105–6). The National Aboriginal and Islander Skills Development Association Dance Company was founded in 1976, four years after the Aboriginal Tent Embassy had been established in the nation's capital. Limited land rights for First Australians were conceded by government, beginning in 1975 with Prime Minister Gough Whitlam handing Wave Hill cattle station back to the Gurindji peoples. In 1992, six months after the Mabo Decision had struck out terra nullius, Keating delivered a speech to launch Australia's participation in the International Year of the World's Indigenous Peoples in which he urged "non-Aboriginal Australians" to acknowledge that "it was we who did the dispossessing. We took the traditional lands and smashed the traditional way of life" (Keating 1992). Amid much controversy, a protracted process of reconsidering Australian identity, its ethnic makeup, and national relations with each other and the landscape, was active throughout the 1980s and 1990s. Despite the presence of dissenters like Hanson, the stage was set for a more sympathetic reception to Japanese arts than ever before, with artistic exchanges between Australia and Japan now being constructed as in the national interest.

8 The Japanese Theatrical Boom in Australia, 1982–1994

Eckersall (2004: 23–54) identifies a "Japanese theatrical boom in Australia" of touring companies and artists, particularly after 1986. As previously noted, Tanaka was the first to reach Australian shores in 1982. Although Tanaka's visit attracted relatively little interest within the theatre community, photographic documentation became available via newspaper coverage, specialist art journals and other sources.

In terms of live performance, Ohno Kazuo's tour of a program of signature works *Admiring La Argentina* (which Hijikata contributed to) and *The Dead Sea* at the 1986 Adelaide Festival was a more significant watershed.[9] Ohno's tour was supported by the Japan Foundation, as were more to come. Byakkosha had a particularly interesting trajectory, beginning with their 1981 performance at the Fifth Third-World Theatre Festival in Korea which prompted them to extend what they called the "World Dance Caravan Through All the Continents", taking them through Jakarta, Yogyakarta, Bali (1982), Manila (the Second Asian Theatre Festival and Conference, 1983), and then Taiwan (1986). Tony Yap would work across many of these locations. A successful tour by Byakkosha to the 1985 Spoleto Festival in Italy led to the company being invited to the sister festival based in Melbourne in 1987. In 1988 and 1989, Sankai Juku participated in what had been the Spoleto Festival and was now the Melbourne International Festival of the Arts (MIFA), as well as the Adelaide and Perth Arts Festivals. Dairakudakan followed suit appearing at MIFA in 1991. The last tour of one of the companies close to Hijikata concluded with a visit from Hakutōbō to Adelaide in 1994. Particularly significant in terms of signalling cultural and political rapprochement was the invitation for the Suzuki Company of Toga (SCOT) to appear at the 1988 festival in Sydney which marked the anniversary of two hundred years since the establishment of the first British colony in Australia. This constituted a highly public statement regarding the change in relations between Japan and Australia nearly forty years since the conclusion of the Pacific Wars. SCOT also appeared at MIFA in 1989. This led to the landmark collaborative production of *Chronicle of Macbeth* (1992) featuring an Australian cast under Suzuki's direction.

All of these events played out against a corresponding global rise in intercultural and multicultural theatre as a whole, which was embraced in Australia despite some critical misgivings. Peter Brook's landmark English language production of the Hindu classic *The Mahabharata*—described by Rustom Bharucha as a "United Nations of theatre" in terms of its syncretic universalising

---

9 *Admiring La Argentina* also included the Dance of Divine which Ohno had prepared for the revised version of Hijikata's infamous premiere of butoh, *Kinjiki* (1959). Baird 2022: 10–11, 120–143.

aspirations (1993: 81)—was staged in Perth and Adelaide in 1988 and the film version was screened on the national multicultural television station SBS. Alongside *The Mahabharata*, Australian audiences were treated to Robert LePage's *Dragon's Trilogy*. Several key Asian Australian theatre makers rose to prominence, notably the Chinese-Australian photographer and monologist William Yang (who premiered *Sadness* in 1992), as well as Chinese-Malaysian dance-maker Kai Tai Chan (artistic director of One Extra dance company, 1976–91, and a regular choreographer for Sydney Dance Company).

Eckersall argues that the 1994 Adelaide Festival marked the "apogee" for Japanese mainstage performance in Australia, as this festival was programmed with an explicitly Asian focus. Some audiences took issue with this, a letter to the *Adelaide Advertiser* attacking a:

> program of esoteric and generally incomprehensible items which appeal to very few and the exaggerated accent on Asian content has arrogantly ignored the artistic preference of many thousands who are more comfortable with a Western/classical orientation.
> ECKERSALL 2004: 40

Significant here is the conflation of national/racial categories with aesthetic ones. It was not simply that these performances were *Asian*, but that the implied role of public institutions to represent the best of art, and hence by implication the *classical* Western canon, had been usurped by these more challenging and *esoteric* non-Western forms. Although such "Asian content" was of great interest to Australian avant-gardists and their heirs, rear-guard actions to keep Australian performance focussed around classic Euro-American and Naturalistic theatre, ballet and Western symphonic musical performance continued. It is was, after all, in 1990 that one of Australia's leading theatre makers, John Bell, improbably claimed that Shakespeare's work was not getting enough national attention, and founded Bell Shakespeare Company. Butoh and Suzuki technique therefore remained minoritarian and not entirely integrated forms of performance even as they gained ground in Australia, and today this remains part of their cultural potency. Butoh and SMAT continue to function to some extent as outsiders within the full panoply of cultural consumption in Australia, just indeed as German tanztheater did when it was brought to Australia by the likes of Bodenwieser.

In the chapters that follow, I trace the development of these oppositional modes of embodiment which butoh and Suzuki brought to the Australian context, starting with Tess de Quincey's encounter with the "magnetism" exerted by the geographic and mythic lands of the central Australian deserts (2021: 322), and reckoning with the legacy of the Australian Legend in performance.

CHAPTER 3

De Quincey Takes Body Weather Inland: Lake Mungo and Alice Springs

1   Introduction

In this chapter, I sketch de Quincey's career and her powerful engagement with the Australian landscape and national tropes. It is my contention that even though de Quincey has not solved the problem she set herself of "How to Stand in Australia" (Grant and de Quincey 2008), her self-reflexive, dialectical attempt to do so has established Body Weather and related practices as key concepts to corporeally investigate Australian national landscapes and cultures. My argument is that de Quincey ventured bravely, perhaps at times naively, into extremely vexed, overdetermined issues in Australian national identity and history, specifically in the inland desert regions of central Australia, where she and her dancers found themselves interacting with colonised lands. As de Quincey has observed, it was "the first time that I really saw the bare bones of Aboriginal Australia and the history" (de Quincey and Eckersall 2012). De Quincey produced through her practice of Body Weather an essentially intuitive and materialist critique of how the forces of history and environment animate the body. Perhaps de Quincey's most important contribution is to situate such animating forces outside of the dancing individual, and to see such corporeal responses as always provisional, divided and dispersive. The national subject is always one set upon by shifting agents which emanate, in the first instance, from outside of itself.

2   De Quincey's Butoh Encounter and Position within Australian Dance

In 1984, Anglo-Australian Tess de Quincey attended a performance of one of the few works from the companies Hijikata himself directed and which toured during his lifetime. The piece was *Nihon no Chibusa* (*The Breasts of Japan*, 1983), devised to feature Hakutōbō's leading dancers Ashikawa Yoko and Kobayashi Saga. Ashikawa performed a range of physical transformations from, "Tired old whore" to "geisha's ghost, doll, grimacing monster, frightened aborigine"—or an Ainu from Tōhoku—as well as a Jōmon "clay statue" (Viala and Masson-Sékiné 1991: 92). De Quincey was awestruck by the performance, finding herself afterwards:

> standing on the street in Copenhagen and thinking: "What the hell was that?" I felt I had to go to Japan and find out why this work was being done, what it was about and what its language is. So I went, had the opportunity to see a lot of different work and then ... joined Min's company as I felt a total and immediate rapport with his way.
> PARSONS AND WYNNE-JONES 1996: 14

De Quincey came to specialise in her own variant of the method developed by Tanaka Min, entitled Body Weather, and which de Quincey herself describes as "not butoh" in a true sense, and hence "different" to some degree from Hijikata's work (Parsons and Wynne-Jones 1996: 15–16). Nevertheless, de Quincey was drawn to butoh and its derivatives by the ability of Hijikata's chosen successor Ashikawa to *transform*, such that the choreography "exploded every concept I had about dance and performance" (de Quincey and Eckersall 2012) including something both "fundamental" but also "destroying accepted form[s]" (Parsons and Wynne-Jones 1996: 14).

De Quincey was the second Australian to work with Tanaka's company of Maijuku (the first Australian was Nigel Kellaway), and she has become an international leader in Body Weather. She has been practicing in Australia since 1989. Her two projects sited in inland Australia, first at Lake Mungo (1994–95) and then Triple Alice (1999–2001), remain the most sustained investigations of landscape and Body Weather outside of Tanaka's practice.

De Quincey has trained and influenced numerous Australian and international dancers. Even those Australians who have worked with Tanaka or other Body Weather artists have usually spent a period comparing or refreshing their work with de Quincey. In terms of geographical distribution, de Quincey had become by the early 1990s the unchallenged leader of butoh-related work in Sydney, a position which she largely maintains, despite the subsequent rise of artists in Melbourne (in the state of Victoria) and Brisbane (Queensland). Many of de Quincey's collaborators were distinguished Body Weather practitioners in their own right, training others. Workshop leaders included Frank Van de Ven (based in Amsterdam, and who has also offered workshops in Australia, Amsterdam and Europe), Stuart Lynch (who has since returned to Denmark), Christine Quoiraud (a French based Body Weather artist who contributed to Triple Alice), Peter Snow, Alan Schacher, and Gretel Taylor.

3 Tanaka Min and Body Weather

Tanaka Min had attended *Nikutai no Hanran* in 1968, but initially developed his practice independently. He trained in Graham technique and Japanese modern dance during the 1960s before striking out on his own as a solo improviser in 1973 (Marshall 2006: 57–58). His aim was to not "dance *in* the place", but to "dance" or embody "*the place*" itself, initially through what he called a "dance condition" or "butai", which he describes as the "vibration or activity of the soul … manifest through the body" (Tanaka 1981 and 1986; Snow 2002: 80). The term "butai" carried clear echoes of word "butoh". In the early 1980s Tanaka reached out to Hijikata by publishing in *Yu* magazine an essay entitled "I am an avant-gardist who crawls the earth: Homage to Hijikata Tatsumi" (Tanaka 1986). Tanaka concluded the article by claiming to be the "legitimate son of Hijikata", and selections from the text were included in Tanaka's program notes for overseas tours:

> I decided to write to … [Hijikata] of my feelings of love. It was quite direct; quite cold but quite direct … A month later he came to my performance. Since that time I became a student of his. I studied with him from 1982 for four years and in 1986 he died.
> in MARSHALL 2006: 59

Tanaka worked under Hijikata's direction with Ashikawa and the two performed a duet in 1983. Hijikata also directed a solo for Tanaka entitled *Ren'ai Butoh-ha Teiso* (*Pure Love Dance School*) in 1984. Tanaka claimed to have learnt from Hijikata and Ashikawa one thousand embodied states which were prompted or described by poetic images or motifs. Tanaka would pass these on through his own training.

Tanaka's working association with butoh dancers predated *The Pure Love Dance* project itself. From 1978, Tanaka had been developing what he called Body Weather (shintai kisho), drawing on a diverse range of influences including sports training (Tanaka had been a professional athlete) as well as yoga, acupuncture, international folk dance, and butoh. Several members of Dairakudakan participated in the early workshops (Baird 2022: 214). Tanaka put these methods into practice through his solos, which passed under various titles, including *Drive* (1977–1980), *Hyperdance* (1977) and the more expressive *Emotion* series (1982–83). Tanaka's performances in New York and Sydney in 1980 and 1982 respectively were billed under the moniker *Drive*, while *Hyperdance* was a series of 120 site-specific works performed in Japan over the course of 70 days (Tanaka 1981: 6–7). As Zack Fuller explains, the locations:

included college campuses, temples, gymnasiums, art galleries, tent theatres, and riverbanks ... stairways and city streets, a factory, an old train station, a hotel dance hall, a lumber yard, many public parks, a bulldozer, a truck, the runway of a local airport.

2016: 77

Perhaps most famous of all were the performances at the ironically named Dream Island (Yume no shima), an artificial island in Tokyo Bay built entirely of noisome urban and industrial waste. These dances were photographically documented by Tanaka's long term collaborator Okada Masato (Tanaka and Okada 2019).

Throughout this period Tanaka's appearance was very much that of a classic butoh-ka, his head shaved, and either naked or very nearly so, exposing his body to the elements such that the distinction between his body and the site became confused. As Tanaka observed:

Face the field in front of you with one fragment of your body—face the cosmos only with your right bun [buttock cheek], or face the water horizon only with your spine ... There is no need any more to be overconcerned as to where lies the boundary of your body.

TANAKA 1981: 7

Tanaka often employed make up, typically grey or ochre-like brown, which commentators have noted drew parallels to Ainu and even African American performers (Aslan 2004: 179–180). Tanaka's body therefore appeared otherworldly and racially ambiguous, not unlike Hijikata himself in *Kinjiki,* for which dark olive oil was painted onto the skin.

Four years after the first Body Weather workshops, Tanaka founded Maijuku, or the Dance School company. This was the first Japanese butoh ensemble with an international membership, approximately half of the dancers being recruited from Japan, and the other half coming to hail from Australia, Aotearoa New Zealand, the Netherlands, Denmark, France, Spain, the USA and elsewhere (de Quincey and Eckersall 2012). In 1985, Tanaka secured a small farm approximately four hours from Tokyo at Hakushu (later Hakuto city). This was Tanaka's base of operations until he moved to Honmura, Shikishimacho (later Kai city) in 2000. Both institutions involved bucolic surroundings just beyond the urban sprawl, lying at the foot of steep, volcanic hills such as are characteristic of the Japanese landscape. Vegetables and later rice and tea were farmed and a number of outdoor stages built, producing what Tanaka's assistant Kobata Kazue described as a space where "Earthy folk art and avant-garde art merged in this highland village" (Tanaka and Bailey 1993). Tanaka's move to the countryside was echoed by several of the artists discussed in this book, including Suzuki Tadashi, who even initially planned to conduct farming at his Toga estate but this proved impractical (Goto 1989: 121–2).[1] Tanaka played the role of Banquo in Suzuki's 1991 Japanese production of *Macbeth* (Sant 2003: 153), the same role which Australian Suzuki expert John Nobbs was to play in the 1992 Australian version (Figure 2).

Body Weather is a structured system, although Tanaka resists allowing it to become fully standardised. Peter Snow (2002) provides the most detailed account of the training regimes of Tanaka and those which Tess de Quincey developed from these. Work at Tanaka's farms generally commenced with the aerobic sessions called muscle/bones or mind/body (MB), in which dancers crossed the floor in rows or diagonals, executing various poses, twists and expressions. Though neither as disciplined as Suzuki's approach nor as focussed on hips and legs, there is some similarity to the variations on processional walking of MB to Suzuki's training. MB was usually followed by the manipulations,[2] in which one partner put the other into involved often painful stretching positions and folds. Then followed exercises which de Quincey has since termed "groundwork" (McAuley 2000: 235–7), and which involves exploring locations so as to map the surrounding environment onto the body, and vice versa. As Triple Alice participant Marnie Kee née Orr and her collaborator Rachel Sweeney observe, there is often an implied cross-sensory and synaesthetic aspect to these interactions, whereby:

> The fingers are smelling the landscape. The tongue listens to a bird on the opposite hill. The ears can feel the distance between the teeth and the horizon. The mouth is an open orbit, revolving eye.
> ORR AND SWEENEY 2011

Gretel Taylor also relates the following examples of:

> Hijikata's images (as I have learned them from Tanaka) ... ants walk in between your teeth; a moth flutters on your forehead; your internal organs are falling out; horses gallop on your back, which is a paddock; your legs and pelvis are a cow's, pissing; your arms are beckoning to a soul.
> 2010: 77

---

1 See chapter seven: "Suzuki Tadashi in Japan & Australia".
2 Illustrations of the positions are published in Viala & Masson-Sékiné (1991: 163) & Pagès (2017: 329).

Larissa Pryce (2017: 54), who encountered Body Weather at Triple Alice, explains that MB serves to displace the dancer and their body, while groundwork—particularly in de Quincey's practice—acts to re-embed within the dancer the specifics of the location. Several exercises involve being positioned or moving blindfolded, and many exercises are referred to using skeletal terminology. Much of the instruction therefore involves placing the body in a near death or coma-like state so that it might take on influences without a will or intent of its own. Another key exercise is bisoku, or moving extremely slowly (less than a centimetre per second), which Pryce (2017: 51) describes as breaking "open a ... phantasmagoric plenitude" in the body and its perceptions. Explorations of weight and gravity are conducted under the title bag of bones (Taylor 2020). Alternatively, Tanaka might give images or phrases for the dancer to embody, many of these being drawn from the vocabulary Tanaka learned from Hijikata and Ashikawa.[3] De Quincey would go on to develop her own, Australianised version of this repertoire which she titled a Dictionary of Atmospheres.[4] As Taylor explains, these various actions would then be conducted again and in combination on Tanaka's open air stages, where "large butterflies" were often "wafting through our workspace" and there was the "occasional interruption" by aggressive bees (Taylor 2010: 75). Exercises were accompanied by what Tanaka calls the "insect musicians of Japan" (Tanaka and Bailey 1993). All this meant that exercises did not necessarily "become more manageable but rather increasingly complex", with many competing sensorial inputs and challenges to be attentive to (Taylor 2010: 75).

Tanaka's training was interspersed with physical labour on the farm, which Tanaka felt was crucial for the development of a sensitive mind and body, dancers becoming attuned both to the environment and to the collective at the farmhouse. Despite the expressive potential of Body Weather, it is in many ways a depersonalising practice, where the dancer becomes an impersonal vehicle for the dance as part of a human and non-human environmental exchange. Tanaka has moreover likened Body Weather to the divinatory trances of Tōhoku's mediums, or so-called "itako", who "brings the dead people into her body, to speak" (Fuller 2017: 269). For Tanaka, the shaman, like the Body Weather dancer, is a type of almost non-human "media, or emptiness ... one of the most talented Body Weather [dancers]. Ancestor of the dancer" (269). It is worth bearing in mind however that what Tanaka promotes above all else

---

3 For a rich autoethnographic account of the act of imaging in the Australian context, see Taylor (2008: 1).
4 For discussion of the production the same title, see this chapter under *Dictionary of Atmospheres* below.

is a dialectic between the *depersonalised* dancer who takes on the forces and, yes, emotions, of the universe itself, versus Body Weather as an *expressive* and highly emotional form. Broadly speaking, different artists emphasise different aspects, with de Quincey's work generally being characterised by an impersonal, abject, puppet like quality, whilst others such as Gretel Taylor insist that because the dancer cannot in fact transcend their own subjectivity, one should embrace the Expressionistic elements of Body Weather practice (Taylor 2008: 127–128). Tanaka's own work is not without expressive elements, and he is well known as an actor of stage and cinema, including working with Suzuki.

4 De Quincey's Development from Postwar Britain to Australia

De Quincey's early life was highly peripatetic and this has left her with a tendency to interrogate the specifics of locations, while also relating different places and sites to each other. In de Quincey's life and practice, the site is never singular but always multiple—a point to which I return below. After a childhood on the rugged coast of Wales, de Quincey's family moved to London where she enrolled at art school at a multicultural college in the late 1960s. She was very taken by the postwar, postcolonial moment, with populations from Britain's former colonies being highly visible. She auditioned for the Royal Ballet school but was not accepted, and she ceased dancing until she moved to Copenhagen some years later. Before that, in the early 1970s, de Quincey's family moved again, this time to Sydney. De Quincey then travelled inland across Australia to Mount Isa and then from the northern Australian city of Darwin and on to the island of Bali where she, like Antonin Artaud at the 1931 Paris Colonial Exposition, encountered Balinese gamelan performance and dancing. "It felt deeply foreign", she explains, "but I felt enormously fascinated" (de Quincey and Eckersall 2012). She would later study Balinese dance drama. She continued moving north through Indochina, Afghanistan and then Europe. De Quincey claims that:

> On the boat … coming into Europe through the Black Sea … the moment I saw Istanbul, I suddenly saw the density and the layering of Europe and its history. And I could feel Australia! I felt that *huge* space. And I suddenly got a summing up of what Australia had been for me.
> DE QUINCEY AND ECKERSALL 2012

It was therefore through an encounter with the historical and spatial vastness of another region—namely Eurasia, the Silk Route and the complex exchanges between east and west that have ebbed and flowed since Indo-Hellenic culture reached Japan—that de Quincey came to see the ancient landscapes of the Australian continent as similarly multilayered, sublime and expansive.

    De Quincey's recognition of Australian space at the gates of Europe provides a clue to her conception of how to engage with the Australian landscape in dance. Places are for de Quincey both specific yet interlinked, possessing a trans-geographic and indeed transhistorical character. De Quincey's own journey of discovery was moreover very corporeally engaged, some of her strongest memories being the smells of the markets, of getting lice in her matted hair, and the sensorial encounter with diverse landscapes and cultures. De Quincey concluded by settling in Copenhagen, where the networks she established enabled her to study with Peter Brook's frequent collaborator Oida Yoshi, whose acting drew heavily on Japanese noh theatre, as well as Eugenio Barba's cross-cultural laboratory the Odin Theatre. Through Odin she was able to study one of the Balinese temple dance forms (topeng masked dance) akin to those Artaud had witnessed. De Quincey also had an opportunity to experience the styles dance of both Cunningham and Graham, neither of which resonated. After seeing Ashikawa in Copenhagen in 1984,[5] de Quincey secured a position recruiting companies from Japan and surrounding countries to tour London and Europe. Through this role she encountered a range of artists, including Australian performance artist Stelarc (then based in Japan), Indian tabla artists (with whom she briefly studied), the Korean music theatre form of pansori, as well as Korean shamanism, Japanese kabuki, noh, gagaku, and of course butoh. Through Ashikawa, who's European tour de Quincey helped arrange, she found her way to one of Tanaka's annual Body Weather laboratories. At this time Tanaka's dancers moved between a former textile factory in Hachiōji on the outskirts of Tokyo, and the vegetated fringes of the city, including the temple mountain of Takaosan. De Quincey took part in two days of Tanaka's laboratory, and as noted at the top of this chapter, she "felt a total and immediate rapport" with his approach (Parsons and Wynne-Jones 1996: 14). She recalls blindfolded walking, running up and down Mount Takao, and other activities, which resonated with her adolescent experience of sports. After arranging Maijuku's trip to Copenhagen, she was invited to join the company, and worked with Tanaka, 1985–1995. De Quincey met Frank van de Ven at Maijuku, de Ven's association with Tanaka's laboratories running 1983–92, before he founded Body Weather Amsterdam in 1993. Stuart Lynch, also active in Copenhagen during the 1990s, was with Maijuku, 1990–93, and would become one of

---

5 See under "De Quincey's Butoh Encounter" at the top of this chapter

de Quincey's main collaborators in Australia from 1991 onwards. Peter Snow, another Australian based artist, would join Tanaka's laboratory for the 1991 season and then follow de Quincey to Lake Mungo and beyond. Fellow Australian Alan Schacher was also at Maijuku, 1989–91. De Quincey also trained with Ohno Kazuo in Yokohama, 1985–86, between classes with Tanaka, and although she notes that Ohno's classes remain "very vivid" in her memory (de Quincey 2022), Tanaka has been a stronger influence.

Initially working with approximately fifty-five other dancers in Hachiōji, Tanaka was still supporting the company by having his dancers perform erotic cabaret and hostess work at the Tokyo bars established by Hijikata and the latter's wife, dancer Motofuji Akiko. These included Bruto club in Roppongi, as well as Caramel, Kitaro and Shōgun. Hostess work and burlesque performance provided a lucrative income for most butoh ensembles, one of Dairakudakan's female dancers responding aggrievedly to a creditor that, "We [the company] have been eating by means of my body!" (Baird 2022: 100). Melissa Lovric, an Australian member of Dairakudakan, reported being:

> suited up in this kind of silicone number ... And then in the performance they gave me a whip and said I had to whip these guys, who were writhing around. I was sort of standing there going: 'what the hell am I doing' ... Some people in Japan think that it is natural that these worlds should go together, but I don't ...
> ROBERTSON 2015: 79[6]

De Quincey herself was ambivalent regarding these activities, but accepted them to hone her skills in episodic physical performance and working with others—and that it could even be quite "fun" and certainly "ridiculous" (de Quincey and Eckersall 2012). Significantly, these on stage burlesques were referred to by the company as "acting", as opposed to true dance (ibid.). Group sequences were choreographed by Ashikawa, but lesbian duets were self devised, and de Quincey reports she enjoyed exploring some of the more "magical sensibilities" (ibid.), such as the aesthetics of erotic smoking. Certainly eroticism and sadomasochism was an important component of Hijikata's examination of carnal nikutai, as well as in the French Surrealist texts which Hijikata drew upon. Tanaka has however claimed to be more interested

---

6 It is worth remembering that no less than the internationally renowned Japanese noise musician Akita Masami (a.k.a. Merzbow) was the author of *Nihon kinbaku shashin-shi* (*A Photographic History of Japanese Bondage*) (1996) and that early French accounts of butoh first appeared in Théo Lésoualc'h's *Érotique du Japon* (1978).

in the "shintai" (the social or mental body) rather than the "nikutai" which so obsessed Hijikata (Tanaka 1986: 155). As de Quincey observes:

> Min didn't want to do the nightclub thing that all the other butoh groups were doing, because he didn't want [necessarily to] have a sexualised body [nikutai]. And I really saw the difference between the Maijuku bodies and the Ashikawa girls [in Hakutōbō]. They couldn't escape sexualisation. They all worked in the nightclubs. And we didn't have that.
> DE QUINCEY AND ECKERSALL 2012

De Quincey worked at the clubs for a period, but she felt that once she returned to Maijuku, "I could shed [all] that" (ibid. 2012). The establishment of the Hakushu farm in 1985 meant Tanaka and his dancers increasingly moved away from these practices.

De Quincey found some of the ways in which the farm and Tanaka's projects were run difficult to accept, but despite her misgivings, she and her peers in the company were always expected to follow Tanaka's lead. As de Quincey put it, "you have no power to make any decisions because you're inside a whole Japanese world" (de Quincey and Eckersall 2012). She became particularly frustrated with slaving to grow vegetables only to see large quantities rot due to lack of distribution. Company members were also obliged to pay for performances at Tanaka's venue of Plan B in Tokyo, and the women cooked for Tanaka and the audience, as well as providing alcohol, presenting the master with a bottle of sake in exchange for his choreography. De Quincey reports that at one stage she was effectively frozen out and not talked to by the whole company because she objected to the fact that only women had to serve as chefs.

The American artist Zack Fuller, who attended Tanaka's laboratories 1997–2000, described Body Weather as devoted to an "anti-hieratic ideal" in that "the workshops were open to people with little or no movement training", including visual artists and writers (Fuller 2014: 198, 202). Dancers were therefore often "asked to learn the movement habits of ... inferior dancers" as part of a series of kata or instructive poses to memorise and accumulate (202). Perhaps most importantly, the act of tending different crops using different movements was seen as a core element of the "dance training" such that Tanaka did "not privilege training over everyday life or human bodies over physical space" (199). Nevertheless, Fuller found Tanaka's claim that there was "no hierarchy at Body Weather Farm ... difficult to support" given the "magnitude of his presence as a visionary leader" (202).

The conventions of Japanese pedagogic authority involving a master who instructed unquestioning apprentices—and which butoh, for all its iconoclasticism, had largely embraced—was a significant challenge for non-Japanese, as it was for some Japanese (Vangeline 2020: 153–5). De Quincey's peer Nikki Heywood found Tanaka had a "demand for a type of 'obedience'" involving submission not just to "the work, but also to the authority of the teacher" (2016: 61). As the Australian Sarah Dunn observed, it was however up to the individual to deal with any lingering effects or psychological challenges of these practices, and many dancers have reported finding the return to the urban environment after so long at Tanaka's farm, or the Australian desert, to be profoundly disorientating (Dunn 2002: 46; Cardone 2002: 19; Pryce 2012: 62). Some of de Quincey's own students in Australia found Body Weather to function as an "assault on the ego" such that psychocorporeal resistance was worn down to enable reconstruction from a non-resistant "'blank' slate", or as Sarah Dunn put it, a "breakdown to breakthrough" which could leave some "mentally dishevelled" and "in a state of shock" (Dunn 2002: 44). Pryce claims that exercise such as muscle/bones were not only "exhausting" but left participants "thoroughly discombobulated and disorientated", all the better to take on new psychocorporeal patterns (Pryce 2017: 46). This same harsh, authoritarian teaching structure was visible in Australian iterations of Suzuki method.[7] Most of the artists discussed in this book however—including de Quincey—accepted this pedagogical model at least to some degree, and certainly were hard taskmasters themselves, akin to the Russian and European ballet instructors who had come to Australia in the years surrounding World War Two (see Grove 1996: 23).

A greater impediment to the uptake of butoh by non-Japanese such as de Quincey was the broader cultural context and upbringing. De Quincey observes that "there was no doubt ... that the Japanese had ... [a] different relationship" with Tanaka (de Quincey and Eckersall 2012). Horikawa Hisako, for example, worked with Tanaka from 1978 and would later be described as co-founder of Body Weather (Amsterdam University 2013; Fuller 2017). While it was not impossible that non-Japanese could develop similarly close associations, de Quincey considered it unlikely. De Quincey claims that Tanaka had moreover become frustrated with working with non-Japanese and wanted to, in her words, "ingrain" himself more into the Japanese context by the time she chose to leave (de Quincey and Eckersall 2012).

Tanaka did however give his approval for de Quincey and other non-Japanese such as Van de Ven to offer Body Weather workshops in Australia and elsewhere. De Quincey presented her first classes in Sydney in 1989. This

---

7 See chapter seven.

workshop was attended by Maijuku regular Peter Fraser, who would later join de Quincey's own company as well as work with Gretel Taylor's Environmental Performance Authority. There was also the Australian dancer Melissa Lovric, who was so inspired that she moved to Japan where she became the first non-Japanese member of Dairakudakan, 1990–96 (Robertson 2015: 79). Nikki Heywood, who had been part of a New South Wales Grotowski group during the 1970s, participated in these early Australian Body Weather workshops too, and later would seek out Tanaka on her own. Mike Mullins, who had facilitated Grotowski's tour in 1974, and had gone on to establish The Performance Space (TPS) in Sydney in 1983. De Quincey used TPS s premises and also performed the solo piece *Movement on the Edge* at the venue. Subsequent de Quincey workshops and laboratories tended to be held outdoors, including a nine day stint inland from Sydney in the Blue Mountains, and another workshop hosted by La Mama theatre in Melbourne. De Quincey's career was in no small part enabled by the ongoing support she received from The Performance Space and similar institutions, including in later years the Universities of Sydney and of Southern Queensland (Toowoomba). Although de Quincey's work was more firmly rooted in Body Weather than the types of butoh represented by Sankai Juku and Dairakudakan, publicity material for her classes described them as an introduction to both Body Weather *and* butoh (Snow 2002: 68). Recalling her work at Hijikata's burlesque clubs in a 1997 interview, De Quincey insisted that "I am butoh" and explicitly rejected the suggestion that she was only weakly "butoh influenced" or "butoh inspired" (Vernon 1997: 2).

5 De Quincey's First Solos in Australia

De Quincey's early solo performance *Movement on the Edge* (1988) was developed by the artist while at Tanaka's farm and premiered at his Plan B space in Tokyo. De Quincey took the work to Copenhagen and Sydney where it was positively received. Within these early shows, de Quincey's face was framed by a shock of "wild red hair" extending down to her waist (Sykes 1990: 10), her visage painted white in the manner of Sankai Juku's dancers, with red lipstick in the style of a Japanese noblewoman or courtesan, sections of the piece being performed nude.[8] Presented in this fashion, I would argue that both de Quincey's performance and her body tended to be read as representative of Japan, partly explaining why Jill Sykes' 1989 review described butoh as "adapted from noh" in

---

8 This image was used on the early fliers for De Quincey's workshops.

addition to being influenced by the Japanese postwar environment and Hiroshima. De Quincey conceded that some of her colleagues in Copenhagen even told her that in *Movement on the Edge* "you even *look* Japanese!" (de Quincey and Eckersall 2012). De Quincey observed that to be "presenting yourself as a Westerner" and yet "coming from an Eastern tradition" such as butoh that "it's a really difficult position" (ibid.).

Movement on the Edge was principally a slow, sculptural, solo exploration of the body, with isolated body parts briefly fluttering into motion, often at obtuse angles. De Quincey's body was intermittently raised up to tumble down. Sykes (1989) described some actions as "jagged" and "savage", noting the rolled up foetal position that so often appears in butoh, and also "grotesque expressions of silent mirth or tragedy". In keeping with de Quincey's intense corporeal focus, the staging was sparse, featuring a spotlight, crumpled white paper, and a number of rocks, to which the body was related and which it recalled.

The next solo de Quincey performed at TPS was *Another Dust* (1989). It was a sequel of sorts. De Quincey described *Movement on the Edge* as a "white piece" (literally in terms of central focus on a pale bodily form) while *Another Dust* was a "black piece" (de Quincey and Eckersall 2012), in that de Quincey used the techniques of black theatre and shadow-play to help further break down and isolate corporeal elements on stage—a practice that would recur with *Nerve 9* (2001–05).[9] Although the piece offered "her white, upturned mask of a face floating in space between white limbs" (Sykes 1990: 10), de Quincey was "anchored in the [reddish] gravel/earth that covers the stage floor ... stamping in the ground so the dust spirals" (Dithmer 1989). Here too there was a tendency to rise and fall. Dance critic Monna Dithmer saw in de Quincey's performance both the depersonalisation of butoh as well as gestures found in European Expressionism, such as the "crater like mouth yawning in silent scream" (evoking Edvard Munch's 1893 painting amongst other sources) or the "deep back-arch with arms stretched to the sides which seems to be a citation from Expressionist dancer Mary Wigman's *Der Todesruf* of 1931—a form of near hysterical bodily extension such as de Quincey later evoked in *Nerve 9* (2001).[10] De Quincey confessed that although she "didn't set out to do a piece about my brother's death" (de Quincey and Eckersall 2012), through the intense psychocorporeal investigations which butoh encourages, this topic became partly what *Another Dust* revolved around.

Although de Quincey's reputation as a butoh expert was opening up opportunities, she was aware of the paradox inherent in her status as a non-Japanese

---

9   See "A Masterpiece of Hysterio-Choreography: *Nerve 9*" in chapter four.
10 See "A Masterpiece of Hysterio-Choreography: *Nerve 9*" in chapter four.

representative of Japanese arts in Australia. She stated that if "butoh is to survive … it has to find a … relationship to … local" as well as to "globalised identities" (Sheer 2000: 142). Consequently, de Quincey elected to "cut my hair off after the first couple of performances at TPS. The history of my hair as a performer lay in Maijuku"—and implicitly therefore in Japan—"so when I left it was important to cut it off … You can't teach Body Weather the same way here [in Australia], you can't push people the same way" (Sheer 2000: 142). Helen Gilbert and Jaqueline Lo claim that after de Quincey had abandoned such "formulaic signifiers" of butoh as long, unkempt hair, "white body paint and slow, tortured movement", it became rare that there was "any mention of her Japanese association in reviews" (2007: 102). De Quincey would come to liken this process of first integrating herself with Japan, and then decoupling from it, to a psychocorporeal rite of passage (de Quincey and Eckersall 2012), such as shamans or Australian Aborigines have practiced.[11] De Quincey did however continue to split her time between Copenhagen, Japan and Australia, making the move to Sydney in 1991. That year was also "the last time I ran workshops with the militant attitude of the Japanese" (de Quincey and Eckersall 2012). De Quincey was looking for something different, and had begun to seek a way to ground herself in this ancient southern continent.

6 Body Weather as an Uncanny Project: Tracing an "Interactive History of the Senses" on Australia's Colonised Lands

In de Quincey's laboratories at Lake Mungo and Alice Springs, the haptic abrasion of the body and its sensorium by features perceptible at the site generated a series of historiographic, critical yet provisional and dynamic responses (Figure 4). De Quincey and her dancers invited landscapes to inscribe traces of ancient remains and hidden subterranean watercourses onto their own bodies, or as one of the participants of the Triple Alice laboratories would later observe, this was "a first attempt at tracing an interactive history of the senses" (M. Harrison 2000: 8).

De Quincey was not the first settler descent artist to go inland in search of the Australian imaginary. Painter Russell Drysdale had visited Lake Mungo

---

11 "I often think about it as a little bit like some of the shamanist rituals. You take people out into a situation where you basically take down everything that they've learned, and then … you know for example, [within] some of the Indigenous Aboriginal traditions … then you incorporate a crystal into the body. And that crystal is knowledge" (de Quincey & Eckersall 2012).

in 1945, and Albert Tucker toured with Drysdale through much of the then drought afflicted country surrounding the dry inland lake.[12] Their peer Sydney Nolan also visited (McBryde 1994: 38), painting *Drought Skeleton* (1953) nearby. Choreographer Beth Dean went Yuendumu in 1953, which is in the Central Desert northwest of Mungo, and whose Warlpiri relations de Quincey and Taylor would also consult. Dean used her experiences to inform her own production of *Corroboree* (1954).

Tucker had earlier promoted an artistic process rhetorically similar to that de Quincey would develop in the Australian deserts. Drawing on many of the same Surrealist precedents as Hijikata, Tucker argued that the artist should employ a "haptic" perception of reality, developing an "apprehension of ... objects and events" via "inner bodily processes; muscular innervations, tactile memory, deep sensibilities ... and unconscious mental processes" (1946: 11). Body Weather's interactive psycho-corporeal logic "tracing an interactive history of the senses" (M. Harrison 2000: 8) followed the same overarching logic.

De Quincey was also to echo Tucker and Drysdale in often describing the Australian desert as a haunted region which took the form of boneyard or a landscape strewn with human remains. The Walls of China are sand buttes bordering Lake Mungo, named after the now departed Chinese labourers who worked on the pastoral lease during the 1860s. As Tim Bonyhady explains, Drysdale:

> conceived the Walls [of China] as part of a larger landscape of skeletons. There were the skeletons of trees and the skeletons of animals. There were also the skeletons of houses abandoned by their owners and the skeletons of windpumps that had lost their iron vanes. Not least, there were the skeletons of the original human occupants of the land.
> BONYHADY 1997: 12

De Quincey and dancer Kristina Harrison would both express their encounters with the Australian desert as one which revealed the "bare bones of Aboriginal Australia" and of the landscape (de Quincey and Eckersall 2012; Harrison 2003: 13). There is therefore a sense in which de Quincey's two inland desert projects reworked themes long established within the Australian cultural imaginary and ways in which artists in these lands have attempted to wrestle with landscapes and histories here.

---

12 Drysdale, Nolan and Tucker were well known to Australian dancers, Drysdale painting a backdrop for Beth Dean, and Nolan one for an Australian production of *Rite of Spring* (Spunner 2005: 158; Potter 2011: 21–23). Drysdale's *Dead Heart* inspired a piece by Elizabeth Cameron Dalman (Tonkin 2017: 29).

The continuity of corporeal imagery and discourse is indicative of the Uncanny effects which interactions with the Australian landscape often had for individuals of settler descent. As Jane Jacobs and Ken Gelder have argued, an "Uncanny" perception of Australian identity has the potential to make visible the "limits" of Australia's egalitarian national ethos. Drawing on Freud, Jacobs and Gelder (1995: 171) explain that: "it is not simply the unfamiliar" experience or location "which generates the anxiety of the Uncanny", but rather the "combination" of "familiar" national tropes—isolation, adversity, violence, and the "austere spirit" which this is said to elicit in the national subject in literature and dance (McKechnie 1991 unpag.)[13]—with becomes "unfamiliar" (Jacobs and Gelder 1995: 171) through an engagement with ongoing Indigenous presence and tenure in the landscape. This Uncanny experience offers settler descent subjects a potentially productive sense of estrangement from and within the landscape even as one engages with it.

The psycho-corporeal explorations which de Quincey and her associates encouraged produced precisely such an Uncanny response, at once haunting but informative, disorientating and yet productive in that these very modes of disorientation allowed for a new, more tentative response to Grant's and de Quincey's chosen task of finding "How To Stand In Australia?" (2008).

7 De Quincey's Lake Mungo Workshops, 1991–92, and Beyond

De Quincey's workshops and performances had gathered a small coterie of interested artists around the new arrival. De Quincey reflected that although she was only just becoming reacquainted with the:

> eucalypt-scented continent in which I found myself, the country itself exerted a magnetism and a pull. I felt a resonance between Body Weather training—and the spirit that it engenders—with the deep, ancient nature of the outback. The hunger, raunchy openness, and sheer willingness of those workshop participants to jump into the unknown, giving themselves entirely to the process, had its own impetus. The land was calling, I had a committed group, and there was momentum. The obvious next step was to go into the outback.
> 2021: 322

---

13 See "Expressive Japanese Performance" in chapter two.

De Quincey asked Heywood to propose a location, and when de Quincey returned from Europe in 1991 preparations began to visit Lake Mungo.

Lake Mungo is located approximately 760 kilometres inland of Sydney, near the intersection of the state borders of New South Wales, Victoria and South Australia. Archaeological remains from the region are of global significance, demonstrating that homo sapiens were practicing post-mortem rituals on the Australian continent at least 40,000 years ago—over 35,000 years prior to the erection of Stone Age mortuary tombs and monuments in Europe at Stonehenge and elsewhere. Lake Mungo held large volumes of water in the past, but is now dessert scrubland marked by sand-blown features. Members of the Paakantji, Mutthi Mutthi and Ngyimpaa peoples maintain cultural responsibilities and live in the region. In 1981, Mungo and the surrounding regions were listed as World Heritage sites with UNESCO, and at the time de Quincey visited Mungo, it had been in the news again as white archaeologists negotiated with First Nations representatives to hand over the ancient human remains that they had obtained years earlier on a field trip. The first such repatriation occurred in 1992.

De Quincey and Heywood initially had no clear knowledge of how to engage in the appropriate cultural protocols with the First Nations peoples and there were few institutional frameworks to support such exchanges. At Mungo, Mutthi Mutthi Elder Mary Pappin and her daughter Alice Kelly had been in negotiations over the UNESCO World Heritage listing and were lobbying for Indigenous control of lands and funerary remains from the region (McBryde 1994: 39). This would eventually lead to the foundation of the Lake Mungo Aboriginal Advisory Group. De Quincey (2012: 323) was referred to Kelly by Australian National Parks rangers and it was Mary Pappin who "gave me her blessing" (de Quincey and Eckersall 2012; also de Quincey 2021: 323–6). Additional exchanges with Paakantji Elder and activist Aunty Lottie Williams were arranged, and the dancers agreed to present a showing at Auley Station, which was overseen by the Pappins and the Kellys. Auley station would later be incorporated as the Balranald Local Aboriginal Land Council. Although Kelly and Pappin had long been in discussion with archaeologists and heritage experts, it seems that they had not been approached by visiting artists before, but this came to be conventional following de Quincey's visit, later serving as consultants for Ros Bandt's aeolian harp sculpture, *Mungo* (1997), for example (Bandt 2020; de Quincey and Eckersall 2012).

De Quincey's early interactions with First Australian stakeholders were tentative, but essential. De Quincey's statements imply that engaging with the landscape itself generated a relationship of some kind to the region's First Nations peoples. "For the first time", she reflected, "I actually felt that I could see the raw bones of Australia" (Rentell 2000)—a reference to both the human remains found at Lake Mungo and the hard, calcified features which protruded from the sands, as well as the many dried animal carcases which dotted the landscape. As we saw in the previous chapter, Shirley McKechnie had felt that the "bones and nerves and muscles" of Australian dancers know of the "harshness" of the Australian inland landscape.[14] De Quincey's dancers adopted this association of the living body with non-living bones and landscapes. Snow (2002: 260), for example, developed an improvisation at Lake Mungo in which he embodied a "face stripped of skin by the wind", "exposing bones which were scarred and whitened and ... a head" with "sand stuffed" into its orifices. De Quincey felt that what was "evident in black Australia is actually vivid there [at Lake Mungo] and you're faced with their history quite clearly" (Rentell 2000). This impression of engaging with the archaeological and colonial histories of First Nations peoples through the materiality of the landscape would be further developed at Triple Alice (Figure 4). Heywood had a similar response to Mungo, reflecting: "I had a really strong experience of the presence of a long prior history. I realised that this was not a big, vacant landscape. It is an inhabited landscape" (de Quincey 2021: 327).

Inland lakes moreover hold an especially potent place within Australian cultural imagination. The Murray Darling and other massive, interlinked river systems empty onto the south-eastern coast of Australia between Adelaide and Brisbane. From the 1810s to the 1850s, George Evans, John Oxley, Charles Sturt, Thomas Mitchell and other white explorers chartered inland Australia. All of these men postulated that the extensive Australian river systems must be fed by an inland water body—but none of them found any trace of such a fantastic ocean (Haynes 1998: 23–57). The idea was largely abandoned by the 1850s, and geological studies came to show that the waters of inland Australia had waxed and waned since the Aboriginal peoples first arrived, leaving salt pans and ancient deposits above and below ground. A number of water bodies today, such as Lake Eyre (Kati Thanda) or Lake MacKay (Ngayurru), fill only every three years or so.[15] Tales of hapless white explorers heading away from the coast in search of a mythic inland sea only to find adversity and death have become ingrained into the Australian national mythology, a narrative celebrated in Patrick White's novel of *Voss* (1957) and elsewhere. As the iconic Australian poet Henry Lawson put it, "An Australian lake is not a lake; it is either a sheet of brackish water or a patch of dry", salt encrusted "sand" (Curthoys 1999: 8). Indeed, the concept of a mythic inland sea features in the rhetoric of

---

14   See "Expressive Japanese Performance" in chapter two.
15   Napangardi's Dreaming is discussed in "Triple Alice" below.

some First Australians, with painter Dorothy Napangardi describing the dry salt lake of her own Dreaming Country of Minamina as an "inland sea" in the title of several of her canvases (Herbert-Nungarrayi, Lewis-Japanangka and Webb, in Webb ed. 2002: 8, 22, 76). De Quincey reports senior First Nations individuals describing the region around Lake Mungo to her as "Edenic" (de Quincey 2023b). There is some precedent for imagery of this kind within butoh, as in Ohno's performance, directed by Hijikata, entitled *The Dead Sea* (1985). Some of Ohno's movements drew on his 1983 visit to Israel's Dead Sea, a massive inland body of saline water, described by his guide to the site, Nourit Masson-Sékiné, as a kind of "suspended landscape" which it is "almost a mystical experience" to visit and hence "which resonates with his butoh" (in Marshall 2020a).

Lake Mungo is a salt bush speckled expanse of hard ground where the visible traces of ancient water erosion pull the body into chthonic imaginings which vex both concepts of colonial domination and the erasure of pre-existing conditions and histories. De Quincey claims that, "One of the strange things about approaching Mungo is that it looks as if there's water there … The sense and weight of the water is ever present"—despite its literal absence. Here, the "undercurrent of the continent" can be deeply felt (in Parsons and Wynne-Jones 1996: 17). For de Quincey and others, "Lake Mungo summons an awareness of geological time" in its "crumbling erosion[s]", bringing up images of "primordial reptiles" dragging themselves onto ancient shorelines (such as Amagatsu depicted in *Jōmon-sho*),[16] as well as human bodies evoked by skeletal forms in the landscape (2021: 330), like Drysdale's tortured trees. As I have argued elsewhere, visibly eroded marks in the landscape elicit in visitors "geological thinking, such that time emerges as a fissure, or a yawning scar-like space of discontinuity, within the mise en scène" of a landscape characterised by "harsh, jagged materials … stones … boulders" and intensely excoriated sand buttes which serve to "materialise these breaks" in temporal and cultural continuity (Marshall and Duncan 2018: 87).

The Lake Mungo workshops consisted of two intensives of twelve to thirty days, 1991–92, followed by additional short stays, and involved eleven participants, at least six of whom had worked with Tanaka (Snow 2002: 74). In addition to her Australian contacts, de Quincey tapped into a growing international Body Weather community. One participant was German, and one Danish (Heike Müller). The location was a degraded historic pastoral lease on the eastern side of the dry lake bed, originally named Gol Gol station, later renamed

---

16   See "Lineages of Descent" in chapter one.

Mungo—from which the title for the lake was derived. The dancers stayed at the shearers' quarters, near the historic Mungo wool shed, which was built in 1869 from termite resistant pine by Chinese labourers (NSW NPWS). It was this prior history of Asian-Australian interactions that gave the name of the Walls of China to the dune and rock structures on the opposite side of the lakebed from where the camp was located. Corporeal knowledge, impulses, and sculptural elements, were sourced at the site, as well as during extended journeys taken by the dancers on foot, sometimes travelling kilometres. These would form the basis of video works and live performances, including the ensemble piece *Square of Infinity* (1992), as well as de Quincey's solo *Is/Is.2* (1994–95). Although there were up to twenty-two participants at any one time, de Quincey and ten other artists remained constant. These included the aforementioned individuals Nikki Heywood, Stuart Lynch, Peter Snow, Heike Müller, and Peter Fraser— in addition to Lynne Santos (a former member of One Extra dance who would later work with Nigel Kellaway, Yumi Umiumare and Tony Yap), as well as Leah Grycewicz, Claire Hague, Russell Milledge, and Phillip Mills. None of the dancers are known to have publicly identified as First Nations Australians.

The workshops followed a standard Body Weather structure of MB (muscle/bone or mind/body), followed by manipulations, groundwork, and exercises. Instructions and improvisations varied. One challenge was to "walk slowly forward" as if "licking the stars with your tongue" (Snow 2002: 213). Omnicentral imaging, which I discuss further below, was included but does not at this time seem to have been seen as a core practice. Rather in Snow's view, the central practice at Lake Mungo were the various collective expeditions and single-file journeys which acted as a summation of the challenges presented within the developmental exercises at the main camp and which took the dancers out as a depersonalised collective to interact with diverse local environments (2002: 75, 221). There were also nightly showings of self devised solo works situated in the landscape, the choice of timing itself reflective of a transtemporal period during which things are in flux.

Another key exercise in the workshops was to focus in almost microscopic detail on a macroscopic universe. De Quincey and Stuart Grant named this exercise "ground being", whereby participants "concentrate on one small patch" (one metre square or so) of landscape or "sand, observing the changing shapes, speeds, and directions in its microtopography, the mounds, the divots, the holes, each grain … taking the texture" of these objects and spaces "into our bodies" (Grant and de Quincey 2008: 251; Taylor 2008: 103). The aim was "to empathise on a cellular level with the chosen element" (Anderson 2014: 15); a kind of bisoku or slowing down of the senses and of corporeal response, or as Snow put it, to develop an "intercorporeal" sense in which the body of the dancer reflects and eventually became confused with the bodies, objects and forces that surrounded it (2006: 238).

Soon after arrival on the first day, de Quincey:

> sent the participants fanning out into the terrain, each following a different trajectory ... they left at 3 pm, returning by 6 pm. I tasked them to record ... what they noticed ... everyone spoke of how, in the empty expanse of the lakebed, they felt watched; they were aware of unseen presences who were observing them. We were all on unknown territory that was deeply inhabited.
>
> DE QUINCEY 2021: 324

This sense of the landscape as mediating an encounter with both human and non-human inhabitants from the region proved a constant for all those involved. Heywood describes how:

> The sustained daily practice of Body Weather in this isolated and captivating place, the embracing bowl of the ancient lakebed, brought about a paradigm shift at a phenomenological level ... Extended periods of time spent alone, and miles from our camp, engaged in tasks of perceptual awareness ... had a profound effect on my sense of mortality, raising questions about the place and consequence—or lack thereof—of a single human being within the vast geological scale of such ancient land, sensing the ghosts of its original people.
>
> HEYWOOD 2016: 73

Even Mills "imagined seeing" his own white "ancestors behind the bushes" at Lake Mungo (Snow 2002: 223).

The experiences of the dancers related above suggest their encounter with Lake Mungo constituted something like a rite of passage, or one of Uncanny estrangement. The encounter with beings both present and absent, and their attempts to transition from being unfamiliar with these landscapes to being deeply in tune with them, encouraged a perhaps naïve but undoubtedly raw and physically immediate way of relating to Australia's landscapes and their histories. The physical challenges of white colonisation, settlement and mastery were here replaced by something less goal orientated and more prone to the wearing down of one's psyche and bodily deportment.

Nor was the laconic individualism and mateship of the Australian Legend entirely sufficient to banish disturbing elements. On the contrary, Body Weather is practiced precisely as a form of challenging discipline. Individual egoistic responses were frowned upon, or as Tanaka frustratedly exclaimed to Fuller at Hakushu, "Your work looks so personal ... It is painful for me" (Fuller 2014: 202).[17] Emptying of the butoh body therefore allowed for the possibility that preestablished colonial attitudes might be eroded—quite literally given the abrasive qualities of the Mungo landscape. As Sarah Dunn wrote of the Triple Alice laboratories "our bodies were cut, scratched, bruised, grazed, stung, prickled, sunburnt, wind burnt, blistered and dehydrated" (2003: 43; Figure 4). These destabilising psychophysical modalities would be further developed at Triple Alice, but it is worth stating here that it was the apparent absence of people or inhabitants at the specific locations where the dancers themselves worked which nevertheless, in a dialectical manner, produced the sensation that the dancers were interacting with other imagined bodies, where the landscape and the relics within it were read as corporeal forms in their own right. All this is implicit in Body Weather as an aesthetic form from the start, but had rarely been an explicit element of Tanaka's practice. Settler descent bodies in Australia came to elicit, and in return respond to, a transhuman, Uncanny and haunted post-colonial landscape.

The rigours of Body Weather and the focus required of it was central to the efficacy of these activities. Heywood admitted to sometimes feeling, as she had in her earlier Grotowski work, that she was "participating in a sadomasochistic cult, with very elastic personal boundaries" between self and other (2017: 204). Especially for novices being inducted into the extreme positions of the manipulations, Body Weather can produce in the practitioner sensations of "great pain ... blind panic ... feeling helpless ... of being defenceless and dependent", to say nothing of injuries (Snow 2002: 169). Nevertheless, Heywood attested that "group bonding with the other performers, our shared circumstances and subsequent trust-building also allowed us to take physical and creative risks" (Heywood 2017: 204). These risks were very real. On de Quincey's first day, she set out for a long journey like the one she gave her dancers, but realised she had not taken enough water and had to return to camp (Sykes 1994a). Fortunately the relatively cool temperature meant that this was not in and of itself life threatening, but later in the year it could have been. Snow, who reached the site slightly after his peers, reported being informed of a blindfold exercise prior to his arrival. Linked only by "a piece of cotton thread, index finger to index finger, they had to journey as a group some five kilometres in the direction of ... the Walls of China" (Snow 2002: 92). One dancer served as the seeing guide. No one was allowed to talk. Instructions had to be given physically "by

---

17 This was not unique to Tanaka, who reported hearing Hijikata chastise Ashikawa, "Must you always dance Yoko Ashikawa?" (Cardone 2002, 21)

means of impulses transmitted along the thread" (92). It was winter's dawn and extremely cold. "Progress was excruciatingly slow" (92), and the party became perilously lost before inching back onto the correct trajectory. Heywood and others also reported feet injuries and a relentless toughening of the skin, such as occurred at Tanaka's workshops, but here given a particular twist by the windswept dryness of the Australian interior. Fraser notes that a group of "young men", perhaps retaining some of the ethos of the Australian Legend, "made a vow to work barefoot ... and ... spent each evening taking splinters and pus out of their feet" (de Quincey 2021: 325).

De Quincey and her dancers therefore had to respond to an environment which was not only very different from that where Tanaka had conducted his workshops, but which was also, counter-intuitively, unlike many cliches regarding Australia's supposedly balmy, sun-kissed conditions. Body Weather in Japan had been conducted on fertile farmland, while de Quincey's major workshop series at Mungo, and then the laboratories at Alice Springs, were both conducted on degraded former agistment lands and desert scrub. Although the area around Lake Mungo was technically a desert, the dancers encountered an abundance of wildlife, including kangaroo, emu, eagle, lizards, and echidna (Snow 2002: 75). While the Hakushu workshops were typically conducted in summer, when it was humid, hot and lacking in shade, Mungo by contrast was actually often very cold. At that time of year, the baking force of the sun was less apparent than the national myth might suggest. Body Weather in Japan was conducted on hard, splintering boards, muddy earth, mountain paths, and grassy, vegetated areas between planted beds. At Lake Mungo, the ground varied from gently sloping clay plans to "soft ... sandy" areas as well as "rough, stony and uneven" portions speckled with saltbush (Snow 2002: 120), large stinging ants (colloquially referred to as bull ants), and stubby, twisted mallee trees such as Drysdale depicted.

Towards the end of the workshops, the showing at Auley Station occurred. The dancers spent the day in a travelling version of the ground being exercise known as "collecting material" (Snow 2002: 7). Corporeal responses were then organised around central themes of birds, journeying, fires, concepts of weather in the landscape, and in the body:

> Come evening we were all gathered in the large shed; there was agricultural machinery, a combine harvester, old motorbikes, a car, tools ... It had a corrugated iron roof ... and a dusty dirt floor ... locals drifted in, a Country and Western tape was playing, lamb chops and potatoes were cooking on an improvised barbecue ... 'til maybe twenty-five [mostly First Nations Australian] people of all ages ... were milling around ... Alice Kelly ...

arrived and was seated ... on an old car seat ... The whisper goes around amongst the performers, start when the drumming starts, keep going 'til it stops ... Tess tells us ... where we should be—birds ... down this line, weather over there behind the fire, journeys ... alongside one wall ... we ... take off our coats—we're dressed ... [in] tatty workshop clothes—the van is turned around, its lights providing a beam of thin light, the drum tape starts and ... we move, each in his/her own time ... not to the music, but alongside it ... we burn ... Half an hour later, exhausted, we stop.
SNOW 2002: 8

Kelly's daughter Mary Pappin enthusiastically responded, "You's [are really] wakin' up the land" (de Quincey 2021: 326). Perhaps the ancestors of Kelly and Pappin were watching on approvingly.

8 Lake Mungo Performance Works and on to Alice Springs

Two principal works were developed out of the Lake Mungo workshops. The first, *Square of Infinity,* was named after the groundwork exercise described above. De Quincey's solo *Is* also made reference to this key exercise. *Square of Infinity* (1992) was initially staged on site by nine performers for spectators who had driven from Adelaide. It was then reworked for performance in Sydney at TPS. A filmic version was made by Roman Blaska. For *Square of Infinity,* de Quincey engaged Jim Denley, Rik Rue, Shane Fahey and Jamie Fielding to perform the score. Tanaka had worked extensively with a range of influential musicians, notably electronic son-et-lumière pioneer Iannis Xenakis—who postulated that musical events might be considered as high density fields of "granular" sonic details (Roads 1988: 11–13)—as well as Derek Bailey, who was a pioneer of extended technique and author of the first monograph on free improvisation (Bailey 1975/1993; Tanaka and Bailey 1993). De Quincey's own musical collaborators were well known figures in the Australian experimental music scene, often collaborating under monikers such as Splinter Orchestra (who would later record a responsive musical project at the same location, released as *Mungo,* 2016), or Machine For Making Sense—co-founded by leading free improviser and saxophonist Jim Denley, together with sound collagist Rik Rue, and concrete poet Amanda Stewart, and which featured Japanese expatriate koto player Odamura Satsuki.[18]

---

18   Julian Knowles too was involved, collaborating with Rue on the score of *Is/Is.2*. For Odamura's collaborations with Umiumare and Yap, see chapter five.

Documentation shows that *Square of Infinity* both conformed to and exceeded butoh tropes. In addition to other instructions, de Quincey asked the performers to create "ancient images" for the production, and this included naked and near naked dancers moving across the sand dunes and other sites (Snow 2002: 225). *Square of Infinity* opened with the performers coming into view, bodies arching backwards, chests rising, as the arms spread.[19] Attired in loose fitting robes, de Quincey's collaborators recalled the members of Hakutōbō in the latter's own ample shifts. Other typical butoh positions included the horse stance (legs bent and apart, the torso lowered down and held parallel to the legs), foetal poses, as well as the pained, gaping mouth and unfocused gaze. One photograph shows a dancer asymmetrically posed, partly kneeling, the torso over the knees while thin, spindly arms and fingers reached forward to stroke the ground, an expression of concentration and perhaps pain on the face (Heywood 2016: 56). Other arresting images included vertically arranged, dark clad bodies juxtaposed against the flat horizon. Stiff limbs twisting about the side of the bodies, the dancers recalled the tormented figures from the finale of Ingmar Bergman's film *The Seventh Seal* (1957), where they jerkily moved in a row along the skyline. Performers sometimes strode amongst the scrub with confidence, but more commonly crept in stops and starts. Filmed sequences included rolling naked down sand dunes, or weaving amongst the "lanoline-drenched timbers of the nineteenth century shearing shed, morning light and a cold wind slicing through the slab walls on to bodies clad in nothing more … than underpants" (Sykes 1993: 23). Here one might recall the photographic collaboration between Hijikata and Hosoe in the farmhouses of Tōhoku, a precedent which would be reworked again by Tony Yap and Yumi Umiumare in their filmic collaborations.[20]

There was no doubt though that the landscape was the leading actor in *Square of Infinity*, and the choreography involved placing the figure within an already dramatic environment, or as Gretel Taylor (2008: 13) observed of her own practice, "by bringing an audience to a site and via my moving in relation to the site, the place itself 'performs'. Attention is drawn to what is already there: the 'dance' that is already underway". As Sykes noted:

> De Quincey had envisaged a fairly slow-paced unfolding of action set against the seemingly endless horizon. Instead … the mood turned into

---

19 As I have argued elsewhere, these epileptoid/hysterical positions, which echo spasmodic opisthotonos, are a defining feature of butoh choreography which links it to various nervous dances, notably German Expressionism, Surrealist practice, and Dada (Marshall 2013, 2020c & 2021b). Similar positions also feature in several of de Quincey's works.

20 See *"Sunrise at Midnight"* in chapter five.

a buffeting confrontation with powers beyond human control set against a sense of rebirth and survival beyond the odds ... rain [had] brought huge changes to Lake Mungo: ... new grasses and a huge number of caterpillars, blue-tongued lizards, baby kangaroos [females have dormant embryos they release in good weather], even shrimps, whose buried eggs can wait for years.
1993: 24

Mungo still had unforeseen dramas with which to surprise non resident artists and audiences. Sykes described *Square of Infinity* in primal terms, finding the movement "savage", "prehistoric" and "elemental", as when, "The performers appear to be buffeted by fire and storm, their bodies ... hurtled in all directions yet held at the precipice [of death] by the will to survive" (1992).

De Quincey also presented a solo performance under the title *Is* (later *Is.2*). The piece included a sculptural installation by Stuart Lynch consisting of walls of corrugated iron against which de Quincey crashed, or which she performed in front of. Also on stage was an old wool bale such as would have come out of the shed at which the dancers rehearsed, as well as a sledgehammer suspended from the roof. The sledgehammer was to give a sense of the weight which the open desert sky imparted onto the dancers. As de Quincey has explained, she often felt as though she was being pummelled into the ground by the sky. She would return to this image in Triple Alice project, the subsequent Triple Alice laboratories concluding with a production entitled *Sky Hammer* (2000). Also dropping from the fly gallery was a "nest of plumb bobs", marking out a one metre square area (Picott 1995). This highlighted the proximity of Body Weather practice to a geomorphological survey, marking out a precise space to develop choreography from, or to nestle within. Choreographically therefore de Quincey's solo moved between a sense of vast, unbounded space, versus more circumscribed, precise, miniaturist events.

An early sequence in *Is* can be read as a direct transposition from the Mungo workshops, with de Quincey moving extremely slowly across the stage while wearing a black blindfold. As in Tanaka's later works, de Quincey performed in an anonymous black suit, as well as in a roughly textured great-coat, which she wore with the back covering her front, producing a shambolic, crinkly silhouette. This was contrasted with de Quincey in a strapless silver dress with black stripes and an elegantly cinched waist, allowing for moments of off centred, sensual self presentation and almost flamenco twists (Figure 5), very much in the spirit of butoh. As in previous works by de Quincey, the body both rose and fell during the piece. Even so, Tanaka's tendency to lie prone for much of the performance and which characterised his early *Hyperdance* works, was absent.

FIGURE 5
Tess de Quincey in *Is* (The Performance Space: 1994). Installation and projections Stuart Lynch
PHOTO: ROBYN MURPHY. IMAGE COURTESY OF DE QUINCEY COMPANY

Clad in heavy boots which gave density and weight to her steps, de Quincey might have waivered and collapsed, but the creature performing here was not quadrupedal or slug-like, as in some butoh and Body Weather productions. De Quincey by contrast depended on a dialectic between horizontal and vertical, between the standing figure, and the expanse it jerkily moved across. This was to become a defining feature of her choreographic response to the Australian interior, and much other Australian butoh.

Knowles' score for *Is* used granular synthesis and other means to translate weather-satellite data from the region into grinding, hissing sounds. This recalled the so-called "bisoku dot-body" which de Quincey and her dancers had developed by mapping the sand and sandstone structures of Mungo onto the architecture of their own bodies (de Quincey 2021: 328). Knowles' aim was to translate, in an arbitrary yet nevertheless structured manner, geomorphological, climactic and environmental conditions into aesthetic form—in this case sound rather than bodily deportment and choreography. To further enhance the presence of the distant site within the performance space, Knowles and Rue infused the space with what one critic described as a "vibrating intensity" of the noise of passing aircraft, thunder, insects, and voices (Ulzen 1994a: 68). Crisscrossing these elements were visual projections of raw data from the weather satellites and selections from Blaska's footage from Mungo, as well as close ups of de Quincey's face, painted white, staring out blankly. The whiteness of the projected body evoked death and bones such as lay in the landscape.

It is worth pausing here to note the innovations which de Quincey had by now brought to Body Weather in Australia. The addition of an Australian context and content was obvious. Less frequently noted is that, unlike most of

Tanaka's own choreographies, the landscape itself has become the *subject* of the dance. Tanaka's early butai solos did indeed turn his body into a medium which expressed landscape and location, but few of his later pieces functioned that way. At Hakushu and the farms, Tanaka and his dancers might perform improvisations in which they invited the landscape into their bodies (such as Tanaka's solos at the Tokason farm; Tanaka and Okada 2019). But most of Tanaka's choreographies after the 1980s did not themselves *portray* landscapes. Rather he employed bodies which had been trained to become responsive to landscapes to depict other themes. One of Tanaka's first major works for Maijuku, for example, was a free interpretation of *The Rite of Spring* (1987),[21] initially staged on the grounds of the Hakushu farm, and which depicted in Tanaka's words:

> a variety of endeavours dictated by the four seasons both macroscopically and microscopically … a natural history of tragedies and comedies of living things … I find feasts and celebrations [i.e. rites] going on every day.
> FULLER 2017: 168

The piece concluded with a particularly charming sequence in which the dancers were wrapped in paper to serve as "presents to the world" (Holborn 1987: 63). The wrapped dancers were also intended to look like weathered "bones" (87), not altogether unlike the forms in the landscape of Lake Mungo. As with most butoh, there was also a fluid exchange between moments of actual signification—dancers as presents for example—and other moments where the body resisted signification. The body was more simply (and ambiguously) presented as a sensually rich object. De Quincey's choreography did this too, but there was a greater emphasis on representing specific locations, or at the very least of evoking the experience of being in another specific space which lay off stage—though there was some prevarication in de Quincey's published statements as to what degree specific *histories* might be being represented here. The overt reference to the highly charged, culturally significant Australian landscapes of Mungo and elsewhere however meant that these performances functioned according to an abstract but ultimately mimetic or referential logic. Landscapes were brought into the theatre by means of a choreographic installation of body, sound, projected image, and sculptural elements—the latter often having a directly indexical quality, having been literally sourced at the site. Tanaka's own work rarely operated this way.

---

21 On *The Rite of Spring,* see "Lineages of Descent" in chapter one.

Despite positive responses from Sykes, Pappin and others, the Mungo workshops were a success almost by default. De Quincey was still struggling with establishing the right balance between the focussed discipline, and a more interactive model which might suit those less inclined to unquestioningly submit to a charismatic male Japanese master who, if he tended to speak at all, did so in short epigrams. De Quincey reflected that perhaps she needed a more "feminine" touch, or as Mary Anderson and Peter Snow explained, de Quincey's teaching came to include far more "precise and detailed" instructions than Tanaka's, as well as the active exchange between participants and instructor (Anderson 2014: 40; Snow 2002: 181). Even so, de Quincey retained what Triple Alice participant Sarah Dunn described as a "minimal style" (2003: 37). Heywood did feel that at Lake Mungo, "something went terribly wrong" and that de Quincey was "disappointed" by the participants' "attitude" (Robertson 2015: 51). Heywood went so far as to claim, "It was a bit of a breaking moment", as indeed it was for Heywood, who would move to train with Tanaka rather than staying with de Quincey's emergent ensemble. De Quincey though remained focussed on the opportunities which continued to present themselves in Australia.

In 1995, de Quincey toured *Is.2* to Alice Springs, in the centre of Australia and near to the famous geomorphic landmark and Aboriginal sacred site of Uluru (then more commonly referred to as Ayer's Rock). A revised version of *Is.2* was performed outdoors at the waterhole beside the colonial transcontinental telegraph station which had led to the foundation of Alice Springs. De Quincey performed beside the waterhole, with the sloping rocky hill behind her replacing the corrugated iron of the TPS performance.

De Quincey and Lynch also included an element which constituted their most overt reference to the mythos of First Nations Australia to date. A back injury had meant that it was unclear how much of the choreography de Quincey would be able to execute. Although she largely recovered, new material developed by Lynch featured at Alice Springs. Here, Lynch attempted to evoke the mimih, a well-known Australian First Nations' spiritual being. Mimih are tall, thin entities of the far north, rocky country which dwell in crevices (Leslie 2021: 24–25). They taught humans aspects of hunting, song, dance, painting, and the use of fire. Mimih paintings have been reliably dated to approximately 20,000 years of age, and designs may go back as far as 50,000 years. Lynch described his character as a ghost (which mimih are not), and he made a striking entrance in *Is.2* after lying almost invisible in the water, submerged up to his neck (Parsons and Wynne-Jones 1996: 27–28). In describing his mimih as a "ghost" (27), Lynch might be implying that the Aboriginal presence in the landscape is only present today as a deceased haunting of times long past. This particular, mimih-like spectre nevertheless made a physically forceful appearance. It "exploded" out of the water giving "vigorous voice" to being present (ibid. 27–28). Some audiences initially thought it was a wayward saltwater crocodile coming in for the kill. There is a degree of naiveite in this performance—whatever Lynch was depicting, it had little equivalence with the mimih of northern Aboriginal rock art. The performance nevertheless represented early, tentative steps towards settler-descent butoh artists coming to terms with Australian landscapes, histories and peoples through corporeal sensations such as the extreme cold of the water and the need to heat up—the latter conditions in fact being the principal motivation for Lynch's energetic opening. Here as elsewhere, corporeal knowledge and bodily responses to *material* circumstances guided an emergent if perhaps incomplete postcolonial consciousness (Figure 4). De Quincey and Lynch felt that they could tap into the primeval forces of the landscape through bodily sensation. Imperfect though such attempts were, they represented a significant intervention into the corporeal politics of the Australian nation and its representation. Marrugeku theatre company would later offer a more nuanced and negotiated theatrical interpretation of the mimih itself, and here too, Body Weather was to play a part.[22] Either way, de Quincey's trip to Alice Springs proved decisive, and the next Body Weather intensives would be staged approximately one hour's drive from the township of Alice Springs, at the gateway to Uluru, in the mythic heartland of the Australian outback.

9 Triple Alice, 1999–2001

The Mungo workshops were ambitious, but Triple Alice was much more so and remains without international parallel in Body Weather practice. Following Tanaka's lead, de Quincey had invited dancers and non-dancers from different backgrounds to her workshops since 1989. De Quincey described Triple Alice however as:

> a new model of interdisciplinary exchange with three annual interlocking but independent laboratories of different practices: Body Weather, writers and visual artists, comprising Indigenous and non-Indigenous artists besides guest speakers and musicians. The aim was to create an interflow between the three disciplines.
> 2023C

---

22   See chapter six under "Umiumare's First Nations Collaborations".

As de Quincey stated in an essay of the same name, de Quincey set herself and her dancers the task of discovering "How to Stand in Australia?" (Grant and de Quincey 2008) by engaging in the Central Desert landscapes on which Triple Alice was sited. This rhetorical phrasing regarding a problematics of standing at ease or upright was derived in the first instance from Hijikata. As Ko Murobushi has stated:

> after the Second World War ... In that moment, our ground became zero. And Hijikata had to start, to stand, with this condition, because he began to think about the crisis of existence, the crisis of standing.
> in SAKAMOTO 2019: 23

It follows then that all nations have their own "crisis of standing", informed both by "the crisis of existence" (ibid. 23) but also the particularities of their historical encounters with modernity and other challenges. In the Australian context, the history of colonialism is inescapable—particularly when located at what de Quincey herself described as a "burning point—geographically, culturally and politically" (2003: 27) for the Australian consciousness.

De Quincey had by now attracted the attention of scholar Gay McAuley. De Quincey was included in an artistic research project at what was then known as the Centre for Performance Studies at the University of Sydney, led by McAuley (see D'Cruz 1996: 36–52). This evolved into a series of exchanges between de Quincey and the university (de Quincey 2023c), with undergraduate or postgraduate students participating in multiple seasons of Triple Alice. In addition to the dancers, Triple Alice included scholars McAuley, Ian Maxwell, Jane Goodall, Edward Scheer, Kerrie Schaefer and the Centre for Performance Studies' technical director Russell Emmerson, in addition to the poet Martin Harrison and his colleague writer/visual artist Kim Mahood, the latter of whom grew up in Central Australia on Warlpiri Country in the Tanami Desert, a bit over 570 km north of Alice Springs. Also participating were new media artist Francesca da Rimini, ethnobiologist Peter Latz, anthropologist Scott Campbell Smith, historian Dick Kimber, artists from Watch This Space gallery in Alice Springs, including founders Pam Lofts and Ann Mosey, visual artist Julia White, and others.[23]

In 2023, de Quincey characterised those involved in the 1999 laboratory as follows:

> the 1999 Lab involved a number of local Indigenous participants including: Uncle Arthur Ah Chee, traditional owner Steve McCormack, musicians

---

23 Comprehensive lists of participants may be found at De Quincey et al (1999–2001).

Nokturnl and Frankie Yama as well as Gallery Gondwana artists Dorothy Robinson Napangardi and Polly Napangardi Watson. Returning to participate in the 2001 laboratory Dorothy Robinson Napangardi brought six of her Aunties from the remote Nyirripi community, Margaret Napangardi, Mitjili Napanangka [Gibson], Minnie Napanangka, Nancy Napanangka, Sarah Napanangka [Daniels] and Ena Nakamarra [Gibson] (de Quincey 2023c; see also Premont 2023).[24]

In a report published not long after Triple Alice concluded, Stuart Grant more bluntly described his peers as principally consisting of "white people", and entries on the website designated those present at a 2001 Triple Alice 3 event as being "non-indigenouse [sic]" (Grant 2003: 79; de Quincey et al. 2001a). De Quincey seems to suggest that despite the complex cultural politics of non-Indigenous dancers coming onto Country, at least at the time, this was not the focus of the research. It is however important to note that dancer Victoria Hunt—one of de Quincey's most consistent collaborators and who was present at all three seasons of Triple Alice—would go on to explore her own Māori ancestry and whakapapa (genealogy) in later choreographies.[25]

At the time of Triple Alice, Dorothy Napangardi was emerging as a leading artist in the region. Her relations were principally Warlpiri and Pintupi, originally from the region of Minamina and Ngayurru (Lake Mackay). This is a massive salt lake system of 3,500 square kilometres between the Gibson and Great Sandy deserts of Western Australia—what Napangardi likened in scale and nature to an "inland sea": bigger than many European nations. Napangardi and her relatives were also linked with two of the foundation sites of contemporary Australian First Nations art and Australian choreography. Fellow painter of the Minamina Dreamings, Maggie Napangardi Watson, was one of those who befriended Beth Dean when the latter came to Yuendumu to research Warlpiri and Pintupi initiation rites to incorporate into Dean's version of 1954 ballet *Corroboree* (Spunner 2005: 146–156; Dean and Carell 1955: 125–138). Australian Body Weather artist Gretel Taylor (2012). would also work and dance with members of the Napangardi kinship group.

Dorothy Napangardi's mentor was Eunice Napangardi, whose husband Kaapa Mbitjana Tjampitjinpa was a founding member of the ground-breaking

---

24 "Napangardi", "Japanangka" and "Japangardi" are what is known in northern Australian Kriol as "skin names" which may or may not correlate with parental relationships, the children they bore, or birth siblings, see Rose 1992; Curran 2017. For a Warlpiri account, see Jones 2014.
25 On Hunt's Māori performance, see chapter nine.

Papunya Tula painting movement of the 1970s (Premont 2020: 61, 72). Dorothy's father was Paddy Lewis Japanangka, a senior lawman and Pintupi custodian of Minamina Country (Artbank nd; Premont 2020 and 2023), who was involved in the creation of the epic 1984 Yuendumu series of thirty painted doors. Her connection to the Country of her childhood was consolidated by a trip to Minamina in 1999: the first she had been able to undertake since she and her kin had been forced off Minamina County in 1957 (Nicholls 2002: 61–67).[26] Napangardi's kin by this time typically lived some distance from the Country they were responsible for, in the settlements of Yuendumu, Nyirripi, Puturlu (Mount Theo), Papunya, and Balgo, hundreds of kilometres from Alice Springs.

The participation of Dorothy and Polly Napangardi in the 1999 laboratory was organised through Gallery Gondwana (founded by director by Rosalyn Premont). According to de Quincey, "staff at Gondwana explained that Napangardi enjoyed the experience of Triple Alice 1 and therefore wanted to participate again in Triple Alice 3," bringing her kin and Aunties from Nyirripi (de Quincey 2023c). The involvement Napangardi and her kin is moreover significant in that their Dreamings—the Kanakurlangu Jukurrpa, or Karntakurlangu Jukurrpa (Digging-Stick-Possessing Dreaming, or Women-Belonging Dreaming)—are not only maintained through dance and song, but are a series of interlinked narratives which are both *about* and *relate stories of* women dancing, or of other ancestral groups such as the Snake Ancestors and the Warlpiri Two Men Ancestors, who spied upon or approached the dancing Digging-Stick-Possessing Women from Minamina (Herbert Nungarrayi 2002: 6; Jones 2014: 63–64, 113–127, 191–192). As Napangardi's father observed, "those Warlpiri ladies, they're mad about dancing, they go round and round dancing, they're always dancing" (Paddy Lewis Japanangka 2002: 22). They danced so much that a dust cloud arose, carrying away some of the licentious Snake Men who had disturbed the women's journeys. The Minamina women also cross gender divisions, representing a time when the ancestral "Women controlled the weapons and sacred objects now associated only with the male domain" and so at least some of the Dreaming iconography may be seen by both men and women (Jones 2019: 117–127). Napangardi moved back to Yuendumu later in life, but when de Quincey encountered her she was living in Alice, close to her immediate family and away from the other Yuendumu and Nyirripi artists. Her style by this time moved from her early colourful canvases depicting the bush banana Jukurrpa and the blossoming of desert food plants to densely tracked, undulating white dots across a black background, whose shimmering

---

26 Paddy Japanangka had attempted to take his family back to Minamina when she was young, but they were apprehended, and forced back to Yuendumu (Tacey 2022).

optical effects evoked the water-like haze and patterned, cracked lines of salt which stretch across the lake at Minamina (McAuley 2006: 271; Webb 2002: 72–76).

Triple Alice ran 1999 to 2001 as a series of three annual laboratories. The project initially had fifty-five participants, later distilled to around a dozen dedicated parties. There was a notable reduction in numbers after the first week when it became apparent that dancers were paying to attend an event that often functioned like a boot camp, with regulated meals and shared sleeping spaces (Dunn 2003: 36). Key figures at Triple Alice included veterans of the Lake Mungo workshops, namely Stuart Lynch, Peter Snow, Frank Van de Ven, Peter Fraser and Lynne Santos. Students from the University of Sydney included Stuart Grant (who edited and co-authored several of de Quincey's texts, and would later collaborate with Gretel Taylor), Snow (completing a doctorate at University of Sydney), Sarah Dunn, Katrina Harrison, and Mary Anderson. Also present were independent Australian dancers Victoria Hunt and Marnie Kee née Orr, as well as Danish dance-maker Karen Vedel, all of whom would continue to practice Body Weather in Australia and beyond. Larissa Pryce, who attended the first season only, would continue to practice as a performer for some years following Triple Alice and would author a thesis on Body Weather.

The Triple Alice laboratories were conducted at Hamilton Downs Youth Camp. Snow described the site as an "old pastoral station" which had been "superimposed on ancestral Aboriginal lands" and which was "now a residential camp" (Snow 2003: 58). Like Mungo, it was another degraded historic pastoral site, consisting of a group of renovated buildings dating back to the 1890s, but which had been abandoned when a better location for the station was selected by new owners in 1948 (Grant and de Quincey 2008: 253). As some of Triple Alice's artists observed, Hamilton Downs was strewn with the "pathetic remnants" of unsuccessful attempts at white settlement (ibid. 253), evidence of which abounds across the Australian outback, but which is rarely recognised as indicating the failure of earlier attempts to profit from, and live upon, the Australian landscape (Marshall and Duncan 2018: 88–89). Since 1992, Hamilton Downs has been managed by the Thakeperte Aboriginal Land Trust, composed principally of local Arrernte peoples.

Hamilton Downs is located on undulating quartz scrubland (unlike the clay and sandy soils of Lake Mungo), backed by West MacDonnell ranges to the south, and the fringes of the Tanami Desert (Warlpiri Country) to the north, or as de Quincey and Grant put it, "shattered quartz country" (de Quincey and Maxwell 2020: 169) of "red dirt, ants, scrappy casuarina, desert gums on the banks of dried up riverbeds, ancient rocks … spiky … desert flora" such as spinifex bushes (Grant 2003: 74), "small marsupials, lizards, crows, galahs, cockatoos and dingoes" (ibid. 74) —in short, a more iconographically classic Australian dryland landscape in the eyes of most whites than the otherworldly barren mounds of sand and rock found at Lake Mungo.

Although images of the Central Desert are a key part of the Australian cultural imaginary, direct experience of this terrain is uncommon for most Australians. Pryce noted that even exposure to widely available tropes such as those developed by Drysdale, nothing had prepared her for "the shock" of "stepping out of the plane" at Alice:

> I was confronted with an immediate visceral, prickling sensation of the body being made porous through the intense heat, the drawing down of energy and absorption of the body's moisture out into the atmosphere ... [an awareness of a] tangible presence resonating from the deep red earth ... this land seemed to have a pulse, moving on a vibrational level ... [a] vast sense of scale, the striking contrast of iron-oxide earth meeting blue expansive sky.
>
> 2012: 43

Hamilton Downs is a one and a half hour drive northwest from Alice Springs, which itself began as a telegraph station servicing the 1872 overland line running from Adelaide to Darwin and which enabled almost instant communication across the British Empire via trans-oceanic cables. The telegraph was a significant achievement in the colonisation of Australia, facilitating further pastoral incursions into Aboriginal lands as well as serving to coordinate armed reprisals against Indigenous resistors (Shepherd 2022). From these beginnings, Alice Springs became a centre where diasporic First Australian populations concentrated. Much of the Alice Springs Indigenous population is semi-itinerant, moving back and forth from communities that are closer to traditional Country, including Yuendumu, Nyirripi, Balgo and Papunya. This partly accounts for the diversity of peoples around Alice and the tensions that exist between them, as well as the fact that many of those who pass through have a fair degree of familiarity with regions which need not be their own principal ancestral grounds, yet to which they may be linked via lineage or marriage (Rose 1992; Carty 2021).

Consider for example the Lhere Mparntwe, or Todd River, which runs north-south through Alice Springs, parallel to the main road. Following the violent disruptions of twentieth century colonisation, the riverbed became a camping ground for Aborigines, including those visiting from distant regions for family, business, legal, and medical reasons. Jim Denley, who would compose music for the showings coming out of Triple Alice as he had for Mungo, reminded participants that the riverbed was a literal bed for many Aboriginal people (Anderson 2014: 24). Police regularly moved Aborigines off the river sands, and even the local Arrernte were unhappy about the damage these often impoverished and occasionally drug-affected populations were inflicting to significant Arrernte sites (Kanamori 2010: 63–65). Participants such as Karen Vedel (2007) identified "two very distinct spatial" and embodied practices active in the riverbed, namely those of the whites such as the "police, who regularly enforced their ... jurisdiction [by] patrolling the riverbed in a motorized van" as well as members of "the local cricket team" who jogged through the riverbed once a week, but did not dwell there. Those who had an ongoing, physical relationship with the riverbed were black, and in the eyes of Vedel, appeared to value the sensorial qualities of the site as well as its location. Vedel observed them, "Moving either *alongside*" the riverbed or along it, "by foot", most choosing yielding sand trails, rather than:

> paved roads ... groups, or 'mobs', of adult and elderly persons from the Aboriginal community, mostly males, settled in the shade of the red river gum trees in the riverbed. Forming circles in the sand ... these groups fluctuated in size during the run of a day with persons drifting to and fro. Perceived from the outside, the groups' main activity was talking, often in quite full voices. And although drinking alcohol in public is forbidden, drinking *did* take place, especially in the vicinity of the bottle shop.
> VEDEL 2007

For outsiders, hearing these elevated voices in the distance raised the possibility that violence might ensue, as it occasionally did. After Triple Alice was concluded, a 2009 by-law prohibiting camping in the riverbed was passed with the support of members of the local Arrernte community (Everingham 2009).

Alice Springs is known globally as the closest township to the sacred site and tourist destination of Uluru. Following the 1970s, First Nations groups came together to prosecute land claims, with the Pitjantjatjara and Central Land Councils lobbying the federal government to return Country. In 1985, ownership of Uluru was formally ceded back to the Anangu peoples, with the land then leased back to the National Parks and Wildlife service. Gratifying though this symbolic exchange was, negotiation continues over the level of First Nations control over the site. It was not until 2019, for example, that the Anangu were able to enforce a ban on climbing the rock.

Although de Quincey and her collaborators made little reference to these specific events, artists at Triple Alice were well aware of pre-existing tensions. The site of the Triple Alice laboratories was, if anything, *more* overdetermined in its relationship to Australian colonial imaginings than Lake Mungo. De Quincey for her part described the region as representing the "confronting heartbeat of the continent" (Finnane 1998). At least one of the dancers involved in Triple Alice has suggested that the laboratories might have constituted a way for them to "create our own Dreamings" (Anderson 2014: 26). In an earlier version of de Quincey's essay quoted above and which appeared on the Triple Alice website, she stressed that it was "inevitable" that any consideration of central Australia must acknowledge the "extensive historical relation to the establishment and function of electronic media in the Central Desert—bush telegraph, radio, television, satellite relay and the Internet" as "integral components within the contemporary environment" of the Alice Springs site and its histories (de Quincey et al. 1999–2001). The local quartz and silica deposits were moreover related to the main components of the silicon hardware that had replaced telegraphy (Grant and de Quincey 2008: 259). In contradistinction to the negative histories around the establishment of the colonial telegraph, the Triple Alice laboratories were envisaged as having a shared, interactive online presence, with ancient materials facilitating the development of a trans-spatial yet grounded techno-primitivist consciousness. Participants were invited to "post statements, texts and journal entries [while] ... At the same time, this website was receiving information from [distant] writers and artists" (M. Harrison 2003: 30). Here and elsewhere, de Quincey found the "Archaic space" of the region to be one which "coexists within everyday time" and what might evolve from it (2003: 23).

Unlike at Lake Mungo, the weather at Alice Springs was often extremely hot. The greatest level of physical exertion was therefore reserved for the relative cool of the mornings, with the hottest part of the day for more conceptual activities. The general pattern was as follows:

06:00–07:00 am	Breakfast
07:30–09:30 am	MB (muscle bone / mind body)
10:00–11:40 am	Manipulations and groundwork
12:00–13:40 pm	Lunch and rest period
14:00–17:30 pm	More manipulations and groundwork; walks and tours; and/or Peter Snow's 4pm performance making sessions (P4)
18:30 pm	Dinner followed by campfire yarning and other activities (Dunn 2003; Snow 2000 and 2003)

The work of the laboratories ran for six days a week followed by a rest day. MB was mostly conducted on the sandy tennis court beside the main building, which was raked daily. This was an echo of the Japanese tradition, continued in the studios at the University of Sydney, where performers wiped down the wooden studio floors with a damp cloth prior to exercises (Snow 2002: 116). Images from Hamilton Downs show how demandingly the MB sessions were, with participants' leaping completely into the air before rebounding onto the ground (Emmerson et al. 2003: 107). Manipulations took place outside under a shade cloth. Walks through the surrounding countryside were sometimes led by members of the group, generally as an alternative to groundwork. Groundwork might be conducted alone, in pairs, or collectively, with time for isolated introspection, as well as for the observation of one's fellows. As Tanaka put it, "You have a big chance to research" by considering "other people's bodies" (Cardone 1978: 20; Fuller 2014: 202). One development from Lake Mungo was the increasing importance of omnicentral imaging, or the strategic fragmentation of the body into a series of connected by not necessarily compatible units, which became a focus at Triple Alice. Tasks involving bisoku, ground-being / square of infinity, as well as blindfold exercises, were included too. In these and other activities, bodies rose and fell, or might lie prone for an extended period, taking on sensations and qualities. Rocks and objects might be piled on the body, or participants might crawl painfully over rough surfaces. Omnicentral embodiment often elicited twisted, contradictory movements, with limbs crisscrossing the body (see Emmerson et al. 2003: 119).

Omnicentral imaging is a central component of Tanaka's dispersal of the body into a weather-field of loosely affiliated units—what de Quincey (2002) calls the swarm body or dot body. Omnicentral imaging consists of the embodiment of diverse images, derived either from the environment (biota, geology, weather, historic remains) or poetic phrases derived from Hijikata and others, which the dancer attempts to situate within different parts of the body simultaneously. At Triple Alice, participants would typically work with three to four images at a time. The body would be divided, often into relatively straightforward units such as head, legs, torso and arms. A sequence used at Lake Mungo for example ran: "your hair is on fire, your arms are feathers, your legs are those of a chicken, your chest is a cloud moving across the sky" (Snow 2002: 213). On Warlpiri Country, Gretel Taylor (2010: 77) would later attempt to embody the images "cracked clay face; spinifex legs; blow-fly elbow".

In other omnicentral tasks, multiple images might be layered throughout the same body part. Legs, for example, might take on the qualities of a lake, but with bird's feet below, and knees which appeared to be "following stairs"

(Snow 2000: 266). These tasks were not strictly speaking representational—as in to make one's feet look and move like those of a bird, in the example just given. De Quincey rather urged participants to feel the distinct "movements, rhythms, weights, textures and speeds" of each image (Grant and de Quincey 2008: 250). Nor is omnicentral imaging an affective or Expressionist challenge in and of itself. Rather, one must "give different sensibilities to different muscle groups and nervous structures" (ibid. 250). Nevertheless, participants have reported "extreme emotional reactions" to imaging, ranging from "Laughter" to "trembling" and "sometimes tears" (Cardone 1978: 16). In many cases, the very logic or poetics of the images was divergent. De Quincey gave as an example the act of locating in the head the "gestalt" of "butterflies", including their insect qualities, their erratic movement, and use of spindly "feelers" for sensing (Grant and de Quincey 2008: 250). Legs however took on the aspects of the ground, including "sharp stones, foliage ... branches" (ibid. 250). Arms then were shaped according to concepts of velocity rather than what the object was, with limbs functioning as "lines of flight" as well echoing the trajectories of mosquitoes, wind-blown grasses, and "flames" (ibid. 250). Finally, the torso was to hold a series of avian or airborne images, namely "galah wings, clouds, birdsong" and even a "serpent" (Grant and de Quincey 2008: 250; one is tempted to imagine the Warlpiri Walyankarna, or snake ancestor, who was lifted up into the skies by the Minamina women's dancing and which came down in the rain to become a soak at Yaturlu Yarturlu, or the Granites; see Herbert Nungarrayi 2002: 6–7). Unlike in Tanaka's classes, de Quincey's exercises could be highly discursive, with the exchange of verbal reflections on what each image might mean and even journaling. De Quincey claims that by "placing" these various forms of "intelligence into different parts of the body ... you explode consciousness" (de Quincey and Eckersall 2012). Echoing the engagement of Japanese butoh with Surrealism, de Quincey further noted that these poetic prompts encouraged the individual to "generate" their *own* "surreal images", harnessing the power of the bodily and its psychic "subconscious" (ibid.).

Snow explains that by developing empathetic exchanges and relations with objects, landscapes, and so on, the dancer becomes "unaware what is coming from where" and hence the "barriers of unitariness ... coherence, and ... individuality" break down such that it seems as if movements and impulses begin to come from beyond the bodies and minds of the individual dancers themselves (Snow 2002: 160). McAuley noted that de Quincey "continually stressed ... the necessity to look out to the horizon and to connect to place as well as partner while undertaking the complex steps, jumps and turns" (McAuley 2003: 106). The site, its largely flat, expansive and hence multi-dimensional quality, and the fact that one shared the site with others both literally and metaphorically, was to be constantly born in mind. Partaking in these and other activities, day in day out, participants did indeed find that the environment seeped into their being.

Amongst other prompts, participants at Triple Alice were told that a young Aboriginal woman had allegedly hanged herself in the old storeroom at Hamilton Downs (K. Harrison 2003: 18). Even in the absence of detail or verification, this archetypal tale of a First Nations suicide carried enormous potency. Other local sites of violence beckoned. Snow was drawn to the old meat-shed, which contained a "long metal [cutting] bench ... I was interested in death and the blood that had been spilt here; of Indigenous people" and the cattle, the latter having been killed and hung to mature (Snow 2003: 60). Snow performed a dance of death and mourning during which, quoting Theodor George Strehlow's reading of an Aboriginal Dreaming narrative, "supernatural beings" violently birthed humanity by slicing a single living mass "into ... infants, then slit the webs between their fingers and toes and cut open their ears, eyes and mouths". Snow concluded that the shed had become "a site of desecration". Katrina Harrison (2003: 15) described a harsh, conflicted "process of placing myself in the landscape" which, in addition to the physical demands of the exercises themselves, involved the corporeal act of "inhaling dust and a substantial number of the local population of flies ... losing myself in the sky, the [view of the MacDonnell] ranges", as well as hallucinatory visions of "underground waterways" akin to those which haunted the dreams of participants at Lake Mungo.

Many spectres visited the camp. Grant claimed that, in addition to Snow, participants Fraser, Santos and de Quincey all "called up ghosts of previous inhabitants whose dreams, desires and daily lives haunted the shadows behind doors and directed ... movement" (2003: 78). After a P4 showing in the old machinery hut, Sam de Silva "left a [written] message for the ghosts to answer" (Snow 2003: 60). Jane Goodall noted that some of the dancers had been spooked by a "wili-wili"—an Anglicised Aboriginal word for a miniature sandstorm—which had started up while "someone was trying to put up a tent ... persistently ripping out the canvas free of the pegs" before swirling the sheeting into the air (2008: 120). Goodall confessed to having experienced a "fearsome dream" in which the dead returned, concluding by citing Jacobs and Gelder that, "If there is an Australian uncanny, it is surely characterised by this sense that we ourselves"—settler descent subjects— are in fact "alien presences in the landscape" (Goodall 2008: 120). As with Lake Mungo, Hamilton Downs was perceived as a profoundly haunted and Uncanny landscape. Exchanges between the participants and these not-fully-present spectres manifest within the materiality of the site (benches, huts, moving sands, dense shadows, sensations of the wind and of electrical storms on the skin and in the air) provided destabilising elements throughout the laboratories.

Another new factor in the training was the centrality of dialogue. The University of Sydney provided a studio for rehearsals between time spent on site. De Quincey gave her participants readings during these periods. Readings included material authored by Indigenous Queensland artist Pamela Croft, as well anthropologist Theodor George Strehlow's *Nomads in No-Man's Land* (1961), in which Strehlow offered a call for the collective Indigenous management of their own affairs (Anderson 2014: 111; de Quincey and Eckersall 2012). Strehlow was quoted by Snow in his performance at the meat-shed above. Also consulted was the biographical novel *Craft For a Dry Lake* (2000), written by Kim Mahood (who attended Triple Alice 3), and which dealt with Mahood's attempt to reconnect to the lands of her childhood and the Warlpiri peoples of the Tanami Desert. For the concluding performance of *Dictionary of Atmospheres* (2005), de Quincey and her dancers also quoted from Germaine Greer's essay "Whitefella Jump Up" (de Quincey 2023). It is not clear at what point during the workshops different texts such as that by Greer were consulted, but it seems likely all were drawn upon from at least Triple Alice 2. Greer's own essay argues that Australia must be reconstituted as an Aboriginal nation, with Indigeneity and its values lying at the core of national identity. Greer suggests Australians "Try saying ... to yourself in the mirror ... I was born in an Aboriginal country, therefore ... must be considered Aboriginal" (Greer et al 2003: 14–15). This passage was quoted by de Quincey's dancers during *A Dictionary of Atmospheres*.

At Hamilton Downs, writings such as these served as a way to refine and conceptualise activities. Hijikata's dancers had reported that when working with him they were often scrawling down text, images, and poetic instructions. What de Quincey instigated was more dialogic though, and not common within Japanese butoh. At Hamilton Downs, Anderson observes that everything was constantly being "transposed" (2014: 97), not just from the surroundings onto the body, but "from body to page, from page to body, from body to ... [white]board, from ... [white]board to body", and then even "from body to body", such that dancer's own bodies became almost decomposed media for inputs, sensations, and ideas. Not quite a blank page, and not entirely hollow or empty, but as Robertson (2015: 48) puts it, "an active receptor ... re-inscribed by place". Circuits of signification, narrative and subjectivity were scrambled to allow repeated inscription and rewriting.

De Quincey's processual, dialogic methodology was given an Indigenous inflection through a pattern of yarning by the campfire which Napangardi and her relations had contributed to in 1999 and 2001—although this crucial model of sociability instantiated in Australia by its First Peoples seems to have been only partially recognised as such by participants. Yarning is an Australian conversational model which crosses racial boundaries, but which is particularly associated with First Nations dialogical processes. As Dawn Bessarab and Bridget Ng'andu explain:

> When an Aboriginal person says *"let's have a yarn"*, what they are saying is, let's have a talk or conversation. This talk/conversation/yarn can entail the sharing and exchange of information between two or more people socially or more formally.
> 2010: 38

This is a mode whereby the exchange of life experiences, thoughts and nascent concepts goes "beyond ... pleasant and informative chats to become a transformative process" of both hearing and talking, proceeding in a freeform, associative manner rather than in a linear, outcome directed way (41). The fireplace is the traditional centre around which yarning occurs, and discussion rarely commences until a kettle or food has been put on the fire, and participants have found a place to sit.

The campfire which the Warlpiri women helped to enrich on the 1999 visit to Hamilton Downs therefore offered a model for discussions, or as de Quincey has put it, "Through their presence and way of being, Napangardi's family thickened the experience and depth of sharing around the campfire" (2023c). When Triple Alice's participants presented thoughts and findings to the collective throughout the workshops, this commonly involved:

> a campfire that either accompanied the presentation or was *part of* the presentation. The campfire was the literal place where bodies could gather and recognize the act the gathering.
> ANDERSON 2014: 96

Anderson therefore argues that, "The campfire was ... a means by which exchange could happen" in an open-ended, egalitarian manner (96). Learning from the site and its peoples was occurring, though not necessarily consciously or in a linear fashion.

When Napangardi and her relations came to Triple Alice 3: "Campfires were lit, kangaroo tails were cooked, and we sat around and ate, talked, laughed and looked at the skies" (2003: 19). Arrernte Elder Steve McCormack, who lived five kilometres from Hamilton Downs, also came to share, yarn and cook on the fire (Grant and de Quincey 2008: 254).[27] De Quincey would instigate a similar ritual as part of the rehearsals and daily set-up for *Dictionary of Atmospheres*, gathering around a pot of tea in the sands.[28] De Quincey and her associates echoed in this sense Greer's own suggestion to "sit down on the ground" of the Lhere Mparntwe and "have a think" in the company of others (Greer 2003: 78). Anthropologists and others have noted that Napangardi's Warlpiri kin have been known to declare "We Warlbiri live on the ground (*walya-nagga ga-liba nyinna*, ground-on we sit)" (Munn 1973: 58; Morphy and Boles 1999: 167).[29]

Yarning and related activities have intuitive timeframes of their own, sometimes rapid, sometimes spread out. De Quincey states that, as she understood it, as soon as Dorothy Napangardi and her Aunties from Nyirripi arrived at the station, they prepared to "sing, paint and dance Minamina into the Hamilton Downs Country" (2023c).[30] This was a way to acknowledge the people and spirits of the lands that they had come onto, as well as to ground their own presence in this location. After some negotiation, Triple Alice's members were allowed to come near the performance as the women moved on to the station grounds.

The communication of Dreamings typically involves negotiation and dialogue within communities regarding what can and cannot be shown in what media and who holds the rights to which images, symbols, phrases and so on—as well as what are the correct expressions and gestures. Correcting each other's recall of choreography and words is part of the act of generating the performance or painting itself. In Warlpiri tradition, the organisation of these exchanges may be overseen by figures called "kurdungurlu" (managers, or even "police women" as de Quincey herself put it [2023c]; Morphy and Boles 1999: 207–8; Dussart 2004; Jones 2014: 14; Curran 2017: 4). The accounts of the ceremony at Hamilton Downs authored by Harrison and de Quincey seems to have

---

27 McCormack would feature in the 2005 film *Living Country*, written and directed by David Tranter.

28 Anderson states: "Tess designed a ritual of having tea in the riverbed, complete with aluminium thermoses and cups for chai that the Company prepared each morning. 'What time is it?' is an ongoing, shared joke between Company members, referencing a desire to abandon perceived Western conventions associated with time and temporality and adopt a perceived Aboriginal sensibility of timelessness" (2014: 188).

29 I am grateful here and elsewhere in this chapter for the advice of Assoc. Prof. Darren Jorgenson (University of Western Australia) for referring me to key authorities such as Nancy Munn and for looking over my discussion of Warlpiri art and culture.

30 Harrison states that dancing occurred after the women had been at Hamilton Downs for some time, but as de Quincey observes (2023c), that was not consistent with what would be expected to happen if the women strictly followed protocols involved in having travelled onto Country which is not one's own.

unfolded under the watchful eye of such individuals.[31] Katrina Harrison relates that the women sat down to make a circle and:

> paint their bodies. We gathered around anticipating the dance that was to begin. As the sun started setting they began to dance their country, Mina Mina. They sang and stamped, with one of the older ladies muttering and directing, correcting and stopping as the women would fall in and out of debate and discussion about the dancing of their land. The dreaming was coming both from their bodies and the constant chattering, ensuring that all was going as it should. ... While the sun was still setting, the women danced and danced, laughed and chattered and when they felt it appropriate they came over to us and we sat together. We sat, letting our buzzing senses exist in the journey we had been taken on, to Mina Mina.
> K. HARRISON 2003: 19

It is not clear what dance was performed at Hamilton Downs, but a comparison of sources with photographic documentation from the event show five women, painted up, carrying sticks. The sticks indicate that the dance was likely part of the Jukurrpa related to Minamina's Kanakurlangu or Digging-Stick-Possessing Women (de Quincey 1999–2001; Webb ed. 2002; Premont 2020; Curran 2017). Senior First Nations scholar Djon Mundine (2002: 68–69) has described Warlpiri women's dance as resembling a kind of "minimalist shuffle", followed by a hop, in which the feet were largely kept upon the earth, scraping and caressing it before a short leap. Elders say "look to the knees to judge a dance" (Mundine 2002: 68–69). "The power of the subject is represented through repetition rather than" through the "impact of scale or colour", sequences typically being performed in "short 30 to 60 second bursts" (Mundine 2002: 68–69). The photographs of the performance hint at all of this, one still image capturing a moment where a dancer seems relaxed, her feet lightly sweeping the earth, whilst her fellow rises, heels off the ground, but toes on the earth, a burst of power lifting her body upwards with an easy authority (de Quincey et al. 2001a). Although one could never confuse butoh for First Australian dance, there are stylistic traits which the two had in common: the reduction of movement, a tendency towards low, ground based positions, precise action blended

---

31 Kirda (right or ownership of a Dreaming or ritual) and kurdungurlu (police or managers of Jukurrpa or ritual) are reciprocal relationships, and though it is not certain, it seems likely Napangardi was one of the kirda of the Jukurrpa painted at Hamilton Downs, whilst others in the party were more visibly active as kurdungurlu (see Curran 2017: 4).

with pedestrian gestures, and in the case of Body Weather, a frequent aspiration towards a quasi-mythic significance of dancing the landscape.

After a period at the camp "laughing at our crazy galavantings ... thinking it was ridiculous in the heat" (K. Harrison 2003: 19), the Warlpiri women sat down a second time, now to paint one of the Minamina stories related above. Napangardi appears to have been a notable presence within the group, but she did not lead the painting, and hence it did not reflect her own unique style.[32] Harrison reported that Triple Alice's own participants "found ourselves in the exciting position of being welcomed to assist" in the act of painting (ibid. 14)—a relatively common occurrence in Central Desert painting, where family groups and others will paint under the direction of senior holders of the Dreaming. This was therefore a gift of sharing from the community, rather than an act led by a singular artist.[33] Napangardi and her Aunties chose not to explicate the story or stories painted with the participants at Triple Alice 3.[34] Communication and communion, if indeed it was achieved, was effected through the intuitive exchange of arcane symbology, and the simple act of sharing space and activities.

Harrison concluded that, "As a kick off, this was a wonderful display of collaboration and conversation" (2003: 19). De Quincey for her part saw this shared performance on sandy ground as a precedent for the final production of a *Dictionary of Atmospheres,* noting that in some sense the encounter had "permeated" into what Triple Alice's artists would later present (Grant and de Quincey 2008: 268). The generous contribution of the Warlpiri women constituted a powerful act of cross-racial yarning which offered an example of how to proceed.

Providing a different perspective on Aboriginal Dreamings to that which the Warlpiri women had offered, ethnologist Peter Latz explained that the area around Hamilton Downs was a woman's or "female place" (Grant and de Quincey 2008: 254), referring to a group of rocks where an Arrernte ancestor had been killed for trespass, as well pointing out the extensive caterpillar Dreaming trail that runs hundreds of kilometres along the MacDonnell Ranges.

---

32 The reproduction of Napangardi's canvas *Mina Mina* (2006) in McAuley (2006: 271) is a different work to the one painted at Hamilton Downs. The latter may currently be seen on the De Quincey Company website (de Quincey 2023c; de Quincey et al. 2001a).

33 Although not in Napangardi's own personal style, we can be certain that Napangardi took an active role in the painting because Julia White remembered Napangardi seated beside her, instructing White to "Fill 'im in" and hence work the surface with dots (2003: 88).

34 An image of this work, now held at the University of Sydney, is online at de Quincey et al. (2001a). It features marks indicating multiple figures seated on the ground, likely both men and women, with implements beside them; see Munn's (1973) lexicon.

Latz guided participants to a waterhole associated with the Rainbow Serpent, a powerful being found in the cosmology of many continental First Australians and which is associated with watercourses above and below ground (K. Harrison 2003: 17–18). As de Quincey observes, Dreaming is "such an underlying facet of Central Australia, because of the Aboriginal culture that is so powerful there", such that "the whole place is imbued" with First Nations culture (2023c). Consequently, everyone is "talking about it in one way or another", all the time. It was therefore not only those listed above who spoke about the Dreamings which enfolded the laboratory, but at some level "everybody" who came and went. In de Quincey's eyes, the role of Body Weather was not to separate these historical, cultural and biological strands, but rather to become attuned to all as part of a sublimely challenging field of interweaving points and fragments.

Social experiences and corporeal sensations such as these accumulated within the participants, especially those who came for more than one season. As Gretel Taylor observed of her own time on Warlpiri Country that even after the "twelve hours" return journey from the location, "I still had orange dust encrusted in the pores of my skin and throughout my clothes" (2008: 155). Mary Anderson felt that the sand was "teaching" her how to stand, fall and teeter (2014: 19). Snow records "tasting the sand in the riverbed" while blindfolded: "It was curiously warm, smooth and thick" (Snow 2002: 220). McAuley described the "massive luminosity" of the generally cloudless skies as being "almost oppressive, creating a kind of vertigo" (Emmerson 2003: 110), and poet Martin Harrison coined the term "Skyhammer" to express this idea of the sky as "a force beating down on the earth and its inhabitants ... its energy almost impossible for humans to bear" (McAuley 2003: 116). Potent though these responses were, they clearly reflected an outsider's view of the Central Desert. There was perhaps more truth than the participants realised in the Elder Muta a Murinbata's statement recorded by W.H. Stanner that "White man got no dreaming" in the way their Aboriginal peers did, and so whites must "go 'nother way ... Him got" a journey across Country which "belong himself" (Stanner 1991: 297). Could Body Weather be a way to shape such a transcultural Dreaming; a "'nother way" for whites to follow? Many of the responses of those who were present at Triple Alice seemed to suggest it might.

The first two Triple Alice sessions were held during the final period of a six year drought. Prior to the third laboratory, unseasonal rain fell, with floodwaters briefly cutting off Hamilton Downs.[35] Snow noted that the Lhere Mparntwe burst into full flow, while lightning struck "in long blue bolts along the

---

35 These rains would inspire Dorothy Napangardi to produce her *Inland Sea* series, documenting Minamina's Ngayurru salt lake in flood (Webb 2002: 76).

[MacDonnell] ranges ... the sky was ... inky dark and very threatening", or as de Quincey put it, "Stupendous, encircling electric storms" crossed the "limitless" sky to "render electromagnetic fields" visible and physically "palpable" (de Quincey and Maxwell 2020: 169). Following the rain, "the whole world seemed gentler, more fragile ... exploratory" (Snow 2003: 56). McAuley agreed that the Country had suddenly become "green and almost lush, not at all the typical image of the red Centre, but this is what happens to the arid country when it receives a good fall of rain"—though she nevertheless admitted that "lushness is a relative term" where green foliage remains "spiky and hard" and the creek bed at Hamilton Downs only showed patches of damp sand and effervescent pools (McAuley 2003: 104). In a typically Body Weather response, Katrina Harrison found herself:

> entranced by life and death in this land: the short life cycles, which would spring up in fresh pools of rainwater, humming and buzzing with the excitement, busyness and rush of peak hour, only to disappear and leave dried, squashed, paper-thin traces of what had been.
> 2003: 17

All these impressions added to a sense that this landscape was one of death and life, of trauma and rebirth. Natural cycles of bloom and collapse were echoed by, and interwoven with, those of history and colonialism.

There were moreover striking examples of "inhabitation" with Hamilton Downs and its creatures. During one of the P4 sessions, Snow describes how:

> Hunt made us follow her quietly up the stones of the river bed until we reached a place where she told us to turn away and wait one minute before turning around. When we did, she was crouched away from us with her head plunged deep in a crevice in the rocks ... Then someone noticed the sleeping snake in the next crevice!
> 2003: 61

Katrina Harrison identified Hunt's companion as a death adder, one of Australia's most poisonous snakes and which is particular to the Central Desert. Snow reflected that when another snake had been found, one of the party (probably the caretaker) had "killed and skinned" it. Harrison herself chose to echo and inhabit "a space next to ... a beautiful gum tree, strangled and wounded by barbed wire tangled around it" (2003: 20). In a more playful manner, Snow and Van de Ven performed an improvised duet in which de Ven danced while Snow recited text. At one point, "Frank plunged his head into a crevice in a rock and came up with a bunch of dried leaves, which he smothered over his face. Towards the end, he stood behind me, lifted my hat, and dropped sweat" onto the dome of Snow's head (Snow 2003: 59).

De Quincey would seem to have concluded that the lands around Alice Springs offered at least some degree of access to the truth of Aboriginality, presenting a sensation that was "massive" in scope but which was "seemingly untouchable" or unattainable "on the coast" (de Quincey 2003: 23). Anderson has noted that de Quincey's journey into the Australian landscape echoed the course of European colonisation itself, with coastal settlements acting as launching pads for the invasion of inland regions (2014: 17). Anderson herself though does not see this as doing justice to de Quincey's multidimensional thinking. De Quincey's essay on Alice Springs as a "burning point" harnesses a range of destabilising spatial metaphors, in which one treads "into an unknown path and an unknown territory" before one "flips an underbelly of fear and a void, the screaming wobble of vulnerability" (de Quincey 2003: 21–22). The Centre is also read as, "An insistent place of undercurrents and absences, of magnetism and invisible forces ... of water, of fire and of deep ground". As at Mungo, there was a sense of a vertical descent as one steps *"into ... a void"* (my emphasis), drawn by the magnetic pull of water, history and culture, which has seeped into the sand to join ancient aquifers and geomorphological structures—"the swell of a giant invisible ocean" (Grant and de Quincey 2006: 259), but which is also crossed by horizontal movements along a "path" which carries the staggering, sensitive body across the surface of the landscape. It is a place where it is impossible to traverse in a "straight line" (ibid. 259). Rather one moves in "Swoops, curves ... jitters of birds ... and foldings" (ibid.: 259). Caught between the vertical and the horizontal, even one's sense of being located at a dominant core was problematised in de Quincey's statement that Triple Alice should act "in stages" via "concentric circles of artistic and cultural exchange" which "build out in ripples ... to establish interchange", rebounding back to modify the central actors. Grant and de Quincey have written that Triple Alice might be seen as composed out of a "series of overlapping swarms, or a swarm of swarms", by which they mean both human and non-human agents (Grant and de Quincey 2008: 259). Anderson observed that in many ways the site acted as a "container", a locus within which things could be lodged—either temporarily or as part of a longue durée (as the Annales historians would phrase it, see Tilly 2017; Anderson 2014: 49).

As noted above, de Quincey's vision of Australia as she passed through the Dardanelles is revealing. The multiplicity with which Body Weather constructs spatiality means that sites are not seen as fixed or singular—also reinforced by Van de Ven, Snow and Taylor (2008: 90–91). These is not indicative of a essentialist perspective, whereby the specifics of the environment might be stripped away to reveal features common to many similar landscapes and waterscapes.[36] De Quincey's model was rather governed by what Anderson identified as a "transpositional logic" whereby every isolated point within the granulated swarm of the site, and one's response, to it "cannot but help speak to another point" (Anderson 2014: 110–14), or as Snow phrases it, de Quincey's dancers are "never simply in one place but always in many places" (Snow 2002: 77). Even as they are attuned to the specifics of what is around them, "any local investigation brings with it an inquiry into global weather ... how do these Australian weathers ... differ from other weathers worldwide" such as in Japan? Through these investigations, "New realms of inbetweenness emerge" (Snow 2006: 238). Sites and bodies are endlessly morphing, perhaps in subtle ways, but without end or rational logic. De Quincey explains that even though Body Weather involves an intense investigation of the place one dances within, through these investigations one paradoxically discovers that "You never arrive" (in Pryce 2017: 58). Such an approach might indeed enable a means for those of settler descent to provisionally engage with First Nations histories and cosmologies, but it is a very different model to those of the Australian Aborigines, and one suspects very different from that of Japan's own aboriginal Ainu peoples (Taylor 2008: 147–9). De Quincey's vision of the site arises then out of a global, multidimensional consciousness. This might find some kinship in the multidimensional and transhuman character of Indigenous links to Country, but the two are not the same. Rather, as de Quincey recognised from the outset, Body Weather exists in a constructively shifting dialectic with such conceptualisations, informed to some degree by the urge to collapse particularities into a universal sameness, while also resisting these tendencies.

10   Triple Alice Performances and *Dictionary of Atmospheres* (2005)

There were a number of work-in-progress showings which developed out of Triple Alice, including the performative report *Skyhammer,* presented at TPS in 2000 (Johns 2000). *Dictionary of Atmospheres* was however the main public performance which came out of Triple Alice. The title had earlier been used

---

36   By contrast, butoh artists Eiko & Koma attempt to "focus on the primal elements" at the site such that the piece evokes "the very essence of the river ... what connects one river to another ... so that River X becomes all rivers" (Kloetzel & Pavlik 2009: 183).

for a 2001 performative lecture by de Quincey and Kristina Harrison, but would later come to refer to the multimedia work staged in the Lhere Mparntwe for the 2005 Alice Springs Desert Festival.

The name originally referred to de Quincey's attempt to echo Tanaka in accumulating a repertoire of prompts and images from which choreography could be developed. Prompts for this riverbed performance of *Dictionary of Atmospheres* reportedly included the smoke body, shadow body, storm body, and other images (Anderson 2014: 16). The outdoor venue of the Lhere Mparntwe was chosen not simply for its combination of sandy grounds, hidden water and spreading river gums, but because of its status as an overdetermined social and political location (Vedel 2007). As de Quincey put it, the riverbed was "such a contested space. Whitefellas very rarely ... walked down it". For the performance, de Quincey's dancers and audiences came right "down to where the blackfellas were camping ... we wanted to be as gentle as possible, and not invade" (de Quincey and Eckersall 2012). Anderson argues that the piece was conceived as a way to bring mixed audiences into this little used "public space to, at least in part, deal with the problem[s]" associated with that site (2014: 62). For the period of the performances, this did in fact happen. In de Quincey's words, the riverbed became a "community gathering spot" (de Quincey and Eckersall 2012). Noticeable in the photographic documentation is the presence of white children, playing in and around the performers, not something normally seen on the Lhere Mparntwe at the time.[37]

De Quincey explains that the final stage of developing *Dictionary of Atmospheres* arose out of a:

> three-week process ... inhabiting the Mparntwe/Todd river bed quietly each day, gradually absorbing and building a greater sense of this very contested, place and exploring how to bring the choreographic material into play in a way that could shape a coherent flow and amplify the different elements of the performance. Then in the last week we started to consolidate all the tech through the crossover between dusk into darkness. Each afternoon cables had to be dug down, lights installed, projector and screens erected to then be dug up and removed each night for the last four days of performances.
> 2023c

---

37 My analysis draws on unpublished photographs kindly shared with me by de Quincey.

The event featured video projections from Sam James and was accompanied on saxophone by Jim Denley. Also accompanying the performance was a musique-concrète or audio-montage backing track consisting of three:

> pre-recorded ... CDs of my saxophone ... which were played on three ghetto blasters carried and placed by Indigenous teenagers who ... [helped] spatialise the sound [by walking and]; spiralling around the audience and place. The recording and playback machines extended me into a cyborgian musician. The effect was a multiplying of the saxophony; an immersion into a spatialized, phase-shifted, microtonal saxophone multiplicity that then engaged with the sonic ecology of the Todd.
> DENLEY 2023

Dancers in *Dictionary of Atmospheres* included Peter Fraser, Victoria Hunt, Kristina Harrison, Linda Luke and Tom Davies. Audiences gathered at the northern end of town near the Schwarz Crescent causeway and concluded on the riverbank near the Totem Theatre with the dancers disappearing around the curve in the riverbed as audiences gathered around a video installation by Francesca da Rimini at the end of the route. Preparation for each evening's performance began with a morning greeting and yarn in the sand before the participants removed rubbish and sharp objects, including glass and needles. Those already present at the site tended to wander off, but Vedel records that the local Aborigines also often shared tea with the artists, exchanged "fragments of life stories" and "greetings", generating a "sense of sharing" (2007).

De Quincey's aim with *Dictionary of Atmospheres* was to continuously reframe views and relations to the landscape and the site (2023b). The event took place along a two kilometre route with the dancers "appearing from and then disappearing at the other end of the riverbed as one long continual thread" which evolved over time. The piece started as the sun began to set and concluded in the dark. *Dictionary* began with Fraser stretched across the curving horizontal of a tree branch close to where the audience had been positioned. He was barely noticeable at first, dressed in sand-stained clothing, slowly unfurling, "like a lizard" (de Quincey 2023b). Hunt appeared in the distance, silhouetted on the boulders at the top of Spencer Hill, which rose a kilometre or so northeast of the site. Three figures became apparent north of the audience, along the curve of the riverbed, wearing brightly coloured, translucent plastic rain ponchos, as they approached at a medium pace before gaining speed. Hunt leapt between the boulders, before eventually joining Fraser and the others by the tree. Photographs show some of the dancers with their arms spread, their bodies arching backwards in a pose similar to one featured at Lake Mungo.

Much of the initial section of *Dictionary of Atmospheres* was highly interactive. Fraser moved amongst the audience whispering scraps of text such as Strehlow's interpretation of the Arrernte concept of the spirit double (1971: 598–601) as well as Greer's essay "Whitefella Jump Up" (de Quincey 2023b). Moving slowly, the dancers carried out Greer's injunction to look at themselves and the landscape in large, rectangular mirrors they held before themselves, while briefly reciting, "I live in an Aboriginal country" (Greer 2003: 14; de Quincey 2023b; Anderson 2014: 29–36, 68–69). The mirrors were "held and moved at different angles" so that audiences could "see different parts of the environment reflected" across their surfaces, before the mirrors were laid on the ground (de Quincey 2023b). Tom Davis dug around the feet of audiences, while Fraser collapsed in front of others. Denley bent enthusiastically forward towards spectators as he played his saxophone. As de Quincey (2023b) observes, these spontaneous interactions were playful but not without tension, with photographs showing perplexed but smiling audience members closely involved with the artists. In one performance, the dancers physically lifted and moved a laughing spectator. It was all "about the life that occurs in that riverbed" (de Quincey 2023b), and the interactions, of both a vexed and a positive nature, which local humans, organisms and entities shared along the Lhere Mparntwe.

Further movement along the riverbed was initiated by several of the dancers taking off with red ribbons streaming behind them, and the audience was encouraged to follow. The dancers pulled yellow hazard tape from under the sand and used it to entangle and corral the audience, evoking the strategies used by white settlers, police, and others who had attempted to manage access to land and Country (de Quincey 2023b). Spectators were then encouraged to burst through the tape and follow the performers who had continued to move down the riverbed, performing various sequences—some of which involved impromptu interactions with local First Nations individuals and others who were camping or resting along the route. Photographic documentation shows that most of these performative offerings were accepted with a sense of fun by locals caught up in the action, smiling at the performers and each other.

As the light faded, the performance moved to a more defined stage (Figure 6), bounded by massive trees, and backed by three video screens. De Quincey likened these to "sails" emerging from the sand "as if a boat had floundered in the middle of the riverbed" (2023b). An expanse of netting was stretched and coiled about the space, and at times the dancers became tangled in it, or moved it about. Themes of aggression, status and domination emerged, with

102   CHAPTER 3

FIGURE 6   De Quincey Co's *DICTIONARY OF ATMOSPHERES* (Lhere Mparntwe/Todd Riverbed, Alice Springs Festival, Arrernte Country, Central Australia: 2005). Performers left to right: Linda Luke, Kristina Harrison, Victoria Hunt, Tom Davies, Peter Fraser
PHOTO: MAYU KANAMORI. COURTESY OF KANAMORI

pairs of dancers pushing each other down using a hand on the head of their partner, or later gently pinching each other. Scuffles and wrestling movements occurred, with dancers at times lifted and tossed bodily across the space. A performer seemed to kick at a prone body, while another buried their head in the sand. By now, everything had become "dusty, dirty and sandy" (de Quincey 2023b). Textures of the landscape and of skin were projected, as well as flames, Warlpiri women rolling human hair into string, and the phrase "Living Systems". Clouds of sand billowed up, at times obscuring the scene, as harsh spotlights picked out tumbling dancers. There was violence, but tenderness too, with groups of three or more coming together to embrace awkwardly across the gritty performance space. More measured poses were enacted in front of the screens, with three dancers forming a line as they bent over, later pouring red sand onto the ground.

Dictionary of Atmospheres concluded with the three dancers in rain ponchos moving slowly through the sand (see Anderson 2014: 30–36). They carried bundles of spinifex just under one metre long and bound together in a shape recalling a coolamon, or curved Aboriginal dish for food gathering (de Quincey 2023b and 2023c). Before exiting, they placed the spinifex on the ground, where it was lit, with the embers providing a possible locus for spectators who wished to muse or yarn over the event. De Quincey recalled that "there was quite a large fire and it was after that the dancers moved away together from the audiences disappearing in the centre of the riverbed as it curved away from view" (de Quincey 2023b). Anderson's interpretation of these departing figures was that they were "the living disguised as ghosts", moving "between worlds" (2014: 30). As at Mungo, the site proved one of the most expressive actors in the performance, one reviewer concluding that the dominant impression was one of "the desert dusk and the ancient presence of the riverbed" (Maher 2005: 11). Although *Dictionary of Atmospheres* was densely woven with allusion to the politically-conflicted nature of the space, these comments from the reviewer suggest that, for some audience members at least, the piece was largely interpreted as an abstract meditation on landscape.

After the season was over, de Quincey discovered that there had been a death close to where Fraser began his dance (de Quincey and Eckersall 2012). Another death occurred in the riverbed shortly after closing night. Nevertheless, some of those with whom de Quincey had become close in Alice felt that the performance had acted as a ritual to "cleanse out that place" just as they had "literally cleaned it" of rubbish each day (de Quincey and Eckersall 2012). Vedel (2007) adds that the Aborigines who had been dwelling there had become "well acquainted with the performance by the time of the premiere" and so were used to withdrawing to the banks of the river for a brief spell as the dance passed them by:

> On one occasion, however, a group of Aboriginal men remained seated ... [and it was] Not until the dancers reached them ... did they get up ... one man remained, entering into a movement dialogue with performers, and as they moved on, he took a bow before the audience.
> VEDEL 2007

Photographic documentation shows the man in a pose which could well be interpreted as a butoh stance, his hips slightly dropped and displaced to one side, knees gently bent and slightly wobbling, his torso twisting around and down to the left as hands splayed asymmetrically from the body, fingers unevenly spread (de Quincey 2023a). De Quincey was particularly gratified when one of the Aborigines with whom they had conversed "came by laughing and waving his hand encouraging us just before the performance began: 'Any Dreaming—All Dreaming—Everyone's Dreaming!'" (Grant and de Quincey 2008: 269). De Quincey took this as an endorsement. If certain members of the transitory First Nations communities in Alice Springs concluded that Body Weather enabled a kind of "other way" or white man's Dreaming, then surely de Quincey's dancers could do so also? My own position is that it is less important how one answers this question, than that de Quincey so insistently asked it of audiences and artists. De Quincey and her peers actively grasped the nettle of how those of settler descent might "stand in Australia", concluding that one way was by repeatedly "falling down" whilst moving into and out of "A central ... holographic point" or moving "cluster of points" at Alice Springs (Grant and de Quincey 2008: 258). No other butoh or Body Weather artist, with the exception of Gretel Taylor,[38] has put so much at stake in attempting to answer this question of postcolonial dance in Australia. Moreover, coming out of an experimental performative research laboratory, de Quincey's work was never meant to answer such questions once and for all. De Quincey's efforts therefore should be studied by those who follow.

---

38   See "Post-Colonial Butoh & Rejecting the Empty Body: Gretel Taylor" in chapter four.

CHAPTER 4

Body Weather Comes Back from the Desert: De Quincey's Urban Works, the Hysterical Body, and Other Body Weather Performers in Australia

1   Introduction

De Quincey's inland site-specific explorations constitute some of the most in depth choreographic engagement with Australian national tropes and landscapes by non-Indigenous dancers. Body Weather has also been deployed to explore a range of other expressions and topics in Australia. In what follows, I move to the urban environment to examine the site-specific works mounted by de Quincey and others which examine contemporary post-industrial metropolitan conditions, as well as her mature investigation of the hysterical body in *Nerve 9* (2001–05). I also consider the work of three of de Quincey's peers in Australian Body Weather, namely Martin De Amo, Nikki Heywood and Gretel Taylor. The work of de Quincey and her peers demonstrates the diversity and sophistication of butoh practice, and the ways one might explore the divided body, the humanimal body, a body moved by forces outside of itself, and what it is to dance place, sometimes evoking scenes of hysterical collapse, excess and abjection.

2   De Quincey's Urban and Industrial Site-Specific Works: *Compression 100* (1996), *City to City* (2000), *The Stirring* (2007), *Run* (2009)

Many of de Quincey's early collaborations with fellow Australian Body Weather expert Stuart Lynch took the form of task based improvisations, typically enacted in a manner responsive to the environment being performed in. Like Tanaka's *Drive* and *Hyperdance* series, the titles of these works varied, sometimes being given as a production by the de Quincey / Lynch Performance Union, or alternatively as a Paradance work. Typically unformed and experimental, these works nevertheless were some of the first to demonstrate the transferability of butoh and Body Weather to Australia's urban locales. Three early examples stand out: *Compression 100* (1996), *Segments From an Inferno* (1997), and *City to City* (2000).

De Quincey's and Lynch's *Segments From an Inferno* was a mediation on Dante's *Divine Comedy* describing the author's travels through Hell. The piece was installed and performed at the former Hyde Park Barracks, where colonial convicts had once been assembled, disciplined, and sent as labourers across Sydney during the early nineteenth century. *Inferno* was a durational performance featuring de Quincey, Lynch, as well as Carmen Olsson and Heike Müller (students at the University of Sydney, Olsson now being based in Sweden, while Müller is Danish and a veteran of the Mungo workshops). Snippets of Dante's text were recited by dancers absorbed in a "trancelike concentration" performing moments of:

> Running, jumping, standing still. Small quick steps ... and long striding leaps. Gravel spraying through clouds of red dust. Bodies curved inwards in the *butoh* language of quivering, dysfunctional looking limbs [and dissociated gazes] ... Slow movements and fast action. Nothing remaining the same for long, but all of it going on for a marathon of six hours.
>
> SYKES 1997

Gay McAuley (2006: 150) noted that the performance "prize[d] open the contemporary reality of the place" in often quotidian and unspectacular moments of dance, thereby "permit[ing] the past to surge into the present" via the bodies of the performers. De Quincey's practice enabled here a kind of doubling and collapse of both time and space, fragmenting realities, moments, and corporeal responses in a collage-like, historiographic dialogue. Here again, Body Weather rendered sites and bodies multidimensional and transhistorical.

De Quincey's and Lynch's *Compression 100* consisted of one hundred and eleven largely improvised site-specific collaborations performed in different locations in Sydney during May 1996, beginning and ending with what Jane Goodall (1996: 35) described as a kind of "forced march" along the so-called "Compression Highway", or Parramatta Road, which follows the original route which the predominantly white settlers took as they moved away from the coast and into the rich grasslands of New South Wales and eventually towards the centre of the Australian continent. *City to City* was a reprise of the first and last days from *Compression 100*, with audiences four years later being invited to join the performers in a kitsch Australiana journey. Publicity material stated that Parramatta Road was the "first intercity road in Australia" dating back to the "earliest years of Sydney's history", prior even to European settlement, the route being travelled by the local Indigenous Eora peoples deep into the past (de Quincey et al. c2000). Echoing Goodall's own comments as a long-term

Sydney resident, de Quincey and Lynch declared that despite this history, Parramatta Road was a route which:

> Sydney loves to hate ... It has been claimed that no road in Australia has had more curses bestowed upon it. In the early years, the curses were provoked by potholes, deep mud or bushrangers. Now the frustrations have changed. Heavy traffic, and a general impression of concrete, steel and noise characterise our experience of the Parramatta Road in 2000. But is it all bad?
> DE QUINCEY ET AL. C.2000

For the 2000 performance, audiences were shown, "some of Sydney's oldest taverns and see the roadside mannequin [at a caryard], the suspended piano player, the pet car" and other quirky sights along the route. Significant here is that, as with Hijikata's relationships with artists and theorists, or indeed Tanaka's exchanges with the writers at *Yu* magazine, critiques from Goodall and others informed de Quincey's own development and conceptualisations through a reciprocal exchange between critic and dancer. Of the opening day of *Compression 100*, Goodall reflected that the experience had made her "feel differently" regarding Parramatta Road:

> I've moved from dissociation to mild fixation. I've developed a perverse sense of attachment to this roaring, ugly, clashing, hot, polluted environment. I've taken to walking along it, sometimes for two hours a time, to writing about it and to driving down it in preference to using the freeway. Now this is perverse and *Compression 100* was, amongst other things, a shared exercise in sustained perversity. Its legacies are likely to be random and widely dispersed. Perhaps all over Sydney there are people who are experiencing altered relations with particular spaces.
> GOODALL 1996: 35

Goodall concluded that it was the "relentless driv[ing] forward" of the cars, modernity and time, which "became the choreography of 'Dancing the Parramatta Road' was in its own way a form of receptive channelling" of the urgent imperative to move inland, to reach the next suburb, to get home, and to more generally get off Parramatta Road itself (Goodall 2008: 119). While Goodall's critique draws more attention to the politics of urban capitalism and consumption than de Quincey's and Lynch's own amused road trip, there remains a sense for all parties of using the body and its travels to investigate and critique urban spaces and their histories. Butoh's proximity to European Surrealism and psychogeography (the latter being a ludic form of urban analysis which developed in part out of Surrealism) is visible here, but in a very different urban space, and within a different national context. All but paraphrasing her Surrealist and psychogeographic precedents, de Quincey concluded that in Sydney and elsewhere, "the body is the city" which could therefore be danced (Gallasch 1996: 4). The open ended nature of *Compression 100,* and the limited engagement de Quincey and Lynch had with most of their collaborators prior to the improvised on site collaborations, made for an uneven but exciting series of odd juxtapositions, closer to Happenings and Performance Art of the 1960s-70s, than mainstage theatre. Tunnels proved literally resonant sites for many of the more striking events in *Compression 100,* where snippets of operatic text merged with sculptural placings of the body, not altogether unlike *Segments of an Inferno. Compression 100* may not have been de Quincey's most successful program, but it demonstrated the ways in which butoh aesthetics might be deployed within the Australian urban context, and hence showed how butoh might become a deracinated practice within the broader field of Australian arts. The concept of localised site responsiveness here overwrit any lingering sense of the choreography's Japanese origins.

Following the desert residencies discussed above, de Quincey returned to urban sites in Sydney on several occasions. I shall limit myself here to two other related examples, namely de Quincey's *The Stirring* (2007) and *Run: A Performance Engine* (2009), both of which were performed at the former industrial space of Carriageworks, to which TPS had relocated in 2007. Following in de Quincey's wake, many other Australian artists would engage in site-specific psychogeographical explorations, notably Tony Yap's work in Javan, Malaysian and Australian cities such as his video-dances immediately before and during the Covid epidemic of *Liminal City* (2021–22).[1]

The land on which Carriageworks stands was granted to the Chisholm family in 1835, who established a farm and dairy, before the site was acquired for the construction of the Eveleigh Railway Workshops in 1880 (Curio 2017). Steam and later diesel powered rolling stock were constructed and repaired at the site, servicing the state of New South Wales and beyond. The workshops were important employers for residents of the surrounding suburbs, and played a significant role in Australian labour relations. When workers objected to what they saw as a coercive, anti-union way of managing efficiency—the so-called Taylor Card System—they downed tools and walked off the job, starting the highly fractious Great Strike of 1917 (Ellmoos 2017). The railyards closed in 1989, serving briefly

---

[1] See "Yap's *Eulogy For the Living, Rasa Sayang & Liminal City*" in chapter six.

as a market before becoming a cultural centre in 2007. De Quincey and her collaborators were commissioned to stage an opening memorialising performance, which was offered as a cross-site durational work. Themes and actions from this piece were reworked for a related theatre piece performed in a single location in front of seated audiences. The principal link, aside from histories of the site, projections, music and voice-over, was the use of massive suspended scaffold supports found in situ. For *The Stirring*, audiences were invited to pull on a rope and make one such object move ever so slightly along a rail. For *Run: A Performance Engine* much of the choreography was performed by dancers located on top of, hanging from, or moving, several such composite iron beams.

The Stirring was more expansive in drawing on what Harrison at Triple Alice had described as a "history of the senses" (M. Harrison 2000: 8).[2] While *Run: A Performance Engine* evoked hardness, cold metal, and above all the effects of weight, gravity and momentum on bodies both industrial and human, *The Stirring* featured a range of elements. De Quincey again engaged a senior member of the free improvisation music scene, in this case flautist Natasha Anderson. Audiences moved through the site and into one of the extremely large, refurbished work sheds, where they found a trough of milk—a reference to the now vanished dairy industry (read by some spectators as indicating a vanished river; McNeilly 2007: 29)—and another trough of dense, smelly oil—referring in this case to the dripping industrial machines that populated the sheds. In one particularly striking section, spectators came upon rocks and steam. De Quincey explains that she "wanted to make one of my archaic [Stone Age] burial mounds" such as she had encountered in her youth in Wales (de Quincey and Eckersall 2012). Employing ten tonnes of stones previously used as ballast around railway tracks, she constructed what was listed in the program as a "Shrine for a Whale" (McNeilly 2007: 29), which in its memorialisation of an animistic god she likened to aged Japanese Shinto shrines and monuments. De Quincey also noted that Indigenous groups along the New South Wales coast have claimed kinship with whales, establishing a link between indigenous Japanese concepts and those of Australia. De Quincey related that:

> The stones are doused in water and heated. Clouds of steam surge and billow out and up, encounter a cool mist, and are drawn into fine turbulences—an atmospheric micro-dynamic. ... The intermittent revving of a motorbike engine sent an explosive sound reverberating through the enormous buildings, a reminder of the ear-splitting noise of the workshops of the steam

---

2 See "Body Weather as an Uncanny Project: Tracing an 'interactive history of the senses'" in chapter three.

age. Hanging paper overalls became the spirit bodies of the Aboriginal past. The suspension of a gigantic iron remnant rigged with a tug-rope engaged audiences in the slow dragging of great weight. An immersive sound composition was juxtaposed with small audio installations, both historic and abstract, including radio interviews on individual speakers.

Five performers functioned as installed bodies, integral elements of the place ... Sporadic guttural voices and chalk writings touched on different cultural spaces and times, from rousing speech reflecting the intense political history to the tracing of Aboriginal names and the nature of crow dreaming. As reflectors and carriers of history and time negotiating and uncovering each moment, the performers' roles were to strike deep into the heart of the place.
DE QUINCEY AND MAXWELL 2020: 171

Intermittent encounters unfolded in the cavernous foyer and elsewhere, with figures standing on, or hanging upside down from, mezzanine levels, as well as ceiling pipes, illuminated by scattered lights amongst shadowy spaces, often glistening with water. Jodie McNeilly (2007: 29) identified Alan Schacher—who also trained with Tanaka but later developed performance installations for his own company Gravity Feed—moving throughout the sheds in a "scurried motion", and screaming out "There are no angels" (McNeilly 2007: 29). As is typical in butoh and de Quincey's works, audiences found the performance to be "haunting" (Needham 2007). Clocks, chimes and alarms such as were used to monitor workers on site echoed throughout the space, "tapping into not only the industrial past ... but also something more ancient" (Needham 2007).

The Whale Shrine was the most evocative site, at which Oguri—a dancer who worked with both Hijikata and Tanaka—toiled, dressed in a "soiled, hooded white [rain] coat" similar to those used at Triple Alice. Initially adopting a hunched position, Oguri began very slowly, his ascent marked by the crunching of ballast beneath his feet. The huge mound of rock "steams steadily. A thin spray of water falls" creating a "weathering of elements ... water, steel, stone and concrete" (Needham 2007). Prancing, crouching, twisting, falling, seemingly walking on burning coals steaming from beneath his boots, Oguri made for a compelling sight. A brief "cheek to cheek duet" between de Quincey and First Nations dancer Henrietta Baird helped bring proceedings to a close, after which the dancers led the audience to a pair of oil drums acting as braziers and around which the spectators were invited to yarn with the artists, as at the conclusion of *Dictionary of Atmospheres* (2005).[3]

---

3   See *"Dictionary of Atmospheres"* in chapter three.

Although drawing on many of the same historiographic materials, *Run: A Performance Engine* was themed around the choreographic implications of industrialised labour and the enforcement of machinic, choreographic and aesthetic principals within society. This topic was the focus of many of butoh's forebears, having been explored by Austrian-Australian immigrant Gertrud Bodenwieser in her landmark production *Demon Machine* (1924), which dramatized the seductive but dehumanising transformation of living bodies into a larger, machinic ensemble (Toepfer 1997: 266–270). Modernist dance and its arts were greatly influenced by late nineteenth century physiological studies of human movement and by those choreographies which went hand in hand with industrial, athletic and military time-and-motion studies (Marshall 2008; Braun 1994). The stop motion photographic analyses of patients, athletes, dancers and workers which were published by Étienne Jules Marey in France and Eadweard Muybridge in the USA were a direct influence on the founder of Eurythmics Émile Jaques-Dalcroze, the Soviet theatre-maker Vsevolod Meyerhold, as well as Frederick Taylor, author of the concept of the scientific management of construction line laborers, and which underpinned the Taylor Card system imposed upon the former workers at Carriageworks (Ellmoos 2017). De Quincey returned to the work of Marey, Muybridge and Taylor for inspiration in devising *Run* (Lancaster 2009), rendering the piece not only a mediation on the relationship of bodies to machines and industry, but also on the history of modernist dance and its ambivalent connection with ideals of becoming machinic and so transcending the human (Marshall 2011a: 261–81).[4] In her typically translocating fashion, de Quincey recalled that the efficiency cards which workers had to fill out at Sydney's railyards were devised by Taylor in the USA, and gazing at the iron beams at Carriageworks, her mind turned to the historic 1930s photographs of construction workers riding massive girders as they were hoisted over New York during the construction of the Chrysler building and other skyscrapers. While alluding to the specifics of the Carriageworks site and its material remains, de Quincey therefore sought to reflect what she called the "global cultural history of the industrial revolution" and of the ambivalent place of the choreographed body in these developments (de Quincey and Eckersall 2012).

Run: A Performance Engine occurred on top of and around six mobile elements. These included a step ladder with a platform at its summit, four massive metal struts sourced on site each of which weighed over one ton and were made up of

---

4   Marcel Duchamp (*Nude Descending a Staircase*, 1912), the Futurists, Dadaists and Surrealists repeatedly used the stop motion photographic studies by Marey, Muybridge and others in their own photomedial outputs, collages, paintings, sculptures, and live performances (see Marshall 2021).

FIGURE 7   De Quincey Co's *RUN – A PERFORMANCE ENGINE* (The Performance Space: 2009). Performers: Tom Davies (left) and Victoria Hunt (right).
PHOTO: HEIDRUN LÖHR. IMAGE COURTESY OF LÖHR AND DE QUINCEY CO.

two heavy, edging lengths with crossed steel between them to make up a braced support (Figure 7), and finally a lone, single cast length of massive iron which was set slowly swinging back and forth during the show as a metronome. Other indicators of the measurement of industrialized time including factory whistles and ticking clocks, repeatedly sounding during the performance, as in *The Stirring*. Recalling a scene from Charlie Chaplin's film *Modern Times* (1936), during which a beaming Chaplin was inserted between a series of massive cogs, *Run* began with the "dancer as robot ... the head slowly being apparently twisted, fitted and tightened by a giant hanging beam that looks like a spanner" (Lancaster 2009). In addition to an amplified, found-object score originally devised by Denley but performed by last minute replacement Dale Gorfinkel, the piece was accompanied by the noise of beams moving about, each of them having its:

> own voice. The weighted sound of the clack of the tracks, or the ratchet of the metronome swing ... disturbingly ominous, threatening, and then ... a gradual slowing ... as ... [the pendulum] unwinds to stillness [and] ... 'death' ... [for] these relics of a great industrial time/age, once created and animated by man, then left to rust.
>   JACKSON 2009

Peter Fraser, a veteran of the desert workshops and who danced in *Run*, described the objects used in the performance as "very tactile and pleasurable ... similar to the body ... they have a very rusty, scaly surface" which he likened to "the bark of a tree" or an insect or a skin, at once anthropomorphising the beams as well as imparting to them a "totally unhuman quality" (ABC 2009). Here, different forms and transhuman entities became objects animated by the human and non-human assemblages which surrounded them.

The dancers gently manipulated the iron structures, turning the production into a danced version of one of the modernist Alexander Calder's mobiles, or alternatively the dangerous yet beautiful self-propelled kinetic art works by the Surrealist Jean Tinguely. As de Quincey put it, much of the "choreography is the risk management" of working with these items (2023b). Victoria Hunt, also a veteran of de Quincey's desert projects, pushed low and from a bent-over position one of the angled beams, while Fraser slowly progressed, his own head lying just below the raised corner of the gently moving scaffold. At other points, the trusses were hung unevenly from the roof as Hunt, Linda Luke and/or Tom Davies, with their legs locked between the cross beams, stretched out and backward from the slowly rotating structures. Relatively little of the dance drew from the conventional repertoire of butoh positions, though Fraser did exhibit a twitching, electrical, zig-zag feel in his hands and arms. It was rather the fragmentation of the body, self-consciously enacted by the dancers so as to emulate the discontinuous representation of movement seen in stop motion photography, which drew the choreography into butoh; a temporal effect of something like omnicentral imaging. Fraser suggested that the dancing produced a multitemporal body, imbued with "different speeds" (ABC 2009) and in this case historiographic resonances. There were a number of active sequences, such as a period of circular running during which the pendulum was spun above Hunt, and various awkward clamberings and apparent conflicts to get over or through each other (Figure 7) such as whenever one dancer confronted another on a single beam. Overall though the ambience was one of a slow unfolding, the gentleness of the movement in contrast to the visibly dangerous aspect of moving about on such unrelenting, massive, hard objects. Like *The Stirring*, *Run: A Performance Engine* constituted "a kind of sensual history exhibition" told in images, bodies and creaking, groaning materials (Needham 2007), the link to the specifics of Carriageworks being at once precise but abstracted.

These projects demonstrated the diversity of de Quincey's career, where site-specificity and the relating of the body to clearly defined landscapes and locations has served at once to ground Body Weather within a recognisably Australian cultural, historical and performative context, without limiting the form to elaborating Australian sites and their corporeal relations. Through Body Weather's engagement with the specificities of the Australian context, Body Weather emerges as a globalised almost historiographic practice in the way it prompts reflections regarding corporeal and cultural histories. In seeking out new ancestors and affiliations, Body Weather can be seen to effectively seed new antecedents for its choreographic outcomes, ranging from Stone Age Wales to the Central Desert of Australia, from the roadside curios of Parramatta Road, to the melancholy remains of once mighty local industrial edifices and the labourers and artists who once interacted with them.

3   A Masterpiece of Hysterio-Choreography: *Nerve 9* (2001–05)

As I have elsewhere observed, butoh was influenced both by neurophysiological and psychiatric modernism, as well as other movements which drew on these discourses. Butoh is therefore one of a series of global aesthetic forms which often generates what one might describe as a hysterical performance text, or self-divided body and subject (Marshall 2013, 2020b and 2021b). The term "hysteria" here refers to the widely popularised features of the historical hysteria diagnosis which were promulgated in Europe and Japan during the nineteenth and early-to-mid-twentieth centuries, and which had a significant influence on Surrealism, Dadaism, Futurism, Expressionism, Modernism, and butoh (Marshall 2013 and 2020b). These variously nervous, spasmodic, ticcing, and abject or formless gestures and artworks act to dramatize the splits and contradictions within and between figures, their voices and their bodies. Tess de Quincey's intermedial solo dance *Nerve 9* (2001–05) is exemplary of such a hysterical performance text, demonstrating a debt to Japanese butoh and Body Weather, whilst refining and clarifying the hysterical aspects of butoh dance to produce a precise dramatization of the hysterical subject functioning in defiance of conventional structures of language, society and gender.

De Quincey explains that *Nerve 9* arose out of a sense of:

> being in a sort of thick, viscous space of non-entity. It's something that I experienced … where I really thought I had no language. I was in Denmark and I had lost enough English so that I wasn't really thinking in English but I didn't have enough Danish to think properly in Danish.
> DYSON 2005: 9

De Quincey describes the choreography in Body Weather terms, as expressing a "cellular understanding" of what "arises in this sort of gently fluent mess" of formless being (in Dyson 2005: 9), stripped of language and much of what organises the individual, their thinking, and hence their bodily logic and gestures. To lose verbal language is in this sense to lose or disrupt the language of the body itself, since—according to Julia Kristeva and other psychoanalysts—the relative significance and pleasures of bodily structures and psychosexual identity develops in tandem with the infant's acquisition of language. Indeed, I argue that Body Weather training is designed to generate an at least a temporary state of hysteria in the dancer, stripping them of their prior conceptual and choreographic structures to present as an abject mass of free-flowing pulsations and ticcing spasms.

De Quincey cites as an influence the writings of Julia Kristeva (Dyson 2005: 9), along with the poetry of Amanda Stewart, a co-founder of Machine For Making Sense and colleague of Jim Denley, Rik Rue and Natasha Anderson, and who was herself greatly influenced by Kristeva. Stewart's recording *I/T* (1998) provided the basis for the score for de Quincey's *Nerve 9* (2001–05). Stewart concedes that much of her own poetry and the extended vocal techniques which she uses such as clicks, growls, cries, and so on, dramatize a "certain hysteria" in the speaking subject (in Zurbrugg 1989: 45). As Stewart explains, the voices featured in her poems and recordings are "urgently trying to understand and oppose the processes that cause 'IT' to be". "IT" here refers to the subject who is speaking the poem, and to the very concept of subjectivity which the first person speech structure of "I am speaking" generates:

> all the voice can do is intone cliches of 'IT', shouting staccato adjectives and high speed blocks of nouns until it finally breaks into an 'IT' incantation. Ironically, the voice makes IT BECOME again through ITself.
> in ZURBRUGG 1989: 45

Nerve 9 may be considered the choreographic equivalent of this repetitive, illogically ticcing, psycholinguistic journey towards a chaotic self-realisation.

Kristeva associates the realm of such non-syntactical and non-verbal speech with the burbling proto-language shared by infant and mother. These are "archaic phenomena" which "have their roots in the first vocalizations and echolalias" which consists of "glottal stops ... stress[es]", spasmodic stutters, squeaks, and so on (Kristeva 1980: 287). This is an abject language, emerging from a state of subjectivity which lacks clear boundaries, just as the infant begins to learn to "abject", or push away, its shit and other unwanted elements, back onto the mother. This hysterical, infantile and hence subconsciously familiar condition, limins death, or as Kristeva (2005) puts it, childhood and birth is "dominated" by a "caesura: that of beginning", and hence acts as "a

FIGURE 8   Tess de Quincey in *NERVE 9* (The Performance Space: 2002). Projections and photo Russell Emerson.
COURTESY OF THEATRE AND PERFORMANCE STUDIES, UNIVERSITY OF SYDNEY, AND DE QUINCEY CO.

conjuration of death" and precursor for when intimations of that experience return in adulthood. As we have seen, this binding of infancy with death, of the embryo with the premonition of the corpse and the forces of the maternal, are key concepts in much butoh dance (notably Ohno's *My Mother,* 1981; Marshall 2020a).

Nerve 9 is described by de Quincey as a "dance score in nine movements" (de Quincey 2023a). The title refers to the ninth cranial nerve which dictates the movements of the oral cavity (Crampton 2005). Eight of the dance's movements are named after concepts from Kristeva's writings, namely "Archaic domains", "Tensile zones", "Flesh of everyday speech", "Porous matter", "Enigmatic hallucination", "Infinity emerging", and "Black continent". The fifth movement, however, named "Tongue of sacrifice at the edge of the Other", comes from Stewart's poetry (Brickhill 2001: 35).

For the production, de Quincey projected the dynamically arranged pages from Stewart's published collection *I/T* (1998). Selections from the recordings originally issued as part of the package with *I/T* were also used in the production. Additional texts were composed by Francesca da Rimini (who participated in Triple Alice). The soundscape was further enriched by audio of women speaking in Chinese, Spanish, Arabic, Turkish, Persian, Indian, French, Chilean and Balinese (Dyson 2005: 9). The staging had de Quincey moving in and under dispersed fields of letters which often crossed her body, between moments where she lay before or to the side of grainy blocks of white and blue video projections. Close up images of women's lips, both closed and talking, were shown, partly as an allusion to Man Ray's Surrealist painting *Observatory Time: The Lovers* (1936). These moist, gargantuan parts of the female anatomy loomed over the figures. Also projected were women's eyes, striated fields of industrial landscapes, and images of smoke and fire. The projections were generally tilted off centre, giving the space an indistinct, asymmetrical quality.

Much of the choreography was acephalic, with the dancer's head folded away or neglected while the arms and hands seemed to project from a decapitated and only sporadically moving body (Figure 8).[5] When de Quincey did lift her head past her shoulders, she variously appeared internally focussed and inhuman, eyes closed, or at times questing and almost ecstatic, as her hands folded about her neck in a gesture of self-supplication. Viewers variously perceived de Quincey's choreography as robotic or "doll like" (Brickhill 2001: 35), mammalian (Crampton 2005), or exhibiting bird-like tendencies (Brickhill 2001: 35). From my own viewing of the 2005 live performance in Perth and the video documentation (de Quincey et al. 2001b), there were gestures which could be read as similar to those of insects, while the often robotic quality of movement harked back to precedents such as Hijikata and his interest in the Surrealist Hans Bellmer's dolls (Hijikata et al. 1993). The dance was highly segmented and omnicentral, with very small, stochastic twists of the wrist, pokes from the fingers, or angular folds and uneven zig-zag diagonals in the limbs. Later, straight armed semaphore-like movements occurred, and the leg struck downwards in a single, paralytic stamp. De Quincey squatted, lay down and ascended. She appeared:

> standing on the sides of her booted feet so that her body is pushed into a tree-like vertical; throwing her head so far back that her body is almost at a backward right angle as she walks; moving so slowly and smoothly that action is almost imperceptible.
> SYKES 2005

---

5   I discuss acephalic butoh, and its debt to Georges Bataille, in a forthcoming essay on Damien Jalet's *Vessel* (2019).

This arching of the body "almost at a backward right angle" evokes one of the classic poses of hysterical and epileptic seizure, often executed by patients and subjects upon the stages of early twentieth century France and Germany, and which were a significant influence upon butoh, Surrealism and modern dance more generally (see Marshall 2011, 2013, 2020b and 2021b).

Nerve 9 opened in darkness before "a slim needle point of light pours downwards, as if from the darkness of a cave", initially picking out only the tips of de Quincey's spikey hair (Crampton 2005). The movement traced expressions of "infantile gestures" with the figure "seeking instinctively for sensory stimuli like a new born marsupial … then moving on—exemplifying growth in a simple but also astonishing transition to full height" (Crampton 2005). The choreography was proximate to the audience's seats such that it felt "almost invasive" (Crampton 2005), and then later the dancer retreated upstage to hide within the projections. At one point, eyes shut, her mouth spasmodically opening and closing, de Quincey captured at the corner of her lips a long red string which was pulled from the ceiling into the space, demarcating areas and entangling her. This was partly intended to be evocative of the use of red and of rope barriers in Japanese temple rituals to mark off areas devoted to living beings, from those of the spirits and the dead (de Quincey 2005 and 2023b).

Despite the abstract nature of *Nerve 9*, it communicated its central concepts clearly, particularly in France, where de Quincey claimed that while women did not pay much attention to the citation of Kristeva per se, they were "voluble" in recognising that the piece evoked "a womb state—they talked a lot about infancy and the unformed" (Dyson 2005: 9). While the at times almost classical precision of de Quincey's execution, as well as the visibly intense focus on gender, distanced *Nerve 9* from most precedents within Japanese butoh, the production nevertheless featured many butoh signatures. Although something of a departure from de Quincey's site-specific and landscape-based studies, *Nerve 9* epitomised other stylistic tropes she had developed, such as an almost architectural and corporeal deployment of a poetic text and abstract recitative alongside a shuddering, hysterical body.[6] This was also a key feature of de Quincey's later multivocal dance theatre work *Ghost Quarters* (2009; Goodall and Stevenson 2018: 139–153). *Nerve 9* demonstrated de Quincey's power as a mature artist, and her ability to blend butoh choreography with a finely honed

---

6   De Quincey worked on a related project as a model for photographer Anne Ferran's project *A Box of Birds*, inspired by photo-documentation of psycho-neurological asylum inmates from the nineteenth century (Ferran 2013), and whose title evoked Caryl Churchill's and David Lan's reinterpretation of Dionysian possession in light of modern psychiatric treatment, the movement theatre work *A Mouthful of Birds* (1986) (see Diamond 1988).

sense of interdisciplinary aesthetics, corporeal mastery and thematic exploration. There was little in *Nerve 9* to mark it out as an example of Japanese aesthetics per se. Indeed, de Quincey claimed that French audiences found the work "very Australian" (in Card 2014: 159), despite the absence of any reference to the Australian Legend, national imagery, or athletic embodiment. *Nerve 9* is ultimately a global, syncretic piece, like most international butoh today.

4   Other Body Weather Artists in Australia

As previously noted, de Quincey has influenced a plethora of Australian artists who have trained in Body Weather, and who have, at one time or another, worked with her. Some have come at Body Weather and butoh largely through de Quincey's workshops and laboratories, whilst many others have either built on these, or consolidated their own familiarity with the form by working for a time with de Quincey. In this chapter, I restrict my discussion to works by Nikki Heywood, Martin Del Amo and Gretel Taylor, each of whom are influential in their own right.[7] In chapter nine, I also discuss works by Victoria Hunt.

5   Heywood and Humanimal Body Weather

Nikki Heywood has explored the utility of deploying Body Weather to evoke animality and the non-human. Despite her extended period of working with de Quincey, Van de Ven and Tanaka—in addition to Ashikawa—Heywood's first exposure to butoh related dance was through attendance at a double bill presentation of *The Dead Sea* (1985) and *Admiring La Argentina* (1977). These were solos performed by Ohno and which Hijikata had significantly contributed to. Heywood attended them at the 1986 Adelaide Festival:

> Ohno was 80 years old. His ancient, chalky white body with exposed rib cage and idiosyncratic skeletal alignment, expressionistic face and hands pleading toward the light accompanied by the sublime voice of Maria Callas discombobulated everything I thought I knew or expected from a 'dance' performance. It was, and still is, radical to see a partially naked eighty-year-old body dancing, full of life and yearning. In 2011 I had the good fortune to participate in a master class with his son and

---

[7] For additional accounts of Body Weather in Australia, see Orr & Sweeney 2011; Sweeney nd; Orr & Sweeney nd; Fraser 2014.

co-performer Yoshito Ohno (b.1938-) who still, as a man in his seventies, devotedly teaches the work.
HEYWOOD 2016: 140

As is evident from this passage, Heywood's training was (like many Australian artists influenced by butoh) a mixed one, including not only time with de Quincey, but an extensive period improvising around Grotowski exercises, and workshops with a range of artists from both inside and outside of the butoh community.

One of Heywood's early works was the dance theatre piece *Burn Sonata* (1996), which she directed. It featured a pathological "family of frightened and frightening animals" (Baxter 1998: 4). Scenes were developed through blended Body Weather and Grotowski modes, including blindfold exercises, imaging, and improvisations themed around uneven power dynamics (Heywood 2016: 34). One scene featured performers tearing at scraps of cloth held in their mouths as if they were dogs. Heywood built on this portrayal of a humanimal family with her 2000 production, *Inland Sea*—an echo perhaps, in terms of imagery, of Ohno's performance in *The Dead Sea* (1985). Heywood's piece offered a "visceral, crazed family" consisting of "six diverse figures [from] the Australian psyche" (Gallasch 2000: 47)—one of whom was played by Martin Del Amo. These characters were found on stage, imprisoned with each other in the "agoraphobic inland" of the desert regions which Heywood encountered at Mungo. Essentially paraphrasing her own experience of encountering the Australian desert, Heywood claimed that *Inland Sea* was "about what happens to our bodies when we move from a state of emotional and physical repression and enter a landscape that is so large and so open that our senses can't really deal with it" (Rentell 2000), or as one reviewer put it: "the timber wall of their house opens and they are suddenly inland, in an alien land. A child is lost/murdered, each of the family enacts some personal drama" (Gallasch 2000: 47). This produces a kind of "fictional history of place" (AusStage entry 28634) in which familial dysfunction allegorises the violence and conflict at the heart of Australian settlement.

Although Heywood's directing work has been diverse, her focus on transhuman animality remained a recurrent theme, as in her own solo doctoral research production *Museum of the Sublime: Relic #5* (2011) which featured Heywood in a bear-like fur coat that:

> enfolds the body in a kind of embrace: the embrace of both the [dead, skinned] abject animal and the illusion … of glamour and luxury … I crawl under the coat to create the illusion of a headless body that stum-

bles blindly around, directionless, until it finds and re-unites with the animal head [a rubber horse head].
HEYWOOD 2016: 101

There is a notable similarity between *Relic #5* and *Nerve 9* in that both de-emphasize the head, together with offering a suggestion of something non-human and abject. Indeed, this is a common thread within Body Weather in Australia and internationally,[8] Gretel Taylor observing that during one improvisation at a river's edge she "felt like an animal" as "My face morphed into my body" (2008: 30). Throughout *Relic #5*, Heywood's body—like Taylor's—was moved by something outside of itself, in this case the shaggy coat. Drawing on one of Hijikata's favourite authors, the dissident Surrealist Georges Bataille, Heywood observes that her use of the bear like coat and masks produces something akin to "the figure of an early shaman", wearing the head of another being, this abnegation of the head proper to the human signifying (in Bataille's words) "'the shaman's voyage into the beyond, into the kingdom of death'" (Bataille in Heywood 2016: 114). Heywood likens this to the chimerical hybrid performances and representations found in the "French caves of Lascaux" and elsewhere, naming the same location that Sankai Juku's director Amagatsu Ushio echoed his own sensibilities and aesthetic (Watanabe 2013).[9]

6   European Tanztheater Meets Australian Body Weather: Martin Del Amo

Dance-maker Martin Del Amo initially encountered butoh through the Australian documentary *Butoh: Piercing the Mask* (1991; Robertson 2015: 71). He had begun training with German dance-maker Katharine Sehnert in Cologne, 1991–2003. Del Amo explains that:

> Sehnert had been a student of Mary Wigman's in the 1950s and worked as an assistant to Pina Bausch in the early 1970s. She was very interested in butoh, had been to Min Tanaka's farm … and frequently invited butoh performers to teach workshops at her studio. It was there, at her studio in Cologne, that I was first exposed to butoh training by … practitioners

---

8 Baird (2022: 6), Marshall (2018: 163–4) and others note that a de-emphasis of the head or face, turning away from the audience to present a headless image of the hunched back, and so on, emerged as a persistent theme of butoh from the 1960s.
9 See "Lineages of Descent" in chapter one.

such as Andres Coacher (a student of Min Tanaka's and member of Maijuku), Masaki Iwana, Anzu Furukawa and later Tess de Quincey and Stuart Lynch.

After moving to Berlin in 1993, I continued to do workshops with butoh performers, notably Minako Seki (founding member of [Tokyo/Berlin group] Tatoeba) and Anzu Furukawa (student of Akaji Maro's and co-founder of Dance Love Machine). I then became student of Anzu Furukawa ... I studied with her in 1994/95 and performed in one of her productions ... Around that time I started doing workshops with Tess de Quincey and Stuart Lynch.
DEL AMO 2005

Del Amo's association with butoh reflects the international networks established in the late 1980s and throughout the 1990s, which bridged Japan and Europe, and via this, facilitated the work of de Quincey, Lynch, Van de Ven, Del Amo, and others.

Del Amo performed in *Compression 100* (1995) and other de Quincey/Lynch projects as well as in Nikki Heywood's *Inland Sea* (2000), before he moved to Sydney in 2002. Del Amo presented solos at TPS and other venues. These pieces reflected an idiosyncratic fusion of European tanztheater and Body Weather. Del Amo conceded that he felt butoh was "essentially Japanese" and noted that he had not himself trained in Japan (Del Amo 2005). Even so, in 2005 he felt that butoh and Body Weather remained "the backbone of the work I'm doing now", at least with respect to the "physical aspects" (ibid.).

Del Amo's solos in Australia during the 2000s were episodic, with sections structured around a slow build-up of material, tension and energetics. Del Amo combined his Body Weather choreography with spoken word sequences such as are more common in European dance theatre. He would later secure Rosie Denis and others to generate text for him, much as de Quincey collaborated with Stewart and Da Rimini to produce texts. In this sense, Del Amo's work was, from an early stage, departing from classic butoh formula and into what one might call postdramatic theatre, in which he would often employ "simple task based actions such as bringing on microphones ... or taking off/putting on clothes" to bridge the text/dance separation (Del Amo 2010: 40). As critic Erin Brannigan pointed out, in Del Amo's solos, "undressing becomes a part of his body's struggle with itself" (2012: 27). Like Yumi Umiumare,[10] Del Amo saw his work as an avant-garde form of "Queer Cabaret" whereby the presentation of

---

10   See also "Butoh Cabaret" in chapter six.

his own ambiguous nikutai, in combination with biographical text about himself as a gay man, unseated simple gender binaries (Del Amo 2019).

In other respects, however, Del Amo's work was consistent with Body Weather precedents. His choreographies were generally based on corporeal fragmentation and the isolation of bodily parts which comes with omnicentral imaging. Del Amo offered the body as the "target of uncontrollable forces, being moved rather than moving of its own accord" (Del Amo 2010: 39). One particularly notable instance which I witnessed at the Melbourne Festival in the early 2000s, was when Del Amo performed a conceptually simple but massively detailed and semi-comedic improvisation in which, with one arm and one side of his body, he strove to stroke an imaginary cat's sensually gorgeous fur, while with the other side of his body, he strove to eat an especially delicious apple. Quivering and prevaricating in different micromovements of the arms, face and body, which caused him to twist and angle crazily, it was a breathtaking performance: a delightfully abject, hysterical bodily struggle akin to *Nerve 9*.

Much like Maro's dancers in Dairakudakan and other groups, Del Amo's movement often exhibited an emphasis on arms, hand and finger details, as well as "compulsion ... repetition ... exhaustion" leading to a "physicalized chaos" (Brannigan 2012: 27). Del Amo would "playfully jump cut between ... states of desire and deterioration", as he put it (2019). The textual interjections provided a space for Expressionist and abstract biographical interludes which imbued the corporeal work with considerable drama and emotion—most notably with *Under Attack* (2005), a piece which dramatized Del Amo's grief for his deceased partner. Again echoing the butoh traditions, his themes often revolved around "physical extinction", "trauma and obsession" (Brannigan 2012: 27). Indeed, Del Amo often dramatized the state of the global butoh dancer itself, forever moving from one show to another as part of a placeless international circuit which therefore generated within the performing individual a sense of loss regarding home, leading to "displacement and failure" (Brannigan 2012: 27).

Perceiving the limitations of the solo autobiographic form, Del Amo built on his experience with de Quincey and Lynch on *Compression 100* (1995), to craft his own work out of his responses to the city. Del Amo here employed such classic Body Weather exercises as blindfold explorations, walking backwards, and crawling throughout Sydney's harbourside district of the Rocks (Del Amo 2019). This resulted in the 2009 production *It's a Jungle Out There.* Around 2010 Del Amo began to choreograph works which not only departed from Body Weather precedents, but which also involved other dancers, sometimes including those with relatively little training. Although figures such as

Del Amo and de Quincey exhibit an at times frightening level of bodily exactitude and precision, Del Amo is one of several Australian butoh artists who, like Taylor, Yap and Umiumare, came to use these stylistic modes to engage with lay performers, a development which is rare but not altogether absent from Japanese butoh. In short, Del Amo offers a paradigmatic example of how Body Weather and butoh have been incorporated into a mixed aesthetic within Australian dance.

7 Post-Colonial Butoh and Rejecting the Empty Body: Gretel Taylor

While Heywood and Del Amo have developed concepts of the humanimal and the fractured queer male body within dance and installation performance, Gretel Taylor has built on de Quincey's work in non-urban and outback Australian environments. Specifically, Taylor interrogates the politics of what it means to "Stand in Australia" (as de Quincey put it in her essay of the same title; Grant and de Quincey 2008), and Taylor continues to engage with First Nations landowners and custodians. Her work is nevertheless diverse, exploring a range of ways to activate communities through their interactions with their chosen or found environments. Here I discuss Taylor's early works which focussed on issues of settler-colonial relations.

Taylor's association with de Quincey is indirect and mediated through her interactions with long term de Quincey collaborators Peter Fraser and Frank Van de Ven, as well as Triple Alice alumni Stuart Grant (Taylor 2022a). Taylor participated in Van de Ven's workshops in the Pays Basque and Czech Republic during 2005, but her principal introduction to Body Weather was by her attendance at the Tanaka's farm, 1999–2000 (Taylor 2008: 21–22, 88). Around the same period she participated in classes in Australia run by butoh artists Yumi Umiumare (ex-Dairakudakan) and Tony Yap (Taylor 2008: 21–22)—neither of whom are Body Weather artists. Taylor's approach is also informed by her training and collaborations with the senior Australian performance artist Jill Orr at Victoria University (Taylor 2022b). Taylor also briefly worked with Ohno Yoshito. Taylor is the co-founder of the Environmental Performance Authority along with Fraser and Grant (Taylor 2022a). She later initiated the BodyPlaceProject. She has been teaching dancers and lay people versions of Body Weather and site-specific attunement for over ten years.

Taylor's (2010: 72–87) major contribution to butoh practice in Australia was to point out the rhetorical similarities between the idea of the butoh body as something that can become "empty" in the landscape, with the Australian colonial mindset.[11] In response to this rhetorical similarity, Taylor makes a point of situating at the heart of her site interactions her own status as a settler descent artist. She prefers the phrase "locating" to describe her approach. Taylor (2008: 112) typically begins from a state of self-conscious settler descent "alienation" from the site when she first approaches it. As she moves to "locate" herself, she seeks to "be as physically present as possible" in the space and so allow the fullness of her own particular psychocorporeal responses to become manifest (2008: 23), or as she puts it "my body awakens to the place I am in" and "we begin to merge" (2012: 8). As Australian scholar-practitioner Jo Robertson says of Body Weather as a whole, the emphasis is one of corporeal "permeability" rather than a bounded empty vessel (2015: 59). For Taylor, permeability is generated through an "embodied attunement or acclimatisation" to the site through what she calls "multisensory listening"—in other words, literal listening, as well as proxemics, skin sensations, and other embodied sensory responses to the landscape (2022a). She seeks a "desired" and ultimately utopic/poetic state of "merging" with the landscape (2008: 24), but she acknowledges that many obstacles to such a blending arise not only from within her subjectivity, but from within her own body, its structure and historical forces. Taylor's process allows for the possibility that the dancer loses herself within the dance (to be "uplifted" and "literally unbounded" as she puts it, but this does not "empty" the body per se, and resistances remain; 2008: 112). Taylor's perspicacious observations provide an important clue to why Body Weather and butoh often produces a state of abjection and hysteria: the human body itself is constitutionally unable to merge with its surrounds in the way desired by the butoh-ka unless it "dies" and gives up its own forms.

There is therefore always something of the character or persona of *Taylor herself* within the dance. Drawing on the work of UK landscape photographer and performance artist Richard Long, Taylor (2008: 109) observes that any journey or walk across the landscape is in some ways a "self-portrait". Particularly painfully, Taylor has brought her own experience of losing a pregnancy into her work, acknowledging that when expressing one's psychocorporeal relations with a site at any given moment, it is impossible for such events *not* to inform the performance, noting that at this time she withheld her "grief" such that when it came out, "My main physical experiences of this withholding were incredible tightness, tension, constriction", acting to isolate and close off the body (2008: 163). She was therefore forced to move beyond "an almost impenetrable dense heaviness" (163). Her movement out of grief and tightness

---

11   See "Emptiness & Possession" in chapter one.

was facilitated by her interactions with the Warlpiri women at Yuendumu, and their own manner of grieving. Puturlu in Walpiri Country is known as a "healing place" and so "it was as if I felt the support of the Country itself, stabilising my post-natal wobbly legs" (2008: 165). Indeed, it was this layering of affects, places and narratives that made and makes Taylor's work so affective: "whilst dancing 'Ode to Miranda', the colonial figure" in her piece filmed on Warlpiri land, "I broke down" and then "returned with tear-stained face, filled with intense emotion and ... proceeded to perform a dance that bore little resemblance to the planned choreography" (2008: 167–8).

If Taylor summons ghosts within her performances, these are therefore largely imagined white colonial subjects, or Taylor's own kin. Her solo site-specific work *Immersion/Excursion: Killeavy* (2007), for example, was performed for an invited audience at the site of a now nearly vanished colonial farm along the Yarra River in Melbourne. Although Taylor does not herself cite Ashikawa as an influence, it is striking that Taylor's performance echoed the translations Ashikawa performed in *Breasts of Japan* (cited at the top of this chapter), the production which first introduced de Quincey to butoh and which was therefore a significant catalyst in the importation of Body Weather to Australia (Viala and Masson-Sékiné 1991: 92; Parsons and Wynne-Jones 1996: 14). Taylor performed her own transformation from "maiden" (a young, unmarried white woman imagined to have lived at the site), "mother" (the deceased female colonial householder), "crone" (the latter's cruel fate), and then "ghost" (2008: 32).

Taylor built on de Quincey's journeys onto the Indigenous lands of regional Australia, and has actively cultivated relationships with First Nations subjects at Yuendumu. Taylor explains that:

> In any performance about place in Australia, I attempt to include Indigenous people, by inviting them to represent themselves in person if possible, and otherwise through consultation during the process and acknowledgement of them in the performance. First Nations dancers were also, of course, the first site-specific dance artists.
> 2020

Taylor renewed the contacts established by de Quincey with Warlpiri women, working principally with Dorothy Napangardi's skin-relations Coral Napangardi Gallagher, Grace Napangardi Butcher, and others, who were Elders and painters in the Warlukurlangu artists corporation. Taylor produced a site-specific exploration near Yuendumu at Purturlu, or Mount Theo, in 2006. This led to the creation of the three-part dance film installation *Still Landing* (2008). Taylor received permission from senior Warlpiri man Japangardi to dance at Purturlu, and then six Warlpiri women "travelled out with me to show me the 'good spots'" and to clarify which sites were permissible and which were off limits (2012: 11). The women were in mourning for one of their sisters, and hence—echoing the butoh obsession with death as a rejuvenating limit—"visiting the Purturlu Country was like visiting a graveyard" (2008: 164). The women "began chanting songs of the Country and wailing" (2012: 11). A fire was lit, goanna cooked and eaten, and the story of a pair of lovers was told:

> All six had become quite upset as they sang the traditional songs of the Country [over the fire] … Apparently the Country and the songs had resonance of sorrow and deeply heart-felt memory for them, to do with relatives both long gone and recently departed. For these women, the Country, its songs [today] and their grief or 'sorry business' were inextricably interrelated.
> TAYLOR 2008: 164

Taylor received permission to include the Warlpiri women's singing alongside her own filmed dance in the installation. Like de Quincey's collaborators at Mungo and Triple Alice, Taylor (2012) found the "dusty orange earth" to be haunted by the voices of these and other women, though in Taylor's case, she had worked more extensively with the Warlpiri and their kin, and was to return to work with them again on Country. She danced at Yuendumu in 2008 when working with Elders and young Warlpiri to encourage the next generation to learn traditional and ceremonial dances. Taylor (2012) reports that in this role, she found herself in the humbling position of having onlookers "guffawing with laughter at my white body painted up in the ochre design, trying to emulate the Elder lady's movements". Taylor has also worked with the young Wurundjeri women of the Djirri Djirri dance group for a series of events activating locations just north of Melbourne in Corhanwarrabul, or the Dandenong Ranges (*Dancing Place: Corhanwarrabul,* 2020). She continues to be guided by Dharug Elder Professor Liz Cameron. In short, de Quincey's pioneering engagement with the peoples surrounding Alice Springs has been extended and deepened by Taylor and others.

Taylor's practice also shares the sense of spatiotemporal multiplicity with that of de Quincey. Taylor's site-specific performance *Blasted Away* (2007–16), at Queen's Bridge near central Melbourne, alluded to the former waterfall at the site where the local Wurundjeri peoples met prior to and during the early years of European settlement. At the same time, she evoked the current crowds of daytime office workers and night-time revellers in central Melbourne, who regularly use the bridge which now stands there. During the dance, Taylor "became a drunk" and later "the waterfall", embodying an image of "rippling rapids" in her legs and body: "Still in my suit I moved with this image to the sounds of the place in the present moment" in a realisation of multitemporal omnicentral imaging. Taylor danced to the noise of:

> trains, traffic, ferries ... a video image of a waterfall was projected onto the bridge and the sound of rushing water was heard ... When the sound and image faded, I was standing on the wharf with a rope around my waist, leaning from a mooring post, wavering ever so slightly.
>
> 2007: 140–1

As is evident here, Taylor engages with the political histories of landscapes more overtly than de Quincey, offering a poetic critique of the colonial violence which led to today's conditions.[12]

8 Evidence of Bodily Emergences

One of Tanaka's key claims is that "images" of body and self which have been "lost can be regained" (1981: 6). As we have seen, numerous reports show that participation in Body Weather workshops, and particularly those dealing with Australia's own vexed history, can have marked effects on artists. Goodall claimed that, despite being a non-dancing participant at Triple Alice, she nevertheless suffered from "fearsome" dreams involving the return of the dead (McAuley 2008: 120). Sarah Dunn stated that following the laboratories, she found memories from her own past to be spontaneously returning, in all their psychocorporeal detail. Most were relatively banal rather than highly affective ones, and there seemed no pattern, with recollections of different times in her life, locations, "moments from travel, moments from work" (2003: 44). If there was anything organising these memories, it seemed to come from outside of Dunn's own subjectivity: "Something else 'within' me was operating this reshuffling of memories":

> one memory was of walking down a main street in [Sydney during] ... summer three years earlier ... the ... feeling [of] the walk, the restric-

---

12   Taylor has also worked on several community engagement projects, where her role was to mentor lay dancers, or to use dance and movement to develop community outcomes; see Taylor 2017; Taylor & Warr 2018.

tions of the skirt I was wearing, the warm breeze flowing over my neck and down into the back of my blouse, the glare of the day, my mood and thoughts, my destination of the cash card teller halfway down the hill on the left.

DUNN 2003: 44

Victoria Hunt recalled vivid memories of herself "walking through monkey forest" in years past (Anderson 2014: 94).

Larissa Pryce however experienced a much more disturbing "memory visitation" shortly after returning to Perth, in which she recalled the sensation of being in her now forgotten childhood home, experiencing it as if she were "a floating being reconnecting to a place that in actuality no longer exists … inhabiting a place that had become lost to me (a place [that] I had unconsciously forgotten)" (2017: 61). Pryce found the experience "deeply unnerving and emotional". In Freudian terms (1973), Pryce's experience of Body Weather was quite literally unheimlich or "unhomely", as "the Uncanny" more precisely translates. These and similar accounts provide autoethnographic evidence that at least some of the poetic tasks and challenges of Body Weather have very real psychocorporeal affects upon the dancer. In short, Body Weather is not simply an aesthetic conceptual heuristic, but a psychocorporeal practice with concrete (even potentially dangerous) effects on the long term subjectivity and perceptions of the dancer. While this has always been contended by Tanaka and other butoh practitioners, the strongest evidence for this comes from Australia.

9   Fragmented and Dialectical Bodies

Snow concludes that ultimately all bodies, even inorganic and non-human ones, carry within them multiple histories. It is this inherent psychocorporeal multiplicity that generates the individual's potential responsiveness or their "semi permeability [and] … openness to the worlds we inhabit" (2006: 238). Body Weather performers capitalise on the fact that in the act of "remembering, we carry with us many places", generating "a kind of 'in-between placedness'" (238). Body Weather is ultimately a methodology to produce self-divided, fragmented and processual body in performance. Despite its conflicted politics, Body Weather in Australia is an inherently dialectical methodology, activating differences and polarised exchanges in order to keep bodies and minds mobile while fantasmatic ancestral possibilities emerge and fade. De Quincey's bold and at times brilliant way of responding to some of Australia's most iconic landscapes and unsettling landscapes ultimately led to an abject hysteria such as was dramatized within *Nerve 9,* performing the deconstitution of the subject itself. While de Quincey and Body Weather cannot be reduced to site-specific dance or landscape performance, de Quincey for her part felt that her thorough examination of these potentials helped her to produce a highly refined form of interconnected yet regionalised butoh. Others have gone on to deepen or blend these findings with other aesthetic modes in the Australian context.

CHAPTER 5

Diasporic Austral-Asian Fusions 1: Early Works by Umiumare and Yap

1   Introduction

In this chapter, I introduce Tony Ding Chai Yap, Yumi Umiumare and Umiumare's former mentor in butoh Maro Akaji, all of whom have had a profound influence on Australian butoh. I survey the early works of Umiumare and Yap, including Yap's Mixed Company, the artists' roles in theatrical productions (*Love Suicides*, 1998, *Miss Tanaka*, 2001, *Meat Party*, 2000), the landmark live Australian butoh production *Kagome* (1996–98), a film which was shot in some of the same locations which Tess de Quincey had used for her Lake Mungo workshops (*Sunrise at Midnight*, 2001), Umiumare's and Yap's long-term collaboration *How Could You Even Begin to Understand?* (1996–2007), and each of their first full length productions as author-creators (*Decay of the Angel*, 1999, and *Fleeting Moments*, 1998). Chapter six deals with the artists' mature works and personal aesthetics in more detail, including Umiumare's character dances and Yap's trance dance.

Across these early works, Umiumare and Yap moved from performing racially or ethnically defined dramatic character roles to more demanding, self devised performances, emerging as significant Australian butoh choreographer-devisers in their own right. Ghosts, demons or yōkai (the latter having already attracted the interest of Hijikata), uncanny restive spirits, acts of possession or trance, and displaced transmigratory bodies, were recurrent features across these works. The two dancers offer a distinctive vision of butoh in Australia defined principally by its historically braided, intercultural nature. Umiumare's playfully exuberant and pop culturally infused version of butoh—derived in part from the influence of Maro's so called "ero guro" style (Umiumare and Eckersall 2012)—was also to characterise her mature work, as well as that of other Australian companies such as Zen Zen Zo and Frank.

2   Umiumare's and Yap's Butoh Encounters

Yumi Umiumare first saw butoh in Japan in 1989, when she attended Dairakudakan's signature work *Kaiin no Uma* (*Tale of the Sea-Dappled Horse*). She reflected that:

> it was an incredible shock ... The dancers' movements were completely different—perhaps even opposite—to what I'd learned in classical and modern dance: knees bent inwards, grounded posture, with incredibly contorted facial expressions showing their suffering and agony ... almost everything that I was taught not to do ... I felt extremely confronted, I did not want to see—but at the same time I felt a great curiosity.
> UMIUMARE 1999: 41

Umiumare was later struck within Dairakudakan's workshops by the fact that company members exhibited little technical excellence. They seemed "slow ... couldn't do steps or anything" (Umiumare and Eckersall 2012). But on stage, Dairakudakan's dancers were "amazingly weird and raw and powerful. So that blew my mind ... I said, 'What the hell is that? Is it dance or what?'" (ibid.).

Umiumare's response to butoh was similar to that of many Australian dancers. She echoed their sense of surprise and disorientation on seeing butoh: it was confronting, especially for someone like her who had been taught to consider ballet as the technical basis for concert dance. There was, in a formal and affective sense, something foreign in the presentation of the butoh body, even for a Japanese viewer. She was most impressed by two aspects of butoh dance, one visible in its outward choreography, and the other only evident indirectly through its affective weight. Butoh was physically challenging, contorted, but also seemed to offer access to deep angst and suffering—as well as to a rich vein of comedy. Despite this, butoh retained its mystery. Though not eliciting a fascination with an Orientalist generalisations, as it did for some of the critics cited in chapter one, Umiumare's principal reaction was one of "curiosity", or a *desire to know more*. Butoh's appeal for the dancer was through what was withheld in this initial encounter. Umiumare would later join Dairakudakan, and help bring butoh to Australia in the early 1990s.

Tony Ding Chai Yap first encountered Sankai Juku in Australia when the group toured their production of *Unetsu* (*Eggs Standing Out of Curiosity*; 1986) to Adelaide in 1988 (Yap and Eckersall 2012). Yap himself was performing in *Far From Where* at the coincident Adelaide Fringe Festival with IRAA theatre, an Australian based Grotowski-inspired company. Unlike other artists discussed in this book, Yap was not so taken with butoh as to position himself as a butoh artist or train in the form per se. Yap's association with butoh came later, principally through the workshops which he and Umiumare ran during the late 1990s, which Yap felt appealed to "lots of misfits" seeking release from "mainstream" theatre and dance in Melbourne (Yap and Eckersall 2012), at least some of whom were as keen to use Yap's workshops as a space for psycho-personal development as they might have been for professional performance outcomes.

Yap admitted that although, "People call it butoh. I didn't" (Yap and Eckersall 2012). Even so, he conceded that the term "butoh" acted as an "umbrella" for a fringe community of actors, dancers, physical theatre artists and interested lay-people in Melbourne and beyond. "I was dancing here before butoh" he stated, "and now I'm still doing similar things. But the term 'butoh' has become an index that people can use to understand my work" (Marshall 2001a). Yap did not experience a shattering encounter with butoh like many of his peers, but butoh became a critical touchstone for his work.

3   Umiumare and Yap within the Context Butoh

For some time, Yumi Umiumare was the only butoh practitioner based in Australia who was of Japanese descent.[1] Umiumare's direct link to the national context out of which butoh evolved gives her an authority over butoh itself (rather than butoh influenced work) which few in Australia can match. Umiumare danced in Dairakudakan's *Sea-Dappled Horse*, which was one of the first pieces to introduce global audiences to butoh in the 1980s and 1990s. When Umiumare began teaching and dancing in Melbourne in the 1990s, butoh was generally taught as part of a mixed program blended with the work of Grotowski, Lindsay Kemp, the Living Theatre, and other modes. Umiumare therefore came to act as a standard, helping to distinguish mixed, butoh-inspired work such as that by Rainsford, Cheryl Heazlewood (Ulzen 1994b: 20), Mémé Thorne and Nigel Kellaway (Sydney Front),[2] and others. De Quincey had described her early work in Sydney as butoh, but came to be seen as Australia's leading expert in the butoh-related sub-discipline of Body Weather. De Quincey was certainly the leading butoh-related artist working out of Sydney, but Umiumare and Yap rival de Quincey in Melbourne. Umiumare and the Brisbane based artist Lynne Bradley worked several times with the founder of Dairakudakan, Maro Akaji, but Bradley only trained with him relatively briefly, and would cease labelling her own work butoh in 2008.[3] Umiumare therefore represents the strongest ongoing link to the cultural, historical, and institutional origins of butoh in current Australian practice. These lineages remain visible in Umiumare's work

---

1   The Japanese born dancer and producer Takiguchi Takashi encountered the work of Yap and Umiumare through MAP Fest and other exchanges, before moving to Melbourne following 2014. Takiguchi has not trained with any Japanese butoh artists other than Umiumare, though he has also studied Suzuki technique.
2   On Kellaway, see also "Suzuki Tadashi in Japan & Australia" in chapter seven.
3   Bradley is the focus of chapter eight.

through her self-conscious exploration of Japanese histories and stereotypes. Umiumare did not initially practice as a choreographer, and many of her early performances were within productions overseen by others. In these contexts, Umiumare was often contracted to devise roles and make them her own, drawing on her eccentric, comedic, yet intense, variant of butoh, moving between dance and theatre. Many of Yap's early roles took a similar form, and in addition to working together on duets and other works, Yap and Umiumare have performed opposite each other in many productions. Both however moved towards self-devising and directing ensembles, which I cover in more detail in chapter six.

Although Yap has no formal butoh training, critics generally viewed his choreographies within a butoh context. This is not only because of his association with Umiumare, but because of Yap's allusions to writings and images from Hijikata and his circle such as Mishima and Hosoe (Yap 2021: 38, 78–81, 108, 133–134). Influential Australian theatre-maker Aubrey Mellor went so far as to see Yap in explicitly Japanese theatrical terms, comparing him to a "noh master" (Stock 2012: 95). Classic butoh poses often occur within Yap's performances (foetal positions, facial grimacing, asymmetric or twisted poses, extreme arching of the back, contraction of muscles about the eyes, among others; Marshall 2013: 72–73). Yap's link to butoh also lies in the fact that he shares with Hijikata and other butoh artists an intense interest in Asian trance forms which approach emptiness and death. As of the 2000s, Yap called his work "trance dance". This involved a complex interplay of forces which arise from inside and outside of the body to move it, often in a chaotic and twisted manner, as in butoh. Umiumare too has explored trance dance, mediumship and magic. Yap and Umiumare have served as mentors and trainers of other Australian artists. Lynne Santos, Matthew Crosby, Ben Rogan, Gretel Taylor, Adam Forbes, Brendan O'Connor, Michael Hornblow, Nareeporn Vachananda, Helen Smith, Jonathan Rainin, Anthony Pelchen, and others have all worked with Yap and Umiumare, or have taken their classes. In addition to highly proficient regulars and professionals, Yap and Umiumare have taught many individuals whose interest in butoh is not necessarily artistic. Butoh is, as noted earlier, an approach to dance and life, and many of those who have worked with Yap and Umiumare have done so because, in the words of Umiumare, "coming to [a] butoh workshop is cheaper than a psychotherapist" (Shiarz and Palmer 2021). The impact of Umiumare's and Yap's teaching therefore extends beyond that of dance and theatre, particularly in the case of Umiumare's jujutsu project discussed in chapter six. Yap's and Umiumare's leadership of butoh in the region is enhanced by their role as festival directors. Yap founded the Melaka Art and Performance Festival in 2008, and in 2017, Umiumare founded the BUTOHOUT!

Both events are hubs for cultural and geographic exchange, drawing performers from not just across Australia, but Malaysia, Singapore, the Philippines, Indonesia, China, Taiwan, Japan, Korea and beyond.

4   Maro and Dairakudakan

As noted in chapter one, Dairakudakan was founded by the sometime actor and student of Hijikata, Maro Akaji, in 1972. The title of the company literally means "big camel vessel", but is usually translated as "Great Camel Battleship", with Maro serving as the "captain of the battleship", allegedly in homage to his father's status as a naval commander during World War Two (Bradley 2017: 15). Maro grew up in the ancient Japanese capital and temple city of Nara, which he identified as "the end of the Silk Route" by merit of its status as an early site for the transmission of Indian Buddhism into Japan, as well as the Indo-Grecian art that supported it (Hoffman 1987: 13, 76). The camel is therefore for Maro a signifier of how Japan received and then repurposed international and multicultural influences.

Maro admits that when Hijikata first saw his work, the senior dancer "didn't like it" (Hoffman 1987: 76). Maro's epic theatricality represented a distinctive stream within the evolution of butoh. Maro stated that he aimed to "add dynamism and drama to butoh, to enlarge the spectacle" (ibid. 76). Tanaka and others have at times dismissed such work as "theatre" based on the "Image without body" and so producing "good pictures" but "not dance" or butoh per se (Stein 1986: 147). Maro however insists that Hijikata came to see that the younger artist was "following a different ... course" and that he "accepted it" (Hoffman 1987: 13, 76). It was moreover the butoh lineage which Maro established which later developed into the highly refined aesthetics of Sankai Juku. More than any other companies, Sankai Juku and Dairakudakan were instrumental in spreading butoh around the globe. In Australia, Tanaka and Maro have been the most influential artists by far (closely followed by Ohno Kazuo and the latter's son Yoshito).

The Australian butoh artist Lynne Bradley, who is the focus of chapter seven, identified Maro's early practice at Hijikata's nightclubs as being particularly important for the development of Maro's aesthetic (Bradley 2017: 16). Maro christened these the "Golden Shows", where men adorned with exaggerated penile prostheses like that Hijikata wore in *Nikutai no Hanran* (1968) were accompanied by women in G-strings, and painted in used cooking oil, to give them what Maro described as a "shiny, dirty gold" look (Bradley 2017: 16). Maro choreographed many of the shows staged at Hijikata's nightclub of Shōgun and elsewhere, before adapting them for Dairakudakan's mainstage productions. This contributed to what Umiumare described as the company's "ero guro" style (Umiumare and Eckersall 2012), short for "ero guro nansensu" or erotic grotesque nonsense. The term arose as a descriptor for the vibrant, chaotic mass culture of 1930s Japan, or what Yasunari Kawabata characterised as a blend of "Eroticism ... Nonsense ... humour like social commentary cartoons, jazz songs ... Women's legs" and the corporeal contortions of Charlie Chaplin (who visited Tokyo in 1932) as well as Chaplin's films like *Modern Times* (Silverberg 2009: xv-9, 28–29). Dairakudakan's ero guro aesthetic would be echoed by not only Umiumare herself,[4] but in Australia by Zen Zen Zo and Frank Theatre.[5] This is part of a global trend in diasporic and cross-cultural butoh, with several companies in France and elsewhere employing a similar aesthetic (see Pagès 2017: 202–3)

Historian Bruce Baird identifies two main contributions to butoh practice which Maro initiated. The first was the concept of "tenpu tenshiki", which Maro explained means "Just being born ... is a great talent" (Baird 2022: 78) and therefore everyone has innate talents waiting to be released. The task of butoh was to make these talents manifest. In practical terms, this would lead to Dairakudakan accepting as performers those who had no formal dance training, as had been the case with Maro himself. Although some of the members of Dairakudakan, like Amagatsu, had studied ballet, most had not. Umiumare was unusual in that she had already developed technical proficiency through her training in ballet, modern dance, sports and physical education. Yap however had no formal dance experience when he first began to perform in Australia, although he did participate in several workshops which greatly influenced him,[6] and both Umiumare and Yap regularly instructed individuals with no prior training. From Maro's model of tenpu tenshiki it also followed that each of Maro's dancers could potentially develop their own choreography. Although Maro exerted strong control over the group, he encouraged dancers to develop material and eventually establish their own companies—"One person, one troupe" was the phrase used (Baird 2022: 78). Umiumare's work with diverse groups and Yap's model for Mixed Company both echo Maro's willingness to grow butoh beyond any technical focus and to include more varied practitioners and participants. It is furthermore worth noting that, following Tanaka's lead, Maro became the second major butoh artist in Japan to

---

4   See "Butoh Cabaret" below.
5   See chapters seven and eight.
6   See "Tony Ding Chai Yap: From Melakan Trance to Australian Physical Theatre" below.

accept non-Japanese members, specifically Australian Melissa Lovric, who also worked with Umiumare.

Dairakudakan was initially domiciled in a communal work space, but Maro and his dancers began to live apart from one another during the 1990s. Since 2002, the company has run an annual retreat in Hakuba, a valley just over 270 kilometres from Tokyo which hosts a number of ski resorts. Despite the communal ethos, Dairakudakan was not egalitarian. Lovric complained: "I can't describe any worse kind of hell than working together for the big shows" (Clarke 1994: 122). As Umiumare observed, there was a clear division of labour, with women making the costumes, doing the cleaning and the cooking, while "man has to make a stage" doing set construction (Umiumare and Eckersall 2012). As with Maijuku, individuals' professional earnings were channelled into company finances, or as Umiumare put it, the men took jobs in carpentry or at the "fish market in the morning. And woman work in the cabaret nightclub" to support the company. This was however changing when Umiumare joined, with dancers moving out and retaining some of their finances.

Maro's productions were typically loud, epic, with elaborate costumes and sets, often drawing together in a Surrealistic manner diverse influences, cultural origins, and historical referents. Maro cited the influence of Japanese folktales such as the twelfth century compilation *Konjaku Monogatari* (which features demonic monsters or yōkai), as well as the influence of Western materials like the music of Bach, and even mass-produced early modern Japanese commodities like hanafuda cards (Bradley 2017: 243). Hijikata had played a modern beastly yōkai in the film *Horrors of Malformed Men* (1969), where he acted the role of the role of a jerky, insane villain experimenting on bodies and subjects.

Dairakudakan's pieces constituted a form of "wordless theatre" in Baird's phrasing (Baird 2022: 84), or as one reviewer put it, works often consisted of:

> different scenes that are a challenge to link mentally but are nonetheless engrossing ... One doesn't exactly "make sense" of a Dairakudakan performance ... Sometimes you get it, sometimes you don't. Whichever, Akaji Maro is a ... compelling performer ... a bit like Charlie Chaplin.
> ARIALL 2008

In productions such as Dairakudakan's *Sea-Dappled Horse* (1980), there was a crossover between drama, theatre and dance, producing what Baird calls "grand seminarrative spectacles" (2022: 90). Facial expressions varied from an entranced gaze, to "imbecilic" grimaces, "orgasmic" expressions, or depictions of pain and suffering such as Umiumare witnessed (Baird 2022: 70). Karen van Ulzen of *Dance Australia* found Dairakudakan's work to exist "on the verge of hysteria" with a similarly "histrionic sound score" of electronic tones, distorted Japanese folk music, horns, Western opera, and other elements, screaming out of the amplification system at a punishing volume (1992: 42).[7] I remember a pair of terrified finches released from cages located under Maro's geta (platform shoes) during *Sea-Dappled Horse* in Melbourne. Desperate to escape the ungodly din, the birds launched themselves into the fly gallery. One however struck a light, dropping to the stage, where it sat, stunned. Dairakudakan's mishmash of cultural references invariably included characteristically Japanese elements, and this helped define the company as it moved to the international stage. Ulzen (1992: 42) claimed that the group "constantly reminds an Australian audience of its absolute foreignness".

Despite the often confusing Surrealistic imagery around which Maro's scenarios developed, they had a logic. *Sea-Dappled Horse*, for example, opened with a striking tableau that referenced Mishima Yukio's obsession with Saint Sebastian, amongst other sources. The dancers were posed in a line stretching across the back of the stage, in front of wooden panels. Arrows, like those which seemed to pierce the near naked Mishima in Hosoe Eikoh's photograph of him as Sebastian, were bound to the dancers' limbs (Hosoe and Mishima 1985). Each dancer held in their mouth a red temple flag, connected to each other by a length of rubber rope. Splaying themselves against the panels in a crucifixion-like pose, they opened their mouths and the rope sprang forward, flying over the front row seating. The dancers then came together in a pulsating mass at the front of the stage, or as Baird puts it:

> on their hands and knees as a group, inhaling and exhaling in yoga cat-cow pose (marjaryasana-bitilasana). They convulse progressively energetically until they are exploding outward and shrinking in repeatedly. Returning to the line, they take the rope in their mouths and back off stage between the panels.
> 2022: 82

Maro's journey in search of the sea-dappled horse therefore began with a violent birth which presaged death (the martyred Sebastian), and which confused

---

7   Not without reason, Jillett (1991: 12) described this as "noise of such brutality that, by comparison, the average rock show sounds like a lieder recital. Enduring this noise ... is like being trapped in a steel drum while someone bashes it with a crowbar". Thompson (1987: 10) similarly characterised the soundtrack to Byakkosha's earlier 1987 performance as "ear batteringly loud" so much so that "it was almost causing pain, and the stage itself seemed a torture chamber". One can only wonder what Australia's early critics would have made of Maro's musical peers such as Merzbow or Fushitsusha.

gender and sexuality, as with the queer imagery of Mishima and the photographic collaborations between Hosoe, Hijikata and others. Pain and pleasure, east and west, Japanese temple flags and Christian martyrdom, collided in a wonderfully spectacular image of throbbing movement which brought to mind anemones, as well as the finale of Kurosawa Akira's filmic adaption of *Macbeth,* which concluded with Mifune Toshiro, bristling with arrows, writhing against the wooden panels behind him (*Throne of Blood,* 1957). The meaning of the opening to *Kaiin no Uma* remained opaque, to be sure, but its elements constituted more than amusingly scattershot juxtapositions. Umiumare too would produce complex juxtapositions within her works, especially in her butoh cabaret pieces.[8]

Like Tanaka and others, Maro was clear that the butoh body took on movements and impulses from outside of it, or as Maro put it, the "space" or "ma" around the individual "has [a] different power and possibility from what we have with just ourselves" (Baird 2022: 80). Moreover, Maro often asked dancers to the identify the general nature of what moved them from outside—air, water, heat, and so on—each producing different qualities of movement (Bradley 2017: 104). The pulsing bodies of *The Sea-Dappled Horse* certainly seemed to be motivated by a force of attraction from beyond the forestage. "Ma" is a highly loaded term in Japanese philosophy, meaning the space between things, which is charged with significance. It is often seen as a defining metaphor for Japanese classical art and noh theatre, where it is the "ma" between things which generates beauty, rather than action or expression per se (see Komparu 1983: 70–73 and passim). Maro was however clear that, "Everything is full of something" (in Baird 2022: 81), so although the choreographic aim was to empty oneself so as to allow outside influences to lodge themselves within the "ma" of the body, Dairakudakan's dancers were not entirely evacuated vessels, but like Tanaka and de Quincey, Maro constructed the butoh body as fundamentally porous (Bradley 2017: 91).

Maro christened his own method "miburi-teburi". Literally referring to hand gestures, the term implied for Maro a movement without purpose which emerged out of daily activity (Maro 1972 and 2008). The Australian dancer Helen Smith—later a key member of Zen Zen Zo who participated in Maro's workshops in Australia and Japan—stated that in Maro's classes:

> The participant starts by miming an everyday activity, such as brushing teeth or cutting vegetables.[9] The teacher makes a sudden loud noise, which shocks the person into frozen stillness. In this moment, all thought

---

8   See "Butoh Cabaret" in chapter six.
9   Although any mundane action will do, brushing one's teeth is a commonly cited example (Calamoneri 2012, 133–4; Coelho 2008).

is momentarily suspended … until something ventures out of the darkness to inhabit the body … a … 'falling into' the state of nothingness, quite suddenly—from a moment of shock or fright.

This technique constitutes a part of Dairakudakan's core training methodology and can also be a tool for generating images and vocabulary for later use in choreographic work.

SMITH 2013: 49

As Maro has put it: "If someone tries to prepare food and cuts his finger, this moment of surprise is the first door of butoh" in which normal time is "stopped" and a new space of experience opens up (in Alison Broinowski 2017: 198). This is in effect a state of altered consciousness akin to that of Surrealist automatism and other conditions, in which seizures and tremors might arise. Maro compared this stopped condition to shamanic possession rituals; a fugue state which emerges as simply as when one unexpectedly trips on a stone and starts to fall (Bradley 2017: 86–90). The crack so produced within daily life was well expressed in the 2000 comedy-horror film by director Sabu (aka Tanaka Hiroyuki) entitled *Monday,* where a Japanese salaryman's drunken behaviour as a suave, sexy, imposing and extremely violent alter-ego climaxes with his transformation into a virtually indestructible monster, which is signalled by none other than Maro and his company appearing out of nowhere, their bodies whitened up, to dance past the bemused protagonist in a corridor. Umiumare often employed the same technique as Maro, noting that her aim was to find the "crack" or "moment of transformation" which was engendered by the "repetition of mundane action" like "brushing my teeth" wherein one becomes "propelled into another world of existence" (Umiumare 2014: 12). Jeremy Neideck, who trained with Maro, Bradley, Umiumare, de Quincey, and others, likens this "crack" to a performance involving spirit possession (Neideck 2018: 349). Dairakudakan's aesthetic of startling revelations within the banal is also echoed by Umiumare's description of her *DasSHOKU* pieces as "shock cabaret" (O'Brien 2005a) or ero guro.

Maro's concept of miburi-teburi is significant for two reasons. Firstly, the term "teburi" suggests a particular interest in limb movements. Dairakudakan's performers are notable for ornate gestures of the hands, wrists and forearms (as in scene six of *Sea-Dappled Horse*). Secondly, Maro's philosophy eschews Hijikata's own model of a deep, chthonic underground of mental, cosmic and social darkness, for something closer to the surface.[10] Dairakudakan slipped

---

10 In psychoanalytic terms, Maro may be seen to echo more closely Pierre Janet's model of the subconscious, rather than the Freudian Unconscious. Surrealism and Hijikata were

from dark tragedy to buoyant comedy more readily than many other butoh companies. As Umiumare reflected, Dairakudakan's workshops had "colours and spectacularness ... it was just fun" (Umiumare and Eckersall 2012). Indeed, Umiumare (1999: 8–9) has described her own butoh as one of moving out of "the dark ... towards the light". Maro's dance classes were punctuated with "laughter and exaggeration" (in Marshall 2001a). This was quite unlike Hakutōbō's classes, which Umiumare found "Very strict. No smile" and where the teaching method was "don't talk, just do it" (Umiumare and Eckersall 2012). Lovric agreed, finding Maro's company to exhibit "a real sense of humour" and "more freedom" despite the strong sense of disciplined group authorship (in Clarke 1994: 122). Even so, while Maro's choreography required dancers to tap into their idiosyncratic impulses, they nevertheless "have a count" and cues to organise the performance. Maro's bouncy combination of darkness and light, structure and chaos, was a decisive influence on both Umiumare, Bradley and the latter's collaborator Frances Barbe, all of whose butoh burlesques had more than a dash of visibly ridiculous impulsive action interwoven into their structures.

5 Umiumare: From Regional Japan to Urban Australia

Yumi Tsuchiya Umiumare spent her youth in the Kansai region in the heartland of Japan. The family was based just outside of Osaka. Umiumare also resided for a period in the nearby city of Takarazuka, the birthplace of the Takarazuka revue: a popular theatrical form from the early twentieth century featuring female chorus lines as well as travesti roles performed by women. Osaka had many old Showa period shops and dwellings, which Umiumare used to frequent. It was also home to the first taishū engeki company—literally "theatre for the masses" (Powell 1991: 109–110). Taishū engeki is a melodramatic vaudevillian performance genre whose popularity has waned since the 1940s. Plots generally offer a "simplified and speeded-up version of the giri-ninjō conflict" of emotional satisfaction versus duty, performed in a broad faux-kabuki style, along with "earthy humour ... song, dance and eroticism, all within a comic framework". Performances were interspersed with popular songs as well as enka standards and dance routines. Cross-dressed as well as gender consistent performers wear, as a pair of American critics put it, "kimonos that Elvis Presley might have worn had he worn kimonos" (Schneider and Schneider 2020:

---

more influenced by Janet's construction (which is cited in the Surrealist manifesto) than Freud's (see Marshall 2011a).

256). As in butoh and indeed many other Japanese performance forms, taishū engeki performers supplement their income by providing companionship to spectators, flirting with them, and soliciting gifts and tributes. Umiumare cites the fun, flashy aesthetics of taishū engeki as an important influence on her own practice (O'Brien 2005a). Australian playwright John Romeril (2001: 4; 535), with whom Umiumare and Yap would later collaborate, was another fan of taishū engeki and Takarazuka revue, both of his plays *Love Suicides* (1997) and *Miss Tanaka* (2001a) referring to the styles. Osaka company Theatre Gumbo were also influenced by taishū engeki, and Umiumare would engage the group to collaborate on two of her *DasSHOKU* pieces in years to come.[11]

Umiumare learned English through her mother, who was an English teacher and later became a calligrapher, while her father worked for radio (Umiumare and Eckersall 2012). Umiumare shared her parents' interest in communication, the dancer's thesis at university exploring the "connection between movement and verbal expression", while her familiarity with calligraphic forms underpinned her first full length choreographic work, *Fleeting Moments* (1998) and the sequence "Tears" from *EnTrance* (2009–12).[12]

Although living near Osaka, Umiumare's father was originally from Hijikata's homeland, namely the Tōhoku region in the north, and Umiumare herself would later tour to Tōhoku with Dairakudakan, as well as journeying there as part of her exploration of trance dance and Japanese possession rituals (Umiumare and Eckersall 2012). Umiumare fondly recalls the leafy, mountainous landscapes she had access to when she was young, both her school and Kobe University being atop of tall peaks (ibid). Since moving to Melbourne in 1993, she returns to the uplands of Japan most years. "The mountains contain their own special spirit", she explains, "an earthy mix of nature and cultural tradition" (O'Brien 2005a). She notes that she grew up with "all sorts of mixed-traditional rituals, social disciplines and modern rituals combined with superstitions" and she has since endorsed the saying that Japanese are "born into a Shinto ritual, get married at a Christian church then" finally have funerary rites in the form of a "Buddhist ceremony" (Umiumare 2014: 12). The Japan of Umiumare's upbringing was therefore defined by a mixture of traditional and Showa culture, popular urban phenomena, and steep leafy glades.

As well as piano, Umiumare began studying ballet as a child under the tutelage of Arahori Riichi, who was influenced by modern dance as well as classical technique and choreographed for the Takarazuka revue (Umiumare and Eckersall 2012; Umiumare 2023; Tano 2010). She began performing at a young age,

---

11   See "Butoh Cabaret" in chapter six.
12   On *EnTrance*, see also "Butoh Cabaret" in chapter six.

and was fairly experienced by the time she joined Dairakudakan, having taken lessons with Kano Hiriko and Tano Hideko, founder of the neo-Expressionist Tano Body Culture Centre in Tokyo. Umiumare began working with radical Japanese artists at an early stage, learning nihon buyō with Genshū Hanayagi, a transgressive classical Japanese dance figure who also performed in erotic films and rejected the hierarchical iemoto system within Japanese classical arts (Umiumare 2023). Like Ohno and Tanaka, Umiumare initially studied sports and physical education as well as dance at university, and like de Quincey, she decided to travel Asia as a young woman, visiting Nepal, Pakistan, China and Korea. It was while she was studying at university that she saw Dairakudakan in Kyoto. Umiumare had been developing her own:

> strange expressive dance and then put that really strange music and just move really weirdly ... Then I started seeing butoh and I thought, "Wow, that's exactly what I was doing".
> UMIUMARE AND ECKERSALL 2012

Umiumare was featured in newspaper coverage of a demonstration against the mourning rules around the 1989 death of the Emperor. The headline referred to a "Masked woman just coming onto the crowd and dancing", and Umiumare admits she wore a "funny white mask ... a bit ... butoh-ish ... disrespectful" (Umiumare and Eckersall 2012). Umiumare was therefore something of a butoh autodidact prior to her encounter with Dairakudakan. Butoh offered her a way to further develop her idiosyncratic version of edgy, expressive dance theatre.

In 1989, Umiumare moved to Tokyo to work for a real estate company. Here she began seeking out performances, including Peter Brook's *Mahabharata* and Shōgo Ōta's silent, slow theatrical production of *Mizu no Eki (Water Station)*— the latter piece particularly impressing her. Umiumare attended workshops led by Ashikawa at Hakutōbō, as well as Sankai Juku, and the butoh duo Eiko and Koma. She found none of them immediately appealing. Umiumare did however consider Dairakudakan "comical and funny" (Umiumare and Eckersall 2012). The company was to restage *Sea-Dappled Horse* for a season in the Tokyo district of Asakusa. The area had been an exemplary site of ero guro nansensu's mix of "eroticized, sensual pleasures" representing a "down-and-out (which is to say 'grotesque') social order" during the early twentieth century, serving as the "home of popular comedy" and taishū engeki (Silverberg 2006: 6; Powell 1991: 107). Umiumare declared that "I have to be in it!" leaving her job to perform in Dairakudakan's revival. The company was still something of a ramshackle ensemble at the time. Umiumare remembers a dangerous incident during the Asakusa performance. There was a scene in which the women entered, bent under futons, before throwing the quilts away to reveal both themselves and Maro made up as hysterically happy young girls in white dresses with pink bows in their hair. One night however "big bolts" began falling from the fly gallery, "so I just kicked" them off the stage (Umiumare and Eckersall 2012). The stage crew commended the new member's initiative. Umiumare also met the Australian dancer Melissa Lovric, who had moved to Japan after encountering butoh through de Quincey's workshops in Sydney. Lovric became the first non-Japanese member of Dairakudakan in 1990. She would collaborate with Umiumare when they toured Melbourne together in 1992. Lovric worked with Dairakudakan for seven years, and remained in Tokyo after leaving the company, where she continued to work in the arts, principally on graphics and projection.

In addition to working at an izakaya, Umiumare subsidised the company through employment at Motofuji's nightclub, Shōgun. Umiumare notes that she was required to perform "topless or some sort of feather dance", as well as acting as a hostess. Umiumare took these activities in her stride, noting that the dancers were often asked to sit with clients, but that they were closely monitored, so patrons were not able to be "doing naughty things" (Umiumare and Eckersall 2012). A mix of direct audience address and playful eroticism would be a key feature of Umiumare's later butoh cabaret.

In 1991, Umiumare came to Melbourne to perform in the Festival production of *Sea-Dappled Horse*. Peter Seaborn, who had been working with Handspan since 1978, met Umiumare through the Melbourne Festival (Umiumare and Eckersall 2012). Handspan had grown out of the 1970s New Wave in Australian theatre and was one of several groups whose members were looking to Japanese and European puppetry techniques. The link to Handspan is significant, as this paved the way for Umiumare's later collaborations with John Romeril, starting with the Handspan coproduction of *Love Suicides* (1997). Following the 1991 tour of Dairakudakan, Umiumare briefly returned to Japan before her personal relationship to Seaborn drew her back to Melbourne (the pair were married 1993–1999; Umiumare and Eckersall 2012). Umiumare took the opportunity to stage with Lovric the playful multi-media dance-theatre duet *Buddha's Banquet* (1992). Seaborn organised the production and for Umiumare to present what would be her first butoh workshop in Australia (Umiumare and Eckersall 2012). *Buddha's Banquet* was described by one reviewer as an "avalanche of beautiful, grotesque, terrifying, funny and often highly erotic images" in which "the two performers play with the idea of what it means to consume" (AusStage entry 17571).[13] Similar themes would return in later works such as

---

13   Umiumare initially performed under the name Yumi Tsuchiya.

DasSHOKU Shake!! (2012–15). The material in *Buddha's Banquet* had been developed while Umiumare and Lovric were performing with Dairakudakan, and the piece was very much in the spirit of the company. Both wore white makeup, employing grotesque facial gestures and twisted body positions.

Umiumare met Tony Yap at a 1992 workshop run by Cheryl Heazlewood. Heazlewood was one of a number of figures beginning to experiment with and teach butoh in Australia. Heazlewood had worked with the Australian Performing Group (APG) and later Murobushi Ko, Ohno Kazuo, the UK avant-gardist Lindsay Kemp, and others (Ulzen 1994b: 20; Heazlewood 1996; Yap and Eckersall 2012; Bradley 2017: 22). Also active was Paul Towner, a.k.a. Rainsford, who was artistic director of the fringe company, Chapel of Change. Rainsford appears to have been the first to offer self-devised butoh-related classes in Melbourne, before facilitating workshops led by Umiumare and Yap from around 1992 (Rainsford nd; Yap 2022–23). Rainsford's own work was a broad fusion of elements inspired by Sankai Juku (Rainsford appeared head shaved with white makeup and in robes for *The Descent,* 1995), Grotowski, and the style of camp, Surrealist eroticism exhibited by Théâtre Panique and others (see Rainsford nd; Ferrier nd). Yap shared with Rainsford a mutual interest in Hijikata, Mishima, Zen and Daoism (Yap and Eckersall 2012). Rainsford directed Yap's 1999 breakout work *Decay of the Angel.* It was also through workshops in Melbourne that Yap and Umiumare met their frequent collaborator Lynne Santos, who had attended both the Mungo sessions and Triple Alice run by Tess de Quincey, but who's own style never fully conformed with de Quincey's model of Body Weather.

Umiumare and Yap were to emerge as the best known and most influential butoh practitioners in Melbourne by the end of the 1990s. The power of their choreographic collaborations was dimly hinted at in that first workshop led by Heazlewood at the start of the decade. Umiumare recalls that she and Yap were paired together, and that in one of the exercises, they placed the palms of their feet together (Umiumare 2023). They met, then, partly through their feet, a unity of flesh at once proximate (palms joined) yet also distant (heads apart). This position would recur in several of Umiumare's and Yap's later works, notably *Zero Zero* (2010–14). Might one then read this prone, oppositional-yet-joined bodily disposition as an alternative answer to Tess de Quincey's question of "How to Stand in Australia?" (Grant and de Quincey 2008), or indeed of the post World War Two "crisis of standing" in Japan and in the face of modern culture which had been identified by Murobushi Ko and Hijikata? (Sakamoto 2018: 525–6). Umiumare's and Yap's position contains such a possibility even if not recognised as such, a corporeal status both supine and yet highly sensitive. More elaborate positions were to follow.

5   Tony Ding Chai Yap: From Melakan Trance to Australian Physical Theatre

Tony Ding Chai Yap grew up in a fishing village in Melaka, over 3,500 kilometres north west of Australia. Melaka lies on the strait which separates the Indonesian island of Sumatra from the Malay Peninsula and Singapore. The strait leads north to the Bay of Bengal, offering access between the South China Sea and the oceans around India, Pakistan and Bangladesh. Melaka consequently has long history of cultural and ethnic exchange. Melaka had a succession of different rulers, beginning with the Islamic Malay Sultanate (1400–1511), who welcomed large numbers of Chinese as well as Japanese merchants and settlers. The city was used as a trading centre and then successively ruled by Portugal, Holland and the British from 1511 to 1942, followed by Japanese occupation during World War Two (Malaysian Dept. National Heritage 2008–11: 9–10; Amat 2019: 9–10). Following World War Two, the states of Indonesia (1945), Malaysia (1957) and Singapore (1965) were established around the Straits. Each of the former rulers and trading partners contributed to Melaka's urban form and its socio-cultural make up. The city retains what the UNESCO World Heritage Submission describes as a rich "living multi-cultural heritage" (Malaysian Dept. National Heritage 2008–11: 9) as reflected by the number of temples, shrines, churches and institutions representing different faiths and historic regimes resting cheek-by-jowl throughout.

Yap is of Peranakan lineage, a mixed diasporic group derived from those of Chinese descent who started to arrive in Malaysia from the early modern period and took wives from the local population. Yap describes his home village as "Very multicultural. We have Indians, Malays and Chinese, all living side by side" (Yap and Eckersall 2012). Yap came from a typically mixed family, his mother being Javan-Indonesian and Peranakan, while his grandfather was a "half-Irish, half-Sri-Lankan" engineer for the British, once possessing "a chauffeur and a grand piano". Yap's grandfather on his father's side came from the Chinese coastal town of Hai'an, before Yap's father moved to Malaysia and was educated at an Anglo-Chinese mission school there. The family had Daoist, Confucian, Buddhist as well as Catholic beliefs.

Yap's family home was located by the beach, and acted as a temple for Daoist-Confucian spirit possession, divination and therapeutic intervention. Rooms within Chinese homes may serve as centres for religious practice. Shen deities or spirits, often "worshipped for pragmatic reasons" (Lee 1986: 199; also Legeza 1975; Chan 2015), include most of the beings in the Chinese Daoist pantheon, as well as local Malay spirits, some Hindu saints, plus distinguished ancestors and notable figures from Chinese history, as well as recently deceased individuals. As Yap puts it, shen mediums "provided remedies to the villagers' problems: physical, emotional, spiritual and even material woes" (Yap 2007). The practice is likely derived from neolithic rituals, becoming more formalised under the Shang dynasty in China during the second millennium B.C. when priest shamans (wu) were often connected with the imperial court (Lee 1986: 199). Later, mediumship came under the support of the Spirit Cloud sect of Daoism with which Yap later associated his work. The practice is now found amongst Chinese communities in Malaysia, Taiwan, Hong Kong, Singapore and elsewhere. In Melaka, the mediums are often "known popularly in Hokkien as *dang ki*, or 'divining youth'", the name signifying the energy which such customs bring to the individual and the community (Lee 1986: 200). Mediums may be male or female. Perhaps more significantly, critics in the region had recognised a kinship between local shamanic beliefs and the primal version of butoh presented by Byakkosha when the company toured the Pacific, writers likening Byakkosha's work to the dangki of the spirit medium tradition which Yap himself drew upon (Byakkosha 1987).

Yap's grandfather had practiced divination. Others from around the village conducted mediumship sessions in Yap's house:

> three times a week somebody would go in trance and then a god would possess the person and ... the villagers would come if there are inquiries of health, money and general questions that they have. And then the mediums would give guidelines.
> YAP AND ECKERSALL 2012

These sessions had a ritual-theatrical character. Incense, chanting, and percussion instruments were employed to help bring on a possessed state (Lee 1986: 203). Bands of cloth or aprons were often put on once the shen entered the body to identify who had become manifest. Mediumship sessions are often held in association with various calendrical festivals, and even performances of Chinese opera. Each god or deity exhibited a characteristic "choreography" or repertoire of actions (Morelos 2004: 98). Yap has described this in Jungian terms, as being like "dream-work, right in front of you—going into the subconscious" as the medium acts to interpret or realise the forms particular to each possessing spirit (O'Brien 2005b). Yap notes that the Peranakans and their peers have approximately:

> sixty different deities, from the Goddess of Mercy [Guanyin] to the Monkey God to the Beggar, to the Warrior, the King and the Child God ... every

archetype ... is represented by a different age, a different animal ... It's like Greek tragedy ...

The Beggar God, for instance, is particularly effeminate ... [but] like a manly rickshaw driver, which reminds me of Mishima's [characters] ... the tori [night-soil] man, because his [Mishima's] rickshaw drivers are always strong men[14]
YAP AND ECKERSALL 2012.

Yap's interpretation of these syncretic practices is therefore transcultural, Yap perceiving a unity between those Dionysian acts of possession which underlay Ancient Greek tragedy, through to Jungian concepts, as well as the queer writings of Hijikata's peer and supporter, the Japanese author Mishima Yukio. Mediumistic performances might be calm, playful or violent, depending on the spirit invoked. Yap is clear that the possessed individual is "definitely someone else". One female medium possessed by a demon, for example, became "was very strong, far beyond her physical means ... they would tie her up and she would just break the ropes, and they couldn't control her" (Morelos 2004: 98).

Yap recalls how he fell ill as a child, and his father contracted a group of dangki. The cure involved writing "a magic word" onto a paper talisman (fu), after which they "burn the paper and put it in this glass" which Yap drank and recovered. Yap also related how:

> At one cleansing ceremony, a huge wok was filled with sesame oil to boiling point. The medium in trance—staring [at] ... me, the youngest in the family—took my hands and dipped them into the boiling oil.
> YAP 1998: 40

Yap was unscathed. Indeed, Peranakan and Indonesian shamans often:

> perform great feats ... from ... acrobatic ... fire-walking, cutting the body with razors, swords and axes, burning the chest with a bundle of lit incense and tossing a red-hot spiked ball between mediums.
> IBID.: 40

It is worth recalling that Hijikata also claimed to be possessed by the spirits, specifically those of his deceased sister (Hijikata 2000d: 71–79). Yap's exposure to acts of possession and mediumship at a young age proved decisive, serving as

---

14   Yap is here referring to a scene in Mishima's semi-autobiographical novel, *Confessions of a Mask* (1949), where the young Mishima fantasises over a powerfully built night-soil man (shimogoe tori).

a primer for his later butoh-related, which would come to focus on the question of what is it to be possessed physically, psychically, and spiritually, by an entity or a force that moves through the body. As implied above, such dance has a trans-historiographic character, in which things are "brought back" from the past or from distant lands and into the multilayered time of the diasporic present. Yap would go on to work intensively with mediums, shamans and entranced performers from a variety of traditions across the Asia Pacific region.[15]

Echoing his father, Yap was educated at Taylor's College, Kuala Lumpur—one of a number of similar schools which Yap identified as "remnant[s] of the English system"—and then at the Australian coastal town of Warrnambool, approximately 300 kilometres west of Melbourne. Yap enrolled at the Warrnambool Technical College (later part of Deakin University) in 1976 as part of an international scheme. Yap majored in the arts and continues to work as a graphic designer. He initially moved around regional Victoria, working in Horsham for a printer, a newspaper, and a regional art gallery.

Yap helped bring together a group of local contemporary artists in Horsham, and with them he staged a short solo performance on a makeshift stage at the town gallery. Informed by Yap's interest in tai chi, the piece was entitled *Transition and Change* (1984). It was "about my life really ... a transitional state" of moving away "from a whole life that I thought I have already left behind", as a recently out gay man from Melaka, now in Australia (Yap and Eckersall 2012; Yap et al. 1984). Viewing video documentation, the piece comes across as slightly naïve but performed with an elegant conviction. Several key features of Yap's later aesthetic had emerged. There was a doubling and multiplication of body and subject, who was drawn to external forces—in this case represented by a selection of mime masks. There was also a marked sensuality of the body, expressed through the removal of Yap's T-shirt and his revivifying self-caresses. In later pieces, Yap would often perform topless, his torso gradually becoming filmed with sweat and energy, like the male mediums he used to observe. Dramatic development and intensity was moreover produced through a journey towards a death-like state, as in butoh. *Transition and Change* featured a coffin which divided the stage in two and within which Yap paused before moving from one side to the other to dramatize a shift in identity. Of this brush with death during the intensity of performance, Yap would later reflect:

> at the strong moments ... I feel I'd die. I am no longer me ... a death of ego and [of] the personality. That is what I mean by dying ... Fears come

---

15 See "Yap & Trance Dance" in chapter six.

> from the ego, expectations come from the ego, and the personality is because of this. But I die because I just don't want this at the moment, [and hence] there is just nothing.
>
> MORELOS 2004: 99

As an early experiment in dramatizing the abnegation of self, *Transition and Change* lacked the intensity of his later work, but it offered a glimpse of what was to come.

Yap moved to Melbourne where from 1984 he worked as a graphic designer for La Trobe University and then the University of Melbourne, 1986–92. In 1985, Simone Forti, a major figure in the New York studio dance scene, presented improvisation classes at Extensions dance studio in Melbourne. The year after, US dance artist Deborah Hay began to give semi-regular workshops in Melbourne, initially hosted by the Victorian College of the Arts and later Dancehouse (Yap 2020).[16] The latter institution was founded by workshop attendee Helen Sky in 1992, and played an important role in facilitating the work of Yap and Umiumare, who often featured at Dancehouse's mixed bill programs such as *Mixed Metaphor* and *Bodyworks*. Dancehouse accommodated Yap's workshops in exchange for the dancer designing the institutions' publications (Yap 2022–23). Yap attended both Forti's and Hay's workshops. Yap has suggested that his own self-taught tai chi and other practices acted to consolidate and streamline these otherwise diverse methods into an evolving whole (Yap 1999: 40). Yap met David McNamara (then known as David Whitmore), an Australian artist who had toured with several Japanese companies and designed sets for Tess de Quincey (*Another Dust*, 1990). It was, Yap observes, McNamara who "brought butoh into the rigour of our training methods", and it is largely McNamara who Yap today credits with introducing him to butoh (Yap 2022–23; Yap 1999: 40). It was also at this time that Yap saw the Australian film-maker and theatre-artist Richard Moore's 1991 documentary *Butoh: Piercing the Mask* (Yap and Eckersall 2012).

6 Theatre of Sacrifice and Redemption: Yap in IRAA, 1988–94

Yap and McNamara encountered the advertisements for workshops being offered by Italian-Australian theatre maker Renato Cuocolo in physical performance and Grotowski (Yap and Eckersall 2012). After attending several

---

16   The dates given in Yap & Eckersall 2012 are incorrect. Yap's curriculum vitae c.2020 is more reliable.

workshops, Yap joined Cuocolo's company, and toured to Adelaide in 1988 with *Far From Where,* the first IRAA piece he performed in.

Cuocolo had founded the Institute of Anthropological Research on the Actor (IRAA) in Rome in 1978. He and the company moved to Melbourne in 1988 after touring to Australia in 1985. IRAA was an experimental group focused on what former IRAA member Paul Monaghan titled "body theatre" (2009: 45). As Cuocolo put it, the aim was "to create a theatre where the actors may express their complete psycho-physical energy" through "the study of the Self; to study the Self is to forget the Self" (in Dolgopolov 1991: 164). In addition to Grotowski, Cuocolo was influenced by Eugenio Barba's model of intercultural theatre anthropology and the Odin Teatret, Julian Beck's Living Theatre, and in later years, the post-apocalyptic memory theatre of Tadeusz Kantor, whose work Cuocolo would go on to adapt. He briefly studied shamanism amongst the Mapuche people in Southern Chile, Japanese noh theatre, and collaborated on a dance project with the Aboriginal community of Mimili, South Australia (Musa 1990a: 33) on Anangu Pitjantjatjara Yankunytjatjara Lands. Cuocolo was also influenced by Zen Buddhism and Sufism, including the meditative spinning dance practice of the dervishes (Monaghan 2009: 45), which he had performers emulate in some of IRAA s productions (Musa 1990b: 21). Yap's experience with IRAA both expanded his horizons, offering him an intense engagement with elements of European performance, but was also paradoxically a homecoming of sorts, based as it was on "a European tradition that studies the eastern languages in theatre" in order to establish its own forms and lineages (Yap 1998: 40). It was also through IRAA that Yap first met Santos, with who he would continue to work after he left the company. Cuocolo claimed that Australia was a version of "the West beyond the East" offering a site where difference turns back upon itself, or wherein the "Other is present within the culture" of the majority itself (Monaghan 2009: 56). Travel writer Bruce Chatwin, whose interactions with Australian Aborigines led Chatwin to coin the term "Songlines", agreed, claiming that it was "not by chance that IRAA has established itself in Australia. This land ... is the perfect receptacle for hallucinations, loneliness and exile" (Monaghan 2009: 56).

IRAA s signature works were interpretations of Ancient Greek classics, such as *Medea: Vision of the Void* (1991), *The Bacchae* (1992), *The Trojan Women: Memories of Pillage* (1992), and *Agamemnon: Dawn of the Darkness* (1993), all of which featured Yap. Drawing on Nietzsche's reading of the interplay between eastern Dionysian forces and western Apollonian ones, Cuocolo claimed that the productions dealt with the "clash between cultures" of "the West and the Other" often focussing on issues of "exile" and displacement (Monaghan 2009:

45–47). The aesthetic was both metaphorically and literally that of Grotowski's "Poor Theatre", and often involved minimalistic but inventive staging. *The Bacchae: Burning by Water* (1994), for example, was performed in a shallow pool of water covering the entire stage. Yap has since claimed that one of the "main insights that emerged at that time" was:

> My dance aesthetics are in deep agreement with the philosophical work of Grotowski, especially in relation to his concept of 'poor theatre'—a theatre with a minimum of accoutrements other than the pure presence of the actor.
> 2021: 2

The poor theatre aesthetic would become defining feature of Yap's own works with Mixed Company. Yap's performances for IRAA developed an "oscillation between an interiority of the psyche and external physical actions" which reflected "the strong influence of trance in the context of my South East Asian heritage" (Yap 2021: 2). Yap, who sported an impressive mane of hair for much of this time, was cast in queer feminine roles, playing Medea, Cassandra, Dionysius and others. Yap had begun reading Edward Said's classic critique of the uneven power relationships embedded in Western representations of Oriental culture (Yap and Eckersall 2012). Looking back, Yap confessed that "it seemed to me sometimes that Renato was perhaps somewhat simplistically using a kind of image of Orientalism" particularly in "how the Asian body was portrayed" (Yap and Eckersall 2012). Yap was after all the only visibly Asian performer in the ensemble, and it was he who was chosen to adopt gender-ambiguous roles. Nevertheless, "playing a woman's part was exciting" as well as challenging. Yap was able to infuse these roles with themes of exile and his own experiences. *Medea*, for example, became "about a displaced Malaysian in Australia" (ibid.).

Yap shone in these works, developing an impressive, vibrating energy which alternated with scenes of deathly sacrifice—very much in the mode of Grotowski's para-Catholic formulation of death being followed by redemption, and not far from butoh's own positioning of suffering being key to understanding life, death and the world of the body. As Yap explained, these roles tended to follow a pattern of "First, I die" and then "For the next hour or so, I'm dead". There was therefore an "unmistakable … trace of trance" and butoh "in my early roles" with IRAA, which varied from:

> a displaced 'dead' soldier (*Far From Where*, 1989); the impassioned priestess, Medea (*Medea*, 1990); the prophetic Cassandra (*Agamemnon*, 1992);

as the illusive demigod, Dionysus (*The Bacchae*, 1992 ... 1994); mad soldier, Woyzeck (*Woyzeck: A Good Death*, 1994).

YAP 2021: 35

However, as Cuocolo began to perform Italian themed memory plays in the manner of Tadeusz Kantor after 1994, these rich and intense roles for Yap dried up.

7 Mixed Company and Tony Yap Company, 1993-Present

Participants in Yap's workshops would become members of what Yap initially called Mixed Company (founded in 1993), and later Tony Yap Company (TYC), in recognition of their mixed training and the fact that most had come to him not through conventional dance training, but other avenues. Key figures included Lynne Santos, noted above, and Matthew Crosby—the latter having worked with Suzuki Tadashi on the Playbox Theatre production of *Chronicle of Macbeth* (1992)[17] and with Shinjuku Ryozanpaku, a group led by Kara Juro's former disciple Kim Sujin (Maro Akaji worked with Kara before he moved to Hijikata's group). The companies also included Yap's long-term associates Ben Rogan, Adam Forbes, Brendan O'Connor, Jonathan Rainin, and Dean Linguey, while Umiumare and Gretel Taylor appeared in some productions. Most of the long term members of Mixed Company and TYC have at one time or another presented their own short solo works or duets; Umiumare and Gretel Taylor went on to develop long-term careers as choreographer-directors.

Yap's early Mixed Company productions from 1995 onwards were often provisionally themed around Greek mythology (Echo and Narcissus, Icarus), offering a more resolutely choreographic outgrowth of the textual interpretations staged by IRAA. In the Mixed Company production of *Saint Sebastian* (1998), critic Philippa Rothfield (1998: 4) noted both the continuity and the development of Yap's work as compared to IRAA, observing that Mixed Company retained "the slow group walk" and the "contained, strained emotion" of IRAA, pervaded by a sense of "cruel enormity". Within this and other productions Yap typically acted as a central organising pole around which sometimes chaotic choric performances would be staged. *Saint Sebastian* itself was, like the opening sequence from *Sea-Dappled Horse* (1980), inspired by Mishima's erotic obsession with Saint Sebastian.

---

17   See "The Australian Production of *Chronicle of Macbeth*" in chapter seven.

As the 1990s progressed, Yap's works began to reflect a number of butoh signatures, such as the interest in flamenco-like movement, combined with his own particular interpretation of possessed performance, or being moved by forces outside of the body. In *The Body and the Double Bass* (1998), for example, Yap transitioned from an explosion of flamenco-like leaping and foot stamping, to a section in which his eyes were either closed or urgently looking, while his body twisted and turned, fell and rose, oblivious to all but the need to move. He seemed wracked by an unattainable desire, agape, hands flying around and into his mouth, but never stemming these needs.

Although Mixed Company featured striking female performers such as Santos, the group exhibited a strong sense of masculine energy, male embodiment, and homoeroticism. Standard attire for the men was to be topless with basic black slacks, bare feet. The clash, embrace and ecstasies of male bodies, often ending heaped together upon the stage floor, featured strongly right through to Yap's late works like *Dionysius Molecule* (2015), or *Strife of Light Bearer* (2017). Yap stated that *Light Bearer* reflected "the uneasy learning of masculinity; the thematic strife … in the absence of fathers" and the search for masculine self definition (Yap 2017). Mourning for an idealised male figure in oneself or in others produced deep introspection and psychocorporeal movement, and this ambience has infused much of Yap's oeuvre.

As Yap developed his aesthetic during the 1990s, he also drew more and more on his memories of Peranakan medium rituals, with repetitive actions such as revolving to bring on a highly focussed, Dionysian fervour. In *Echo* (1996), for example, the dancers rose from amongst the audience to repeatedly throw "themselves passionately at each other" and then push each other away, before "crashing to the floor" and start the cycle again (Christofis 1997: 51). In short, the basic elements of Yap's aesthetic were established by the late 1990s, but continued to grow in rigour, sophistication and lyricism, with entranced performance and a more ornate mise en scène rising in importance.

8 Umiumare and Yap in *Love Suicides* (1998), *Miss Tanaka* (2001), and *Meat Party* (2000)

As Umiumare and Yap developed their choreographic trajectories, they performed several roles within pieces developed by others. Umiumare has described much of her work as "character dances" (TRU 2021). Ohno's own major works tend to be themed around characters such as La Argentina, his mother, or a foetus. One of Umiumare's early engagements was as an actor in Mary Moore's 1998 theatrical adaptation of Togawa Masako's 1962 novel

Masterkey (*Oi Naru Genei*), which dealt with the interracial intrigues of an apartment block catering to young single women working in Tokyo during the 1920s (Holledge and Tompkins 2000: 121–127). Umiumare performed the role alongside Takai Tomiko—who had worked under Hijikata from as early as 1959 before working with Dairakudakan (Holledge and Tompkins 2000: 122; Baird 2022: 30–32; Baird and Candelario 2019: 2).

Umiumare's collaborations with Yap in the works of others included a pair of puppet plays written by Australian New Wave author John Romeril. Romeril had undertaken research in Japan (Romeril 1994, 2001a and 2001b), and had composed a dark theatrical expose of Australian anti-Japanese racism and lingering war trauma in veterans of the Pacific War with the play *Floating World* (1975). Like many New Wave artists, Romeril was heavily influenced by the theatrical traditions of late nineteenth and early twentieth century Australia, specifically pantomime, melodrama and vaudeville. Japanese forms such as kabuki, kyogen, bunraku, as well as taishū engeki and Takarazuka revue ("Japanese vaudeville" in Romeril's phrasing; Romeril et al 2001: 4–6; Romeril 1994: 535) offered appealing parallel forms still being regularly produced in Japan. Discussing the style he was aiming for in *Miss Tanaka* and *Love Suicides*, Romeril has claimed:

> Unlike spoken drama in the west that has become more and more naturalistic, in Asia there are still a myriad of theatre forms that don't mind using dance.
>
> Again, this is an example of how I've found it very liberating, in terms of my imagination, to see as much Asian theatre as I have because you look at it and say "Hey, that works". You learn how to echo it or borrow it. As luck would have it of course it relates to the kind of performance form you find in Aboriginal Australia, where moving to song, moving to rhythm and moving to a form of acting or story telling that is very much in your face is integral to the culture. Perhaps it's the kind of theatre that sits best in this continent.
>
> ROMERIL ET AL. 2001: 4

Japanese influences became for Romeril a way to re-examine and come to terms with Australia's own traditions, including those of Indigenous Australia. In Romeril's own work, this involved a combination of blending songs, musical accompaniment, stylised text and heightened drama that moved beyond western Naturalism. Yumi Umiumare and Tony Yap were to play a part in this.

Romeril wrote two plays for actors alongside puppets which were staged by Playbox, a Melbourne theatre company led by Carrillo Gantner and with a commitment to cultural exchange between Asian arts and Australia. The first production was Romeril's free adaptation of a double love suicide kabuki play by the Edo era Japanese playwright Chikamatsu Monzaemon. Romeril's protagonist was Mark Paris, a dubious Australian businessman who once worked in Tokyo but was now "pursued by demons and creditors" (Spunner 1998: 11). Ohatsu was a young Osaka-born woman forced into an arranged marriage. Upon meeting in Perth, they realised "they share a desire to escape the present" and the action moved to a series of reveries across time, animated by their conflicted desires (ibid.: 11). The roles of Paris and Ohatsu in *Love Suicides* (1998) were played by human actors—the latter role performed by Japanese-Australian Izawa Asako—as well as by visibly onstage operators who each manipulated a stylised bunraku-style puppet. The music was also Japanese in tone, composed by Peter Neville and performed with Odamura Satsuki on koto. Umiumare played the spirit of Ohatsu's deceased childhood friend and former lover Keiko. As Denise Varney observes (2011: 132), Umiumare served as a spectral figure whose actions "draw attention to the co-presence of the timeless world". This timeless world was one not only of "memory" but also:

> the dead … As a shamanic presence, Keiko's drumming, dancing, storytelling, magic-making, mask and costume evoke the ancient [Japanese] practice[s] of prophecy and healing.
> VARNEY 2011: 132

Although much of Umiumare's performance cast her as an observer of the actions of the protagonists, elsewhere her character functioned to highlight moments where worlds from the past or beyond death threatened to break into the here and now, such a fusion of life-in-death being a characteristic of butoh. In short, Umiumare's casting dramatized how the role of Keiko within the play as a "shamanic presence" was very close to that of a butoh dancer.

Romeril's second collaboration with Playbox and Handspan was a lighter work, *Miss Tanaka* (2001a), which featured both Umiumare and Yap. Here the score was by some-time shakuhachi player and electronica composer Darrin Verhagen. The staging employed black theatre effects and puppets tended to represent non-human elements such as an oversized sea turtle (with which one of the characters was identified, as a crippled former diver), as well as a mystical black pearl which appeared towards the close of the piece. The play was set in the racially mixed, kriol world of Broome's early twentieth century pearling industry in Western Australia.[18] Characters were a mix of Anglo-Aus-

---

18 See "Troubled Relations Between Australia & Asia Prior to the Japan Theatre Boom" in chapter two.

tralian, Japanese, Malaysian and First Nations Australian. Although Umiumare at times played Mrs Tanaka senior in a graceful, non-verbal dance sequence drawing on buyō and obon dances honouring the dead, the younger "Miss Tanaka" was a comedic travesti persona, adopted by the male mixed descent Aboriginal-Japanese protagonist Tanaka Kazuhiko, as a ruse conceived by his crippled, in-debt father to extort a bride price from two other pearl divers. Umiumare, also cross-dressing, played the male Japanese pearl diver Sakamoto, while Yap played opposite her the role of Sakamoto's male competitor, friend and rival, Malaysian diver Hanif. As Romeril observed, "I've based a fair bit of Hanif's and Sakamoto's ... banter on elements of 'kyogen,'" the comedic sequences which intersperse noh performances (Romeril et al. 2001: 4). Kyogen actors typically also train in elements of noh, and are specialists in broad, physically stylised methods. Butoh has some similarities with kyogen, notably in the tendency for facial grimacing and the adoption of a low, wide-legged stance. The extended joke on misrecognised gendering in *Miss Tanaka* owes at least as much to Anglo-Australian pantomime as it does to taishū engeki and Takarazuka. The more serious and potentially queer implication of having a male character seduce another man dressed as a woman (Kazuhiko and his boss Mott) was also briefly toyed with in one scene but remained unconsummated (Romeril 2001: 45–56), and was not pursed in later scenes. The casting of Sakamoto and Hanif by Umiumare and Yap was indicated by Romeril's requirement that the two have a "readiness to *move* into dance" (Romeril et al. 2001: 4). The script has them enter by *"swinging in on ropes, 'Tarzan-style"*, or in the mode Australian-born actor Errol Flynn, coming *"from opposite directions"*. In addition to engaging in a series of comedic bouts of sumo wrestling, they *"fight a swashbuckling battle that combines both Malay and Japanese martial arts"*, namely a combination of silat and karate (Romeril 2001: 10–11). Photographic documentation shows that the role fitted Umiumare's talents well, though Yap noted that he was to become frustrated at being cast as the "Malaysian pearl diver" or other ethnic character roles, and not in the complex leading roles which he had performed with IRAA (Yap and Eckersall 2012).

Yap was more satisfied with his role in Duong Le Quy's *Meat Party*, also scored by Darrin Verhagen, and directed in 2000 by Michael Kantor.[19] As well as serving as *Meat Party*'s choreographer and movement director, Yap played Vietnamese national, poet and survivor of the war between the US and the Viet Cong named An. An was enlisted by white Australian citizen Mary to help retrieve the body of her father from a fictional haunted, war-scarred Vietnamese

---

19   Kantor became artistic director of the Malthouse theatre (formerly Playbox) in 2005.

landscape called the White Sand Desert (standing in for the real Mũi Né sand dunes where a large graveyard now stands). Le Quy and Kantor drew heavily on Teshigahara Hiroshi's *Suna no Onna* (*Woman of the Dunes*, 1964), which featured a treacherous sandy landscape of memory and introspection which could entrap the unwary.[20] Projections of a woman's eye hovering over the landscape in *Meat Party* also drew on the Japanese yōkai film *Kwaidan* (1964).

In *Meat Party*, Umiumare played the woman found at the heart of this sandy landscape: the Crone, a chanting, damaged madwoman who "prowls the sands, collecting whitened bones ... nursing [those] ... of her children" (Herbert 2000). As with Umiumare's role in *Love Suicides*, Umiumare's Crone was a yōkai-like shamanic figure, using bones as percussion instruments to communicate with the dead. Also in the cast were Matthew Crosby, as well as Nareeporn Vachananda, both of whom had participated in Yap's workshops. Yap's role included spoken text as well as an "exquisite [choreographic] sequence that served to express ... the aesthetic beauty that is war's antithesis" (Thompson 2001: 162). *Meat Party* demonstrated how the community of butoh-influenced independents fostered by Yap and Umiumare were attracting the interest of larger theatre companies and institutions. The involvement of Yap, Umiumare and others also signalled an interest in non-Naturalistic physical theatre by Australian theatre makers such as Kantor and Romeril.

9   *Kagome* (1996–98)

In the early 1990s Melbourne was home to circle of musicians trained in Japanese forms. As a Japanese dancer, Umiumare soon came into contact with them. Anne Norman and Odamura Satsuki formed Nadoya Music and Dance Company in 1993. Norman had trained in the shakuhachi, or Japanese bamboo flute, 1986–92, while Odamura was a Japanese-born expert in the koto or twelve stringed zither. Norman, Odamura and later Umiumare catered largely to audiences for classical Japanese music (Duffy 2001: 154), although all three were skilled in experimental cross-cultural work, Odamura also working with the Sydney based experimental musicians Jim Denley and Amanda Stewart, music by these two being crucial to de Quincey's own butoh productions.[21] Nadoya also consisted of percussionist Peter Neville (composer for *Love Suicides*), and bass player Michael Hewes. Umiumare has reflected that "originally

---

20   The piece was staged in Melbourne as a play by David Pledger, the year before Pledger performed in Suzuki's *Chronicle of Macbeth* (1991; Waddell 1992, 31).
21   See chapters three and four.

I had a little bit of reaction": "I'm come to Australia, working [with] koto and shakuhachi ... 'Oh my god!'" (Umiumare and Eckersall 2012).[22]

The four piece version of Nadoya premiered as part of the outdoor public program in the 1993 Melbourne International Festival, where Umiumare performed a shifting character dance as a yamamba-like crone such as she would later present in *DasSHOKU Hora!!* (2005–06), complete with a wildly streaming green shock wig (Nadoya 1993). After a creative development in 1994, Yap and Lynne Santos participated in subsequent public Nadoya events, such as the Moomba festival, in 1995. Costuming had a Japanese styling, and the dancers were covered in gold and white make-up (Norman nd). Umiumare and Odamura began to performed as the duet Shashaten, featuring semi-improvised dance alongside composed and improvised koto. Norman, Odamura and Umiumare were to work on many productions together, such as the spoken-word and photographic projection work *Chika: A Documentary Performance* (2012) and other pieces. Umiumare would also later collaborate with Melbourne sanshin (Okinawan banjo) performer Ayako Fujii (*Fudo*, 2018). Yap too experimented with his own dance-music ensembles, engaging Norman and others for his own production of *The Body and the Double Bass* (1998), before Yap developed a long term collaboration with Umiumare on a series of entranced duets and works supported by musicians Madeleine Flynn and Tim Humphrey.

Nadoya's sketches coalesced into the full-length work *Kagome* (1996–98), co-directed by Norman and Umiumare. *Kagome* featured Yap and Umiumare opposite Santos with Nadoya's musicians visibly present on the periphery of a curved performance area. Material was developed out of improvisations which took as their starting point the Japanese children's game and song, "Kagome Kagome". Lyrics vary, but those used by Nadoya ran:

> Kagome, kagome
> When will the bird in the cage meet/escape?
> When the sun rises at midnight?
> The crane and the tortoise slip.
> Who is in front of behind?
> NADOYA 1996 and 1997; RT 1996: 34

---

22   A good example of Umiumare working on some of the more sentimentalised versions of Japanese classical and folk repertoire includes a c.1994 video of her mugging and dancing to Norman (voice and shakuhachi), Odamura (shamisen) and Neville (hand drums), performing Hibari Misora's title song from the 1952 film set in Aomori, Tōhoku, "Ringo Oiwake (Oiwake Apple)". The artists are dressed in classic yakutas (Nadoya 1994).

To play the game, children form a circle and the child in the centre becomes "it", or "oni"—"oni" also meaning a yōkai or demon. The oni covers their eyes while the other children rotate around them, reciting the song. At the end of each repetition, the oni attempts to name the child standing directly behind them. If they do this correctly, the oni exchanges places with the other child, and the game continues. In a gloss on early ethnological studies into children's games, Iijima Yoshiharu claims that kagome is a children's version of ancient rituals "known as Jizo-asobi or 'invoking Jizo' (the guardian deity of [dead] children) that were practised until recently in parts of the Tōhoku area" (Iijima 1987: 46). Iijima cites Sakurai Tokutarō's (1975) claim that the game was:

> was apparently used in cases of sickness or to find lost possessions. The housewives and old women of the village would gather and sit down in a circle. In the centre of the ring they would place a dull child with a paper wand (gohei) in his hand. They would then chant time and time again the words "Hail Jizo, Great Buddha, possess, possess, Jizo-san, Jizo-san, Jizo-san." Eventually the child in the centre would fall into a kind of trance and begin to shake.
> SAKURAI, qtd in IIJIMA 1987: 46

After this, the women would ask the child-oni to divine for them. The game also had an existential character. The word kagome refers a hexagonal pattern of woven bamboo strips, such as a basket or cage might be made of. Norman observed that the concept of a cage as something which "both imprisons and protects" provided much of the choreography (RT 1996: 34). Repeating the word "kagome", it eventually became non-sensical, this meaningless invocation helping to induce a dissociated state and access to the subconscious. Ethnologist Matsuda Osamu (1975) went so far as to argue that the oni is, in effect:

> alienated from those around him and, turning towards the Other World, experiences a kind of "death". Then, on guessing the name of the child behind him, he changes places with him, rejoins the circle, returns un-harmed to this world, and experiences "rebirth".
> MATSUDA qtd in IIJIMA 1987: 46

Hijikata had been photographed in 1968 by Hosoe Eikoh playing the role of a kamaitachi-demon, emerging from inky shadows to drag a girl into the undergrowth, or to steal an infant and charge across darkened fields with it (Hosoe and Hijikata 2005). Norman claimed that the lyrics "refer to a time when the gate to the supernatural world opens" (RT 1996: 34), and so a red torii gate, such as one finds at the entrance to Japanese temples, stood at the back of the stage for the production. As in the *Kamaitachi* photobook by Hijikata and Hosoe, *Kagome* drew on the experiences of Tōhoku children as a way to allude to contrasting themes of death, life, possession, playfulness, and energies which extend beyond the control of the human.

Kagome was divided into fourteen sequences, rapid crescendos alternating with more lyrical moments where the three dancers came together, arms held high in sweeping, curvilinear gestures, as they slowly turned back and forth. The movement was devised by the dancers themselves, and while all of them shifted from playfulness to terror, entranced possession to outward curiosity, each dancer remained distinctive. Umiumare was perhaps the most ludic of the trio, often moving in leaps and bounds, her face ever responsive. Atop of the torii, Yap performed an intense possession dance, stamping one foot before urgently and tremulously pointing forward with one arm, his eyes tightly focussed. His energy moved in quick, stabbing shivers through his form, bringing out darting movements in and out of a wide-legged stance, fingers held in an uneven, triangular spread such as one sees in Malaysian classical dances, while his demonic laughter echoed into the space. Yap's role here echoed to some degree the "sickle weasel [kamaitachi]", the mischievous and demonic yōkai which Hijikata played in the photobook referred to above. Santos was by comparison the most grounded of the trio, her eyes generally glazed over and beaming out into the space, as she rolled her arm in front of her chest, as though spinning a massive ball. The most explicitly butoh touch was provided by Santos at the commencement of the work, which started with her in a foetal ball centre stage, wrapped in a tunnel of white gauze falling from the ceiling. She gradually uncoiled and explored the space as Yap came up behind her to a standing position, while Umiumare entered under the tori.

Although Japanese motifs provided core organising elements, everything about the piece suggested a modern multicultural fusion. In addition to an African thumb piano, Norman used a ken tieyu or Vietnamese oboe, to inject a feeling of intensity to one particularly chaotic scene where the dancers ran about and leapt over and between each other ("Who is in front behind?"). The circularity of the performance space and of the choreography was echoed by the circularity of Neville's kettle drums, as well as a Trinidadian steel drum around which the cast rolled marbles, and even the spherical shape of the knobs on the end of the percussion sticks which the dancers took from the musicians and which they rubbed in awkward, blurry swipes across the kettle drum, before delightedly and then in a horrified manner forced into and out of their mouths. This crossing between instrumental music and dance was a marked characteristic of the work, with Umiumare crouching over a block of light striped with black lines and which she ran her fingers over to be echoed by Odamura on koto. The piece concluded with Umiumare playing a whirly-gig child's toy which made a sound like a bird or cicada.

Kagome was a landmark production for Australian butoh in many ways. Although early reviews were mixed, Nadoya followed up with a successful national tour. The production introduced a cohort of artists who would go on to collaborate on numerous shows beyond what had until then been a circumscribed community of Melbourne physical performers and Asian music aficionados. Moreover, unlike the Playbox productions discussed above, *Kagome* had no spoken English text, placing the work in dance theatre rather than scripted drama. Within this piece, butoh was deployed as a dramaturgical heuristic; as a way of organising disparate performative modes and forms (dance, percussion, sound effects, strings, mime, etcetera) as well as cultural material from diverse homelands (Afro-Caribbean, Vietnamese, Malaysian, Chinese, Japanese, Euro-American). Umiumare and Yap would both build on, and depart from, these strategies in years to come.

10   *Sunrise at Midnight* (2001): a Sequel to De Quincey's Mungo Workshops

The first sustained engagement with the Australian landscape which Umiumare conducted was her performance in Sean O'Brien's dance film *Sunrise at Midnight* (2001), which also featured Yap in a central role. The piece is comparable to de Quincey's early outback works due to its setting.[23] The title came from a line in "Kagome Kagome". The film was shot in black and white, like Hosoe's *Kamaitachi* (1968–69), the photographic series featuring Hijikata in Tōhoku, which O'Brien cited as an influence. The cinematographer took advantage of the intense light of the Australian interior to develop a bleached, chiaroscuro version of Hosoe's photography. *Sunrise at Midnight* thereby suggested that central Australia might serve as a Tōhoku or homeland for Australians, yet it did this by way of two protagonists who are themselves strangers to the landscape.

Sunrise at Midnight begins with a voiceover, spoken by Umiumare, which introduces her as a butoh dancer. We see her whiting up her face prior to her transformation into the role. Relating Umiumare's fascination with the Australian landscape, the film cuts to reveal Umiumare staring at her double in the

---

23   See "Lake Mungo" in chapter three.

FIGURE 9 Yumi Umiumare (left) and Tony Yap (right) in *Sunrise at Midnight* (writer/dir. Sean O'Brien: 2001)
ARCHIVAL VIDEO STILL COURTESY OF O'BRIEN

mirror—not made up in a typically butoh fashion, but rather wearing a vintage Japanese kimono, her hair in a bun. In the film, Umiumare related that she had:

> seen an old photograph, a group of karayuki-san, poor Japanese women from the countryside taken to work in a foreign land. These women were entertainers, travelling around the Australian outback.[24]
> O'BRIEN 2001A

The film cut from a historic black-and-white photograph showing four dour looking Japanese women, to a close up of the head of one of these figures, who is identified as Noriko. Umiumare states that she has "heard a story about one of the entertainers" who "wandered away from town and got lost

---

24 Karayuki-san, or "one who goes to China", was a term applied to impoverished rural women, often from Kyushu, who travelled overseas to work, sending money back to their relations. This very often involved sex work, though during the nineteenth century the category was more flexible; see Mihalopoulos (1993); Killoran (2015).

in the bush" (Figure 9). From this point Umiumare-the-performer disappears behind Umiumare-ghost-of-Noriko, and the rest of the film offers Noriko's meditative wanderings, as she moves through different scenarios, before finally disappearing into a sandstorm, killed, or possibly assimilated into the landscape.

The locations for the film were many of the same ones used by de Quincey six years earlier for her first major workshop series set in the Australian interior at Lake Mungo national park.[25] Umiumare is shown in the film traversing windblown sand dunes, open stony landscapes, scrubland, piled rock, and channels in the excoriated eroded landscape which lay before the feature known as the Walls of China. Although not mentioned in the film, the landforms were named after the Chinese workers who built the woolshed during the nineteenth century. Umiumare takes refuge within the historic wool shed at Mungo within which de Quincey's dancers worked. Reprising elements of both *Kamaitachi* and *Kagome*, Umiumare as Noriko enters the Mungo wool shed originally built by Chinese labourers. There she meets with Yap as a version of the sprite or "sickle weasel" which Hijikata played in *Kamaitachi*, which showed Hijikata, hunched and pensive, peering intensely out of the shadows of an old style Tōhoku farmhouse. Umiumare first encounters Yap resting in a deep crouch, dreaming of Melaka, and muttering to himself "I built this place ... with my own hands". As Yap's fingers flutter about his face, he establishes a transhistorical linkage akin to that being performed by Umiumare. Where Umiumare is transformed into a questing, haunted version of Noriko the deceased karayuki-san, so Yap becomes a version of the Chinese labourers who built the wool shed, adding his own Peranakan identity to this, murmuring in Malaysian and English. Early in Noriko's transit across the rocks, the viewer hears the call of an Australian raven. Umiumare moves in a low position, the sleeves of her kimono hanging from her arms as she holds them out stiffly, like wings. In the voice-over, Umiumare paraphrases "Kagome Kagome", asking "When will the bird"—which Noriko through her wing-like has gestures become—be able to "escape? When the sun rises at midnight. You may go through, but you might not come back knowing that place" which you have "gone through" (O'Brien 2001a). Umiumare, crouched under a rock escarpment, folds in on herself, like Yap, before reflecting of the landscape: "How vast it is! There is nobody out here. It goes for ever and ever". Umiumare as Noriko does, however, stumble into a rock shelter where she finds signs of human activity. It is decorated with ancient painted hand prints, causing her to reflect: "There

---

25   See "Lake Mungo" in chapter three.

are many hands in this cave. Who put them here?" Her encounter with the First Nations landowners, though indirect, is corporeal—through the bodily imprints they left on Country.

Yap and Umiumare each present a short, dance sequence in the film. Umiumare stands upon the dry lakebed of Mungo, hunched and twirling, her body and limbs enacting a complex set of changes in direction, left-right, up-down, while glancing anxiously upward and sideways at the intensity of the sun. In the wool shed, Yap attempts to communicate with Noriko. He places one foot forward, bringing his fluttering hands to his chest—a gesture of greeting and self-naming perhaps—his body rising and falling in small jerks. He turns away and looks intensely out of the shed towards the landscape, making small, stochastic changes in position, head twitching, hands flicking, embodying an almost insect-like or reptilian modality—and then he vanishes, leaving Noriko alone.

Sunrise at Midnight was promoted as "both a documentary portrait of Yumi Umiumare" and a "Japanese ghost story set in the Australian desert" (O'Brien 2001b). Hauntings are a common theme in Japanese noh theatre, and this link was enhanced by classical Japanese music from Odamura (koto) and Norman (shakuhachi). Critics at the time seemed unaware of *Sunrise at Midnight* as a response to de Quincey's earlier engagement with the same site, shot as the film was in many of the same locations. The region near Lake Mungo became a locus for Australian butoh performance; Takai Tomiko (who worked with Hijikata) and Mary Moore conducted research for the 2000 Adelaide Festival production *Exile* in the area also (Aston and Case 2007: 121–31). Although in many ways *Sunrise at Midnight* reproduced clichés regarding the desert in central Australia as a place of mystery and self-discovery, the substitution of Asian protagonists for white subjects disrupted these tropes. What is it that a karayuki-san, a forcibly transmigrated Japanese subject, might find in Australia? Umiumare became Noriko, while Yap became one of the Chinese employees who constructed the wool shed—though it remained an open question within the film as to whether Umiumare becomes more at home in Australia now that she has joined with her virtual ancestor Noriko, or whether the similar filiation which Yap establishes with the Chinese labourers at Mungo enabled his body to move easier in this Country. Umiumare and Noriko may perceive the landscape as empty, but given the uncertainty of both figures as performers or actors from distant lands, they are unable to overwrite it through colonisation. Both Umiumare and Yap were presented as displaced spectral bodies moving over the landscape.

11   Duets by Umiumare and Yap: *How Could You Even Begin to Understand?* (1996–2007), *In-Compatibility* (2003) and *Zero Zero* (2010–14)

From 1996 through to 2014, Yap and Umiumare worked on a number of what they described as an evolving "devotional" series, initially based on the "philosophical principle of yin and yang"—the mutually interacting "oppositional elements" that create cycles of dynamic chaos and which give way to balanced "harmony" in Chinese philosophy (Yap et al. nd). These yin-yang interactions provide the "possibility for spiritual transformation" (ibid.). Through embodying this concept in performance, Umiumare and Yap hoped to stage a new type of "expression of Asian identity" (ibid.). Having been pigeonholed as an "Asian" performer following the winding up of IRAA s interpretations of Ancient Greek classics, Yap decided to adopt the Asian label being projected onto him, but on his own terms. "For a long time I wanted to work on non-Asian performance", he reflected. "Now I want to bring things back" (Eckersall 2000: 149). The choice of yin-yang theory was moreover significant as it is both something of a "cliché of Asian culture" and yet its details remain opaque and nearly impossible to rationally decode. Critic Hilary Crampton claimed of Yap's and Umiumare's work that in "exploring mysticism and the spiritual dimension so appealing and so unattainable to Western eyes, their performances have journeyed to a place" which "we", as white audiences, "can never find" (2019: 4). In this view, the bodies of Asian subjects "from Malaysia and Japan respectively" were placed as beyond rational comprehension (4); a subjectivity which could only be approached by the outsider through sympathetic kinaesthesia—a concept which resonated with de Quincey's use of Body Weather in the Australian desert—hence the production's ironic title *How Could You Even Begin To Understand?* Within the performance, yin-yang philosophy was translated into a staging of Asianness which was difficult to read as unambiguously Asian, because these are metaphysical concepts, beyond any signification, Asian or otherwise. The performed identities exceeded understanding, and hence emerged as dynamic, shifting and unstable. Such a modality echoed the core aesthetics of much Japanese butoh.

How Could You Even Begin To Understand? (1996–2007; hereafter *HCYEBTU?*) was followed by the closely related *Zero Zero* (2010–14; Figure 10), in which Umiumare and Yap explored the act of attempting to reach a "zero state", or condition of complete emptiness in a Buddhist sense, thereby moving into "liminal spaces between the visible and invisible" (Papas nd). Umiumare and Yap performed both of these series as the company "-", meaning the space in between, or ma.[26] As such, the "emptiness" they were striving for, if attained,

---

26   See "Maro & Dairakudakan" in chapter five.

FIGURE 10   Tony Yap (left) and Yumi Umiumare (right) in *Zero Zero* (2010)
COURTESY OF YAP

could paradoxically lead to a state of totalising fullness, a oneness with that which surrounded the human. These performances were structured around attempts to go beyond individual subjectivity precisely by exploring the differences and distinctions between two performative subjectivities and what surrounded them on stage. The depth of this relationship between Yap and Umiumare was proven in an incident in 2001 when they were performing the piece as an outdoor durational performance at Mount Arapiles, outside of Melbourne. The two gradually moved towards and then past each other along a trail of hessian sacks. Umiumare was overcome with emotion as she crossed one, which she later discovered was where Yap had been crying some hours before (Marshall 2001a).

Umiumare explained that *HCYEBTU?* generally began with a focusing exercise in which the two sat facing each other, holding incense between them. It made the performance:

> ancestorial ... like going to the temple [or a] ... shrine ... sometimes we focus on a friend who died ... we've lost a lot of friends in the last few

years ... So ... we ... dedicate [the performance] to the dead; dead but they're not separated from us. We are still living with them.
UMIUMARE AND ECKERSALL 2012

In the program notes, Umiumare was more explicit, recounting a trip to the Tōhoku temple complex of Osorezan:

for me, dance/theatre/performance is a ritual in itself. It creates a gateway for performer and audience, to move from the ordinary to the extraordinary. Conducting rituals together, we sometimes successfully transform or even provoke an altered state of consciousness.
UMIUMARE 2014: 12

Like Maro, Umiumare sought to activate such "shocks" or "cracks" in banal movements such as cleaning her teeth—an action which featured in *Zero Zero* (Umiumare 2009). From out of this mundanity, Umiumare claimed to have found herself "channelling the memory of a blind shaman" or an itako from Osorezan (Umiumare 2014: 12). Butoh is not a religious form per se, but the dead and themes of possession are always close by during butoh performances. In *Zero Zero*, Yap adopted one of his characteristic foetal positions, evoking the yin-yang cycles of death and rebirth which animated the psychocorporeal dialectic of the performance.

Umiumare and Yap performed over thirty versions of these pieces, in galleries, churches, outdoor locations and performing arts venues, across Australia, Malaysia, Japan and elsewhere. Spatially, most functioned according to a polar, linear logic, with the dancers sometimes beginning right and left of each other in the wings (*Zero Zero* and some performances of *HCYEBTU?*), or directly in front of each other (*HCYEBTU?*), and then gradually processing away or towards each other, with intermediate swirling sections and solos delivered simultaneously or while one dancer remained largely quiescent. Performances generally ended when either the pair had come together—prone, with palms of the feet joined, as in *Zero Zero*—or had swapped places. This was in a sense another answer to the riddle of *Kagome*: "Who is in front of behind?" It is in fact one's other self, or in Hijikata's sense, the sister who lurked within his own body and who made him sit up by falling down (Viala and Masson-Sékiné 1986: 77), who turns out to be "in front of behind". *HCYEBTU?* and *Zero Zero* functioned as structured improvisations, though the latter was more closely choreographed and with a more composed mise en scène. *Zero Zero* featured a bowl of water which Umiumare crouched over at the beginning, and a swinging light globe under which the audience found Yap. A third variant on these pieces was performed as *In-Compatibility* (2003) with three additional dancers.

In all of these works, Yap channelled characters, emotions and expressive tones, producing a hard body of strained musculature. Eckersall states that Yap's:

> body assumes the ... [trance] dance form ... with such strength and concentration that it seems to explode—eyes popping, every tendon visibly pumped, even the act of standing motionless makes his body perspire profusely.
> 2000: 148

Yap's embodiment echoed that of Suzuki's injunction that the performer be like a jet plane, about to take off, but with the brakes on (Carruthers 1993: 184)[27]— but in Yap's case, this repressed energy visibly agitated the body power, whilst Suzuki's actors hold it in reserve. Umiumare, though quite frenetic in parts, presented a comparatively soft-bodied performance. Whereas Yap was intense and serious, Umiumare tended to be gamin and playful. While Umiumare offered a multidirectional twisting and curling of limbs in on themselves, Yap fell to the ground to lie there, spasmodically arching his back, "twisting and crying out in turbulent dreams" of possession (Alison Croggon ctd on Papas nd.). Yap then:

> rises on the balls of his feet in a delicate, ritualised walk, hands tilted upward, watching his arms as pulses of life tremble through them. Sometimes he twists inhumanly, fingers spasmed.
> DAWKINS 2014: 12

These gestures wove sweeping cycles and rippling patterns about his torso. At one performance I attended, Umiumare stopped to recline on a spectator's lap, and at several other times she abruptly ceased to move so as to smile or stare about the space. In *Zero Zero*, Umiumare also included quotidian gestures of awakening, first carrying a glowing digital clock and then brushing her teeth until this gesture morphed into a "controlled frenzy of shoulder-tensing, near-robotic movement" (Dawkins 2014: 12). Later, as Yap's movement became more intense, she "moves like a crazed praying mantis, arms paddling the

---

27 See "Suzuki Tadashi in Japan & Australia" in chapter seven.

air; then caught in some invisible wind she begins to saw and flail" (ibid. 12). Although the pair came close together and sometimes embraced, they did not seem fully aware of each other. They were present but absent, interacting but apart, tense yet supple.

It was above all twinned antitheses which characterised all these works (Figure 10). Critics identified a combination of "quiet composure" with "frenzied ecstasy" (Hillary Crampton, qtd on Yap et al. nd), as Yap seemed to "both absorb spiritual forces" and to be controlled by them (Dawkins 2014: 12). Alternating impulses moving across the dancers' bodies rendered them—in classic butoh fashion—"puppet-like" (Lynne Lancaster, qtd on Yap et al. nd). *HCYEBTU?* and *Zero Zero* represent the pinnacle of Umiumare's and Yap's projects, and although the dancers continue to regularly work together, the intense focus on a dialectics of exchange is no longer such a feature of their work. The projects drew on butoh and other forms to categorically stage the complexity of Asian and diasporic subjectivities. Gone was the image of "crazy Japanese" against which Dairakudakan has sometimes been read, replaced with something more subtle but no less intense. Umiumare would however return to a blend of historical and contemporary popular Japanese culture in her ongoing series of character dances.

12   Umiumare's *Fleeting Moments* (1998)

Fleeting Moments was Umiumare's first full-length choreography. She stated that after living in Australia, she was "a bit nostalgic, thinking about" the "old world" of Japan (Umiumare and Eckersall 2012). Umiumare had been performing to classical Japanese music, and these butoh performances had often been read as a representative of classical Japanese culture. Gina Lewis, a poet helping to promote Odamura, introduced Umiumare to the writings of Lady Sarashina and Izumi Shikibu, two women of the eleventh century Heian Court in Kyoto (Coslovich 1998). Their work had inspired Lewis' own composition "Flowered Lake". Umiumare admitted that while it might be something of a cliché, she wanted to revisit the "medieval … time of Japan" in which one might be "Very quietly reading [a] … poem, watching [the] moon, feeling the world, smell the cherry blossom … quiet, silence" (Umiumare and Eckersall 2012). Shaped by the Heian popularity of Zen aesthetics and philosophy at court, the poems reflected on the "transient nature of all things" (Eckersall 2000: 146). Drawing on these poems, Umiumare created a group of sequences she contrasted with more frantic moments representing life under modernity.

The piece began with dancer Sarah Potter dressed in a kimono poring over a book of Japanese script. Umiumare engaged her mother to make a film showing Umiumare's mother inscribing exquisite calligraphy, which was back projected. Potter was reading, seated on tatami mats, which served as the veranda of a Japanese house. Atop of the house rested Odamura, playing classicised Japanese folk music on a shamisen, and later koto. Odamura was accompanied by classically trained Western vocalist Deborah Kayser (who also sang in Yap's choreographies) and Rosanne Hunt on cello, performing compositions by Australians Anne Norman and Liza Lim, as well as by Japanese composer Takahashi Yūji. Santos entered to sit on the forestage with Potter, bathing her face. Yap began to walk behind them, left to right, and then back again, his focus introspective. Eckersall credited the opening choreography with a sense "controlled movements reminiscent of noh performance" but also offering:

> a pervasive atmosphere of playful sensuality ... a kind of focused meditation on loss punctured by moments of extreme physicality ... languid movement and glorious kimono costumes.
> 2000: 147

After a duet between Yap and Umiumare, Umiumare, Santos and Potter retrieved three ornate kimonos and started to fondle and play with them. They turned about in the gowns and peered over them in a slow game of peek-a-boo in a childlike fashion not unlike Umiumare's performance in *Kagome*. This was replaced by a depiction of modern freneticism, in which the three female dancers were attired in vinyl miniskirts and 1960s style wigs. They attempted to answer their mobile phones, play leap-frog, or enact high energy acts, which spilled into the audience. Although not entirely successful as a production, these moments of excess and audience interaction would provide a model for Umiumare's later butoh cabaret works. *Fleeting Moments* ended with what Eckersall described as an "imaginary return to ... [a] place of contemplation" or in the words of Sarashina quoted in the program, "I yearn for a tranquil moment, to be out upon the sea of harmony" (in Eckersall 2000: 147).

As a performance of nostalgia, *Fleeting Moments* was purgative for Umiumare. Following this production, Umiumare's work was to become explicitly diasporic, mixed and contemporary—rather than classically "Japanese", let alone historicist per se. As Eckersall observes, the advance of international modernism as a whole was characterised by a sense of "vanishing" and a poetics of the "fleeting" (Eckersall 2000: 147). The high energetics of the second half of the performance suggested that memories of a once tranquil Japanese condition constituted an alluring "phantasm"; another attempt under modernism to imagine ancestors. "Am I lost", Umiumare asked in the program, "in the rush of twentieth century modern life, here in Australia, far from Japan? All around me, moments, fleeting. Memory is not perfect, it can only bring back images" (in Eckersall 2000: 146–7). Like the Farewell Cult of Suzuki's *Chronicle of Macbeth*,[28] Umiumare attempted to bid, "Farewell to memory!"

Fleeting Moments was therefore a transitional work. Nearly all of the pieces Umiumare subsequently choreographed or directed have continued to feature explicit reference to Japanese identity. The playfulness of Dairakudakan remained present. Such explicit allusion to classical Japan and pre- or early modern markers of Japanese national identity such as the Heian court or Zen aesthetics have, however, became a less visible feature in her oeuvre, replaced with an energetic combination of historic and contemporary Japanese popular culture. Umiumare would increasingly *play with* Japanese identity, rather than *depict* it.

13 Yap's *Decay of the Angel* (1999)

Decay of the Angel was a solo dance performance which Yap performed under the direction of Rainsford from Chapel of Change. *How Could You Even Begin To Understand?* would later attract positive reviews and eventually tour, but in the late 1990s Yap was still disillusioned with his status as a relatively underground performer. Yap secured an award for his performance in *Decay of the Angel*, and this proved decisive in developing his profile and buoying him to continue dancing.

Rainsford and Yap took their initial inspiration from the novel *Decay of the Angel* (*Tennin Gosui*, 1971) by Mishima Yukio, an influential Japanese author of queer literature who knew Hijikata well. The text revolved around Honda Shigekuni's obsession with his boyhood friend Kiyoaki, whom he believed to be reincarnated as the sixteen-year-old orphan Yasunaga Tōru. The aging Honda adopted Tōru as his son, yet the young man turned the tables by humiliating Honda and breaking down the latter's sense of self. Yap and Rainsford developed these themes into a mediation on life, dying, and the loss of Yap's own father, or as they stated in the program: "Trapped inside a personal chamber

---

28 See "Suzuki Tadashi in Japan & Australia" in chapter seven.

FIGURE 11 Tony Yap in *Decay of the Angel* (Chapel of Change: 1999)
PHOTO: RAINSFORD (PAUL TOWNER). REPRODUCTION COURTESY OF YAP

in peculiar isolation an angel waits, the angel is in decay, and it is fascinatingly beautiful" (Rainsford nd). Echoing the philosophy of Hijikata and Ohno, Yap has since observed that:

> The body in this zone of trance [or performance] is illuminated with an aura … it also suggests a presence or something visual that is continuously morphing. What colours does an aura exude and how bright is it? Yukio Mishima in his final book, *The Decay of the Angel*, [drew] … from old Buddhist scriptures that there is … a diminishing aura [which] indicates an angel is beginning to die. This aura, this trans-illumination, must also have its link to life itself. In this sense, the aura [of one's dying] can be indicative of the force of life.
> 2021: 133–34

The piece was divided into three acts: one focussed on the "joys and pains" of family; one on the "challenges of flesh and … desire"; and one on the moments before death where "breath hovers between desperation and desire" (Rainsford nd). The aim was to dramatize a decay and fragmentation of both the subject as well as "of the dance itself".

Several features made *Decay of the Angel* one of Yap's most butoh inflected works. Aside from the inspiration of Mishima and the meditation on the powerful energetics of a near death state, there was a corporeal division and fragmentation. Yap's queer erotics also recalled butoh precedents. He was costumed for much of the performance in a bandage wrapped about his genitals, a convention used by Tanaka in the latter's early dances. Photographic documentation shows Yap in a pained foetal position, with white, flaking pigment on the skin like a mask across his face (Figure 11; this also recalls *Transition and Change,* 1984). Butoh and Mishima therefore allowed Yap to express a divided, oscillating sense of body and self, moving between states of pain and those of ecstatic fullness.

14   Conclusion

Love Suicides (1998) and *Miss Tanaka* (2001) provided an initial entrée to mainstage Australian theatre for Umiumare and Yap, with both performers being assigned dramatic speaking roles defined in large part by the racial-ethnic identity of the characters they were playing. Although not butoh in a conventional sense, Yap's and Umiumare's acting roles demonstrated what butoh-inflected performance offered to Australian drama more broadly. As we see in chapters seven and eight, this drive for a haunting, epic, neo-Expressionist theatre was a key factor in the spread of both Australian butoh and Suzuki technique within Australian theatre—the performers' "readiness to *move* into dance" which had been identified by Romeril (Romeril et al. 2001: 4).

Umiumare and Yap moved beyond their early character roles to emerge as collaborative authors of their own performances. Over this period, Yap was to develop a distinctive trance dance aesthetic. Umiumare too was to carve out an oeuvre as both a soloist and as a choreographer-director, wherein Japanese referents abounded within her productions. The work of both artists has something of a hysterical character. The fun, garish aesthetic of Maro was also to become a feature of much of Umiumare's work, as well as that of Zen Zen Zo and Frank.

The formal and conceptual mixing of the products of transmigration within the performer's body has come to define the model of butoh offered by Umiumare and Yap. *Sunrise at Midnight* (2001) and *How Could You Even Begin To Understand?* demonstrate how the *identity of the butoh performer*—searching for ancestors through dramatized acts of performance and possession—changes how the body interacts with the colonised landscapes of Australia and elsewhere. Umiumare and Yap repeatedly embodied figures dwelling within a haunted landscape, proximate to death, dramatizing the effects of history and memory upon corporeality and memory—key concerns of butoh as a whole, and which recur throughout the oeuvre of both artists. In these and other works, Umiumare and Yap remain restive multi-temporal spirits, retaining their difference and mystery for each other and for the contexts within which they move.

CHAPTER 6

Diasporic Austral-Asian Fusions 2: Yap's Trance Dance and Umiumare's Butoh Cabaret, Character Dances and First Nations Collaborations

1 Introduction

Yap and Umiumare navigate a line whereby their status as syncretic diasporic artists provides a crucial context for their works, which represent bodies and cultures in movement, acting within a space of layered, dialectic and mnemonic time. Both reflect butoh's nervous, hysterical traditions, in Umiumare's case through an increasingly over-the-top performance style by stunned and stunning beings, while Yap's possession dances exhibited the flutters, arcs and micro-seizures which wrack bodies or those who have otherwise taken on external influences.

Umiumare's work critiques as well as celebrates Japanese culture, blending early modern yōkai with radical ganguro chic to confuse and provoke audiences. Building on their open training workshops in Melbourne and Yap's practice with Mixed Company, Yap and Umiumare offer inclusive and diverse models for Australian butoh. Umiumare has collaborated with First Nations performers through her roles with the transcultural performance groups of Marrugeku (*Burning Daylight,* 2006–09) and Big hArt (*Ngapartji Ngapartji,* 2007–12), and has since moved on to explore her own relationship with Australian landscapes and Country through a series of ongoing in situ workshops, sometimes framed in terms of personal spiritual development ("coming to butoh workshop is cheaper than a psychotherapist"; Shiarz and Palmer 2021). Umiumare's discourse constructs these psychosocial aims as compatible with Dairakudakan director Maro Akaji's "ero guro" style (Umiumare and Eckersall 2012), or grotesquely kitsch, episodic theatre, Umiumare's performances featuring artists from diverse training backgrounds, non-dancers, as well as members of Osaka company Theatre Gumbo.

Yap's own collaborations have involved masters from entranced dance traditions practiced in Melaka, Malaysia and Indonesia, specifically Bantengan bull-trance possession, as well as the entranced Javan royal court dances of Bedoyo and Srimpi. Despite the growing depth of Yap's cultural practice, his physical performance style has remained relatively constant—though it has become more refined and lyrical, with the corporeal frenzy contained within a wistful demeanour. The eulogising tendency, visible in Yap's *Decay of the Angel* (1999), has become more pronounced, echoing both Yap's grounding in summoning up spirits of history and the deceased, as well as in his personal biography, having dedicated performances to the spirits of each of his parents (*Decay of the Angel*, 1999, *E1: Evocation of a Lost Boy*, 2004–05, *Rasa Sayang*, 2010 and *Srimpen Lost*, 2015), his collaborators (*Animal/God: The Great Square*, 2021) and to the spirits of sites and their histories (*Eulogy For the Living*, 2009–17; *Rasa Sayang*, 2010). In these performances, a state beyond human experience, close to Deleuze's construction of "becoming animal" (Yap 2021: 145), or of releasing the animal within the human, is often evoked.

Yap has convened the Movement And Performance Festival (MAP Fest) in Melaka and Melbourne since 2008, while Umiumare's has managed Melbourne's ButoHOUT! festival from 2017 onwards.

2 Butoh Cabaret and Hystericised Character Dances: Umiumare's *DasSHOKU* Series (1999–2015) and *EnTrance* (2009–12)

From 1999, Umiumare developed what she called "butoh cabaret", premiering *Tokyo DasSHOKU Girl* in 1999 and touring the piece until 2004. Elements from *Tokyo DasSHOKU Girl* were reworked in a subsequent show entitled *DasSHOKU Hora!!* (2005–06), and then a joint show with Theatre Gumbo entitled *DasSHOKU Cultivation!!* (2003) which was succeeded by *DasSHOKU Shake!!* (2012–15). Gumbo are an Osaka based company influenced by Lecoq clowning as well as taishū engeki, the Japanese genre of popular theatre.[1] If *Hora!!* was perhaps the most coherent piece in the series, *Shake!!* featured the most ornate and grotesque costumes of the series. Umiumare's solos in these pieces led to an invitation to participate in *The Burlesque Hour* (2004), produced by long-term collaborators, director Jackie Smith and performer-devisor Moira Finucane. Umiumare performed several of her *DasSHOKU* characters within *The Burlesque Hour,* itself a mixed bill which went through several iterations.

Slightly misleadingly, the Japanese term Umiumare employed here—"dasshoku suru"—means "to bleach", or to strip away coloration. Umiumare has characterised these works as "strip[ping] back the candy-coloured surface of Japanese culture" (Umiumare nd), revealing the madness behind the apparently "happy face of [Japanese] consumerism" (Baxter and Gallasch 2003: 8)

---

1 Zen Zen Zo were also influenced by Lecoq; see chapter eight.

and so thereby exploding "commonly held views of cultural stereo type—e.g. Japanese women as cute, polite and submissive" (Yano 2013: 170). Umiumare wanted to examine the "weird yet internally fragile quality of Kawaii (cute) Girls", and how such cultural tropes in globalised Japanese culture unite both "Love and Obsession. Cute and Creepy" (in Yano 2013: 169–170). The style of the *DasSHOKU* series is however less one of a reduction to hidden, essential features (stripping), but more an outward movement of energy and endlessly morphing, perverse related typologies. If culture and the body are "stripped" within these productions, what emerges are ever more numerous onion-like layers concealing monstrous yōkai-like types, which grow and proliferate to reveal a range of energetic, subterranean desires.

The capitalisation in the title *DasSHOKU* referenced the extremely popular performances of the Tokyo Shock Boys, who had toured the Adelaide Fringe and Melbourne Comedy Festival in 1994–1998. The Shock Boys consisted of five men performing "dangerous and crude stunts" such as "smashing fruit" on themselves, "setting off firecrackers" lodged in bodily orifices, and "putting a scorpion in their mouths" (VC nd). The Shock Boys offered mainstream Australian audiences their first entrée into Japanese shock television—one of a series of works internationally which tended to represent Japanese culture as a land of bizarre extremes. Umiumare was inspired to use this pun after her friend Anne Norman did the same for her 1988 collaboration with a trio of distinguished Japanese flautists under the title *Tokyo Shakuhachi Girls*. Umiumare had initially taken a "rather serious approach" with *Fleeting Moments*, but found "audiences really wanted a laugh" (TRU 2021). Melbourne's image as the comedy capital of Australia, where the international comedy festival had been staged every year since 1987, played a part in this decision. Umiumare built on the ultra-cool but manic modern Japanese characters she developed for the second half of *Fleeting Moments,* as well as her work with Dairakudakan at Shōgun nightclub and her knowledge of taishū engeki, to devise a radical burlesque.

Umiumare's various productions in this mode consisted of a series of episodes of compressed action, each focussed around a novel character. Sequences were short, Umiumare recalling that when she was working with Finucane, the latter would protest: "'Too long! Come and do [it in] three minutes!'" which Umiumare found quite unlike "the slow build you [often] find in butoh!" (Umiumare 2020). *DasSHOKU* s characters took the form of hystericized archetypes of Japanese culture and identity. Umiumare (nd) described the pieces as "homage[s] to the roots of butoh as an anarchic dangerous and at the same time beautiful dance form". The series constituted a raucous, in your face collision of Japanese popular culture references, shlock performance art, Japanese folk tales and yōkai. As Eckersall observed, at times it was "almost ... like a parody of" the dancer's own "experience of being an intercultural performer", with her playing a "butoh queen" who directed the other performers in over the top actions (Umiumare and Eckersall 2012).

One character central to the first *Tokyo DasSHOKU Girl* production was a cyborgian, fetish woman, with Umiumare dressed in black vinyl straps, boots and extendable inverted plastic funnels over her breasts—a dark and ridiculous version of Madonna's *Blond Ambition* tour persona, for which Madonna premiered her pointed cone bra, designed by Jean Paul Gautier, in Chiba, Japan, in 1990 (Hess 2020). While it is doubtful many in the audience were aware of the Chiba connection—neither myself nor anyone I spoke to at the performance at the time raised it in conversation or in later reviews—the demonstration by a Japanese-Australian dancer outdoing an American artist at outrageous couture was evident. Pulling out the concertina style tubes over her breasts to render herself as a phallic woman—a trope that recurred throughout Umiumare's works—the character both flirted with, and threatened, her audience. This piece combines catwalk performance, as found in Madonna's Blonde Ambition tour and her pretensions to high art couture, with the weird body morphing Japanese film *Testso II: The Bodyhammer* (1992)—a movie which purported to reveal the darkness within the average Japanese urban inhabitant (Brown 2010: 55–110).

The second production in the series was named *DasSHOKU Hora!!* (2005–06), from the word "hora!" meaning "look out!" It opened with Umiumare as a shadowy figure crouched on a shrine, her face hidden under a veil of unkept white hair which streamed over a cobweb-like white scrappy dress. This was a yamamba, a well-known Japanese yōkai, or demonic being of one kind or another. Precedents within butoh for allusions to yōkai include Hijikata's 1969 *Kamaitachi* photobook (Hosoe and Hijikata 2005), Yap's part in *Sunrise at Midnight* (2001), and Umiumare's role from Nadoya outdoor performance in the Melbourne International Festival, where Umiumare also menaced the audience whilst dressed in a garish shock wig (Nadoya 1993).

Yamamba are mountain crones, their skin tanned from living outdoors. Yamambas appear in one noh play named after them (Uchida nd), as well as Miyazaki Hayao's film *Spirited Away* (*Sen to Chihiro no Kamikakushi,* 2001). The term was also applied as an epithet by critics of the "ganguro", or "black face", fashion adopted by young women in Tokyo's Shibuya and Ikebukuro districts, 1998–2000 (Kinsella 2005: 144–5). Like the yamamba, Umiumare was a child of the mountains,[2] who celebrated the proximity of her work to Ainu identity. Speaking about the subsequent production in the series of *DasSHOKU Shake,* she noted that the "Japanese indigenous Ainu people consider [that] 'shaking the spirit'" which yōkai, butoh and natural disasters can effect "as simply 'thinking'", functioning as "a modern ritual for both calming and provoking the souls" (Fearn 2013: 37). Umiumare's harnessing of butoh to Ainu belief, yōkai horror stories and their so-called "ero guro" style representations in modern media (erotic grotesque nonsense; Silverberg 2009) echoes Hijikata's summoning of kamaitachi in his photobook, as well as on screen roles adopted by Hijikata and Maro in *Horrors of Malformed Men* (1969) and *Monday* (2000), respectively. The ganguro girl was a racially and ethnically transgressive figure, at once modern and primitive, Japanese and miscegenated. Yōkai as diffused through contemporary popular culture in the form of ganguro chic or butoh therefore represent outsider identities; bodies strategically deployed by butoh artists and young Japanese women against cultural and national norms. The status of the yamamba-cum-ganguro girl therefore parallels Umiumare's own status as a long-term immigrant in Australia, not yet fully integrated into her new context, but no longer entirely at ease in her homeland of Japan.

At the start of *DasSHOKU Hora!!* Umiumare revealed her tanned, twisted visage, before moving forward, hunched over, "all jerky limbs and electric tension", the near hysterical nervousness of the character's embodiment mounting (Bailey 2006: 7). The yamamba then laughed maniacally at the audience, before Umiumare fell backward and gave birth to two enthusiastic and idiotically bouncing hairy white-skinned men wearing fluffy white nappies, black shocks of hair covering their faces. The male characters were played "almost like twins", as Umiumare put it, by Matthew Crosby and Ben Rogan, butoh-Suzuki crossover artists who had previously worked with Umiumare in Yap's Mixed Company (Umiumare and Eckersall 2012).[3] Umiumare threw to each of these flapping, running figures a white laboratory technician's coat, as well as the anonymous black suits and white shirts of Japanese salarymen, which also recalled the costumes of Tanaka Min, Charlie Chaplin, or Alan Schacher's company of Gravity Feed.[4] The pair fell on the clothing, throwing it clumsily across their bodies, and layering all the items so that at first they were in suits with white tails protruding from underneath (Umiumare nd).

---

2 See "Umiumare: From Regional Japan to Urban Australia" in chapter five.
3 See "Mixed Company" in chapter five.
4 On Schacher, see "De Quincey's Urban & Industrial Site-specific Works" in chapter four.

Umiumare departed to return as a ganguro girl, in a short, green fluffy dress, tall suede platform boots, red patterned coat, dark facial make-up and white lipstick, topped by the yamamba's white wig (see the image on the cover of this book). She later removed her dress to reveal a sparkling bikini, though after flirting and showing off, quickly turned on the audience to ask, "Are you looking at my bum?" Ganguro girl opened by dancing a heightened samba with one her sons, and then danced semaphorically, making angled, repeated, stop-start gestures in the air, releasing her energy in nervous or robotic bursts. Ganguro girl's main performance consisted of an extended monologue, developed in part out of a similar confrontational passage offered by the less culturally specific Japanese party girl which Umiumare played in the earlier *Tokyo DasSHOKU Girl*. Deep with irony, and broken by interjections and questions directly addressed to the audience, ganguro-yamamba was nothing if not corporeally and dramaturgically divided. As Nikki Spunde claimed of the final piece in the *DasSHOKU* series: "The only consistent element is dissonance. Happiness is aggressive, sexuality is grotesque, pleasure is tainted and pain revelatory" (2012).

Umiumare as ganguro girl related several "disturbing anecdotes" drawn from Japanese news reports and urban myths—the folktales of today—such as a "young girl stumbling in on her father and her best friend" having sex in a Love Hotel as part of an enjokosai relationship of "casual ... teenage prostitution" involving sex with older, generally married men, "in exchange for brand name gifts" such as handbags, clothes, phones, watches, and money (Boucher 2009: 41–42). The dancer offered other tales about "a schoolteacher squashing a pupil to death because he wished to shut the gate on time" (Boucher 2009: 42), about "children injuring themselves climbing fences trying to get in to school because so much face is lost by not being on time" (Hadley 2011: 11), and of a girl who was "so upset" at being told she was fat that she "killed her best friend with a Stanley knife" (Umiumare nd). Here the subjects of frightening folktales from the past such as those collected by Lafcadio Hearn in *Kwaidan* (2006) were metamorphosed into the latest dark folktales and contemporary yōkai such as the ganguro girl, the female adult-child murderer, or the demented salaryman.

Umiumare's performance throughout was marked by dissonance and division. In her more yamamba moments, she controlled the narrative and threatened the audience. In her girlish characters, she seemed unable to take it all in, offering a rictus smile. She was "Wide-eyed and innocent one minute, jaded woman the next" (Boucher 2009: 40). Umiumare drew attention to the mediatised representation of these girls as "'moron black faces' (kbaka no ganguro)" of whom "taciturn specimens were filmed replying to probing questions from [Japanese TV] anchor men with the single monosyllable '..*eeeh*' ('I dunno..')"

(Kinsella 2005: 146). Ganguro girl's key defining interjection was "What The Fuck??!!!" Umiumare's own phrasing was double-edged, at once suggesting that the speaker did not care at all because it was simply outside of their existence, as in: "WTF", "Who cares", "Over it", and so on. The phrase also conveyed genuine outrage, directed at the audience. By presenting outwardly there was a suggestion that it was the mediatised scrutiny of individuals like the spectators themselves that drove Umiumare's characters to outrageous acts akin to earlier mediatised representations of yamambas and their like depicted in early modern illustrated scrolls and *Hyakki yagyō* or yōkai parades which had influenced Maro (Foster 2015).

Umiumare's next character in *DasSHOKU Hora!!* was the mujina described in Hearn's *Kwaidan* (2006: 51–54). The original story is distinctive in that it joins ancient yōkai such as the yamamba with more recently described ones like the mujina or nopperaboh,[5] who was said to haunt the urban fringes of early modern Tokyo. Mujina/nopperaboh's presence in both *Kwaidan* (originally published in 1904) and *DasSHOKU* shows that yōkai have not disappeared, but rather have metamorphosed into butoh like figures haunting public consciousness. Nopperaboh was not only terrifying because her face was featureless "like unto an egg" (Hearn 2006: 54)—but also because she was moving into our fashion-conscious world of consumption. Umiumare's nopperaboh was a contemporary of the ganguro girl and the schoolgirl prostitute whom Umiumare had played. The dancer depicted nopperaboh initially faceless, with a stocking obscuring her features, but in the act of drawing her features back on with modern make up, accompanied by that distinctive soundtrack to so many Japanese thrillers set in the countryside: summer cicadas. The performance therefore staged a conflation of times, locations and bodies whereby human imagination, terror and greed kept yōkai—and the butoh forms that assisted in their embodiment—present in our lives today.

Umiumare's selection of possible national types in the *DasHOKU* series included that more mundane, consumerist yōkai: the Hello Kitty fan. Umiumare appeared dressed in a red, prepubescent girl's dress, adorned with a love heart across her breast, knee high socks, and cat ears. Hello Kitty was created by illustrator Shimizu Yuko in 1974 as a tool for merchandising and by the 1990s had become an international icon of kawaii culture, which was expressed through accoutrements ranging from Hello Kitty products, to anything "girly", with frills, detailed decorations, pink or glitter, dolls and doll-like items or

---

5 Umiumare and Hearn (2006) call this figure a mujina, which refers to a shapeshifting animal. Nopperaboh by contrast refers to a faceless yōkai. Many (but not all) nopperaboh are mujina in a different guise.

behaviour, tiny, delicate objects, and so on (Mezur 2004: 77). In Umiumare's performance:

> child-like and excitable ... Hello Kitty skitters on to the stage ... She babbles incessantly in Japanese and squeals "Kawaii!" ... and "Sagoi ne!" (It's great) ... "It is fantastic. Delicious! Beautiful!".
> BOUCHER 2009: 42

Umiumare's Hello Kitty implored the audience to "Speak Englishhhhh!" while Crosby and Rogan went into frenzies, chanting "Hello Kitty!" In the end, however, Hello Kitty adopted an archetypal kawaii pout and frown to declare: "But I don't feel anything!" As with ganguro girl, the contradictions were important in showing how, as a butoh-yōkai, the Hello Kitty figure resisted reading. It remained unclear if the complaint of a lack of affect constituted a true aside which broke free of the rhetoric of consumerism and the monstrous performance thereof, or if this was the ultimate kawaii irony, a girl who manipulated the audience to sympathise with her because her childish dreams of kawaii and child-like authenticity cannot be realised.

If Kitty seemed at first like a subject sacrificed at the altar of male desire and capitalist exploitation, the gender politics were reversed in a scene where salaryman Crosby was given a birthday cake by a schoolgirl stripper which she then crafted into the shape of a Hello Kitty head on top of him. With the Kitty cake moulded across his face, salaryman moved bowed-legged, up and down, chanting in an entranced fashion "Kitty ... Kitty ... Hello Kitty!" before Umiumare, Rogan and even Crosby began to tear hunks out of his nominal Kitty cake-face and eat it, smearing cake everywhere. As salaryman's body was grotesquely consumed, Umiumare returned to her yamamba persona, blood running down her chin. It was Umiumare as schoolgirl stripper who effected this revenge upon the salaryman who desired her. Alluding to the clubs that Umiumare had performed in, the stripper appeared dressed in sailor garb. Umiumare ripped pantie after pantie from her loins and threw them to the increasingly demented man who watched her. The sheer number of panties offered was ridiculous. The schoolgirl then assisted salaryman-Crosby to release his penis, represented by a pink and white fluffy boa-like appendage, which she then removed to castrate him—although his beatified expression showed that the act was so extreme, so overwhelming, that it in fact conformed to his own hysterical desires.

In interviews regarding the *DasSHOKU* series, Umiumare confessed that while she found the act of immigrating from Japan to Australia "confusing", she concluded—in terms characteristic of butoh —"This confused state is mine, and that's quite powerful" (Boucher 2009: 44). In other words, Umiumare's transcultural experience of migration offered her privileged psychocorporeal insight into the confusion of contemporary global life. The *DasSHOKU* performances transferred this condition back onto the audience to create a "productive confusion for its spectators" (Boucher 2009: 41), akin to the "crack" in worlds or "shock" which guides Maro's technique.[6]

DasSHOKU Hora!! had a hysterical freneticism (Bailey 2006: 7). Acts were short and sharp, with frozen, hyper-extended smiles and grimaces. Energies repeatedly rose and exploded, as when the two men began reciting as if it were poetic dialogue the lyrics to the Tom Waits' song "Big in Japan" (1999), one first stating: "You've got the style", before the other replied: "But not the grace" and eventually fighting between each other over the consolation that: "But I'm big in Japan!" "No! I am big in Japan!" and so on, followed by a recording of Waits' himself. There was an overall nervous exuberance infused with concentrated bursts of characterisation, each scenario being accompanied by enervating musics. The men varied from over-stimulated to pathologically entranced, notably in another poetic duologue which they delivered to the audience about the yamamba coming down the mountain. The psychocorporeal states of the forced, the spasmodically over-extended, and the epileptically confused, all pervaded the work. As one audience member commented, the "monstrous is portrayed with such glee and exuberance that you can't help being infected" (Born Dancin' 2005). Umiumare's critique functioned—like much butoh—through a near hysterical oscillation generating sympathetic psychokinetic ambivalence in the audience, as with the spectator quoted above.

There were moreover many moments in the show which were just plain weird. Rogan and Crosby for example delightedly danced to the then popular Ricky Martin song "Livin' la Vida Loca" (1999) with their pants around their ankles. Crosby tended to play his role with precise ticks and sweeping, guttural gestures, resembling the walking special effect that was Hugo Weaving in the film of *The Matrix* (1999), while Rogan was at once more relaxed but with an angsty, tightly sprung feel. They called out "come, little girl" to entice their victims, and when Umiumare performed a quick costume change from yamamba to ganguro girl, they cried out in infantile loss, "Where's mummy?" (Boucher 2007). Although Umiumare's characters also reflected a hysterical sense of excess and corporeal energetics, the men were hysterical in a Freudian way, in that their sexuality was perverse, infantile and fixated. Their destruction, such as that Crosby endured, was ecstatic because it perversely but effectively moved

---

6 See "Maro & Dairakudakan" in chapter five.

them beyond puerile fixations into something so violent and all embracing that it erased the Crosby salaryman's corporeal identity. Indeed, this was the message of *DasSHOKU Hora!!*: extremes may both liberate and destroy.

In Umiumare's neo-taishū-engeki collaborations with Gumbo—*DasSHOKU Cultivation!!* (2003) and *DasSHOKU Shake!!* (2012–15)—she added to this repertoire various characters defined in part by their outrageous costumes. There was a pair of dancing shitheads, complete with a coil of turd atop the head of each, dressed in brown leotards, gyrating at their waists and winking at the audience. Matthew Crosby played "An extravagantly robed priest [who] preaches consumerism" (Spunde 2012). Salarymen played by Gumbo's performers lost control of their bodies, jerking about, stretched out in an almost epileptic pose, back arched over a chair. The salaryman's floppy cloth bowels were pulled out by Umiumare and used by another dancer as a skipping rope, as he exclaimed: "Oh! My intestines are rotten!" There was a pair of dancers holding massively oversized consumer fast-food props (an echo of *Buddha's Banquet*, 1992),[7] a kawaii mother who vomited at the smell of her unconvincing toy baby before spraying her face with air freshener. Most striking of all was a monstrously desirable woman adorned with multiple fake breasts which the other excited dancers—male and female—crawled after, attempting to suckle; a somewhat more literal realisation of the thematics offered in the duet Hijikata choreographed where two men suckled at tubes leading between their bodies (*Rose-Coloured Dance: À la maison de M. Civeçawa*, 1965). This led to each of Umiumare's performers finding a phallic symbol, be it a breast torn from the woman, or simply miming sex with a gigantic pole, the entire ensemble becoming both infantile and phallically endowed, leading to a chaotic, multi-pleasured orgy.

DasSHOKU Shake!! was inspired by Umiumare's trip back to Japan in the wake of the 2011 Fukushima earthquake, tsunami and nuclear reactor failure.[8] Umiumare took the audience on a hallucinatory journey to the "Land of Shakes". It was a "chaotic realm" in which the "tribulations and distractions of modern Japanese life" were represented via: "bizarre set pieces" (Spunde 2012). Helen Smith,[9] formerly of Zen Zen Zo, was also in the cast. As one critic observed, the performers were most impressive "when they shake from their core" such that "they seem almost inhuman" (Fearn 2013: 37). The yamamba,

---

7 See "Umiumare: From Regional Japan to Urban Australia" in chapter five.
8 In 1996, Umiumare had staged the solo *INORI-in-visible* (*In-Visible Prayer*), in which she re-enacted trying to phone her relatives during the 1995 Hanshin earthquake, and hiding under fragments of wood falling from the ceiling (Marshall 2000).
9 On Smith's work with Zen Zen Zo, see chapter eight.

played again by Umiumare, was more of a post-nuclear, cybernetic figure in *DasSHOKU Shake!!*, a spasming performer dancing to harsh electronic glitch funk who was dressed in strips of black foil with soft plastic spikes across her back. Versions of Hello Kitty, the schoolgirl stripper and ganguro girl also appeared, together with a spoof of Romeo and Juliet. Performances even included recreations of Franco-American artist Loïe Fuller's historic Serpentine Dance, which used coloured lights on moving fabric and whose own 1900 Paris venue had hosted a number of Japanese modern dance pioneers (Umiumare nd; Berg 1995: 147–156).[10]

DasSHOKU Shake!! was bookended by a scene in which another yamamba figure, Umiumare dressed in a crinkly gold foil dress and with long, stringy gold hair obscuring her face, entered bearing a mirror, in search of light. This echoed the mirror called "Yata no kagami" from Shinto mythology which had been used to lure the sun goddess Amaterasu out of the cave, where she had hidden herself, casting the world into darkness. Yata no kagami is part of the Japanese Imperial regalia. Umiumare returned with this glowing mirror at the conclusion of *DasSHOKU Shake!!*, dressed in a rough white dress, her head shaved, sweat and tears causing her mascara to run, twisting and turning while breathlessly echoing a voiceover recording which urged all present to "turn into light". "Here Comes the Sun" then played on the PA while the cast sobbed uncontrollably, and Umiumare was left standing, uncertain, centre stage. Despite the carnivalesque tone of *Shake!!*, the piece functioned as a complex burlesque ritual, "provoking the souls" partly in order to pay "homage to the departed" who entered this realm of light and disorder (Fearn 2013: 37).

Umiumare's later, less raucous collection of solo character works, *EnTrance* (2009–12) followed the same pattern of episodic character dances referencing Umiumare's earlier performances. The production arose out of a series of creative developments Umiumare conducted with Finucane (who was also dramaturg for *EnTrance* as a whole), Yap, Melbourne choreographer Lucy Guerin, and ex-Dairakudakan member Tanaka Mutsuko. Conceived as a self-portrait of sorts, the aim was to showcase the main influences upon Umiumare of modern dance (assisted by Guerin), butoh (Tanaka), trance dance (Yap), and cabaret (Finucane), though the overall production was Umiumare's conception. The piece was divided into five sequences, beginning with spoken word piece "Maze", followed by a classic modern dance study of alienation entitled "Cityscape", the quasi shamanistic "Cracked Mirror", the grotesquely comic "Punk

---

10   The Serpentine Dance was a special addition to a 2014 fundraiser, which also included Japanese clown dances performed wearing hyottoko and okame masks (crooked faced man and broad faced woman).

Medusa", a second meditative work of text and projection entitled "Tears", concluding with a return to butoh in "Shiro hebi" or "White snake".

As critic Jonathan Bollen explained, *EnTrance* began with Umiumare relating:

> watching dust particles wander in the sunlight and a dream ... of slicing off two finger tips and running outside to find them before they are eaten by her cat. The violence is softened by reflection; the mood is calm and contemplative ["Maze"]. Then the performer is sideswiped by [an image of] a bus ["Cityscape"]. A mirrored cityscape of pedestrians and passing traffic ... She seems squashed by the images, trapped between their flatness.
> 2009: 10

Umiumare, attired in a stylish, short white dress, executed a series of rapid fire, staccato, spinning and twisting gestures, often pushing out with limbs extended before folding back in on herself (Umiumare nd). Guerin's typically clean, skeletally-based articulations were rendered somewhat more urgent and tremulous in Umiumare's butoh-inflected execution. For "Cracked Mirror" had Umiumare donned a flowing, black dress, offering a fluid, wild dance in which she repeatedly became caught in the fine string-tassel curtain hanging from the roof. She was transformed into a "dark, rat-like woman-creature scuttling through the drapes with gaping mouth and tortured movement" (Herbert 2009). She spun around, eyes rolling, arms held straight out, or her body bending rapidly down and up at the waist, which dropped her onto the floor, ready to eat the world (Umiumare nd). Umiumare then jumped to "Punk Medusa" where she held a video screen displaying an image of her head in front of her actual face, dressed in a short black dressed studded with white, pinprick lights, and flailed about gloriously. In "Tears" she posed in a plain white coat over which was wrapped a luscious red kimono and she held a bamboo parasol onto which Japanese characters fell like rain. Umiumare explained the different onomatopoeias of crying in Japanese, where different types of tears are designated by words which make a sound like that the body makes when producing these tears, riffing on her interest in signification which she explored in *Fleeting Moments* (1998).

EnTrance concluded with "Shiro hebi". White snakes are considered good portents in Japan, and at least one critic read Umiumare's embodiment as that of another yamamba or "sorceress" (McNeilly 2012: 5). As she explained, Umiumare ended with a piece which was truly "bare" and which therefore returned her to her "initial influences which was butoh" (O'Brien 2005a). The dancer stripped naked and spattered flour upon herself as make up. The performance was a virtuosic execution of the Dairakudakan style: eyes nearly closed, arms coiling up, out and in-front in a series of complex interweavings. Umiumare grimaced as she moved rapidly back and forth, before breaking off to pull the tasselled curtain down altogether, arching her spine backwards and forwards, and then backing out of a doorway streaming light. "Shiro hebi" was performed to a pulsing electronic soundtrack of beats, digeridoo, and squealing distorted bird sounds. Also projected during *EnTrance* was video of Umiumare floating on the surface of an Australian river, originally filmed for the short installation and meditation on death, *Sakasama* (2007). Umiumare had become a mysterious yōkai herself, a white snake traversing the Australian countryside. She was to turn to the landscape again soon.[11]

3 Umiumare's First Nations Collaborations: Marrugeku's *Burning Daylight* (2006–09) and Big hArt's *Ngapartji Ngapartji* (2007–12)

Umiumare's performance of a Japanese woman living in Broome during the early twentieth century for Romeril's *Miss Tanaka* (2001)[12] made her the ideal choice to play a similar character in *Burning Daylight* (2006–09) staged by the intercultural dance theatre company Marrugeku. Trevor Jamieson performed in *Burning Daylight*, and Umiumare played another Japanese character alongside Jamieson in the Big hArt productions *Ngapartji Ngapartji* (2007–12), *Namatjira* (2009) and *Hipbone Sicking Out* (2013–14), with Umiumare collaborating on the choreography in all cases. In these productions, Umiumare worked directly with Australian First Nations artists and communities. Although her function was framed largely by her Japanese origins, these were all culturally syncretic works. They demonstrated again that in the practice of Umiumare and others, butoh has been deployed to both destabilise and expand definitions of Australian national identity, in part through a negotiation with those issues of place and Indigenous ownership which have vexed Australia since British settlement.

Marrugeku's first production had portrayed the mimih spirits of far northern Australia in collaboration between the then newly formed Marrugeku

---

11   Umiumare continued these precedents to stage a number of other character dances and performative events themed around tea and the founder of kabuki, dancer Okuni, namely *Pop-Up Tearoom* (2015–19), *Tea Break* (2017) and *Buried Teabowl: Okuni* (2022).
12   See "Umiumare & Yap in *Love Suicides, Miss Tanaka & Meat Party*" in chapter five.

company and its parent organisation Stalker.[13] The latter was an interdisciplinary acrodance ensemble. Although neither Stalker nor Marrugeku employed the techniques of butoh or Suzuki in a systematic way, these ideas informed the artists' practice, with Marrugeku co-director Rachael Swain having "sampled everything from Body Weather to Suzuki technique to Lecoq work" (Gough 2021: 336). Swain first encountered Body Weather in the country of her birth, Aotearoa / New Zealand, before taking Suzuki classes led by Nigel Kellaway of the Sydney Front.[14] At one time or another members of Stalker and Marrugeku also trained or worked with Tess de Quincey, Peter Snow and Frank Van de Ven (Swain and Eckersall 2012; Gough 2021: 336; Swain 2024).[15] Kellaway directed Stalker's second production (Gough 2021: 358), while Katia Molino, an actor in the 1992 Playbox Suzuki production, performed with Stalker and Marrugeku before joining Not Yet It's Difficult (Swain 2021: 33).[16] Adam Broinowski was also with Stalker, before moving to Japan to work with Tanaka and post-butoh company Gekidan Kaitaisha.

Burning Daylight was a landmark work for Marrugeku, signalling new directions for the company. After staging *Mimi* (1996), Marrugeku became based in Broome, producing a solo work for co-director Dalisa Pigram (*Crying Baby*, premiered in 2001) and later a portrait of Broome itself with *Burning Daylight* (premiered 2006). *Burning Daylight* was themed around how to represent regional cross-racial identity in Australia. The production was also the first of a series of global collaborations from the company, with Marrugeku's artists working with a choreographer who practiced within European dance theatre as well as within an explicitly (post)colonial context. This was Serge Aimé Coulibaly, from France's former African colony of Burkina Faso, and who was a regular collaborator with Belgium's Ballets C de la B, a company Swain and others identifies as having arisen out of "extension of post-war German *Tanztheater*" (Swain 2020: 75–83) which had also been a key influence on butoh.

---

13   On mimih, see also "Lake Mungo Performance Works & on to Alice Springs" in chapter three.
14   As a young artist, Swain participated in a two week masterclass with Tony Burns (who had studied with Tanaka) and Bert van Dijk (who studied with Burns), before doing some of de Quincey's workshops in Sydney. Stalker shared a venue with the Sydney Front, Gravity Feed, Legs on the Wall, and others, and the companies would often train together, including in SMAT. Stalker also toured with Russian butoh company Derevo, and through them, were invited to a private showing of Ohno Kazuo's *Admiring La Argentina* at his Yokohama studio (Swain 2024).
15   On Body Weather in Australia, see chapters three and four.
16   See "The Australian Production of *Chronicle of Macbeth*" in chapter seven and "NYID's *The Dispossessed*" in chapter nine.

Coulibaly and Marrugeku co-director Rachael Swain devised *Burning Daylight* in association with the cast.

Burning Daylight consisted of a series of episodes occurring around a Broome bar offering music, drinking and karaoke. The title comes from a local kriol term for wasting time. The pub was modelled on the Roebuck Bay Hotel, which lies in the old part of Broome referred to as "the Bronx", bordering the Asian section of Broome (Chinatown), as well as the former Anne St Native Welfare Reserve, which included both state run and private housing (Birdsall Jones 2013: 315–330). Dramatic tableaux involving three interracial romances featured, each of which had its own karaoke moment of a live song performed alongside a film made by Indigenous Australian film-maker Warwick Thornton. The films and other elements offered Broome as a setting for a "noodle Western" playing out within an "Asian Wild West" (Lo 2021: 95). Thornton was strongly influenced by Wisit Sasanatieng's *Tears of the Black Tiger* (2007) and the candy coloured Thai Westerns and action films which Sasanatieng evoked, as well as the *Something More* photographic series (1989) by Australian First Nations artist Tracy Moffatt, which had featured Moffatt dressed in a Chinese cheongsam in front of various menacing and enticing males of Aboriginal and Asian descent (Savage and Strongman 2002). Moffatt's series also influenced Swain's thinking. Alongside these videos were projections of "Old style film posters announcing films" to be screened at the Sun theatre in Broome's old Chinatown, which had originally been owned by the Yamasaki family. The three fictional film features were *Stir Fry, Troubled Waters,* and *Black Pearl.* Through a montage of image and text, they documented the history of Broome, the town's racist journalistic coverage of the couples depicted in these films, and their place in the ongoing stage narrative (Chandler 2009).

Kerrie Schaeffer summarises *Burning Daylight* as follows. The performance opened on a set representing a "pub hung with red lanterns and calligraphy screens for karaoke night". The bar had a pair of US saloon-style swinging wooden doors:

> It is crammed with bodies dancing, stumbling, drinking and singing. Two young men take over the karaoke machine. As they warble away a fight breaks out ... The bar lady breaks up the fight and expels the pugilists out from the bar and onto the street. Other bodies follow ... [they] head over to the bandstand, and pick up an electric guitar and African twin drums that are already there and begin to play. A group of .... five performers begin to dance a vernacular choreography made up of traditional Aboriginal, contemporary European, African dance and Asian martial arts forms. The free-flowing dance serves as an introduction to the dynamic

> and hybrid world of contemporary Broome. The party continues ... in mostly humorous, good spirits though there is a fractious edge.
>
> SCHAEFFER 2009: 64

A large four wheel drive arrived, and Jamieson as the stockman stepped out. His open shirt revealed his rippled chest, his belt was adorned with a large bright buckle, and he carried a whip which he first placed on the ground to dance around, before he cracked it in virtuosic displays of masculine grace and aggression. As Rosemary Sorensen put it, "Jamieson's character shrieked trouble, an embodiment of sensuality wrapped inside a body taught with desire" (2021: 87). Jamieson's arrival stirred the cast into action and to perform physicalised reveries, bringing memories, histories and ghosts into the dance.

The choreographic dramaturgy featured not just dances of memory occurring *within* the bodies of individual dancers, but memories enacted *between* dancers and characters, who performed alongside embodied ghosts from their past. Umiumare became a young Japanese woman clad in a kimono whom Jamieson wooed. A second black cowboy (played by Sermsah Bin Saad) entered. The two men duelled, Jamieson gunning down his rival. Umiumare's character was described in the program as a "geisha", but there was little in Umiumare's performance to indicate she was anything other than a charismatic Japanese woman. Umiumare's other characterisations moreover undermined any classification of the performer according to simple models. She later appeared as a geisha caricature, twirling a pair of folding fans but dressed in a short white bob wig, sunglasses and a bikini, a beauty queen's sash across her shoulder as she burlesqued so-called "geisha" gestures. She later returned dressed in the outfit of a Malay worker holding a Chinese-Malay style short sword with which she attacked Jamieson between tumbling and rolling in a style reminiscent of the Asia Pacific martial arts style Umiumare first encountered in *Miss Tanaka*—silat, to be specific—but not in the style of those better known Chinese or Japanese combat forms such as wushu, kung fu, karate, jujitsu, or the arts of the samurai and the ninja. Umiumare here crossed racial boundaries to perform both as Japanese and as mixed descent. As most of the cast climbed and clambered over the set, Umiumare came centre stage, wrapped in a fishing net, to blow bubbles over a menacing Jamieson. Indeed many of the interactions between characters took a competitive format, with Umiumare in her "geisha" persona facing off against Jamieson while their eyes locked. Both went into deep, sideways crouches, before bouncing back, and then performed an ambivalent tango—a dance long marked by both affection and combat. After Umiumare performed sections of an obon dance honouring the dead, *Burning Daylight* concluded with a scene set at Broome's Japanese graveyard, where

Jamieson laid ikebana-like cherry blossoms on the grave of Umiumare and that of the black cowboy he had gunned down.

Ultimately it was the dramaturgical weaving of Umiumare into these at once powerful and traumatic sequences that rendered her performance butoh-like, rather than any signature butoh gestures or poses. Although reflecting a darkness and violent histories, there was a pop-cultural irreverence not altogether unlike Dairakudakan's aesthetic, reflected in the colour-saturated advertisement for *Stir Fry*, starring Umiumare and Jamieson, bearing the text: "She was a caged bird in a foreign land. He was a lonesome cowboy. Could he set her free?"

Coulibaly and Swain had developed the choreography through tasking, where the dancers were asked to draw on their "memories, embodiment and family stories" so as to create "space for ... mixed race" and cross-cultural forms (Swain and Pigram 2021: 148). Dancers began by working on a "signature move" or "memory of tradition" which had been "entrusted" to them during their lifetimes. Improvising around these actions, their movements were transformed into transhistorical memories located across each dancer's body; choreographies from the past (memory, tradition, culture, history) which had been pitch-shifted into the present. This approach produced a different sense of embodiment in each of the dancers, despite some movements being shared—as where Pigram and her kin taught the Malay-Sumatran martial arts form of silat to the others. Marrugeku's ethos for *Burning Daylight* was therefore conceptually and politically similar to butoh. In both cases, ancestral memories fictional and real returned in altered forms to dramatize a latency or gap in historical and cultural experience, disrupting corporeal and dramaturgical continuity (Caruth 1991: 181–92; Marshall 2013: 60–85). Bodies performed that which could not be fully realised even when the source event had occurred. Racism is too inchoate and destructive, it hurts, baffles and lingers. Swain (2020: 82–83) has characterised much of Marrugeku's aesthetic as representing a form of "choreopolitical neo-expressionism" which reworks and repositions influences running from German tanztheater (Swain cites Mary Wigman), butoh and "Modernist expressionism". Elements and influences from these forms were here refashioned into an alliance with Australian transcultural and First Nations dance. Swain championed the "unsettled ... at-home/not-at-home-ness" which this diverse elements produced (2015: 506), a phrasing which has some degree of kinship with Hijikata's claim that butoh dancers perform on "faltering ... stammering" and "bowed legs" (2000: 78–79). Marrugeku's music involved conflicting antitheses too, with Indian Carnatic violin set against Australian Indigenous hip hop (Perth artist Dazastah), the bouncy Euro-Caribbean style of Manu

Chao, as well as the sound of cattle trucks and bar room chatter (Fargher 2021: 135).

Umiumare's work on *Burning Daylight* (2006–09) led to an invitation to contribute to Big hArt's almost coincident project *Ngapartji Ngapartji* (2007–12). Big hArt ran multifaceted community engagement projects, involving language preservation, intergenerational strengthening, as well as the promotion of Aboriginal values and histories. This project had already led to the 2002 production *Career Highlights of the Mamu* as well as several in-development showings of what was to become *Ngapartji Ngapartji*. These preliminary works featured Trevor Jamieson and Japanese-Australian actor Izawa Asako, who had performed opposite Umiumare in *Love Suicides* (1997).[17] Umiumare's involvement in the concluding production and tour of *Ngapartji Ngapartji* (2007–12) however enabled a more sustained use of choreography in the work, which was credited to Umiumare, with Jamieson's gestures as a performer now balanced by Umiumare's highly physical performance.

Ngapartji Ngapartji (2007–12) and *Career Highlights of the Mamu* (2002) both dealt with the ongoing consequences of colonisation and the testing of atomic weapons on Aboriginal lands, 1956–63, in the region known as Maralinga. Both works drew parallels between the intergenerational trauma of the Spinifex peoples of the Australian interior (Anangu, Pitjantjatjara and Yankunytjatjara language groups), and Japanese subjects who survived the 1945 bombing of Hiroshima. Jamieson's history of dispossession was both typical and exceptional. Typical in that he was part of a diasporic lineage which has lived in many locations across the Australian desert, and whose peoples' physical remains were stolen by whites so that they might conduct dubious, racially biased medical studies. Exceptional in that these First Australians were directly subjected to nuclear assault—although as Helen Gilbert (2013) observes, it is the lands of First Nations peoples internationally which have been the preferred sites for uranium mining and testing, rather than the cities and homelands of colonising white populations. Jamieson's childhood was spent on Spinifex Country in what is known today as the Great Victoria Desert, located on the border of the states of South Australia and Western Australia. Jamieson's family often visited Ooldea soak for water, ceremony and relaxation, but were later encouraged to live on the nearby mission. The soak became a watering point first for cameleers servicing the transcontinental telegraph line leading through to Alice Springs[18] and then a railway station,

---

17 See "Umiumare & Yap in *Love Suicides*, *Miss Tanaka* & *Meat Party*" in chapter five.
18 See "Triple Alice" in chapter three.

both of which facilitated colonisation and land theft. Ooldea is also where the author of *The Passing of the Aborigines* (1938), Daisy Bates, lived and worked. As with the region about Alice Springs, Ooldea is therefore a site of considerable significance for Australian race relations, and its invocation in Jamieson's performance gave the piece a weight of which many audiences may not have been fully aware.

Jamieson's family were warned of the impending dangers that would come from the over six hundred nuclear devices detonated in the Maralinga region (Rankin 2012 passim). Jamieson's family moved 1400 kilometres to Cundeelee Mission (also written as Cundalee), 150 kilometres east of Kalgoorlie in Western Australia (Casey 2009: 125; Rankin 2012: 58–63, 69–73). The 1985 Australian Royal Commission showed that the British government administering the nuclear tests had been remiss not only in failing to protect the interests of white Australian servicemen involved in these actions, but had been even more cavalier and ignorant in their treatment of Spinifex and Pitjantjatjara peoples. The Spinifex peoples received compensation with which they built a road to their ancestral lands at Tjuntjuntjara (in Western Australia, halfway between Kalgoorlie and Ooldea), and Native Title to these lands was granted in 2000 (Casey 2009: 126–7; Stephenson 2007: 139)

Jamieson's Elders had met survivors from Hiroshima at an international anti-nuclear conference. The two groups were struck by "the commonality of their experience" (Stephenson 2007: 138). Jamieson's Elders insisted that he should travel to Hiroshima, which he did. In Jamieson's view, when the Elders went to yarn with the Japanese people, they primarily used non-verbal communication and empathy to interact. This was therefore an *embodied* interaction first and foremost. The survivor groups "'could see in each other's eyes" and in their "mannerisms, it was their body language … they didn't have to use much [spoken] language'" (ibid. 138). The trip was discussed in the play, and it led to a series of two-way kinship alliances. Reciprocal exchange is what the term "ngapartji ngapartji" means, or "I give you something, you give me something". As Jamieson stated in the play, Izawa and Umiumare each "come from Japan, we call her 'sister'" (Rankin 2012: 57), or as Jamieson clarified in an interview, his relations went on to adopt both women "into our family" and that "It's the same, vice versa. When I went there", as Hiroshima survivor Mr Fujimoto stated: "'Now I treat you like my son, this is your country'" (Stephenson 2007: 140). Video documentation of Jamieson's trip to Hiroshima was included in the production, showing Jamieson and Fujimoto retracing the steps Fujimoto took on the day of the attack. Fujimoto noted that a snake lived on the grounds of his old primary school, but after the school was razed, the snake was frightened away (Stephenson 2007: 139). Jamieson imagined a "huge snake" like the

Rainbow Serpent which his people believed kept the water flowing at Ooldea. His Elders believed that the bombs had poisoned the watercourse at Ooldea, driving the serpent away (ibid. 139). In these exchanges, Jamieson echoed de Quincey's version of Body Weather where here becomes there, or distant locations are collapsed together even as individuals attempt to dramatize geographic and cultural difference. The distinction in this case however is that it is a shared emotional intensity, psychocorporeal scaring and healing at two different sites of trauma that drew Australian First Nations experiences into a familial and empathetic exchange with distance. Setting Umiumare's butoh aesthetic in counterpoint with Jamieson's contemporary First Nation's choreography helped to dramatize and embody these relationships.

Ngapartji Ngapartji's mise en scène had some features in common with the installation aesthetic of early butoh and much contemporary performance across different genres. Jamieson performed stage left upon a curved set made of rusted metal such as one might find in an abandoned desert settlement, and the floor was covered with dark sand. This enabled the creation of sand designs in the mode of traditional Australian First Nations ceremony as well as allusions to Japanese sand gardens, as when Umiumare entered to mark out an Indigenous Australian sun pattern (Rankin 2012: 75). A pyramid of white ceramic bones lay piled upon the sand, and to the right sat Jamieson's relatives and Elders around a firepit, grinding the ceramics into white powder, which was later poured onto the stage and shared with the audience, representing the bodies and bones of both black and white children removed from local gravesites by British authorities to test radiation levels ("Australian scientists steal the bones of dead children during autopsy, white children, black children, without asking. They grind them into powder for analysis"; Rankin 2012: 57). Three screens rested above the stage for the projection of films and historical images, notably footage of Jamieson's trip to Hiroshima, other atomic tests, radiation poisoning, and "upbeat Movietone news footage" featuring statements about the purported "emptiness" of the Country around Maralinga (Bramwell 2002: 15).

Ngapartji Ngapartji opened with the sound of a shakuhachi off stage, before Jamieson introduced the audience to a women's choir of his relatives and Elders (Rankin 2012: 55). Staged in combination with Pitjantjatjara language classes for Indigenous and non-Indigenous subjects, the choir's first act was to lead spectators in the childhood mnemonic of "Head, shoulders, knees and toes", sung in Pitjantjatjara ("Kata, alipiri, muti, tjina"). This was accompanied by the usual gestures of bringing one's hands to the relevant part of the body as one sang. The performance served to identify the body as a locus for

FIGURE 12   Trevor Jamieson (left) and Yumi Umiumare (right) in *Ngapartji Ngapartji* (Belvoir Street Theatre: 2008)
PHOTO: HEIDRUN LÖHR. REPRODUCTION COURTESY OF LÖHR

experience, identity, language and memory, a theme which recurred throughout, with press materials stating that the project was structured according to the four pillars of Pitjantjatjara society: Anangu (body), Ngura (Country), Waltja (family) and Tjukurpa (law and culture; Casey 2009: 128). Although initially reassuring, the repetition of the song gradually transformed into a disturbing and Uncanny motif, not unlike the use of children's song in *Kagome* (1996), notably in a sequence where Fujimoto explained that just prior to the detonation of the bomb in Hiroshima, he listened to the sound of his granddaughter reciting "A nursery rhyme" (Rankin 2012: 64). The movements that had been performed with the song returned as signs of compulsive trauma in Umiumare. She danced after a voiceover related the character's experience of the bomb detonation. Umiumare became the daughter, reciting on stage "Head, shoulders, knees and toes" while the recording narrated there was "A flash of blue wind" and people were:

> Flattened, pushed to ground, houses sucked high, fall as shrapnel rain. I wipe my face, I … wipe my face off, lace skin dripping. Calling her. My daughter wanders, without lips, with no face, tongue burnt … People … Not people. Pumpkinheads, zombies …

> ... That day, sky dark at noon ... poisoned river [and] ... my poisoned daughter. Crying, I, drown her. And watch soldiers throw her body on a funeral pyre.[19]
>
> RANKIN 2012: 65–67

Throughout this, Jamieson was on stage, "Listening intently". Umiumare squatted and leaned to one side, starring out, lost in the fog of memory (Figure 12). She held her left hand to her forehead and across her glazed-over eyes, with her right hand grasping her left forearm, as though to steady it. Jamieson sat squatting behind and to her left, holding both hands to his head, as in the children's song, and peeking out from under his fingers to watch Umiumare. Later Umiumare crossed the stage *"rolling slowly across the floor as if by a huge force in Hiroshima ... or like spinifex across the Australian desert. She rolls into* TREVOR *and they both roll off"* (Rankin 2012: 90).

As Gilbert (2013: 207) observes, the choreography literally enacted "the ethics of the play: *Ngapartji Ngapartji*", here translated into a butoh-esque dialogue. Jamieson placed "his own body around hers in a protective embrace" (ibid.: 207), at once shielding her and helping to heal himself. Umiumare danced also when Jamieson narrated a burlesque history of the invention of the atomic bomb, in which he noted that in the "nation you call America, Apple-pie young men are dying" (Rankin 2012: 63), and so the mothers there, like the mothers of the Spinifex people and those in Japan, seek to protect their children. American moms "Beckon big brained, pink skinned scientists, Hunkered down in bunker, in desert deep, till, An atom spat miracle secrets and split, An answer to mamma's prayers at president's feet" (Rankin 2012: 63). Here and elsewhere there was a transhistorical alignment of survivors, mothers, Indigenes, whites, Japanese, and different desert landscapes: New Mexico, where the first atomic bomb was developed, and Maralinga, where Britain's bombs were tested. Umiumare's movements were consistent with those of butoh, but rather than generating a new butoh-like aesthetic, the diverse strategies functioned to dramatize a dialectics of intersubjective relationships, internal traumas, and indeed of history itself, suggesting a transhistorical, transracial perspective. As Stephenson put it (2007: 137), the return of the Spinifex peoples was rendered "dialectically, through an encounter with another people"—the Japanese—"who have suffered atomic invasion". Therefore the Spinifex peoples' act of going back to Country now involved "incorporating outsiders" like Umiumare (ibid. 137), Izawa and Fujimoto via performance and empathetic exchange.

---

19 The script formats this as discontinuous, fractured poetry. For the purposes of quotation, I have simplified the punctuation and joined two discontinuous passages.

Umiumare found cultural parallels between working with First Nations individuals and her career in Japan. As noted above, the mise en scène of *Ngapartji Ngapartji* was designed to echo an Indigenous yarning session, with an imagined fire at its heart.[20] In *Burning Daylight* it was the dramaturgy, rather than the set itself which echoed the yarning exchanges. Adopting these modes, Umiumare claimed she found in both it was "like working with Asians", not least because whenever the artists and collaborators decided "let's talk" this also meant that they would gather for the sharing of food and nourishment (Umiumare and Eckersall 2012). Umiumare suggested moreover that she could almost see the landscape in the bodies of the Elders. She felt that the "gravity" of their bodies was "low … twenty metres" below the ground, tying them deeply into the land (Smith et al. 2017). More significant than any similarities between the choreographies of Aboriginal dance and those of butoh were these ways of being in the body. Umiumare was therefore able to "translate" these actions in some sense to the "Japanese body". Dropping her torso down in a hunch and stepping forward, Umiumare has reflected that "my grandmother walked this way" (A. Carroll 2014) and while the bodies of the Japanese peasantry and of First Australians were not the same, the two did have some degree of corporeal similitude which made for productive exchange.

In 2017, Umiumare followed up on these experiences to work on a series of butoh and Body Weather residential workshops in regional and outback Australia, first in the Wimmera and Yandoit (Victoria), then Broome and Roebourne (far north of Western Australia), as well as Alice Springs (Umiumare and Kondo 2020). Umiumare participated on these workshops with Anthony Pelchen—a regular collaborator in the productions of both Umiumare and Yap, who made one of the videos for *EnTrance* (2009–12)—as well as de Quincey's close peer Frank Van De Ven. Classes were conducted in lightly forested landscapes, rock fields and other terrains. Umiumare has concluded from these experiences that butoh in this context becomes a fundamentally spiritual practice, in which one feels out the "spirit of ancient land"—or lands, including both Australia and Japan—as well as the spirit of "nature" (Umiumare and Kondo 2020). She claims that as a result of these experiences, when she returns to Japan, she is aware of how her own gait is now more open and spatially expansive than it previously was (Umiumare et al. 2017). Bodies transmigrate, in form, dance, and in butoh itself. Even the Unheimlich subject can come home it would seem, if they accept the lessons of butoh in Australia.

---

20 On Indigenous yarning, see "Triple Alice" in chapter three.

4   Yap and Trance Dance; Umiumare and Jujutsu

Yap described his practice as "trance dance" as early as 2003 (Baxter and Gallasch 2003: 8), and he has also used the term "trance migration" to highlight how the entranced states which he adopts allowed him to commune with distant locales and temporal experiences. Trance then offers a different way to link distant spatial and affective conditions as compared to the work of Umiumare described above.

From 2002, Yap formally investigated his heritage of divinatory, therapeutic, and religious dances from the Asia Pacific, initially focussing on shen-possession rituals and mediumship, as mentioned in chapter five. By 2009 Yap had begun actively comparing his knowledge of these practices with other ritual and performance forms of the region. Yap has worked with the artist and cultural leader Mas Agus Riyanto from the East Javan city of Batu, where Riyanto revived the Bantengan bull-trance festival in 2008. In 2013, Yap explored Javan royal court dances of the Bedoyo and Srimpi styles, which although delicate, also involve a willed dissociative state in order to harness choreographic forms motivated by a possessing deity or spirit. In 2021, Yap completed a doctoral thesis investigating these choreographies. Yap's current methodology constitutes a refinement and clarification of the Dionysiac approaches which he has been harnessing since his early work with IRAA. While Yap's earlier productions were, as previously noted, generally intense, the depth of his psychocorporeal skills today means that the work is often lyrical and soft, with surprising small flicks and waves which arc through a still powerfully stimulated corporeal form. In addition to shaping Yap's methodology, these investigations led to a suite of collaborative works involving the master performers of Bedoyo and Srimpi, namely Ibu Kadar (a.k.a. R. Ay Sri Kadarjati Ywandjana) and Agung Gunawan, as well as Riyanto. These works include *Srimpen Lost* (2013), *Kesupen,* (2015), *Shadow's Light* (2018–21), as well as events in the MAP Festival. As with Mixed Company works, Yap often performs in parallel with his collaborators, each offering distinctive embodiments. The productions are in this sense akin to the Odin Teatret's laboratory works. The choreographic dramaturgy, while organised into sections, tends to be various and empathetic, rather than unified.

As in the ritual performances he has studied, Yap frequently employed sensorial stimuli to aid going into trance, or to move from an initial preparatory state into a deeper one. Methods included incense, evaporative oils, droning music as well as sharp percussion. From 2002, Yap developed a long term collaboration with Melbourne sound artists and improvisers Madeleine Flynn and Tim Humphrey, who provided the soundscape for many of these productions. Humphrey's and Flynn's scores combined percussion akin to that commonly used in temples, together with amplified found sound, electronics, as well as Western instruments such as piano and flute. Their accompaniments have tended to be spare and subtle, providing a gently atonal bed punctuated by small sonic interruptions. In this sense, the music echoes and enhances the energetics of the body itself, making audible the constant thrum of power and vibration which Yap performs, as well as spikes and eruptions. From around this period Yap increasingly began to give voice to fragments of text in Malaysian, English, and other languages, derived either from the scripts and stories which each piece alluded to (the Japanese noh play *Atsumori*, for example), as well as exclamations appropriate to the deities, fictional characters, or historic entities coming into play.

Echoing the language of the modernist European dramaturgs James Gordon Craig, Heinrich Kleist and others (Marshall 2011a), the ethnographer Jane Belo has identified what she calls a "puppet complex" within Asia Pacific performance, or as Kathy Foley puts it: "Gods and demons descend to earth and, via trance, make 'puppets' of people" (Foley 1985: 37). Foley argues that this approach may be found not only throughout the geographical space of Indonesia, Malaysia and surrounding locales, but also within different styles of performance: "Puppet, mask, and trancer are alike in that each is an empty vessel waiting for the vital energy of the other to fill it. In trance this 'other' is a predetermined spirit summoned into the trancer" by a shaman or guide of some sort, while "in puppetry and masked drama it is a preset character brought to life" through the intercession of the overseer and the manipulator themselves (Foley 1985: 37; also Bourguignon 1995; Kartomi 1973).

Yap explains that in his own practice, in classic butoh mode, he begins by evacuating himself to drop into a supple state of physical and mental relaxation. He expels tensions and thoughts. He then gradually becomes aware of tremors which begin to fill him and so animate the body. "First there's a total relaxation; a kind of emptiness", he observes, "and then a shiver starts, like shaking" (O'Brien 2005b). Early physical expressions often include fluttering, quivering or stuttering movements. Yap describes this as coming from a "vibration" which can often be "quite high" in frequency as the body begins to flex. Yap tends at this point to rise and fall, sometimes in abrupt leaps. These movement are multidirectional, and so the body may fold in or across itself in contortions. These electric quivers often give way to brief moments of quietude, which act as plateaux or hiatuses within an increasingly frenetic launching of the body into different acts, tics, gestures, and verbalisations. Yap has described the movement as expressing pulsations which are "atonal, unknown, unbridled, exposing blockages, fears … abjection … [and] a touch of graceful compassion … [like] lines of poetry" (Yap et al. 2023). Trance dance may be seen in this sense as a type of "dream-work" which brings out that which flows through the subject from out of dreams, histories, affiliations, fantasies and terrors (O'Brien 2005b).

Rachel Fensham and Odette Kelada provide a useful description of the physical effects of trance in their account of Yap's 2004–05 production, *E1: Evocation of a Lost Boy*, which was based in part on the noh play *Atsumori*. Yap's later collaboration with Bedoyo/Srimpi master Ibu Kadar *Srimpen Lost* (2015) was to some degree a reworking of *E1: Evocation of a Lost Boy* but as a collaborative performance, focussing on the themes of being lost, of mourning a lost person (the character Atsumori, the lost boy of one's own past, or one's lost father or mother), and of meditation (Yap 2021: 53). In *E1: Evocation of a Lost Boy*, Yap walked in an unassuming manner centre stage. Using supple, measured gestures, he divested himself of his glasses and his shirt:

> Delicate, sporadic finger actions draw attention to his hands. The energy continues into the arms and shoulders as if he is plugging into a current and now it is travelling through his body. He moves in a writhing action that combines flowing rhythms with stark abrupt movements. The transitions between poses are rife with short, fluttering muscle actions—constantly interrupted gestures. The frenzy of Yap's dance increases, momentum building as he leaps across the floor. Coming to his knees, his arms wrap around his torso—a cocoon gesturing loss. Hands over head, breathing as though crying, he wails. Falling on the floor repeatedly, Yap convulses in an epileptic-like fit—back arching and body in apparent pain transfixed by emotions and possessed by sensations, interpretations of which are abstract but evocative of language, loss, grief.
> FENSHAM AND KELADA 2012: 404

While the specific thematics of productions have varied greatly, as has Yap's mise en scène, the basic corporeal structure and energetics of the body described here has tended to recur in various iterations throughout.

Yap continues to collaborate with Riyanto on Bantengan bull-trance events at different locations. Here in addition to smoke, incense, horns, the chanting of the crowd, and other stimuli, Riyanto deploys a long, heavy whip which he cracks above participants. The banteng is a type of undomesticated cattle (*bos javanicus*), and whips are used to marshal both actual bulls and possessed individuals (Yap 2021: 61–62). Yap sees this possession ritual in the terms of Gilles Deleuze's model of "becoming animal" in that it is not a fully rendered, discrete bull spirit that comes inside the human to move it. Rather the ritual brings out the bullness located within the human itself (Yap 2021: 63–73, 147).

This is supported by Riyanto's insistence that before the banteng spirits had become bulls, they were the souls of ancestral humans who lived in Batu and surrounding districts (ibid. 68). The possession enacted within this ritual is, in this sense, a corporeal return, where something which is now more-than-human comes back into the body to show its accumulated ancestral and animistic strength. Bantengan performance exceeds the human, even as it occurs within a performer who remains recognisably human-yet-bull-like. Yap named his first Banteng study the *Minotaur Series* (2013).[21] Of his transhuman, minotaurian performance alongside Brendan O'Connor, Yap has written:

> Our necks softened, bodies limp and vision blurring, we were anesthetized … whilst a tremor built in the core. The body began to quiver, and at the crack of whips, we exploded in spasms with muscles clenched and quivering to unbridled sequences of movements. Banteng bull trancers leapt in the united frenzy. Brendan and I danced the beast as our Banteng group began its last kilometre of carnival stretch towards an arena at the finish. Sporadically the group would erupt in ecstatic delirium … Physically exhausted from our three-hour long bull trance … shamans … splashed water onto our faces, chanted mantras, and pressed and flicked our … foreheads, eventually taking us out of trance. We were in … a euphoric daze. The body no longer quivered and a softness returned with the exhaustion.
> 2021: 77

Yap recognised in this event a combination of apparently primal—or at least historic—cultural forces within a new found contemporeity. The ceremony constituted a revival of a lapsed form in the present. There was moreover a self conscious attempt on Yap's part to enhance his own cultural memory through psychocorporeal and spiritual interaction with other groups in the region. This was the start of a trance migration in which Yap himself served as a "bridge" joining choreographic and cultural expressions between the Asia Pacific and Australia (O'Brien 2005b). Yap has only rarely danced the Bantengan itself since—his focus has been on collaborative works with multiple artists of diverse traditions—but the force of the Bantengan was in a sense already familiar to him. To dance it helped to consolidate his own psychocorporeal heritage as well as allowing him to experience different types and levels

---

21   *Minotaure* (1933–39) was the name of the major Surrealist journal edited by André Breton. Bruce Baird describes a key work by Dairakudakan which features a minotaurian figure (2022: 2–10, 103–5).

of ecstatic involvement, including that of a frenzied minotaurian spirit. The simultaneous manipulation of such shifting energetics and phantom memories, combined with a willingness to give in to them, lies at the heart of both Yap's idiosyncratic practice and global butoh.

In Umiumare's case, it was not until 2022 that she publicly launched a related project nascent since her early collaborations with Yap on *How Could You Even Begin to Understand?* (1996–2007) and *Zero Zero* (2010–14).[22] Umiumare has named this the *Jujutsu Project* on "the Japanese notion of shamanism" (Umiumare nd). The title comes from Okamoto Tarō's famous dictum that "all art is magic (jujutsu)" (Umiumare 2023; Umiumare nd). Drawing on Marcel Mauss and others, Okamoto argues that magic functions as "a secret rite producing a transformation … often through" possession and, via possession, to enact a sacrifice of one's self or subjectivity to allow other things to become manifest (Winther-Tamaki 2011: 88; see also Okamoto 2009).

Umiumare has related that in 2010 she went to Melaka with Yap to witness shen possession and other practices (Umiumare and Eckersall 2012). After this they went to Japan's mountains where she was brought up, and then on to the "Buddhist temple[s] of Koyasan and Osorezan". Located south of Osaka and Nara (Maro's hometown), Mount Koya (in Japanese, Koyasan) was the centre for the development of the esoteric Buddhist tradition of Shingon Buddhism in which truth and enlightenment are seen as ineffable and hence to be accessed through tantric prayers or contemplation of edifices such as Koyasan's Okunoin cemetery. Mount Osore (Osorezan) is another group of shrines in Tōhoku. The site has inspired butoh work before. Hanaga Mitsutoshi produced a photographic series there with butoh dancer Iishi Mitsutaka in the 1970s (Viala and Masson-Sékiné 1988: 155–7). Osorezan lies on a sulphurous volcanic lake said to provide access to hell and to the deceased souls therein—especially those of children, who are protected by the deity Jizo (alluded to "Kagome Kagome").[23] Osorezan is famous as the gathering place for Tōhoku's itako, or female mediums, who enact possession rituals to make contact with the dead, particularly deceased children, so as to help put them at peace and relieve parents of guilt and anguish (Lakić Parać 2015; Eckersall 2016: 17–18). Itako are usually blind and manipulate ritual objects while praying in order to fall into ecstasy and speak as the deceased (Sasamori 1997: 85–96). Umiumare's visit to Osorezan represented the start of her own studies into Japanese mediumship.

In addition to the solo "Cracked Mirror" (choreographed by Yap) from Umiumare's mixed bill of *EnTrance* (2009–12), the main performance outcomes of

---

22 See chapter five: "Duets by Umiumare & Yap".
23 See "*Kagome*" in chapter five.

these explorations has been Umiumare's participation in MAP Festival events such as *Eulogy For the Living* (2009–17). Umiumare has also begun workshops with syncretic shamans and transhuman communicators inspired principally by American First Nations practices. Facilitators of the 2022–23 iterations included Tsuchiya Shia (a Japanese expatriate and "animal communicator" based in the USA), Hideki Hamada (a leader of Japan's "Eagle Tribe"), and Amara Kyoko (a channeler and practitioner of shamanic drumming who led participants in accessing their shamanic "power animal"; see Umiumare nd). Although Eckersall was rightly sceptical of naïve Westerner patrons to workshops and productions who choose to see in butoh a "'new age' quasi-mystical mode of operation" addressed to "the individual neurotic subject" rather than the broader, politically "dysfunctional social body" (1999: 44–45), it is clear that butoh has offered many individuals a space for self reflection ever since it arrived in Australia. Umiumare is today highly qualified to offer butoh as a form of psychocorporeal "counselling" whilst at the same time emphasising the form's radical aesthetic politics (TRU 2021). The first major performance outcome of this research, *In-Vocation* (2023), premiered at the time of writing.

5 Yap's *Eulogy for the Living* (2009–17), *Rasa Sayang* (2010), and *Liminal City* (2021–22)

Starting with *Decay of the Angel* (1999), Yap's oeuvre has become increasingly eulogistic. His dances are cross-temporal and often motivated by mourning, and by the joyous recall and movement forward which this can facilitate. *Eulogy for the Living* (2009–17) began as a choric work directed by Yap, initially featuring Umiumare, regular Tony Yap Company (TYC) members Ben Rogan, Adam Forbes, Brendan O'Connor and others. The media release states that it was inspired by the small "wooden tablets that hang in the Cheng Hoon Teng temple" in Melaka which "commemorate loved ones who have passed on" (Yap et al. nd). In the cosmology of Yap's birthplace, the dead are not absent, but proximate, and may be accessed via temples, monuments, stones, rituals and performances. As in all of Yap's trance works, the performance was directed both inward and outward, the choreography evoking "the fleeting transience of contemporary life. We the living both preserve the past and allow things to pass—we eulogise ourselves" and others "in each moment" (Yap et al. nd). The dancers walked in slow, ritualised lines, shoulders dropped, their bodies and faces relaxed, as they gazed "into the middle distance" (Power 2010). Gradually moments of turbulent chaos emerged in which each performer adopted their own, idiosyncratic ticks and entranced movements.

Eulogy for the Living premiered in the ruins of St Paul's Church, Melaka, the hub of the annual MAP Festival (discussed below; Hornblow 2009–22), before being presented in 2011 at the open space of the old Mining Exchange in the Australian regional city of Ballarat. These locations serve as foci for differing community recollections, rituals of memorialisation, and histories which linger into the present. Yap's methodology was not that of de Quincey's Body Weather,[24] yet both employed butoh for site-specific projects such that history, colonialism and race acted as subtextual disturbances within their performances.

While *Eulogy for the Living* focussed on mourning and the linking of the body to immaterial pasts summoned up by sites today, Yap's *Liminal City* (2021–22) was more impulsive, motivated by sensorial responses to landscapes more than specific conceptual or historical ones. Yap has described the dances as "psychogeographic" responses to the sites, a model which again recalled de Quincey—specifically her idea of a "dictionary of atmospheres" prompted by a site and which could serve as a choreographic score—as well as the post-Surrealist concept of psychogeography, or one's affective response to localised "psychic atmospheres" whereby "The imaginary is that which tends to become real" for the subject moving through the site (Debord 1955).[25] Yap's psychogeographic series began with ten short videos designed to explore what the media release described as the "hidden potency" of a "marginalised", banal or neglected sites within urban Melbourne, including back alleys, the docklands, steps leading up to Spencer Street station, and other locales (Yap et al. nd). Casually developed through improvisations with free guitarist Roger Alsop, the pieces often had a spritely aesthetic, with Yap leaping, bouncing, crouching, sitting or leaning across barriers and other features of the sites. Yap continued to post online improvisations throughout the lockdown period imposed in response to the Covid epidemic of 2021–22 and the film series has no projected end. Yap's improvisations have become increasingly lyrical, while the discontinuation of lockdown has meant that non-urban spaces feature more often. These short works offer no deep political or cultural engagement, but rather focus on bodily impulsiveness in the landscape.

---

24   See chapter three, particularly "Lake Mungo" and "Triple Alice".
25   Despite incautious use of the term by some artists, psychogeography has the precise meaning of "the study of the ... effects ... consciously or unconsciously [of a] ... geographical environment acting directly on [the subject's] affective behaviour ... [or a] science fiction" approach to the study of sites, landscapes, and our responses to them (Khatib 1958).

Rasa Sayang (2010) was a more complex eulogising work, a companion piece of sorts to *Decay of the Angel* (1999), in this case mourning Yap's mother rather than his father. "Sayang" was Yap's mother's first name, which translates as "love" in Malaysian. The title of the work comes from a popular folk song of the Asia Pacific region, the lyrics of which are:

> Rasa sayang ... rasa sayang sayang
> Eeee lihat dari jauh rasa sayang sayang
> Feel the love ... feel the love
> Look from afar feel the love.
> PAPAS ND

Often seen as a song of romantic attraction, the verbal refrain of feeling love from across a distance expressed Yap's own concept well. The set design was one of the most ornate to feature in Yap's oeuvre. It was conceived by Japanese-Australian sculptor Naomi Ota (who also designed Umiumare's *EnTrance*), and it situated the production's thematics geographically and culturally. The constructed forms referenced the indigenous megalithic monuments of the Malay peninsula known as "batu hidup" or "living stones". Standing stones, dolmens and capped tombs were erected throughout the area in prehistoric times and in some places the practice continued to the early twentieth century. Stones were said to be alive, containing spirits, often those of the ancestors, and so grew when appropriate rituals were maintained (Taha and Osman 1982; Jusoh et al. 2018). Critics described Ota's renditions in corporeal terms, as "pillars wrapped in cocoons of white webbing, strange sculptures that erupt from the ground like sun-bleached bones" about which were scattered "shards of plaster" making up shattered "stark mosaics on the floor", here evoking other archaeological traditions, such as Greek and Roman mosaics in Europe, and which Yap arranged as the performance proceeded (Vincent 2010). The audience was invited to wander amongst the installation before and after the performance (Yap et al. nd). John Bailey (2010: 29) noted that although the dancer "seemed to work through memories of Yap's mother and the intimacy of memory, regret and grief", there was insufficient narrative detail for it to function as an "autobiographical work" per se. Rather Yap offered a more abstracted sense of "precisely controlled expression that channelled great emotions" and their psychocorporeal power "into tiny gestures". As Jordan Vincent put it (2010), Yap seems to "transform into a man possessed by evil spirits" whereby his body became a "battleground" which "vibrates with tension and emotion: joy, grief, alienation". Yap was "exorcising demons and cleansing the spirit".

6 A Trance Dance Masterpiece: Yap's *Animal/God: The Great Square* (2021)

The culmination of Yap's exploration of trance dance so far has been the solo *Animal/God: The Great Square* (2021). The piece was originally designed as a live performance for the examiners of Yap's doctorate, but due to Covid restrictions, Yap drew on his extensive experience in dance film (dating back to *Sunrise at Midnight,* 2001) to transform the production into a short recorded piece. It has since been offered live at the Australasian Drama and performance Studies Association Conference (ADSA, 2022) and elsewhere. Yap's conception of the dance refers to the foundational writings of Daoist philosophy. Writing in the sixth century BC, Laozi used the term "the Great Square" to describe how one should strive for knowledge of that which can neither be seen nor fully attained:

> The Great Square has no corners.
> The great vessel is late in completion.
> The great music is imperceptible in sound.
> The great image has no form.
> The Dao [or the Way] is hidden and nameless.
> Yet it is only the Dao.
> That excels in giving and completing everything.
>   YAP 2021: 141

In *Animal/God,* Yap strove to approach in his dance that which cannot in fact be comprehensively embodied or even endured. If someone were to host a powerful god as a totalising manifest presence, this would kill the medium and leave only a pained, dead body. Yap seeks a series of shifting states within his performances, or what the dancer calls "becoming animal / becoming god" (145), skipping between glancingly present intensities of body and spirit. In Deleuze's and Guattari's phrasing: "We believe in the existence of very special becomings", of "animal[s], traversing" the boundaries of what it is to be a human being, and hence "sweeping" the human "away" to leave a shimmering fullness (Deleuze and Guattari 2008: 261). Drawing on his more recent filiation with Bedoyo and Banteng trance dances, Yap here aimed to corporealize a spiritual state through a swooping, lyrical struggle with presence and the finite nature of life and the body. Unlike much of Yap's earliest work, *Animal/God* was not a dance of anguish or pain, but one of love and compassion ("love without condition", as he puts it). While it included the characteristic shakes and small leaps of Yap's previous works, there were more sympathetic ripples

FIGURE 13   Tony Yap in *Animal/God: The Great Square* (2021)
COURTESY OF YAP.

through the body than there were shattering quivers. At several key points the body was placed flat, directly opposite the camera, open, as Yap's hands reached out to us in gifting, before fists clenched about invisible poles as if wrenching open a threshold.

Developed in part through Yap's increasingly fine attunement to sonic stimuli as a gateway to altered consciousness and gestural response, the online version of *Animal/God* was performed to a track composed and played by his collaborator on *The Body and the Double Bass* (1998), the violinist Ezio Bosso. Yap notes that Bosso was "passionate … about the idea of trance states utilised in the improvisation of music and dance". Yap reflects:

> This piece of music, *Unconditioned: Following a Bird* is one of Ezio's final pieces before he died … In my state of trance I had a glimpse of a lost being [Bosso's spirit] taking the flight of a little bird for a guide out of darkness. I, too, followed that bird … *Unconditioned* pointed to a love without condition.
>
> 2021: 148

The sound of the video was recorded live rather than being dubbed. Shot in an aged, distressed venue, the space literally echoed with other voices as Yap began to move. He was haunted throughout, and he greeted these spirits with empathy. As Yap elsewhere noted, in the flow of performance he often feels as though he had died: "I am no longer me" as there is "a death of ego and … personality" leaving "nothing" (in Morelos 2004: 99).

The butoh subject, in Yap's interpretation, performs out of a state of "love without condition", closely related to the philosophy which drove Ohno

Kazuo, who, as the butoh author and photographer Nourit Masson-Sékiné has observed, always "seems so distraught when he speaks of so much wasted effort spent by millions of sperm, when … one egg only, will climb the podium for the gold medal in the procreation games", while the rest of the sperm die (in Marshall 2020a). Even conception is joined to death. For her part, Umiumare (2009) observed that in Buddhism, the realms of "Life and Death are described as two shores; one is 'the near shore' (the world of [suffering and of] the living), and the other is 'the far shore' (the world of after-death)" which lies beyond suffering. Butoh is an exploration of the crossings back and forth between these shores.[26] What is at stake here is not just the link between suffering and dance, but the association of life with death and joy. For Yap, as for Umiumare, it is by embodying these interminglings that one feels joy and so moves towards transfiguration.

7   Conclusion: Yap's MAP Fest (2008-Present) and Umiumare's ButohOUT! (2017-Present)

In 2008, Yap founded the Melaka Art and Performance Festival, or MAP Fest. This was the same year that Melaka was declared a UNESCO World Heritage site of both built history and living multicultural history. The hub of the festival was the ruined Dutch church of St Paul's, situated atop of a hill surrounded by historic Eurasian structures—a location that served as the seat of power for each succeeding government until recent times, from the Malay Sultanate to the Catholic Portuguese, the Protestant Dutch, the British, and finally the Malaysian state—the British having departed twelve years after the end of World War Two (Malaysian Dept. National Heritage 2008–11). Since then MAP Fest has often concluded with the "2-hour durational improvisation" *Eulogy For the Living* (2009–17; discussed above). Artist-scholar Cheryl Stock has characterised MAP Fest overall as "a summoning" and "an invocation", whereby the hill calls to the performers with "its spirits and stories of those who had walked upon it and those buried beneath it" (2015: 398–403). Where Hijikata developed his early works in the degraded and bombed out imperial ruins of postwar Tokyo, Yap convokes a gathering of nationally and racially diverse bodies open to different local spirits in the no less problematic ruins of empire and global capitalism left in Melaka some sixty years after the end of World War Two. MAP Fest provides a

---

26   Butoh in this formulation is counter to most Buddhist doctrines, since in Buddhism the aim is to strive for the state of satori (enlightenment) and nirvana which lies *beyond* suffering and rebirth.

space to dream and dance anew amongst the detritus of empires. This might be seen as a function of butoh more broadly, from Tess de Quincey's *The Stirring* (2007) to Francis Barbe's *Fine Bone China* (2004–06; Figure 3).[27]

Umiumare's own semi-annual ButohOUT! festival in Melbourne has been compared by Umiumare not so much to a summoning per se, but to a Japanese matsuri festival (TRU 2021). These are the carnivalesque seasonal events found across Japan which involve the procession of local gods in a shoulder-born mikoshi or palanquin,[28] as well as dancing, the wearing of masks, feasts, drinking, competitions, and so on. Umiumare's butoh matsuris echo Hijikata's celebration of the "aimless use of the body, which I call dance" (Hijikata 2000b: 44), or in Umiumare's own words, staging a corporeal "return to our non-functional selves" (TRU 2021). Here, as Umiumare explains, it is "nothing to do with technique", but rather "the body's presence revealing itself" (TRU 2021). ButohOUT! and MAP Fest today serve as global hubs for a multicultural network of butoh, trance and contemporary dance artists located across the Asia Pacific. Through their work and their programming, Umiumare and Yap have established themselves as leaders in butoh and related arts. Each has filiations to historic butoh, seeking out energies located in temporal zones both distant and proximate, developing butoh as a mode of contemporary transcultural diasporic practice. Butoh today is both festive and critical, transcultural and localised.

---

27 See "De Quincey's Urban & Industrial Site-specific Works" in chapter four and "Frances Barbe's Tōhoku australis" in chapter eight.

28 Hijikata used just such a palanquin in *Hijikata and the Japanese* (1968).

CHAPTER 7

Stomping Downunder: Suzuki and Frank Theatre

1   Introduction

In this chapter, I shift to the examination of the other Japanese physical theatre form attracting attention in Australia at this time—namely the practice and writings of director Suzuki Tadashi. The work of Suzuki and those influenced by him raised many of the same issues regarding national placement and a desire to naturalise down-under what began as Japanese forms. Coming from an explicitly Japanese transcultural position, Suzuki offered a non-Naturalistic, Expressionistic and montage-like approach to physical theatre. As noted in chapter one, the central link between butoh and Suzuki's Method of Actor Training (SMAT) is the focus on the lower body, and in Suzuki's claim that stamping serves to summon external energies which might possess, entrance and animate the performer. Suzuki's early productions were famous for the "shocking" physical "frenzy" of the performers (Goto 1988: 78–79). Suzuki would go on to cast influential butoh dancers Ashikawa Yoko and Tanaka Min to perform in key productions (Carruthers and Takahashi 2004: 49–56, 159–165, 191, 262–3; Sant 2003: 153). The Brisbane-based dancer John Nobbs encountered Suzuki's oeuvre when he played the role which Tanaka had created for Suzuki's original staging of *Chronicle of Macbeth* (Figure 2). Nobbs developed his own variant of SMAT which he entitled Nobbs Suzuki Praxis (NSP). In it, there are exercises which strive to realise a "discombobulated", "freeform", "crazy" or "spastic dance" (Nobbs 2010: 260, 53) of "controlled epilepsy" and "bodily chaos" (Nobbs 2006: 56, 46), all of which makes NSP proximate to butoh. While such expressions tend to be restricted to the training, rather than being visible in the more curtailed performance aesthetic, NSP and SMAT performers have within their range something close to Hijikata's "aimless use of the body, which I call dance" (2000: 44).[1] Moreover, Nobbs, Umiumare, Suzuki and Maro share elements of an ero guro aesthetic, blending international commodity culture

---

1 Nobbs often repeats in his books material from his previous publications, as well as text from oral presentations which he and Suzuki have given at SCOT or elsewhere, in addition to interviews with himself and with Suzuki, sometimes conducted by Jon Brokering. Nobbs considers Brokering the foremost author on Suzuki, and hence has republished much of Brokering's otherwise difficult to access work, notably in Nobbs & Brokering 2016.

with explicitly Japanese, over-the-top cultural expressions, musical choices, costumes, and settings.[2]

In this chapter, I offer a portrait of Suzuki's oeuvre and training, with a focus on Suzuki's landmark Australian production *Chronicle of Macbeth* (1992). Jacqui Carroll and John Nobbs in Brisbane were the most consistent and faithful importers of SMAT into Australia. Carroll and Nobbs began training with the members of what was to become Frank Theatre in 1992, premiering their work in 1993 (Nobbs 2006: 10). I examine how the careers of Carroll and Nobbs led them to take on Suzuki's method, survey their major productions, and discuss Frank's staging of the classic Australian play *Summer of the Seventeenth Doll* in their pop-cultural noh-theatre-like adaptation *Doll Seventeen* in 2002. This production demonstrates how, in the hands of Nobbs and Carroll, the techniques of Japanese physical performance derived from butoh and SMAT dovetailed with the stoic masculine values and muscular intensity of the Australian Legend, described by Russell Ward (1958), where instead of staging the central protagonist's hysterical collapse, Carroll "let the terror out" (Leonard 2002: 35) to hystericize the production as a whole.

2   Carroll's and Nobbs' Encounters with Suzuki

Jacqui Carroll saw Suzuki Tadashi's work in 1991, at a workshop he was using to recruit Australian actors for the landmark production *Chronicle of Macbeth*. She reflected:

> the experience was exhilarating. Here, at last, I saw actors striving physically, working hard and being judged. I saw … actors speaking chorically, as one voice. Speaking with energy.
> 1998: 38

John Nobbs, was also at Suzuki's Australian workshops. He was "struck" by the actors' "simple and profound power", immediately concluding that he was "born to do this!" He saw his previous "dance career, which was not inconsiderable" as "preparation for this Suzuki stuff!" (Nobbs 2006: 6–7). He had been, in his own words, a "very grounded dancer", a "Martha Graham style dancer" (Nobbs 2006: 116). Consequently, Nobbs felt "comfortable" with the choreography

---

[2] While Suzuki's tendency for extravagant combinations alluding to often tawdry elements of popular is well known, his work has not, to my knowledge, been linked to ero guro aesthetics before.

Suzuki offered (Nobbs 2010: 114).[3] For Carroll and Nobbs, encountering Suzuki was a "Turning Point" (ibid. 6). I myself attended the 1992 Playbox production of *Chronicle of Macbeth,* and its startling powers of minimalism and physical presence helped put me on the path that led me to writing this book.

Carroll's and Nobbs' responses to Suzuki were similar yet distinct from the first impressions of butoh formed by the artists in other chapters. As Robertson observed (2017: 121–137), Australian encounters with Japanese physical performance were characterised by a combination of alienation and familiarity. Carroll's background in Australian Expressionist dance, show dance, and actor training, meant that she had been exploring ways to bring bodily precision to acting, and vice-versa, for some time. Suzuki's approach fit that bill, offering her a discipline akin to ballet in challenging the actor to be "striving physically, working hard and being judged", to speak and to hold themselves "with energy" (Carroll 1998: 38), and to go beyond an egoistic focus on producing a psychological performance. With Suzuki, actors performed more like the corps de ballet, or the chorus in Mary Wigman's tanztheater, "as one voice", with a unified and hence largely impersonal physique. Nobbs' response was similar. Nobbs would play Banquo in *Chronicle of Macbeth,* a role in Suzuki's adaptation which spoke no text (Figure 2). Ironically then, Nobbs' "not inconsiderable" dance career (2010: 114) prepared him perfectly to take on a dramatic non-speaking role. Suzuki's work did not present, at least at first glance, any of butoh's grotesquery, and hence neither Carroll nor Nobbs exhibited any of the shock or momentary repulsion which Australian viewers of butoh have felt. Nevertheless, the manner in which Suzuki's psychocorporeal approach was both familiar and yet unlike what the artists saw in most Australian performance at that time was significant. As I argued in chapter one, Suzuki technique often served as a distorted double of butoh in Australia, a mode of performance which appealed to Australian artists for many of the same reasons butoh did, even as it remained distinct. Nobbs has noted the proximity of butoh to his version of Suzuki technique, particularly in the more "freeform" tasks which actors are assigned (2010: 258–263). Something, however, which both Carroll and Nobbs saw in Suzuki—which butoh, at least on the surface, does not exhibit—was a sense of choric discipline and corporeal unity, with moments of tightly choreographed unison movement and drilled rehearsal. Suzuki technique offered a more visibly disciplined, centralised and homogenising aesthetic when compared with the organised chaos of Dairakudakan and its "One person, one troupe" model (Baird 2022: 78). Suzuki's alleged "samurai" or "military" discipline (Chapman

---

3 Nobbs and Carroll have repeated these comments in many publications.

1993; Allain 2002: 50; Carroll 1998: 31; Loth 2001: 37; Beeman 1982: 78) was to be something Australian performers struggled with, leading many like Nobbs, Carroll and Zen Zen Zo to rework Suzuki technique for a broader and less submissive theatrical community.

Frank's artistic directors distinguished their work from Zen Zen Zo's butoh fusion,[4] though links persisted due to exchanges within the Brisbane performance community. Most of the senior artists who worked with Carroll and Nobbs also worked with Zen Zen Zo. Led by Lynne Bradley, Zen Zen Zo employed Maro's teaching in its methods, as well as techniques developed by Suzuki. It was therefore rare, with the exception of Nobbs and Carroll themselves, to find Brisbane artists who had not had some training in both butoh *and* Suzuki. Even some of Umiumare's collaborators such as Matthew Crosby combined the techniques. Frank introduced Suzuki to Brisbane at the same time Zen Zen Zo was founded, and members of both companies have taught at both the University of Queensland (UQ) and Queensland University of Technology (QUT). The issue of how to localise or Australianise SMAT offered many of the same challenges as those which arose in bringing butoh to Australia. Nobbs' reformulation of Suzuki technique for the Australian context provides a cogent comparison with how butoh travelled a similar path. The main difference is that issues of voice and vocalisation became more foregrounded in the translation of Suzuki than in butoh, and that the disciplinary aspects of Suzuki's technique provided a more visible stumbling block to Australians' uptake than was the case with butoh (see Woods 2006).

3   Suzuki Tadashi in Japan and Australia

Along with Maro's former mentor, Kara Juro, together with Terayama Shūji and Satoh Makamoto, Suzuki Tadashi was referred to as one of the "four kings of angura", the Japanese underground experimental theatre movement which arose after the 1960s in opposition to the dominant Naturalistic theatre of the earlier shingeki groups. Suzuki began in 1958 directing social realist plays for Waseda University's "Free Stage" company (Waseda Jiyū Butai)—including a production of Gorky's foundational Naturalistic script *The Lower Depths*— before shifting in 1961 to Absurdist works (Goto 1988: 37–80). In 1966 Suzuki established the Waseda shōgekijō (Waseda Little Theatre) with Absurdist playwright Betsuyaku Minoru. His production of *Waiting For Godot* toured

---

4   See discussion of Zen Zen Zo in chapter eight.

Paris in 1972. Soon after founding Waseda shōgekijō, Suzuki met Hijikata via the latter's 1968 performance of *Nikutai no Hanran* (Akihiko 2000: 62). In 1970, Suzuki directed *On the Dramatic Passions II* and then *The Trojan Women* in 1974. Hijikata attended both (Akihiko 2000: 63). Several prominent butoh artists performed in Suzuki's productions—notably Ashikawa Yoko (1988–89) and Tanaka Min (1991). Some of the earliest performances from Suzuki's troupe were notably wilder and more physically extreme than would later be the case, rendering some of these stagings close to butoh. In 1969, a critic credited Suzuki's star performer Shiraishi Kayoko with a "shocking frenzy" in which her:

> wide-opened eyes are crossed, her widely twisted mouth spitefully twitches, her cheeks in extreme strain quiver convulsively, her stiffened fingers tremble slightly as if grasping at the air …. It … resembled an epileptic fit.
> GOTO 1988: 78–79

Suzuki's father had managed a lumberyard in the forested foothills of Shizuoka (Nobbs and Brokering 2016: 25), and Suzuki heard from some associates of his who were anthropologists about the now rare gassho-style farmhouses, with triangular peaked roofs, still extant in the sparsely populated rural mountain village of Toga. The village had no road access until 1969, and had once been a place of exile for a disgraced samurai. As Nobbs observes, "Anything that's flat" in the village is "a paddy field, and the rest is trees" which have grown back since World War Two (Nobbs and Brokering 2016: 244–47). From 1976, Suzuki sought release from the highly urbanised environment of Tokyo to work in Toga, founding SCOT (Suzuki Company Of Toga). A complex of more than six main stages were erected, the highlight being the main farmhouse renovated as a spacious, rustic theatre (the Mountain Stage). There were also plans for SCOT members to engage in agricultural work, but unlike at Tanaka's Hakushu estate, this proved impractical (Goto 1989: 121–2).[5] Suzuki stated that he hoped to create something like a "religious shrine [honza]", close to where gods once dwelt—but perhaps no longer did in this modern age—and which could be "purified" and ritualised (Goodman 1988: 357; Suzuki 1986: 12). Suzuki claims that by approaching "a European play" such as a Greek tragedy or Chekhov via "the unique means of bodily expressiveness and theatrical sensibility available to Japanese", he might "paradoxically" discover a theatrical form which was "universal" (Hoff 1980: 43).

---

5 See "Tanaka Min & Body Weather" in chapter three.

As Nobbs observed, Toga became an internationally renowned theatre centre akin to Wagner's Bayreuth (Nobbs and Brokering 2016: 238). Suzuki later served as artistic director of the Shizuoka Performing Arts Centre, 1995–2007, and continues to work across multiple locations. Toga and Shizuoka remain pilgrimage sites for his followers, as Bayreuth was for Wagner enthusiasts. Suzuki claimed that maximising manual activities has often "been touted as a means to rehabilitate" not just the citizenry, but also "the actor" and the dancer, building on Suzuki's contention that the Japanese and many other non-Western cultures were descended from essentially "agricultural people" with their feet firmly "planted in the earth", both physically and spiritually (Suzuki 1986: 31; Goto 1989: 113). Suzuki therefore aimed to maximise the use of "animal energy" from the body (Suzuki 1984: 29), training in the mountains with only limited use of machinic power or electricity.

When touring *Godot* to Paris, Suzuki had a transformative theatrical encounter of his own (Goto 1989: 104–5). Suzuki had been critical of the codified nature of classical Japanese theatre, founded as it was on the conservation of established choreographies which members of the major iemoto theatrical families recreated for audiences new and old. As Suzuki explained, "in Japan the classics are not part of the modern theatre's normal repertory" in the way that the works of Shakespeare, Racine or Euripides are for Western theatre makers (Hoff 1980: 44). Scripts by masters such as kabuki author Chikamatsu or noh's Zeami were staged almost exclusively by kabuki and noh actors in the classical style. Attending Paris' Théâtre des nations festival, however, Suzuki witnessed Kanze Hisao give a noh demonstration at Jean-Louis Barrault's unadorned, four-sided studio stage. Absent were the regular accoutrements such as live noh musicians, chorus (jiutai), ensemble members, and the classical stage—though Kanze used Japanese kimonos, masks and audio recordings. Suzuki was astonished at the strength of the performance. The action had a "brilliant liveness" and "theatricality" (Suzuki 1986: 71). Suzuki recognised that if one stripped noh back to its corporeal and rhythmic energies, it became amenable for a diversity of modern and historic scripts. Kanze, who was unusual amongst the noh fraternity in performing in experimental European works, performed in Suzuki's 1974 production of *The Trojan Women* (Woods 2006: 44). Bradley and Woods of Zen Zen Zo studied with members of the Kanze school of noh, 1993–95.

Suzuki was therefore influenced by both early modern Japanese forms and the Euro-American avant-garde. His principal works have taken the form of a memory-theatre, or a theatre of ghostly recollection and madness, drawing on Existentialist philosophy and Absurdism (including Samuel Beckett, Eugene Ionesco, Jean-Paul Sartre, and Albert Camus' *Myth of Sisyphus,* all cited by Suzuki)—in addition to mugen noh, a form in which a central spirit retells their past life. Suzuki describes how "the entire world" becomes a "hospital" or asylum, "and we are all the patients", dreaming of our lives prior to our incarceration (Sant 2003: 156). Many of Suzuki's works recall in this sense German Expressionist works (themselves influenced by Eastern precedents) whereby the stage becomes the expression of the psyche of an alienated and tormented everyman or everywoman.

For Suzuki, theatre "functions as a kind of cultural memory ... of an ethnic group" as well as that of humanity (Sant 2003: 152). To achieve this, Suzuki argued one must ground the performer. Actors accumulate and store energy at the core of their body by pressing down on the earth and absorbing the literal and metaphorical forces which bounce back. Where Hijikata urged dancers to descend downward into themselves and their flesh by placing a ladder within their own nikutai (Sas 2003: 24), Suzuki called on the performer to arrest this descent through a dialectical balance of standing upright even as energy moved downwards, before this energy returns upwards, towards the centre of the body.

Suzuki's metatheatrical construction of the stage as a hallucinatory space of haunted memory was nascent in his 1970 performance *On Dramatic Passions II*, described in publicity as presenting:

> a solitary madwoman [who] recalled fragments of numerous plays from the past, performing them one by one. Through the fiction of the drama, the passions which she was never able to satisfy in real life exploded with dreadful force.
> CARRUTHERS 1996: 222

As Suzuki said of his 1990 production *Dionysus*, "Consciousness is a prison and the walls ... are history" (Playbox 1992: 16). Suzuki's suffering psychomachic figures behaved according to psychoanalytic postulates, with characters suffering a traumatic compulsion to repeat their history because each repetition remained incomplete and unresolved.[6]

Suzuki's works also brim with Japanese signifiers. In one of his Japanese language adaptations of *Macbeth* from 1991, the thane was at times positioned as Japan's wartime emperor Hirohito, holding out against Allied forces amidst a burnt out stage (Mulryne 1998: 85–90). Overall however Suzuki's characters and their settings may be recognisably "Japanese", while "at the same time, his work is not a slavish translation" of a national "tradition" or history (Goto 1989: 119). In various writings and pronouncements, Suzuki has bolstered his deep knowledge of Japanese theatre, culture, religion, architecture and body

---

6 On traumatic compulsion in history, theatre and Expressionism see Caruth 1991; Marshall 2013.

language, with international modernist anthropological research, to position himself as broadly humanist rather than narrowly nationalist or historicist.[7] As observed in chapter one, Suzuki was influence by Jungian anthropology. In his essay "The Grammar of the Feet", Suzuki mused that there had once been:

> a tribe, now vanished, in Tasmania that possessed a secret device for bringing rain. They threw themselves down and rolled on the ground, beating with their hands and feet ... Or they leapt up high into the air, guiding the energy of nature to the earth ... This ancient ritual seems to have existed in older German dance as well.
> GERHARD ZACHARIAS 1964 in SUZUKI 1986: 15[8]

These rituals had affinities to Suzuki's own practice, and the theatrical realms which Suzuki crafted consequently tended to be populated by primal archetypes, rather than precisely drawn, socially-located individuals. Suzuki states that he was drawn to "Greek drama" because it offered "an archetype of the fundamentals of what it means to be alive as a human being ... I find this in Shakespeare, Beckett, and Chekhov" (Sant 2003: 151). His oeuvre echoed in this sense Carl Jung's and Gerhard Zacharias' contention that primitive mythic figures and cultural practices recur across ancient myth and art into the present (Jung 1980: 21, 117–26, 158–9, 184, 258–60). Suzuki's kinship with Jung has subsequently been developed by Nobbs (2020) in the latter's own writings.

Suzuki claims that, as in ancient ritual and noh, the actor summons spirits from below the ground and elsewhere to inhabit the individual:

> The gesture of stamping on the ground, whether performed by Europeans or Japanese ... is a gesture that can lead to the creation of a fictional space, perhaps even a ritual space, in which the actor's body can achieve a transformation from the personal to the universal.
> SUZUKI 1986: 12

Suzuki argued that his training helped the actor to "discover the primal sensibility of the character by feeling with one's interior bodily energy" (qtd in

---

7   Suzuki cites Claude Lévi-Strauss, Shinobu Origuchi, the Research Society for Japanese Arts, Curt Sachs, Gerhard Zacharias, Tatukichi Irisawa, Shirō Kondō, Kunio Yanagita, Kinji Imanishi, Mircea Eliade, Jirō Kamishima, Friedrich Nietzsche, Konrad Lorenz, Sartre, Camus' *Myth of Sisyphus*, Max Weber, Yasusuki Murakami, Zeami, Beckett, Ionesco, Brook, Grotowski, Merleau-Ponty, and others (Suzuki 1986).
8   Gerhard Zacharias (1964) is in turn drawing on Curt Sachs's (1933) *World History of the Dance*.

Nobbs and Brokering 2016: 84). Suzuki wanted his actors to access a "precognitive, preverbal" state close to shamanism (ibid. 78). It is less a "transformation of the body" than a "revelation of the body" and what this allows access to (ibid. 88). Suzuki's metaphysics here comes close to butoh. Suzuki may not argue the theatre is *literally* of site of religious transformation, but he is emphatic that his approach is designed to "restore" a "magical" and indeed "mystical" or "shamanistic sense to ... acting" (in Beeman 1982: 89). For Suzuki, the forces put in motion by the stamping of the feet may be considered a way of "calling forth of the spiritual energy of the place, a summoning of the ancestral spirits to come and possess the body of the performer in a kind of hallucination" (1986: 14). In Nobbs' words, the Suzuki trained actor is a "spiritual athlete", often more "watchable not for what he is, but for what he might turn into" (Loth 2001: 141; Nobbs 2019: 17). Hence the space which the actor's body brings on stage may be seen as a "sacred space" (Suzuki 1986: 91), akin to that which was generated by the mediums which Tony Yap worked with.[9] As Australian actor-director David Pledger observed, in Suzuki's productions:

> you always play to the eye of God [which] ... may in fact be ... your lover, or someone important to you, or something more metaphysical. This object, this thing that you set out for yourself, is a thing which can look at you, perceive you and consider you doing whatever you are trying to do at any given moment. What the audience watches is this relationship between yourself as a performer and this eye of God ... That's what ... make[s] you engaging as a performer.
> WADDELL 1992: 30

This led to the adoption of a frontal performance style, known in classical Japanese theatre as shōmen engi, where the chest is orientated outwards towards the seating banks, eyes fixed over the audience's heads, even when the actor is addressing characters to the left or right (Goto 1989: 116). Suzuki's version of shōmen engi gives scenes a stochastic, broken structure, with the habitual position of the actor facing outward interrupted by sharply demarcated short passages where actors briefly turn to each other, recite text, and then revert to centre. Moreover, in performance and training, the voice and its forceful expression is seen as equivalent to energy itself. In the "possession-like state" called for by Suzuki, one employs a "nondaily use of language" such that the voice itself seems to be conjured from so deep within the core of the body that it exceeds

---

9 See "Yap & Trance Dance" and elsewhere in chapter six.

such a locus (Allain 1998: 81). Suzuki calls this "utterance" (ibid. 81). If not quite the same as the hysterical, tremulous quivering of butoh or Yap's trance dance, it does produce a nervous, otherworldly ambience, with the performer acting, in Suzuki's own words, like a "puppet" (1986: 11), manipulated by external forces, sometimes going into "convulsions, groaning, relentlessly piling up phrase upon phrase" of speech and movement, such that the on stage subject is visibly shattered and broken (Carruthers 1996: 217). As Suzuki explained to the actor playing Macbeth in the Australian production, "At the very beginning of the play ... your personality is already ... broken ... It is the end of your life" (Carruthers 1996: 221), and therefore "everything taking place ... on stage is a visualization of your inner world ... naturalistic mannerisms aren't needed" because "You're possessed"; Carruthers 1992: 620). This parallels Yap's comments about his own entranced performances with IRAA, where before the commencement of the play, "I die" and then "For the next hour or so, I'm dead" (Yap 2021: 35).

Suzuki has described his approach as "bricolage" (Suzuki et al. 1984–2009) or "collage" (in Nobbs and Brokering 2016: 126), wherein elements from diverse sources are juxtaposed with each other. Indeed, much of Suzuki's later work has taken the form of portmanteau productions, quoting elements of his previous stagings. The collision of sources and concepts generates a vacillating uncertainty or duality of meaning. Despite the statements above, none of Suzuki's characters can unequivocally be read as simply deranged or hallucinating. As possessed individuals, it always remains possible that their own inner vision is in fact the true one. In the Australian version of *Macbeth*, the thane was attended by a figure dressed as a cook, possibly from a hospital or prison, who offered Macbeth a bib and fork when the king asked for his sword and armour (Wischusin et al. 1993). But given the metatheatrical construct of the performance as a dream, there is no reason to give more credence to the reality of the material goods brought on stage over Macbeth's strongly held internal convictions. In short, the assembled on stage elements act to comment on, undercut, or render ambiguous the meaning, often producing a sense of dark, grotesque comedy.

This sense of a jarring panoply of shifting fragments from diverse sources and genres had been a feature of Suzuki's selection of music too (Goto 1989: 118), which ranged from enka ballads and saccharine pop songs, to the angular twang of noh's shamisen accompaniment, electronic tones, Western Romantic musics, Afro-Cuban styles, and more. As Suzuki explained:

> Within me reside a number of layers ... from popular songs to Beethoven, from comic books [manga] to Dostoyevsky and Henri-Louis Bergson. Indifferent to accepted standards of value.
> in NOBBS AND BROKERING 2016: 82

The Australian production of *Macbeth* was in this sense atypical, being performed to a single through-composed score authored by French composer and metteur en scène Serge Aubry, featuring a drum machine which Aubry combined with electronic organ and staggered, thrumming notes on a harpsichord-like instrument. This was played back on the sound system at a punishing volume only slightly below that employed by Dairakudakan in their Melbourne production the year before (Wischusin et al. 1993).[10] While *Chronicle of Macbeth* was relatively constrained in terms of formalistic contrasts, Frank Theatre and to a lesser extent Zen Zen Zo Physical Theatre echo Suzuki's use diverse and often ironic musical choices, in some cases choosing tracks which the Australian artists became aware of through Suzuki's productions.

The Suzuki Model of Actor Training (SMAT) has, however, had the greatest influence on Australian theatre practice, rather than Suzuki's work as a director. The dramaturgical aspects of Suzuki's productions are reflected principally in the work of Frank and Zen Zen Zo, while SMAT has been widely adopted to diverse ends—although the distinction between SMAT and Suzuki's dramaturgy is fluid, with many of the exercises initially being movement sequences developed for the productions. The practice known as "standing statues" for example evolved out of the tableaux devised for *Dionysus* (1990), and later would form the basis for the choric movements of the Farewell Cult in the Australian production of *Chronicle of Macbeth* (1992; Allain 1998: 66). Many of the walks began as marching sequences performed by the soldiers in *Trojan Women* (1974; Woods 2006: 45). Frank Theatre would also develop activities out of rehearsals, adding the use of teddy bears, mirrors and other items to their training from various stage works and demonstrations (Nobbs 2010: 85–93, 276–284).

Following the rise of Suzuki's reputation during the 1980s, several Sydney based artists initiated workshops in SMAT, drawing both on written accounts and oral descriptions from those who had visited Toga. Nigel Kellaway of the Sydney Front was the first Australian to train with SCOT (1984–85), though he also spent an extended period with Tanaka as well as a shorter spell with Ohno. Kellaway founded the confrontational performance art/theatre group the Sydney Front with John Baylis in 1986, where they became famous for staging

---

10 No notes on Aubry's music appeared in the program or press coverage, and although it is likely Aubrey's score was composed on an integrated system such as Australia's Fairlight synthesizer, it is possible the harpsichord was recorded using an acoustic instrument and then translated into the amplified electronic soundscape. Suzuki has used the music of mambo legend Perez Prado, sentimental classics like "Sadame Gawa" (Goto 1989: 118–121), post-punk band Public Image Limited (Allain 2002: 166–7), and more.

"unspeakable acts" such as shoving cream buns up the performer's fundament (Hamilton 2011: 56). Kellaway was also the first Australian to study with Tanaka and then dance with Maijuku, which he did during the same period.

Kellaway claimed that Australian artists did not need to ponder overmuch how to define "Asia" and its cultures, because all performance "comes from the same roots" namely "ritual, and Asian theatre has kept touch with it", while Western theatre after Shakespeare exhibited a more attenuated relationship with its ritual origins (Alison Broinowski 1996: 155). Kellaway (2016) had a very mixed career, including training in contemporary dance with Margaret Lasica in Melbourne before working with Kai Tai Chan in One Extra dance, 1981–84, and later with Leigh Warren and Jonathan Taylor at Australian Dance Theatre in Adelaide. A chance encounter with Russell Dumas in Tokyo in 1984 led to Kellaway studying for a period with Tanaka. Unlike the other students though, Kellaway did not live at Tanaka's studio, and this was before Tanaka had established the first farm. Following this, Kellaway worked for a period with Suzuki, whose productions Kellaway found "highly melodramatic and expressionistic and [sometimes] … over the top"—characteristics which Kellaway was however keen to echo (2016: 11). Kellaway and some of his peers such as Mémé Thorne and John Baylis ran their own versions of Suzuki stomping classes in Sydney during the 1990s (Heywood and Gallasch 2001), these exercises informing such productions from the Sydney Front as *Don Juan* (1991–92), which Kellaway described as a "contemporary dance-theatre work within the framework of a Rococo comic opera" (Kellaway 2016: 560). Despite this grounding in Suzuki, Kellaway's pained, cross-dressed choreographic routines tended to be closer to butoh and the work of Ohno Kazuo (Kellaway 2000: 886). In *The Pornography of Performance* (1988–89), for example, Kellaway "resembled a masochistic court jester" as his "naked body twitched and jerked as he awkwardly clambered along the edge of the [bath] tub half filled with water" (Hamilton 2011: 58). Kellaway nevertheless would continue to see his musical performances as influenced by Suzuki, whereby "the act of pianism" and other displays of instrumental mastery served as a form of "theatrical action" (Kellaway 2016: 121). Kellaway shared many links in the world of Sydney performance, working at various times with Lynne Santos (a participant in the Lake Mungo workshops), Amanda Stewart and others. Suzuki's instructions regarding impersonal critical self-observation and outward performance were important influence for Sydney Front's work interrogating the audience's gaze and the act of public performance, but the physical regimen of the Front was very much focussed on a "'hybrid' vision of performance" (Kellaway 2016: 559), and showed few overt signs of Suzuki's impact beyond being described by one commentator as somewhere between "slow dance or really fast sculpture" (Taylor 2010: 185).

Richard Moore, who went on to make the influential 1991 documentary *Butoh: Piercing the Mask* (which includes excerpts of SCOT s production of *The Bacchae*), performed with Suzuki's company in the 1990 production of *King Lear* before mounting his own classes in Suzuki inspired dance and theatre in Sydney and Canberra (Kingma 1989: 21). Don Mamouney, artistic director of Sydney's Sidetrack theatre, offered what he described as a "naïve version of Suzuki", producing an acting style which was "not quite dance, and it's not mime" but might rather be considered a "physical spatial language" (Taylor 2010: 186). Also significant was the Suzuki trained intermedial artist and physical theatre performer Deborah Leiser-Moore, who would go on to teach SMAT in several countries (Leiser-Moore nd). In 1995, Australia's premiere theatre publisher Currency Press issued a commentary on the prevalence and utility of stomping by community arts director Neil Cameron (1995: 8, 74–76), in which the author—like Suzuki—linked his understandings of First Nations Australian dance with diverse practices such as those exercises by monks in Japan, as well as Cameron's own reading of Suzuki's pronouncements. Cameron developed a number of exercises in running and stamping with Lecoq trainer John Bolton, then based in Melbourne.

Localised Australian interpretations and fusions of Suzuki techniques encouraged many other artists to visit Toga, and four Australians who had arranged their own trips to Toga—Joel Markham, Katia Molino, David Pledger, and Bruce Naylor—would join Playbox's 1991 training session for *Chronicle of Macbeth* (Playbox 1992). Suzuki's physical regimen was not always the sole factor in this choice; many Australians—including Nobbs—were partly drawn to him through his anti-Naturalist rhetoric (Nobbs 2019: 23–24). In a 2003 essay, Suzuki claimed that the "Stanislavsky system" cannot be considered to have any true "concept of the body" because it simply "relies on the body of [the] everyday" individual and their normative physical dispositions (Sante 2003: 157). Suzuki's work reached Australia at a time when theatre critics such as Michael Billington were still reciting neo-Zola-esque rhetoric regarding the superiority of Naturalistic theatre because if, like Suzuki claimed to do, "you exclude daily realism from drama you denude it of what gives it juice and life" because action only "happens because of the context in which people live: the social context, the historical context, even the economic context" (in Chapman 1993).[11]

SMAT was assembled from a range of influences, including not only Japanese theatre and dance, but also sports training, kendo and other physical

---

11   Chapman's film includes short interviews with critics, artists and audiences.

and martial disciplines. Suzuki wore a kendo uniform during teaching (Allain 1998: 87) and adapted the gliding walk of noh titled "*Suri-ashi*" for his own work (Suzuki 1986: 33). As Suzuki refined his method and from as early as the 1980s, he used his fame to offer workshops and masterclasses in order to spread SMAT internationally. By 1980, SMAT had become a "staple" of training in several US institutions, including Juilliard, and in 1982 and 1988 respectively Suzuki's productions of *The Bacchae* and *Tale of Lear* were performed with US actors (Coen 1995: 30). The foundation of the Saratoga International Theater Institute, New York (SITI), in 1992, by Suzuki, Ellen Lauren and Anne Bogart was a key part of SMAT's internationalisation. Suzuki taught SMAT less himself, licencing alumni to do so, with sporadic interventions by the master at Toga. After a number of international seminars on SMAT and its global spread, Suzuki revisited the teaching method in 2010–12 to reduce it to a restricted palette of six main acts which might guide a range of studio exercises (Nobbs 2019: 223; Crothers 2021: 13).

Suzuki has described his acting method as the "art of walking", and there are six main walks which make up the core of SMAT, including the famous stomp (Allain 1998: 71). This is a "basic exercise" which Suzuki used to assist the actor in developing:

> energy and control. The stronger the stamping, the more the energy generated—but the harder it becomes to maintain control. The actor must try to prevent ... "shake" or "wobble" in the upper body ... This can be done by learning to "block" or control this energy in the area between the hips (the actor's centre of gravity).
> CARRUTHERS 1992: 624

Akin to de Quincey's model of butoh, SMAT offered an explicitly material and corporeal experience of the metaphysical relationships which the artists cultivate. Performed on sprung wooden floors or similar surfaces, actors felt the energy of the downward blow from the feet bouncing back into the legs. This literal reverberation of physical force from the body, into the ground, and back into performer's flesh, actualised the sense of groundedness and energisation which Suzuki wished his actors to imaginatively embody. The body should be poised within an arc of forces and affective energies running in multiple directions across, below, and throughout body and stage. As Nobbs puts it, during stomping the body "establishes a powerful reciprocal relationship with the ground (and by extension the cosmos)" (2020: 87), and so in Suzuki's words, actors' "very beings" may be considered "part of the ground" or "the earth", the dynamics of ritual and acting fusing the energetics of the two into a dynamic unit (1986: 9). Nobbs observed that the repetitive aspect of SMAT was itself "transformative", much as is the case with military drilling or ballet: one performs an exercise over and over until there is a threshold moment of revelations and it "clicks" psychocorporeally (Nobbs 2006: 112). It does this by taking the trainee through a state which Nobbs recognised as proximate to butoh aesthetics, labelling this "the body in crisis" (2006: 149). Sensitivity is developed in SMAT by repeating the act of crossing the stage or completing other exercises while responding to different musics, changes of pace, direction, axial alignment, positions held in the body, attempting to speak while executing an especially difficult action, and so on (Brandon 1978; Allain 1988; Allain 95–112). There is some similarity with Tanaka's use of moving lines of dancers in training as part of muscle bones.[12] Other exercises involve imagining an external force that lifts, pulls, or holds back the performer, as in the exercise named "tenteketen" (Allain 1998: 71). Commands from Suzuki and other workshop leaders include "Fall like a puppet with the string cut", or "Let the music move you" (Brandon 1978: 31). Standing statues might be varied with a number of additional tasks layered on to the basic instructions, as where actors are told to rapidly freeze and hold a position in an energetic manner, and then to try it again, but starting to move while retaining the position or deforming it in some way. As in butoh, a key position is a foetal pose resting on the buttocks—although the muscular tension required to retain in SMAT this state differs from the shattered, tremulous effect of butoh. Many of Nobbs variations on SMAT in NSP are additional options placed in dialogue with basic SMAT exercises.

SMAT is famous for its unforgiving discipline. Suzuki's approach was for example characterised by Carrillo Gantner as "Samurai training for actors" (in Chapman 1993). Suzuki has been likened to daimyo (head of a samurai clan) or "shogun" (military and political rulers of Japan, twelfth to nineteenth centuries; Lim 1998: 14; Nobbs and Brokering 2016: 9), a cult leader (a comparison made not only by Australian actor Peter Curtin [in Chapman 1993], but from which Suzuki himself explicitly defends himself [1986: 66–67]), a fascist, a drill sergeant overseeing a "quite militaristic" class (Heywood and Gallasch 2001 unpag.), and other similes. Instructions are delivered to performers in blunt, high volume bursts, accompanied by the resonating thwack of a wooden staff beaten on a matt or on the floor, which marks time and signals to the performers to make abrupt leaps from one action to another. As Paul Allain explained, the exercises are "punishing, the stamping hurts, and the stick serves as much

---

12 See "Tanaka Min & Body Weather" in chapter three.

to strike fear in you as to strike a rhythm" (1998: 80). Australian actor Michael Cohen described one of his co-nationals as having to "soak his feet in iced water each day immediately after the morning's session" (1996: 54). Students "cannot rest unless told to nor refuse to do an exercise ... comments are not encouraged. You learn with your body ... You can [only] talk" when "you leave class" (Allain 1998: 73). Students quickly come to "expect a high level of commitment, instruction, and even humiliation" (Allain 1998: 86), with "shouted criticism, slaps on the head, [and] calls of 'damned fool' (baka yaro)" (Brandon 1978: 30). As Nobbs put it, Suzuki often switched between a "good cop / bad cop" persona (2019: 45), praising actors before attacking them. There was certainly a "masochistic" quality to performing SMAT—as was true for some of de Quincey's participants at Lake Mungo.[13] Jeremy Neideck and Katherine Kelly (2021: 452) have gone so far as to suggest that the popularity of SMAT in the Australian state of Queensland might be attributable to a switch in complying with one authoritarian regime—namely the repressive Queensland state government of Premiere Joh Bjelke-Petersen, 1968–87—to another. Suzuki himself is unapologetic regarding this aspect of the training, claiming that "pain can be viewed as a physical device that could bring" about a "revelation to the actor" (in Nobbs and Brokering 2016: 92).

It was however apparent that SMAT is designed not only to shape corporeal control, but that it "alters mental processes, the performer's inner life ... the state of mind" (Allain 1998: 80). SMAT is, in Japanese terminology, a form of shugyō, in which devoted training and repeated acts serve to shape body, mind and spirit (Baird and Candelario 2019: 90). Kellaway's peer Clare Grant recognised that it was not the instructor who was "threatening me with that stick if I don't do the exercise properly" (Taylor 2010: 189). Rather the stick acted as an impersonal agent to move both instructor and student. "For somebody whose ego is in the way, that's a hard exercise to take on", she confessed, and perhaps such a threat of disciplinary violence might indeed be implied if SMAT was carried out as a "fascistic contest of wills" (189). However the exercise was most successful, and hence least threatening, when there was a "lack" of egoistic "will" being applied "on both sides" (189). Many of the Western performers who have taken best to Suzuki training had prior experience of depersonalising disciplinary corporeal regimes. Paul Allain considers it significant that Suzuki's leading US exponent, Ellen Lauren, "originally trained as an equestrian competitor and is from a military family" (1998: 86). Kellaway saw his own background in the drilled virtuosity of classical music as linked to what he learned

---

13   See discussion of De Quincy's work at Lake Mungo in chapter three.

from Suzuki. Nobbs and Carroll both had extensive training with some of Australia's stern, European-educated ballet mistresses, and Suzuki has stated that he often finds ballet dancers easy to work with (Sant 2003: 157). Nobbs has gone on to liken the Suzuki stomp and other basic exercises for actors to barre work in ballet, and claimed that Suzuki training, like ballet, aims to produce archetypal "representational absolutes" via the highly trained body, much as sports and athletics does (Nobbs and Broking 2016: 313–18; Nobbs 2010: 76–78). Frances Barbe, who would later train with both Suzuki and Nobbs as well as performing with Zen Zen Zo, also felt that her ballet background helped her to adapt to Suzuki's method (Allain and Barbe 2009: 152). Joanne Loth of Frank claimed that one of the "great" aspects of SMAT is the way it "brings ... to Australians" and other non-Japanese the "value of hierarchy" where the "Sensei" is able to say "shut up, students" and just "do what I say" as a positive exercise in self learning (Neideck and Kelly 2021: 463).

The aim of SMAT overall then is to establish a range of dynamic tensions across and within body and mind. Allain has noted that during the workshops, "Lauren urges us to 'fight' with ourselves" (Allain 1998: 75). Lauren explained: "All of the exercises are basically impossible" (in Carruthers 1993: 182). For example, "he asks you to maintain ... steadiness as if you held a glass of water inside your body which you don't want to spill" even while stamping (ibid. 182). Lauren reported initially feeling stumped by this, thinking: "'Wait a minute, you want me to slam my feet into the ground and yet NOT'" spill the water? (ibid. 182). Consequently "the audience [is] watching you fight to control the uncontrollable", and this produces drama (ibid. 185). For all of the martial control which Suzuki's actors exhibit, like their peers in butoh, they are perpetually teetering on the edge of failure. The aim is to overcome what are often termed "obstacles" which Suzuki sets up within this corporeal exchange (Allain 1998: 80). As student have sometimes observed, the trainer acts as merely another obstacle (ibid. 80). Because of the contradictory nature of this energised psychophysical model, comparisons are often made between the SMAT trained body and high performance motors, with allusions to racing cars and aircraft common. Suzuki offered "the image of the Boeing 747, its brakes on and engines full-throttle just before take-off" (Carruthers 1992: 626). It was also important to develop within the actor's body a repertoire of psychocorporeal memories—not unlike the "dictionary of atmospheres" developed by de Quincey, or the series of corporeal images taught by Hijikata to Tanaka—which actors might draw upon in performance; what Nobbs (2006: 152–3) calls "a catalogue of physical action, which he [the actor] can then draw on at any time throughout his future". All of the exercises and images described above also appear in Frank Theatre's adaptation of SMAT.

4   The Australian Production of *Chronicle of Macbeth* (1992)

The commission of Suzuki's production of *The Trojan Women* for the festival celebrating the 1988 bicentenary of the commencement of British settlement in Australia was a significant act of cultural diplomacy, publicly trumpeting the rapprochement of the Australia with Japan after the end of the Pacific war. The 1988 tour was followed in 1989 by the presentation of SCOT s version of *The Bacchae* in Canberra, the Australian national capital, and in Melbourne's Spoleto international arts festival. The production featured Hijikata's leading performer Ashikawa Yoko who performed a frenzied "dance of horror" in the role of the possessed Agave (Carruthers and Takahashi 2004: 177). Impressed by these productions and by Suzuki's reputation, the artistic director of Playbox theatre in Melbourne, Carrillo Gantner, negotiated for Suzuki to train a group of local actors with a view to mounting a piece in Australia. Suzuki initially proposed an all-male cross-dressed version of the play *Madame de Sade* by Mishima Yukio, but rights were not available.[14] In what Robert Reid (2023) identifies as "notes that Suzuki prepared for the cast and the company", the director recorded that he suspected that importing a canonical "Japanese play into Australia" could be viewed by some as an "act of colonisation" issued against Australia, whereas if he adapted an "English language classic" this would not be seen to be the case (Reid 2022). Gantner and Suzuki agreed to devise a new version of SCOT s 1991 Japanese adaptation of *Macbeth,* for which Tanaka had played the ghostly non-speaking role of Banquo (Sant 2003: 153; see Figure 2). Ten additional male Australian actors were selected, including Nobbs and Gantner. Gantner insisted on some female actors. Ellen Lauren was commissioned to play Lady Macbeth (Carruthers 1996: 218). Australian actor Katia Molino, who had trained with Suzuki since 1990 (Playbox 1992), joined the chorus. Lauren was already known as Suzuki's leading US exponent, performing the role of Agave in Suzuki's *Dionysus* in the same year. Lauren's presence had a meta-performative function within the Australian production, her superior expertise in SMAT meaning she "provide[d] a useful mark for the Australian actors to aim at" whilst also giving audiences a visible "measure" of how effective the Australian performers had been at adapting to Suzuki's aesthetic (Carruthers 1992: 219). A film of the production was later screened on the public television channel of SBS, as was a documentary dealing with rehearsals and critical reception, ensuring a wide audience for this pioneering exchange (Wischusin et al. 1993; Chapman 1993).

---

14   Suzuki directed *Madame de Sade* in 2008.

Playbox's version of *Macbeth* was stripped back and simplified in comparison to the Japanese production, which had featured twenty-seven performers and elaborate scenic effects. Suzuki's previous adaptations of the play, of which this was the third, had been assemblages. Ian Carruthers notes that Suzuki's 1975 interpretation included:

> role-playing among asylum patients, all vainly attempting to become Macbeth ... selected passages from *Chushingura* (the Kabuki classic about the revenge of the forty-seven Ronin) ... Tsubouchi Shoyo's turn-of-the-century kabuki-style translation of *Macbeth* ... an aged man, confined to the asylum since 1941, gloomily uttered ... "Alas, poor country! Almost afraid to know itself!" ... [and] then dismembered a grotesque-looking doll and scattered its intestines over the floor while passionately singing ... mid-seventies pop song ... "O Night in Ginza"
> 1992: 215

The Melbourne production was considerably more focussed on the Shakespearean text itself, with all explicit of references to World War Two and other texts dropped.

Suzuki retained however the setting of *Macbeth* within a pathological therapeutic environment as part of what he designated the "*Osarabakyô no ryûsei* (*The Rise of the Farewell Cult*) trilogy" (Carruthers and Takahashi 2004: 58). Suzuki's version of *The Bacchae* had dramatized the "rise" of this deranged, ritual group, *Macbeth* the "over-reach" of its members like the thane in his quest for power, and Suzuki's soon-to-be-staged 1992 version of Chekhov's *Ivanov* presented the "disintegration" of the cult's authority (Mulryne 1998: 89). Inspired by Jim Jones' doomsday cult of the 1970s in addition to other obsessive, authoritarian communities, the Farewell Cult's acolytes acted as a chorus, dressed initially in nuns' habits with thick rimmed glasses, and later Japanese-like loose robes, headscarves and Ray-Ban sunglasses. As Leonardo Pronko explained:

> the cult members, now as witches, now as murderers, now as themselves, occasionally weave in and about the stage, sometimes chanting "Double double" and striking the stage floor emphatically with their skull-topped staves as they march thunderously, then stop to pose with staves held at various angles.
> 1993: 112[15]

---

15   The "Double, double" speech is also often used in training.

During rehearsal, the thumping of the staffs tore to shreds the tarkett dance-floor which had been rolled out across the stage and a new solution to how to protect the feet of the performers had to be found (Chapman 1993).

After entering like sleepwalkers, each of the cult members sat at one of twelve mismatched, vintage chairs, irregularly spaced about the stage. Suzuki composed a new text for this opening sequence, drawing on the broken, on-running textual structure used by the speaker of Beckett's radio play *Cascando* (1963), in which an unidentified figure hoped to eradicate the act of storytelling itself (Beckett 1990). Gantner and Lauren stood centre at the rear of the space, acting as leaders of the ritual.[16] Gantner guided the chorus in the following speech, which they chanted after him:

> History / If only it could be thrown away /
> We could rest / ... / But until then /
> ... A thousand and one and many, many times that / That's all there is /
> Of my life /
> Farewell to history / Farewell to memory /
> But once it's finished / That's no good either /
> Can-not rest now / Will ... not ... rest ... now! /
> Right away, another one! /
> But *this* one / Is different from always /
> Finish *this* one / Then ... there can be rest /
> [and so] ... /
> Farewell to history / Farewell to memory.[17]
>   WISCHUSIN ET AL. 1993

This speech was followed by the chorus intoning "Tomorrow ... and tomorrow ... and tomorrow / Creeps in this petty pace from day to day". In order to bid farewell to this endless repetition of tomorrow, and tomorrow, and tomorrow, Lauren instructed that: "Today we shall do *Macbeth*. Begin reading". Lauren and actor Peter Curtin henceforth took the roles of Lady Macbeth and her husband, dressed in more distinctive flowing robes than the chorus. At the end of the production, Curtin/Macbeth joined the chorus in their "Double double"

---

[16] Although the characters of Gantner and Lauren were identified in the program as the Reverend Father and Mother, neither were named or addressed as such on stage, and hence this programmatic designation can only be considered conjectural rather than definitive.

[17] Nobbs recited this passage when he played the same role as Gantner in Suzuki's touring production of *Dionysus* (1994–95).

stamping dance, with the staffs in this case mimed, each holding a bound copy of the script as if it were the shaft of Suzuki's thyrsus-like sticks (Wischusin et al 1993). Lauren then pronounced, "This concludes today's labours" and the cast exited, presumably to replay another story the following day. There was no indication that the much sought after "rest" or disposal of history had been achieved.

As Carruthers explained, *Chronicle of Macbeth* was "narrowly" focussed on the "psychological world of the Macbeths" rather than the events or machinations of political rivalry, staging as "vividly as possible the inner landscapes of their fears and desire" or as Suzuki put it, "What we're trying to achieve is a visualization of the unconscious of the person who plays Macbeth" through the bodies of the actors (Carruthers 1992: 219, 229).

Responses to the production in Australia were guarded but supportive, especially amongst those critical of Naturalism and of textually driven performance. Japanese audiences also responded positively, one commenting that "as a Japanese" she found the Western "performers' physiques" to be "strong", with "pronounced facial features" which enabled them to "make an impact Japanese actors" do not (Chapman 1993). J.R. Mulryne concluded that the "composed, anonymous, sculpted" staging of Suzuki's other productions was here inflected with a greater degree of "urgent expressiveness" (1998: 90). I myself found the rapid juxtaposition of tragic Existentialism and grotesque comedy was unevenly realised—although Molino and David Pledger gave impressive turns as the nurse and doctor (Wischusin et al 1993). For her part, Rosemary Neill (1992) from *The Australian* newspaper railed at what she called a text "gutted" of "psychological insight". Although she recognised that the performance depended on the "sudden emission and suppression of physical and vocal energies", she concluded "the effect is staccato, loud—and often unintelligible". In an interview, *The Age*'s critic Leonard Radic stated that he found the introduction of the cult confusing and unnecessary, claiming that "no one in the audience understood what the purpose of this strange group was", distinguishing Suzuki's "invalid" addition of the cult from other "legitimate" changes the director had made (in Chapman 1993). Radic confessed he would have preferred a more conventional use of "traditional Japanese elements" such as "ghosts", or more explicit reference to "kabuki ... noh ... or ... kyogen" than simply the ghost of Banquo (which Radic identified as a kabuki-like detail; Figure 2), causing him to conclude that, according to these criteria, the production did not seem very "Japanese" at all. Radic did however concede that, "At [its] best, it is strong, compelling theatre ... simply ... performed ... with military precision". But with "no steaming cauldron, no blasted heath, no Birnam Wood ... and no parade of kings", it remained "oddly uninvolving" (1992:

12). Michael Billington, of *The Guardian,* like Radic, also felt that the framing device of the cult rendered *Chronicle of Macbeth* a "meditation" rather than a "realisation" of the play (in Chapman 1993). Some responses went beyond such cultural protectiveness, straying into xenophobia, one commentator arguing that Suzuki should stick to "his own" culture and "stop attacking Western classics", whilst another critic accused him of "transcultural plunder, Suzuki has savaged, even brutalized the text" (Carruthers 1996: 218; Reid 2020).[18]

Like Neill, many critics had attacked the vocal qualities produced by Suzuki's actors, even in Japan (Allain 1998: 83–84; Nobbs 2019: 69). From attending the production in 1992, I recall spumes of spittle emanated from Gantner's mouth every time he uttered, even Lauren struggled in Melbourne at times. Woods (2006) also identified vocal strain as a common weakness of SMAT actors. Many critics would describe the vocal style of Suzuki's performers as being akin to "powerful barking" (Allain 1998: 80). Jo Loth, who trained and performed several times with Carroll and Nobbs as well as running workshops for Zen Zen Zo, would go on to develop a fusion of Suzuki technique with Linklater voice training, concluding that, "In the West, additional impulse-based work" such as Linklater's system "seems to provide an effective complement to the highly structured nature of Suzuki's system" (Loth and Pensalfini 2021: 92). Even so, Pronko felt that even after the relatively short period that the Playbox cast had spent learning SMAT, they played "as though possessed" (1993: 112). Also particularly impressive in the video documentation of the performance is John Nobbs, gliding about the rear of the stage as the ghost of Banquo—replacing Macduff's character in a sense—his bald pate and face whitened with make up like a butoh dancer, smiling horribly as he bore down on Macbeth, wielding an oversized, wooden sword (Wischusin et al. 1993; Figure 2).

Although many Australians would go on to train in SMAT after *Chronicle of Macbeth* (1992), most employed Suzuki's methods as part of a mixed aesthetic, to be combined, adapted or supplemented as appropriate to the needs of the work. Nobbs however has argued for SMAT as a master discipline, and hence he can, with some reason, claim his own faithful rendering of Suzuki's teachings renders him the true "begotten son of SMAT" (Nobbs and Carroll nd.2).

---

18 Purdon's excoriating review (1992: 33–34) was particularly notable, given that despite familiarity with a wide gamut of performance tropes from Kurosawa's films to kabuki and the Euro-American avant-garde, the author likened the production to poor take-away Asian cuisine, calling it a "karaoke version" with "synthesisers, and the actors … wail along [to] … It's Japanese and disciplined, and it's all served up to gullible occidentals with the inscrutability of a restaurant chain presenting noodles with sushi, icecream and tomato sauce" meaning the production "reeks of the fascist, authoritarian and double-talk elements in Japanese society of which the Pacific region would well be rid".

5 Foundation of Frank Theatre

Carroll and Nobbs both had early training in ballet and modern dance, particularly in those forms of dance theatre which developed out of the work of Martha Graham. The dance experience of both artists was extensive, though Carroll had a broader background including choreography. She has worked and trained with many foundational groups in Australian modern dance, such as the Bodenwieser Company, Borovansky's former students, and others (Carroll 1998: 2, 19, passim). Nobbs' career had mostly been with two companies: Australian Dance Theatre (ADT) and Sydney Dance Company (SDC).

From 1971, Nobbs trained and danced with the ADT, based in Adelaide, initially under the direction of company founder Elizabeth Cameron Dalman. In 1973, Jaap Flier—a founding member and ex-artistic director of Netherlands Dance Theatre—became co-director with Dalman, while Flier's wife, Willy De La Bije, was rehearsal director (Carroll 1998: 5–12). In 1975, Flier and De La Bije moved to Sydney to revamp the SDC and Nobbs joined them. Nobbs noted that SDC was in a state of "transition" (Nobbs 2006: 4), causing the frustrated Flier and De La Bije to return to Holland after only three years. After training with Ballet Rambert in London for a year, Nobbs' came back to ADT in 1980 to work under Jonathan Taylor, formerly of Ballet Rambert (Carroll 1998: 14). Nobbs served as a dramatic "character dancer … well known for playing heavies", his muscular physique and broad shoulders often featured (Nobbs 2006: 5; Nobbs 2010: 317). Nobbs ceased dancing in 1983 and toyed with acting, claiming he was "looking for a way to amalgamate" the two (Postle 1996a: 6), before he successfully auditioned for the Playbox Suzuki project.

Carroll's initial training was in "pure and undiluted classical ballet" but "Upon graduation" she realised that the "best source of employment … [was] popular theatre" (1998: 1). From early in her career, Carroll moved between major Australian dance companies specialising in ballet or modern dance, as well as "dancing on television, in theatre, in musicals, clubs, cabarets" and other outlets (1, 17–18). In short, Carroll's career was more similar to the genre busting practices of butoh than commonly the case in Australian concert dance. During her spell with the Bodenwieser company in the mid 1960s, Carroll began teaching movement to actors. After Flier joined ADT, Carroll became a guest artist, dancing and choreographing for ADT while building her expertise in Graham technique. Here she met Nobbs. During the 1970s, Carroll rose to become a major teacher of Graham across multiple institutions (Carroll 1998: 6, 19). In 1975, Carroll joined Flier in Sydney, working on a broad range of choreographies, from Glen Tetley to Nannette Hassall and Anna Sokolov. Although Carroll would collaborate on a number of postmodern works, she resisted the "all encroaching ... presence" of Dumas and his allies, defending what she felt was by contrast a "European" model based on "vigorous disciplines" (1996: 8), rather than the democratic pedestrianism and instructional task work practiced in much postmodern dance. In the wake of Flier's replacement at the SDC by Graeme Murphy, Carroll came to resent being instructed to "just teach the steps" rather than the "complete interior identification with the movement" (Carroll 1996: 8). In 1977, she left SDC to freelance. She took the opportunity to combine her familiarity with commercial dance and popular culture with mainstage concert dance. John Cage, an iconoclastic composer who had a longstanding collaboration with the post-Graham choreographer Merce Cunningham, toured Sydney in 1976. Carroll staged an interpretation of Cage's *Song Books (Solos For Voice;* l970), which was an erratic series of electronically distorted vocal provocations. In Carroll's staging, it featured musicians dressed as superheroes playing draughts while the singer, equipped with a megaphone, was carried on and off stage (Carroll 1998: 11–12). Carroll also choreographed a "fruity melodrama", which included Laurel and Hardy style "knockabout comedy and the broadest [of] burlesque" for ADT under the metafictional title of *The Missing Film* (1980; Carroll 1998: 14). Although restrained compared to the garish eroticism of Frank, Carroll was already developing an interest in approaches which departed from corporeal discipline to blend popular culture and dramatic references in an ironic manner.

This led to Carroll's proto-Frank production for Brisbane's La Boite, scored to the avant-garde vocals of Diamanda Galas, entitled *Briefings For a Descent Into Hell* (1991). The piece featured young, near naked performers from QUT and a Suzuki-esque mix of texts from Euripides to Kafka, Eliot and others, in which hell became, in the words of Queensland theatre academic Adrian Kiernander, "a ritual, a male playground based on power: rugby match, wrestling bout, initiations rite, prison camp" (Carroll 1998: 30). The production's combination of edited texts, gendered choreography, powerful physicality, and erotic charge, would define much of Frank's work. From this period Carroll and Nobbs would regularly teach at QUT, securing long-term institutional interest for Suzuki technique in Australia. They later presented their work at the National Institute of Dramatic Art and elsewhere (Carroll 1998: 47), and Frank was resident company at the Queensland Performing Arts Centre (QPAC), 2004–05 (Neideck and Kelly 2021: 458).

In 1991, Nobbs arranged for Carroll (1998: 31) to sit in on Suzuki's classes for Playbox with the Australian actors. As Carroll explained, Graham's influence had been waning in Australian modern dance, yet Carroll found classical ballet itself an "asexual world of form, lightness and ... beauty" (1998: 52). The "use of the floor to drive the work" gave both Graham's and Suzuki's approaches an "earthdrawn" or "adult, sensual relationship with movement" (52). She read

Suzuki as "the masculine" to the "feminine" of Graham (52), the two combining in her own work to produce a rich, sexually dimorphic model of movement driven from within. Carroll attended as many of Suzuki's performances and workshops as she could. Nobbs then toured with *Chronicle of Macbeth*. When Carroll and Nobbs returned to their base in Brisbane in 1992, the two offered biweekly sessions in SMAT. By 1993, "a small group of performers were coming together", leading Carroll and Nobbs to found Frank Theatre (Carroll 1998: 35). Early members included Frances Barbe, Joanne Loth, Lisa O'Neill and Caroline Dunphy. Carroll directed the majority of the works, while Nobbs performed. Nobbs became the main theoretician and leader of the workshops, with Carroll also vitally involved in the training. Loth would sporadically run classes for Zen Zen Zo, while Barbe, who was a founding member and regular choreographer for Zen Zen Zo, establishing from the inception of Frank their close filiation and exchange with Zen Zen Zo. In 1994, Nobbs became the second Australian invited to perform with SCOT in Japan (after Richard Moore), taking Gantner's role from *Chronicle of Macbeth* in Suzuki's touring adaptation of *The Bacchae* (1994–95). Nobbs also performed this role again in SCOT s *Nightmare* (1999). Nobbs was also one of the first Australian whose classes in SMAT were endorsed by Suzuki (about the same time as Mémé Thorne was in Sydney; Heywood and Gallasch 2001), eventually designating his own variant of SMAT as Nobbs Suzuki Praxis (NSP)—though the titles of the training and of the company changed over time. One or both of Frank's artistic directors reconnected with Suzuki and his company most years (Nobbs 2006), and SCOT company member Noriaki Okubo performed with Frank, 2005–06, often reciting his lines in Japanese. Frank have toured productions to Toga and Shizuoka, including *Salome* (in 1998), *Heavy Metal Hamlet* (2000), and others.

6   Larrikin Orientalism: Frank Theatre's Early Works

Key works from Frank's production history include *The Romance of Orpheus* (1993–95), *Macbeth: Crown of Blood* (1995, 2009), *Salome* (1997–98), *Heavy Metal Hamlet* (1998), *Rashōmon* (2000–04), *Oedipus* (performed as *The Tragedy of Oedipus* in 1995 and then revised for an international tour as *Oedipus rex*, 2003), *Romeo and Juliet* (performed as a ghostly tragedy in 1996, and then as lightweight comedic sketches as *Midsummer Night's Romeos*; Carroll dir. 2003c), and *Hamlet Stooged!* (Carroll dir. 2007). I briefly outline these productions below, before moving to the most overtly Australian work by the company, *Doll Seventeen* (2002–03) in the next section. These works chart the consolidation of Frank's combination of Japanese and Orientalist tropes with

Nobbs' and Carroll's interpretation of Australian cultural traditions—notably the "ocker" or "larrikin" type so beloved of Australia's New Wave artists.[19]

Carroll and Nobbs initially followed Suzuki's model in adapting classics from the Western canon, especially ancient Greek theatre and Shakespeare. Zen Zen Zo would perform much the same repertoire. Frank's productions became more exuberant over time, employing a greater degree of comedic burlesque. This was part of a strategy on the part of Nobbs to render the company's interpretation Suzuki's method explicitly Australian, by allying it with Australian traditions of humour, verbal patois and masculine tropes. Although Frank's productions were not site-specific, the company did experiment with outdoor locations and working in the Australian landscape, staging a version of *Orpheus* on a platform situated between two water tanks in the Bunya Mountains, 240 kilometres inland of Brisbane (Carroll 2023).

Frank's first production was *The Romance of Orpheus* (1993–95). The chorus included Joanne Loth and Frances Barbe, who were also to become Zen Zen Zo regulars. *Orpheus* was an accomplished beginning for Frank, reflecting Nobbs' and Carroll's experience in dance theatre. Nobbs described it as an "operatic tribal ritual" (Nobbs 2010: 344). Functioning largely as a showcase for Nobbs as the bewitched tragic figure of Orpheus, and supported by a chorus of five Furies including Loth and Barbe (Wittenberg dir. 1994), the general ambience recalled a slowed down version of Ruth St Denis's whirling Orientalist "delirium of the senses" as staged in 1906's *Radha* and other works (Desmond 1991: 31). Nobbs' actions were accompanied by repeated, invocation-like text, and a combination of vibrant live percussion and electronic tones (composed by Lorne Gerlach, who later performed in Zen Zen Zo's *Cult of Dionysus*). Carroll employed material from the libretto for Christoph Gluck's opera *Orfeo ed Euridice* (1762), Aeschylus' script dealing with Orpheus' death at the hands of the Bacchic Furies, and other texts. *Romance of Orpheus* introduced a number of signatures of Frank Theatre: a restricted cast of principals supported by a chorus speaking a distilled, essentialist text; a sparse mise en scène enhanced with lush (and in this case, explicitly Orientalist) details in costume; choric vocal work; and mannered movement sequences (Figure 14). The production opened with a sequence derived from Carroll's and Nobbs' exercises which in turn drew on the meditative mystical dance of Sufism's whirling dervishes (Pippin 1998: 25; Nobbs 2006: 84). Nobbs later used a track from a 1993 compilation of Turkish dervish music for Frank's 2006 production of *Manga Ulysses* (Carroll dir. 2006). Carroll drew in this respect on Suzuki's similar, dervish-like choreography for the death of Pentheus in Suzuki's version of *The Bacchae* (1982).

---

19 See "Bodies in Opposition to the Australian Legend" in chapter two.

FIGURE 14   Frank Theatre's *Romance of Orpheus* (Princess Theatre: 1994; dir. Jacqui Carroll). Image left shows John Nobbs (Orpheus, at the left) and Irena Haze (Euridice, right). Image right shows Nobbs (forward) with chorus of (left to right): Lisa O'Neill, Frances Barbe, Christina Koch, Sonia Davies
IMAGES COURTESY OF CARROLL AND NOBBS

As Veronica Kelly observed, the tableau of spinning cast members established a "weirdly entropic energy", driving towards a final "transcendence of individual griefs and passions" with which the piece concluded (Carroll 1998: 39). The choreography, reflecting this narrative trajectory, was orbital, dominated by a sense of return and repetition. Dressed in colourful robes and with bindis stuck to their foreheads (Nobbs 2010: 345; Figure 14), the performers emphasised the Oriental otherness traditionally associated with Bacchic figures. The Furies held staffs to perform a stamping dance adapted from that in *Chronicle of Macbeth,* their "grotesque dreadlocks" heightening their "bizarre appearance" (Pippin 1998: 32). The bow-legged stance of the Furies gave them something of a butoh-like ambience, a characteristic which would be extended by Zen Zen Zo, most notably in Zen Zen Zo's own Bacchic study, *Cult of Dionysus.*[20]

A sense of violent sensual otherness also pervaded *Salome* (1997–98), the cast dressed either in "semi-Japanese costume" or Byzantine like adornments (V. Kelly 1997b: 21). *Salome* was created for dancer Lisa O'Neill. As Kelly explained, the "concept" of a "ritualistic dance pervades" both this production, and indeed much of Frank's oeuvre, the performers "moving with the hieratic and focussed energy that is the company's trademark". Accompanying the dance of the seven veils was:

> hypnotic percussion with hokey snare drums … O'Neill performs a quirky and menacing piece of spiky choreography, somewhere between a pub strip show re-created by a teenager who has learned sexiness from

---

20   See "Fusing Butoh With Suzuki: Zen Zen Zo's *Cult of Dionysus*" in chapter eight.

> exercise videos, crossed with the angular arrogance of a posing catwalk queen. While powerfully sexual, O'Neill is sinister and weirdly inhuman: Lolita with attitude, a Bond-girl clone turned dominatrix.
> V. KELLY 1997b: 21

The diversity of references cited by Kelly aptly described Frank's mixed aesthetic and its debt to the tendency of Japanese artists to juxtapose popular culture with historical and Classical allusions.

Frank's *Macbeth: Crown of Blood* (1995, 2009), echoed Suzuki's Playbox version of the same play in its restrained ethos, performed by four actors dressed in "matching plum, velvet gowns" (Carroll 1998: 41). Kelly described it as an "exercise in aesthetic minimalism" which, like Playbox's *Chronicle of Macbeth*, was focussed around the thane and his wife, and in which "actors move to percussive sounds in dreamlike, controlled movements, like animated friezes" (1995b: 15). Other critics identified the "heightened ... declamatory performance" which Frank had developed, together with "slow movement" which produced "a searing ritual of horror" in which actors were seen "sinking to the ground and rising as if by levitation" (Carroll 1998: 41). Similar effects were visible in Frank's ghost version of *Romeo and Juliet,* Kelly noting the manner in which the "performers glide through doomy shadows, drifting across the stage ... with the uncanny floating effect of wraiths in a Chinese [or Japanese] ghost movie" (Carroll 1998: 44). The presence of SCOT member Noriaki in *Macbeth* heightened the link to Suzuki, while white face make-up evoked Japanese traditions from kabuki to butoh. Lady Macbeth was initially played as an onnagata role by a male actor, before being performed by Tracy Shoemaker in the restaging. The piece was the clearest homage to Suzuki staged by Frank.

Frank's productions of *Oedipus* in 1995 and 2003 were more ritualistic than *Macbeth* (Carroll dir. 2003b). Staged as a mesmeric largescale "physical oratorio", the 2003 adaptation premiered in a Croatian castle with a cast of fifteen, hierarchically arranged on multiple levels and featuring archaic jewellery and wristbands close to the design from Paolo Pasolini's 1969 filmic production of *Medea* (Nobbs 2010: 352–53; Frank nd). The music featured flute accompanied by taiko-style drumming and ended with a furious shamisen solo (Carroll dir. 2003b), locating the action at the intersection of the near and far Orient. Drawing on Jean Cocteau's libretto for Stravinsky's opera, in addition to Sophocles' script, it featured both live percussion and synthesiser. In the outdoor staging, 240 kilometres inland of Brisbane, parts of the production were lit by firelight. Characterised again by an entropic sense of dramaturgical stalemate, Kelly notes that the entry and exit of the cast as a unified group gave the production the feeling of a "dance" accompanied by "sonorous poetry" (V. Kelly 1995a: 14).

Tiresias was played by Lisa O'Neill as a shamanic figure, undergoing convulsions as the words of the gods entered her (Carroll dir. 2003b).

Frank also staged two productions of *Hamlet,* one as accompaniment to a selection of heavy-metal tracks by the likes of Deep Purple (*Heavy Metal Hamlet,* 1998), and the second a garish burlesque, entitled *Hamlet Stooged!* (2006). The physical techniques developed by Suzuki in Japan were here grounded by reference to Australian speech patterns and tropes of identity (Carroll dir. 2007). As observed in chapter two, popular constructions of Australian identity have often posited the national character as essentially working class, populist, anti-intellectual—and hence, by implication, muscular and male (Ward 1959; Ward 2009).[21] Nobbs' own description of *Hamlet Stooged!* was very much consistent with this, being, in Nobbs' estimation, "unquestionable[y] Australian ... burlesque, anti-authoritarian, puerile, rude, larrikin ... deviant", performed by characters who were recognisably "fair-dinkum Aussies" (2010: 47). Nobbs' framing of his Japanese influenced aesthetic within the larrikin traditions of the Australian vernacular and its values is also evident in his voice as a critical artist-commentator, which was often close to how his on stage characters represented themselves. Nobbs has issued six self-published texts, each overflowing with larrikin-style anti-intellectual attacks on famous artists and unnamed academics.[22] Nobbs' critical texts are written in a laconic conversational mode, echoing diatribes by John Romeril and his peers (Davidson 1978: 300–12), drifting from one thought to another—more like a chat at the pub than a coherent aesthetic statement. Nobbs' self-amused, conversational approach is therefore just as much a part of his positioning of the company as Australian, rather than Japanese, as the manner in which he and his collaborators approached the texts which they recite on stage.

Nobbs transposed Shakespeare's language into expletive-filled, staccato larrikin language for *Hamlet Stooged!* wherein Shakespeare's lines from "the great soliloquy" starting with "That this too, too solid flesh would melt" has become "'*so soggy, stale, sinking and slack seem to me all the burgers at big Macs*'" (Nobbs 2010: 28). This "ocker" phrasing of both Nobbs' critical voice and the scripts which he produced for Frank drew upon the slapstick Australian television comedy *Fat Pizza* (2003; Nobbs 2010: 18–19; Carroll dir. 2006). *Fat Pizza* had pillaged Australian ethnic stereotypes and slapstick humour to present an energetic and deliberately outrageous collection of larger-than-life urban types, including Greek, Italian and Lebanese working class immigrants, involved in

---

[21] See "Bodies in Opposition to the Australian Legend" in chapter two.
[22] Nobbs offers diatribes against Jerzy Grotowski, Eugenio Barba, Peter Brook, Robert Wilson, David Mamet, Anne Bogart, and others.

all manner of ridiculous, dodgy activities, and scams. The term "stooged!" was a key part of the show's patois, meaning to be one-upped, or taken advantage of. In Frank's *Hamlet Stooged!* the ghost of the former king's jester, Yorick, was cast as a comedic master of ceremonies. Gertrude was played by Nobbs himself, "in a tarty dress ... fishnets [and] ... red curly wig" (Nobbs 2010: 26). Hamlet was also in "punky tights ... to match Ophelia" (26). The piece included a "playful dogfight over a plastic steak", Oedipal conflict, and a scene set in a massage parlour. Music featured one of the bands favoured by Suzuki, specifically Public Image Limited (PIL), and their track "This Is Not a Love Song" (1983), as well as music from the Tokyo Shock Boys and the original 1960s version of "Locomotion"—a cover of which represented the inauspicious debut of the soon to be Australian superstar Kylie Minogue in 1987. Frank's garish visual and sonic style here went even further than Suzuki and Dairakudakan to produce an ocker version of the Japanese ero guro aesthetic cited by Umiumare (Umiumare and Eckersall 2012).

Frank's debt to Japan was also staged through an adaptation of the short story which inspired Kurosawa Akira's film, *Rashōmon* (1950). Nobbs played the primal, muscular bandit (actor Mifune Toshiro in the film; Carroll dir. 2000). The sequence in which the spirit of a deceased samurai was summoned by a medium suited Frank's "shamanistic" aesthetic well, and Nobbs added a trio of "sly, psychedelic cleaning ladies" in kyogen style to bring out the comedic aspect of the piece (Nobbs 2010: 350). A pitch-shifted version of PIL s track "This Is Not a Long Song" acted as a framing device, while the rest of the music made explicit the Japanese origins and setting, offering a stylised version of kabuki accompaniment and the type of music which often accompanied Kurosawa's films (Carroll dir. 2000).

Several features manifest in these works exhibit Frank's debt to Suzuki in Japan and the proximity of the company's aesthetic to aspects of butoh. As in Suzuki's practice, there is a tendency to employ an invocatory recitation of text as though in a dream or as part of a ritual. Central characters are supported by a chorus, which sometimes took the form of a grotesque, butoh-esque collective. There is a reduction of on stage objects and aspects of the script to core themes and lines. This is typically coupled with a sense of excess, burlesque and carnival which rivals even that of Suzuki and Dairakudakan. This tendency towards excess often leads to an over-the-top presentational style inflected by Australian comedy and cheap jokes. Frank's productions seesaw from wildly carnivalesque pop-cultural assemblages to slow, refined, hypnotic dirges, both styles being found in their Japanese antecedents. Carroll also tended to break up dramatic scenes with extended abstract choreographies, often performed to popular music tracks, especially those from the 1960s, placing her work close to dance and hence butoh, much as occurred for Suzuki himself (particularly when he coopted butoh dancers as actors). As we shall see in the next chapter, Carroll and Nobbs have been keen to distance their practice from that of Zen Zen Zo, while the latter company exhibits most of these general characteristics, particularly in the use of a butoh chorus.

7 Universalism, Localism and Racial Hierarchies

Nobbs has stated several times that he sees the training method of Nobbs Suzuki Praxis (NSP) as one of "many regional variants" (Nobbs and Brokering 2016: 309) of the system devised by Suzuki which has a "universality" in application (Nobbs 2006: 22). Nobbs and his associates nevertheless concede that Suzuki's persona and values remain "very Japanese" (2006: 22). Loth recalled encountering SMAT at the workshops run by Nobbs at QUT in 1993, observing that, "At that stage I'd never been to Japan and to me it felt Japanese—it was Japan as I imagined it" (Neideck and Kelly 2021: 456). Otherwise, Nobbs has tended to construct the perceived Japaneseness of SMAT as a problem which might lead to the practice becoming "ghettoised" (Crothers 2021: 212–23). Nobbs strove to devise novel exercises that he felt were "less likely to be stigmatised as Japanese" by Australians, hoping that through NSP, "SMAT will no longer be seen as a Japanese style of acting" (Nobbs 2006: 94; Nobbs and Carroll 2015). Nobbs has also confessed that he felt it was necessary when teaching "within a Western context to provide much more information—within a Japanese context they just say 'Do it again.'" In Australia, however, Nobbs wanted to be "more inclusive" and let the student into the thinking behind each exercise while the training itself was being conducted (Loth 2001: 142).

Nobbs is clear that, for him, one does not visit Japan or practice Japanese performance training to "become more Japanese", but that rather "we go [to Japan] to discover our Australianness" (Aldred 2001: 21), which Nobbs has likened to Suzuki travelling to Paris to come to terms with his own national inheritance (Nobbs 2019, 37). According to Nobbs, it is only really possible to recognise what is Japanese about Suzuki's training, and what is not, if one conducts some of the training in Japan itself (Loth 2001: 133). Consistent with Suzuki's own dialectical thinking, Nobbs' characterisation of Suzuki as both "Japanese" *and* timelessly "universal" maintains a productive oppositional tension between the local and the universal. If the SMAT is fact universally applicable, as Nobbs contends, it is unclear why one needs to develop "regional variants" (Nobbs and Brokering 2016: 309). The alterations which Nobbs has made, while arguably minor in scale, are significant in their *national* implications.

Nobbs sees the alleged national affinity for outdoor athletic activities and sport as giving Australians an advantage in learning SMAT.[23] He claims that "Australians have always understood space", and that this is "why we make such great sportsmen and such great dancers" (in Lewis and Sweeney 2019: 88). Likewise, Loth claims that the "respect for athleticism ... and sporting culture" in Australia made it easier for the company to attract audiences (Neideck and Kelly 2021: 461), while David Pledger—who appeared in *Chronicle of Macbeth* and would later draw on SMAT to stage a production with Not Yet It's Difficult entitled *The Austral/Asian Post Cartoon: Sports Edition* (1997)—felt that part of the appeal of Suzuki technique was that it was the first "place where my sports background and ... physical performance practices ... met" (Hadley 2007: 5). For Nobbs, this experience of the Australian landscape and its sporting embodiments have enabled him to match "the core values of Suzuki because we're actually about space" in a sense (Lewis and Sweeney 2019: 88). Here, Anglo-Australian traditions of exploration and exalting the body under the sun and at the beach are translated into a spatially sensitive form of embodiment suited to Japanese theatrical modes.[24]

More problematically, Nobbs argues that the transcultural character of SMAT was "verified" by its consistency with other "universalist theories" such as Jungian psychoanalysis, which proposed that humanity shares a "collective unconscious" populated by "archetypes" found across time, race and culture (Nobbs 2020: 13). In short, Nobbs places SMAT and NSP in opposition to postcolonial relativism and difference, rejecting critiques of the socioculturally specific nature of psychoanalytic constructs and the historical nature of the emotions and the psyche (Porter 1996). Nobbs is a selective reader, cleaving to older theoretical materials for support, much as Suzuki himself did.

Nobbs' theorisations also imply a hierarchy of cultural sophistication, knowledge and power. He states that Frank's exploration of "a dialectic between Primitive stimuli and Civilised restraint" is necessary because "Without [Western civilised] restraint it is [simply] primitive piled upon primitive" or, as he elsewhere states, "transformational art is made by western societies when they channel transgressive primitive energies" (Nobbs 2020: 143, 161). Nobbs likens his multifocal approach to theatre to the work of Pablo Picasso, adding that Picasso was "inspired" by African art, able to perceive the "archetypal models that moved ... primitive" people; yet, for Nobbs, the sophisticated

---

23   See "Bodies in Opposition to the Australian Legend" in chapter two.
24   Suzuki did not initially agree, claiming that for "Australian actors ... There's no sense ... of [a] knowledge within [or of] the body" (Chapman 1993).

African wooden and bronze works which Picasso collected were not, in and of themselves, "art", but rather "craft" products which had to be "ingested by Picasso's mind and fermented with the yeast of his European heritage" before they "emerged" in a refined form as "universal" "transformational art" (Nobbs 2020: 147).

Discussing Suzuki's interest in the account of Tasmanian Aboriginal performance, Nobbs repeats one of the more invidious and false claims made against this group, namely that they were a "stone age hunter gatherer culture" and did not cultivate "crops" (2019: 32).[25] In these statements, Nobbs shockingly ignores nearly one hundred years of subsequent historical criticism made of settlers' often highly dubious accounts about the Tasmanians and of other Australian First Nations groups, as well as decades of sensitive art historical discourse rejecting the art/craft divide in African and European arts (Torgovnick 1990). Nobbs' piecemeal use of sources and knowledges as reflected in his writings—if not necessarily Frank's aesthetic works—demonstrates that invidious racial hierarchies can reappear through the medium of such discourse about primal arts (also Marshall 1995). Nobbs' creative acumen is commendable, but Frank's ideological position within intercultural arts in Australia has some lapses.

8 Nobbs Suzuki Praxis (NSP)

NSP is largely consistent with SMAT, and most of what I have said about SMAT applies to NSP. The main difference is how rigour is enforced, and the relationship between teacher and student. NSP is less authoritarian. Nobbs and Carroll employ a liberal dose of irreverence, humour and childish play to make NSP accessible to those who might otherwise reject Suzuki's authoritarian tendencies ("Samurai training for actors" as Radic put it in Chapman 1993) or to berate his students ("slaps on the head, calls of 'damned fool' (baka yaro)"; Brandon 1978: 30). There is, in the phrasing of Nobbs and Carroll (2015), an "intermittent whimsy" to NSP. This is not however to say NSP is easy to perform. Nobbs has also added a number of what he calls "bridging tools", which he likens to those found in Australian sports training such as flags planted into the training ground, cones, swimming kickboards, and so on (Nobbs and Brokering 2016: 343; Nobbs 2019: 193–94). Suzuki already used staffs, umbrellas and blunt wooden swords (kendo bokken). Nobbs has

---

[25] Pascoe (2014) provides a compendium of colonial writings recording continental Australian First Nations plant and animal husbandry and cultivation.

added brooms (which have a different centre of gravity to the staffs), feather dusters, badminton rackets, mirrors (ideally placed in the centre of a badminton racket or otherwise held away from the body on a stick) and toys (teddy bears, rubber chickens, and other items). These objects are employed in walking, stamping, statues and other exercises for a number of reasons, beginning with how they affect balance and the sense of the body's extension in space.[26] Nobbs' tools also prompt more complex psychophysical reactions. Mirrors enhance the ability of the actor to imagine the eye of God, or of the audience, and to intensely self-scrutinise whilst moving and speaking. The "person in the mirror" acts as an externalised Id-being for the actor, not only effecting a "doubling", but allowing the actor to be "witnessing himself talking to himself" as well as seeing himself as a kind of living "sculpture" (Nobbs 2010: 85–93). Nobbs claims that this serves to "'de-civilise' the actor" revealing their "primitive grace" through a "'primeval' experience" of para-cosmic self-reflection (Nobbs 2010: 88). The aim is to "access [a] ... primordial self", akin to "Shamanism [which] is an invocation of primitive unconscious forces" (Nobbs 2006: 52; Nobbs 2020: 79).

Teddy bears are also for Nobbs archetypal symbols, which even adults project ideas onto. In keeping with Nobbs' Jungian beliefs, he draws on post-Freudian psychoanalytic children's therapy, specifically the work initiated by Melanie Klein, D.W. Winnicott and their successors, who began to observe and stimulate different forms of play in children and adults as a way to reveal repressed behaviours and thoughts.[27] NSP students are instructed to relate physically to their bears, to speak for them in different voices, and to blend the bear persona into their own in speech (Nobbs 2010: 276–84). Other physically and conceptually difficult exercises in NSP are undercut by ludicrous or incongruous juxtapositions, reflecting Nobbs' construction of NSP as an anti-intellectual Australian practice. For example, Nobbs has trainees walk forward while adopting different positions and swinging badminton rackets in the most complex trajectories they can manage, at the same time reciting "Whop! Whop! Whop!" (Nobbs 2010: 291). This sense of irreverent but serious play is emphasised by the use of eccentric or culturally loaded historic music tracks as accompaniment. The mambo music of Perez Prado, for example,

---

26 The use of rods in NSP and SMAT is similar to their use at the Bauhaus during the 1920s (see Gropius & Wensinger 1961).

27 Winnicott claimed that "Playing is itself a therapy", and so, "to arrange for children to be able to play is itself a psychotherapy that has immediate and universal application, and it includes the establishment of a positive social attitude towards playing" (1971: 50). Playing is intimately linked to the sense of "enjoyment" and, for children at least, is "intensely real", promoting "self-healing" (1971: 50, 46).

also used by Suzuki, has become a recurrent feature of NSP training as well as Frank's productions (Nobbs 2006: 168). Other key tracks include the cover by comedic blues-voodoo artist Screamin' Jay Hawkins of "I Put a Spell On You!" (1956; Nobbs and Carroll 2015).[28]

Nobbs also attempts to localise NSP by drawing on Australian music in the training, specifically the reverb-enhanced twang of 1960s surf music, which was highly popular in Australia, with local artists such as Normie Rowe and the Playboys recording covers and their own tracks as US surf culture was taken up here. Nobbs uses in training Rowe's cover of "Shakin' All Over" (1965), as well as Australia's The Delltones' "Hangin' Five" (1963), together with "Peppermint Man" (1962), a track recorded by the original Del-Tones: the band of pioneering Los Angeles surf guitar artist Dick Dale. Nobbs argues that surf culture is to Australia what "noh and kabuki" are for Japan (2006: 99): nation defining cultural practices with deep roots in Australia and Japan respectively—though Nobbs omits mentioning that surfing became a global phenomenon which developed out of a series of crisscrossing trans-Pacific exchanges of the post-World-War-Two era.[29]

Other variances between NSP and SMAT have been described by sometime Frank performers Chelsea Crothers (2020), and Frances Barbe (Diedrich and Barbe 2023), who conclude that the main differences include a willingness to allow students to depart in class from set training choreographies so as to improvise or "freeform" more than is typical in SMAT, as well as a flattening of the hierarchy of exercises, whereby there is a focus on entry level exercises which might offer tangible improvements over a relatively short time, rather than Suzuki's systematic arrangement in which basic exercises lead to upper level challenges only offered to those who have attained a certain level. As Nobbs puts it, he wished to "expand the training" such that it might more directly inspire "imaginative shifts and levels", so that the work in the studio would become "more self-generative", rather than always being driven by an adversarial sensei. The "actors were 'teaching' me" he says (2010: 52–54). Nobbs and Carroll (2015) also omit those exercises which could "exclude some people", insisting—quite unlike Suzuki—that "all exercise vocabulary should be inclusive regardless of ability".

---

28   Hawkins had a significant Australian following, touring as early as 1985.
29   The Hawaiian Olympic swimming star Duke Kahanamoku introduced surfing to Australia with an exhibition display at Freshwater Beach, Sydney, in 1914. On Australian surf music, see Palao (2002). On earlier Australian dance works aligned to surfing, see Potter (1996). On the sometimes exclusionary, racist character of Australian surf culture, see Cubby (2006).

9 Butoh Incursions, the Hysterical Body, and Emptiness

Frank shares with butoh a fascination with that which borders on possession, figured in the discourse of Nobbs and Suzuki as a "shamanic" body. The stable, hypnotised physique of the NSP performer differs considerably to the shuddering, spasmodic and butoh-ka. Nevertheless, the two forms share many common sources for these motifs. A key NSP exercise is the "Bacon swipe". Inspired by the work of one of Hijikata's favourite painters, Francis Bacon, NSP's Bacon swipe has the student bring their hand across their face and as they do so, transform their physiognomy to "highly deformed, extreme grimaces, holding said facial sculptures" while they "say three speeches" (Nobbs and Carroll 2015). Hijikata too used Bacon's giblet-like imagery to bring out extreme distortions of the body and the face, though in NSP, the exercise is focussed on bringing *speech* and body together, allowing one's corporeal condition to shape *utterance*, rather than solely breaking down and reconstructing corporeality. In combination with the use of mirrors discussed above, this allows the performer to "witness" and reflect on their own "grotesqueries" (Nobbs 2010: 87–88).

Some NSP activities are derived directly from butoh. Loth notes that Carroll had performers experiment with adopting "butoh-esque" positions of the hands and mouth, which aided one performer in producing a voice which "sounds eerie and disturbing" (Loth 2001: 91). Nobbs (2006: 45) also related how in 1999, he and other members of SCOT attended a performance by Kasai Akira, who trained and danced with Hijikata and Ohno during the 1960s before moving off as an independent (Baird 2022: 159–182). During training the next day, Suzuki instructed the company to do an exercise "like Akira Kasai did last night". Nobbs relates that this produced what he called "discombobulated" movement, elsewhere all but quoting Hijikata in arguing that "the body/voice learns most about itself when on the verge of collapse" (Nobbs and Carroll 2015). Nobbs and Carroll continue to use a standing version of this exercise, in which actors shift from "almost total bodily chaos to complete stillness in a nanosecond" (Nobbs 2006: 46). The "manic, high speed crazed improvisation" of the Kansai task brings butoh directly into the practice of NSP. Nobbs has also reflected that NSP recalls in some ways the work of former Byakko-sha dancer Kan Katsura, particularly in his use of "freeform" or "crazy" (illogical/purposeless) movement (Nobbs 2010: 258–63). Something like Hijikata's vaunted "aimless use of the body, which I call dance" or the "purposeless" body which Maro took from Hijikata is therefore a part of NSP too (Hijikata 2000b: 44; Bradley 2017: 86–87).

Frank's actors and training tends to employ those moments where the upright frontal composure of the actor breaks down or is disturbed by hysteria-like tics. Nobbs (2010: 53) instructs students to perform a freeform "spastic dance" in response to Screamin' Jay Hawkins, or to execute a form of "controlled epilepsy" in answer to the lyrics of Rowe's "Shakin' All Over", which provides a series of distributed localised images for them to interpret ("quivers down my backbone, ... shakes to my kneebone, ... tremor in my thighbone, shakin' all over") (Nobbs 2006: 54–56). Nobbs and Carroll (2015) have students render these movements even more frenetic and freeform at the command "Spasmodic!" Actors are also invited to perform small, pained, hysterical or melodramatic sketches to these tracks, imagining the moment one's leg is bitten off by a shark in "Hangin' Five", for example, and then hopping about in "paroxysms" (Nobbs and Carroll 2015). Relatively few moments in Frank's performance repertoire are quite as seizure-like as what is encouraged in the workshops, but the NSP body is certainly capable of butoh-esque movement.

Like many butoh artists, Nobbs at times employs metaphors which imply that the body is a vacant space within which to house impulses. Actions, sequences and bodies are sometimes thought of as being akin to a "void" which the performer attempts to fill. Nevertheless, Nobbs concludes that "the word *void* can be misleading, as it implies 'empty', whereas the opposite is true" given that the SMAT or NSP body ideally should be brimming with unrealised energy at all times (2010: 107–8). Where Yap realised such a charged presence in his own dance through producing massive tension and quivering expression in his body,[30] Suzuki asked the performer to present such power as latent but not expressed. Nobbs (2010: 108) therefore describes the NSP body as an "empowered neutral" one. This suggests a dialectical opposition between presence and absence, action and inaction. The dualist structure itself recalls butoh very strongly, even if Nobbs constructs this opposition in a different manner. Nobbs is however unconcerned with colonial implications of this formulation. Nobbs insists that Australia is empty in a way which the NSP body is not, stating that "Australia is a land of space and no culture; Suzuki comes from a land of time"—by which Nobbs means historical continuities—"and culture" (2010: 214). The unstated implication is that Japanese culture might help fill the supposed cultural void that is the spatial expanse of the great southern continent. Nobbs contradicts this principal elsewhere, as when he argues that surfing culture is to Australia what noh and kabuki are to Japan, but there is a clear sense

---

30 See accounts of Yap's dance throughout chapter five.

of national anxiety and insufficiency embedded within these statements, and that Australian cultural history is seen by Nobbs as more shallow than that of Japan. In the absence of significant engagement with First Nations culture, Nobbs solution is to turn to the body itself to build a materially concrete and resonant model of national identity. Akin to de Quincey's early experiments with Body Weather in Australia, Nobbs sees the physical sensation of the stomp itself, of the rebound of energy into the legs and body from out of the earth, as the only way to ground those of settler descent to the essence of this "land of space".

10 Frank's *Doll Seventeen* (2002–03)

In 2002, Frank staged for the Brisbane Festival an adaptation of what is often seen as one of Australian theatre's foundational plays, the *Summer of the Seventeenth Doll* (1955). Entitled *Doll Seventeen,* the production represented the most concerted effort from Carroll and Nobbs to localise or Australianise NSP and Suzuki practice. As Carroll explained, playwright Ray Lawler "gave us permission … to dissect his text, to rework it as a mythic, iconic work using a powerful music base" and "movement" (P. Kelly 2002: 36), or what might be characterised as an ironic, carnivalesque tango between tortured souls caught in competing affections and illusions.

Eschewing the Orientalist ambience and mise en scène of Frank's early works, *Doll Seventeen* was located not only within an Australian mythos, but also that of Carroll's and Nobbs' own working environment: the tropical northern state of Queensland, with its largescale cane industry and extensive uncleared lands. In *Summer of the Seventeenth Doll*, Lawler scripted a loving eulogy for a world in which muscular working class masculinity provided a fading but not entirely inaccurate model for Australian labour, especially in rural colonial settings. Echoing their pioneer forebears, protagonists Roo and Barney expressed their masculine mastery over the landscape and their rivals by working as seasonal harvesters on the Queensland cane fields, spending this time in a homosocial environment defined by "mateship"—the close filiation of one man for a particular chosen "brother" in their shared struggles and laughs. Nobbs characterised the play as "ocker" for this reason, its language and ethos suffused with Australian working class terms and values (2010: 9). Roo was the acknowledged leader of the two mates, serving as a "ganger", or head of a crew, while Barney was the jocular ladies' man. Each year, in the words of Roo's lover Olive, they acted like, "Two eagles flyin' down out of the sun, and comin' south every year for the matin' season", enjoying an extended relationship with a pair of Melbourne women (Lawler 2012: 100).[31] Carroll staged this poetic image by having:

> Roo (John Nobbs) and Barney (Conan Dunning) enter the stage … down a pathway of sunlight, bringing with them the myths of mateship and rural testosterone that still resonate nearly 50 years after the original play's creation
> BUZACOTT 2002: 18

Although returning to their off-season home, the placelessness of the protagonists was emphasised by a chorus member playing wistful blues on a harmonica as accompaniment, while Barney raised a leather bag above one shoulder, and Roo a cardboard case held at his side. Their presence on stage was provisional: a stop in an epic journey from one ill-defined, off stage site, to another.

Barney explained in an early monologue that in this, the seventeenth year of the lay-offs, Roo had been bested on the fields by a younger rival, after which Barney deserted Roo to follow the victor. Barney's former lover Nancy had moreover chosen the security of marriage to another man, Nancy being replaced by the less at ease but elegant Pearl. Pearl was played by Leah Shelton as more sympathetic and confident than typical, serving as an echo or reflection of Olive, the pair circling each other while staring into hand mirrors such as each had used to fix their appearances before the men arrived. Shelton's character however saw the writing on the wall and eventually departed, a bag at her side, like the men when they arrived.

In Lawler's original, Olive lived in a rooming house with her mother Emma, who although supportive, made insightful criticism regarding the relationship. In Frank's version, only the two pairs of lovers appeared and Emma's lines were distributed amongst three chorus members, who echoed and reinforced the protagonists' lines, or acted as prophetic voices of unspoken thoughts—much as characters do in Suzuki, noh and Greek Classical theatre. As critic Douglas Leonard observed (2002: 35), it was Olive's "fabricated recollections" of the previous summers which sustained the "fragile" emotional architecture

---

31   Canecutters had initially been recruited through "blackbirding" or the capture of Pacific islanders for forced, indentured labour. Although largely replaced by whites after 1901, these settler-descent yet darkly skinned throwbacks to modern Australia's origins in the seizure of land from First Nations Australians often functioned as a primal racial Other for sophisticated metropolitan whites, or as Wal Cherry put it: "'The difference between the cane-cutter and his city brother is his aggressive manliness, his closeness to the earth, his coating of tan. He has the earth to go back to until he is too old" (1956: 83).

FIGURE 15   Frank Theatre's *Doll Seventeen,* by Ray Lawler (Visy Theatre, Brisbane Powerhouse: 2002; dir. Jacqui Carroll). Left to right: Lisa O'Neill (The Doll), Conan Dunning (Barney), Leah Shelton (Pearl), Caroline Dunphy (Olive), John Nobbs (Roo)
IMAGE COURTESY OF CARROLL AND NOBBS

of the protagonists, who "Strikingly ... often fell asleep", seeking to recapture through dreams the previous lay-offs. Frank's treatment thereby mythologised this richly detailed socio-cultural portrait of Australian gender relations, class, work, and sexuality, transforming it into a neo-Expressionist study of souls apparently lost in a trance, moving through a fantastic, carnival-like space constructed from Olive's desires and imaginings (Figure 15).

Lawler's original described a worn working class house in Melbourne. Frank instead offered an exaggerated black, white, and red fantasy of 1950s popular culture, or as Leonard put it, "a hedonistic 50s Australian suburbia run amok" (2002: 35). This was accompanied by achingly painful Argentinian tango and the exuberant lounge music of Yma Sumac and (again) Perez Prado. Leonard noted that in Frank's *Doll Seventeen*:

> Pink, 50's boudoir pink, was everywhere: scintillating in the costuming and the fake fur-lined wall denoting an arch female "interior" from which

> exits and entrances took place via a revolving mirror door signifying an anterior reality, not a conventional "exterior".
> 2002: 35

Also featured was "a recurring cow print" found in the costumes and design, "inflatable furniture", and small, red "dodgem car" armchairs on rollers (Treyvaud 2003: 13). Simplified or abstracted designs have been relatively rare in canonical stagings of *Summer of the Seventeenth Doll*. The 1955 premiere, for example, as well as the major revivals in 1976 (staring *Chronicle of Macbeth* actor Peter Curtin) and then 1985, all featured detailed, realist settings. In several productions however—including Frank's—colour and a sense of escape from everyday urban reality was signalled through garish objects from popular culture, specifically the kewpie dolls Roo gifted Olive each year. Carroll's approach was to expand these elements into the broader dramaturgy, featuring a life-size kewpie doll, played by Lisa O'Neill, initially wheeled on by the chorus, and later manipulated by Roo and others. Carroll described this as "a device" to "let the terror out", or in Leonard's phrasing, "a pink tulle creation on pointe who can only repeat with fractured ferocity the sentimentalised jargon of popular love songs; the Doll with which Olive finally fuses" (2002: 35).

As critics have acknowledged, *Summer of the Seventeenth Doll* itself was conceived as a "Method actor's play" in which "stage directions indicate a level of gesturality, a dimension of hystericization, [and] an excess of the body of the actor" (O'Regan 1988: 118). In many Australian plays of the period, there was a "propensity for inarticulate violence [which] entangled men in their relationships with women" and with each other (Bollen et al. 2008: 33). In 1956, Wal Cherry concluded that Lawler's play was "dominated by a sense of ... energy suppressed or lost or dissipated", as in the off-stage battle "on the canefields", or the "fight in the parlour" between Roo and Barney (84). In Frank's *Doll Seventeen*, however, the physical falling out of Roo and Barney was conducted as a verbal conflict staged between the men while they were dressed absurdly in black and white boxing attire. NSP s style proved ideal to maintain Cherry's sense of urgent, potentially violent energy throughout the play, whilst simultaneously creating a sense of dramaturgical checkmate. The staging of violence itself was unnecessary in the presence of Nobbs' monumentally grounded, powerful form, matched by the concentration of his peers on stage. As Leonard put it, Frank's characters were "circumscribed" within a "mythic" space and time, the audience being "witness to eternal recurrence rather than linear exposition" (2002: 35). The conventional climax of the play occurs where Roo, crushed by Olive's refusal to give up the layoffs and accept conventional married life, goes into a:

> baffled insensate rage, starts to beat the doll down on the piano, smashing it again and again ... until it is nothing but a litter of split cane ... Only when it is in this state does it drop from his hands, and only now does the tremendous energy sustaining him ... drain away ... he slowly subsides to sag down on the piano stool. Something breaks deep within him, but there is no outward sign.[32]
>
> LAWLER 2012: 182

As critics observed, these directions call for a complex level of psychocorporeal nuance (Bollen et al. 2008: 47–49), but Carroll and Nobbs eschewed such physical excess, instead dispersing their energies throughout the garish set and multi-modal performances of dancerly interludes, dumbshow to mimed musical numbers, and ritualistically intoned text. Because it was Olive whose dreams sustained the mise en scène, Carroll staged only *her* physical collapse, not Roo's (Carroll dir. 2003a). Caroline Dunphy flung herself backward whilst seated in one of the red armchairs, rejecting Roo, seated opposite her. At the climax of the scene, she stood in shock, at the centre of the stage, before falling to her knees, divesting herself of her coat and jewellery. A tremor passed through her, and she ran left and right, before shakily retreating to the rear of the stage and exiting, almost crucifying herself against the fur trimmed, glass door (Carroll dir. 2003a). The men's subsequent trancelike exit was by contrast sedate, inevitable and anticlimactic, suggesting a return to the condition they entered from, rather than a rupture.

The "terror" which Carroll identified in the work was therefore not localised but omnipresent, and with the exception of Olive and a few scattered moments where she or Roo raised their voices, *hystericization* was not a feature of the performers' bodies, but rather a quality which *suffused the mise en scène as a whole*. The piece opened with O'Neill miming to a high-pitched, chipmunk like rendition of the Cher song, "If I Could Hold Back Time" (1989). The lyrics expressed the desires of the protagonists to resist their own corporeal aging as well as changes in society and labour. The production ended with the clock which had been resting above the action throughout finally sounding, its chimes signalling the end of all dreams. "No more flyin' down

---

32   Bollen et al (2008) cite the 1957 edition. I quote from the 2012 edition. Nobbs and Carroll negotiated directly with Lawler before staging the production, so likely were working with one of the revisions published after *The Doll* had become a trilogy.

out of the sun—no more eagles", as Nobbs repeated to Olive and himself (Lawler 2012: 179).

Carroll has extolled the "non-realistic form" of her production (Nobbs and Carroll nd.1). It served as an exemplar not only of Nobbs' and Carroll's opposition to Naturalistic dramaturgy, but also how classics from the Australian socio-realist canon could be successfully translated into neo-Expressionist productions through NSP and the techniques developed by the company. The central motif of Roo as an idealised masculine archetype, insistently defining himself through the act of physically working the land, meant that Carroll's and Nobbs' aim to transform *Summer of the Seventeenth Doll* into a "universal" work cannot entirely succeed. Carroll's compression of dramatic themes and energies into this stripped back performance only had resonance if one has the requisite cultural knowledge to decode allusions to national stereotypes—just as Suzuki's 1991 Japanese production of *Macbeth* set in the wartime ruins of Japan's cities requires a familiarity with Japan's vexed history of imperialism and occupation to be fully appreciated (Mulryne 1998: 87–90). Nevertheless, it was Frank's *Doll Seventeen* which signified that Carroll and Nobbs had moved past drawing on Orientalist imagery and the appeal of Otherness to take NSP and Japanese performance into an explicitly Australian context. Devoid of allusions to non-Australian cultures beyond mambo (an American and Afro-Caribbean phenomenon) and post-World War Two exotica music (through Yma Sumac, who claimed her vocal fantasies constituted a form of Inca language), *Doll Seventeen* rested comfortably within the national mythos of Russell Ward's Australian Legend, as manipulated, critiqued and celebrated by Lawler and his peers. As in Lawler's original, Frank's production was ambivalent regarding the reality, let alone the desirability, of the Legend. It did however produce a paradoxical dramaturgical effect, in how such a distinctively white, Anglo-Australian model of gender, sexuality and subjectivity was expressed through an otherworldly acting form derived in large part from Japan. *Doll Seventeen* remains one of the company's most successful intercultural fusions, and was one that balanced the artists' tendency towards excess and humour with a sense of restraint and clear direction.

11   Conclusion: The Way Forward is Mixed

Paul Allain has speculated that for SMAT outside of Japan, the "future may lie in an intercultural fusion rather than wholesale appropriation", pointing to the international uptake of the technique developed by Anne Bogart in collaboration with Lauren and the US company Suzuki helped establish in Saratoga

(Allain 1998: 85). While Nobbs (2010: 240–241) scorns SITI s method of scenographic construction entitled Viewpoints,[33] the latter is widely taught across Australia, often deployed in combination with elements of SMAT, NSP and even butoh (Marshall 2022a and 2022b). Institutionally at least, NSP has not had wide uptake as a master discipline, though Carroll and Nobbs still offer guest sessions, workshops and masterclasses for arts academies. At my own institution of the Western Australian Academy of Performing Arts, Carroll and Nobbs have had a direct influence on the training of actors and performance makers, with Suzuki training seen in large part through the prism of Frances Barbe's explorations in butoh, NSP and SMAT (Barbe 2011; Allain and Barbe 2009: 156–7; Barbe 2019: 179–201). Others such as former Frank member Joanne Loth and sometime butoh performer Jeremy Neideck also employ Viewpoints in association with Body Weather, NSP, SMAT and other methods, including, in Neideck's case, the Korean sung drama form pansori (Loth 2001; Loth and Pensalfini 2021; Neideck 2016). Within teaching at many of the major training institutions, NSP is present as a locally blended fusion, with butoh elements often prominent. Frank however would seem likely to remain the only group in Australia solely committed to this method of localising SMAT within the national and cultural context, and as we shall see in the next chapter, for many other artists, butoh itself has often provided an explicit part of what can be used to broaden the appeal and efficacy of Suzuki's vaunted method.

---

33   "V/P's [sic] were devised as a post-modern dance tool, a DIY paint by numbers kit for choreographers that had nothing to say, but thought they should be saying something … VP's are for artists that … don't believe in anything but themselves" (Nobbs 2010: 240–241).

CHAPTER 8

Butoh in the Southern Tropics: Zen Zen Zo and Associates

1   Introduction

In this chapter, I examine the work of the company Zen Zen Zo Physical Theatre—created by Carroll's and Nobbs' peers in Brisbane. The company was founded by Lynne Bradley and Simon Woods; Frances Barbe choreographed several sketches in the company's early mixed programs of short butoh performances, as well as contributing to the development of the choreography for later text based works. I survey Zen Zen Zo's productions, with an emphasis on these early butoh works and the emergence of a recurrent trope of the butoh chorus within their work. As a company employing from the start multiple blended techniques, including butoh, Suzuki, and Lecoq clowning, Zen Zen Zo reveals the trajectory of butoh in Australia, showing how quickly butoh elements diffused within other practices to the point that the butoh influence became difficult to recognise. Zen Zen Zo's *Cult of Dionysus* (1994–96) is a significant mid point, a highly accomplished work employing mostly Suzuki concepts to build the performance, which used butoh to create corporeal and dramaturgical counter trends, including sinuous, feminine or queer bodies and a sense of dangerously exhilarating, primal wildness. I also examine works by Barbe herself—notably her expatriate portrait of white Australian identity *Fine Bone China*—and Helen Smith.

2   Bradley's and Woods' Encounters with Japanese Performance

Lynne Bradley first saw butoh in Japan in 1990, by accident, when the piece being staged at Kyoto's Minami-za theatre turned out to not be kabuki, but rather Dairakudakan's landmark production *Kaiin no Uma* (*Tale of the Sea-Dappled Horse*).[1] She recorded her impressions in a journal at the time:

> I went expecting to see traditional Japanese theatre. But what I saw … was unlike anything I have … witnessed … twenty five seminaked bodies

---

1   See "Maro & Dairakudakan" in chapter five.

painted white with shaved heads or masses of wild hair, convulsing in a trancelike state with eyes rolled up, to a cacophony of strange sounds and music … Lengths of tattered red material spilled from their mouths … like fountains of blood. As they slowly convulsed forward I saw the series of imprints their bodies had left upon the walls, like the nuclear shadows left behind in Hiroshima and Nagasaki. As the show unfolded there was a parade of surreal and shocking images, grotesque figures, and inexplicable encounters. It was like being inside a Salvador Dali painting or witnessing firsthand a Rabelaisian Carnival. I don't know what it was (dance? theatre? performance art?) but I feel COMPELLED TO DO IT!.[2]

2017: 2

Bradley's reaction to butoh echoes that of the other artists discussed earlier, but differs in that she invoked a number of key art historical referents to ground her reading—specifically "Rabelaisian Carnival" and Surrealism ("Dali"), both of which would guide her own practice. As elsewhere, butoh was encountered by Bradly as both confusing yet also having familiar elements which might provide an entrée into the work. Bradley also recognised that butoh was not easily defined in terms of form, moving between the conventions of dance, theatre and performance art, including elements of nakedness, and images which evoked both violence and beauty ("fountains of blood"). Bradley's reading of butoh as offering a range of moods and stylistic references created a space for her to rework the form for her own purposes, since its nature was so amorphous.

Simon Woods, who co-founded Zen Zen Zo Physical Theatre with Bradley in 1992, was less struck by his early interactions with butoh, which came in the form of his involvement in the company's inaugural productions. He nevertheless described seeing Suzuki Tadashi's production of *King Lear* in Toga, Japan, 1993, as a "'gestalt' experience", where the combination of setting, architecture, as well as the "technical mastery … precision … pure passion and intensity" of the deeply trained actors was "overwhelming" (2006: 145). Even so, Woods' immediate realisation was that it was not so much the outward "forms", positions, and mise en scène that mattered, but the "principles and philosophies" that underpinned them (Woods 2006: 145). This meant it should be possible to translate Suzuki's concepts into other national settings. Woods and Bradley stayed up all night at Toga's bus stop discussing these and other possibilities.

---

2 Bradley has given variants of this account multiple times; see, for example, Woods (2006: 142).

3   Zen Zen Zo's Foundation and the Development of Its Aesthetic, 1992–98

Lynne Bradley pioneered the practice for students at Brisbane's tertiary theatre courses to travel to Japan to study performance. From 1988 to 1993, Bradley lived in Kyoto. From 1990 she trained in noh and nihon buyō under Jonah Salz of Noho Theatre and Yasuchika Urata of the Kanze school (Bradley 2017: 27; Zen Zen Zo 2008: 148).[3] As she became aware of the Japanese iemoto system in which hierarchical patriarchal family lineages dominate the classical arts, Bradley realized: "I was never going to be a [professional] noh dancer because I wasn't male, I wasn't Japanese, and I wasn't born into a noh family" (Robertson 2015: 70). It was at this time she saw *Tale of the Sea-Dappled Horse*. From 1991, Bradley switched to butoh, initially working with Kan Katsura (Robertson 2015: 20). Kan had danced with Byakkosha, one of the many companies seeded by Dairakudakan, with a similar and if anything wilder aesthetic than that of Maro. Though most influenced by Maro and his former students, Bradley did not become a student of a single teacher, and while in Japan she also interacted or trained with the Ohnos, and Iwashita Toru (formerly of Sankai Juku). In 1992, as part of her studies at University of Queensland (UQ), she produced *Never the Elephant*—a rough translation of "Zen Zen Zo"—choreographing several pieces which featured alongside works by Barbe, a fellow student at UQ who had attended ballet classes from the age of six to twenty-one, but found that this had "left me with a somewhat rigid style in my body" (Barbe 2011: 3, 23). Helen Smith, who joined Zen Zen Zo slightly later, shared with Barbe and Umiumare a frustration with ballet which could be resolved through the adoption of butoh. Smith "felt very restricted by the fact that I didn't have the perfect [ballet] body" (Robertson 2015: 68), and so as a tall and imposing dancer, butoh offered her a way to express both her power and the collapse of this strength. Butoh similarly provided Barbe with a means for to reintroduce flexibility and transformations into her dance, and one of her first butoh sketches for Zen Zen Zo—"Hysterical Angels"—consisted of "a butoh version of the mad scene from *Giselle*" (Barbe 2011: 22). Many of the early members of Zen Zen Zo such as Bradley, Barbe and Smith met working on student productions directed by UQ

---

3   In this chapter I draw extensively on *The Zen Files*, a collection put together by the company which includes often rare interviews and reviews, as well as otherwise unpublished notes, principally authored by Bradley; these sections are cited as Zen Zen Zo (2008). I also cite by individual author published materials which are reproduced in *The Zen Files*, such as Beckey (2004).

theatre academic Adrian Kiernander (Zen Zen Zo 2008: xi–xvi, Beckey 2004: 118; Neideck and Kelly 2021: 456).

Barbe's familiarity with ballet and modern dance gave her the confidence to choreograph short butoh works to go alongside those by Bradley, even though Barbe's exposure to butoh at this time was only through Bradley and the documentation reaching Australia. Simon Woods, with whom Bradley would form a professional and personal relationship, was recruited as lighting designer. Following the success of *Never the Elephant*, Zen Zen Zo Physical Theatre was founded, with Bradley and Woods as co-directors. Carroll and Nobbs were present at the company's 1992 premiere, inviting Bradley and Woods to train with Frank before the younger artists returned to Japan the following year (Woods 2006: 143–7). It seems likely that it was through the influence of Frank that Bradley linked her interest in Japanese performance to the theories of psychoanalyst Carl Jung (Bradley 2017: 29–31, 81–89, 100, 118), as Nobbs is one of small number of practitioners in the field to frame Japanese physical theatre in Jungian terms. Bradley contended that she was one of the "first major translator of Maro's Method ... into the Australian performing arts landscape" (2017: 176), her own interventions occurring shortly after Umiumare began to offer workshops in Melbourne.

Barbe's choreography appeared in Zen Zen Zo's *Never the Elephant* (1992), *Way of Mud* (1993), *Macbeth* (1995), *Unleashed* (1996–2000), *Steel Flesh* (1998) and *Zeitgeist* (2008–10). The same year Barbe first worked with Bradley she started training with Carroll and Nobbs, performing in Frank's premiere production of *Orpheus* in 1993. Barbe maintained an ongoing relationship with Carroll and Nobbs, characterizing her mature work as "butoh-based exercises with a yoga-based warm-up, and exercises from the repertoire of Suzuki Tadashi's actor training method, as practiced by my teachers, John Nobbs and Jacqui Carroll" (2011: 112). Barbe deepened her relationship with butoh, SMAT and other techniques when her career took her to Europe, the USA and Britain from 1997. I discuss Barbe's career in more detail below.

Barbe, Bradley, Woods and Loth, all offered classes in butoh and Suzuki under the umbrella of Zen Zen Zo at one time or another. From 1996, Zen Zen Zo's workshops ran almost every week. Bradley described becoming a teacher of butoh so early in her career as "very strange" (Robertson 2015: 44). This was barely three years since Carroll and Nobbs had begun offering public workshops in Brisbane to train their own cohort of collaborators. Bradley oversaw Zen Zen Zo's butoh training, while Woods focused on derivations of SMAT, though they blended the two in many instances.

In 1993–95, Bradley encouraged company members to train in Japan and then with SITI in the USA. Bradley, Barbe, Woods, and Helen Smith joined for some or all of these sessions.[4] They trained in SMAT principally with SITI's trainers Ellen Lauren and Leon Ingulsrud, rather than with SCOT's actors at Toga, though Bradley and Woods attended many of Suzuki's productions and observed Suzuki's training at Toga (see Bradley 2017 and Woods 2006 passim). Bradley would also take advantage of Australian opportunities for training and exchange, a 1996 workshop with Tess de Quincey introducing her to the concept of "omnicentral imaging" (2017: 101–102) used by both Tanaka and Hijikata. Bradley also drew sparingly on ideas developed by Hijikata's star performer Waguri Yukio (with whom she interacted briefly at NIDA), as well as Nakajima Natsu, who worked with both the Ohnos and Hijikata. After their initial spell with SITI in 1993, Bradley and Woods returned in 1998 to participate in intensives run by Bogart, Lauren and others at SITI. John Nobbs was present at SITI's SMAT classes in 1993 (Woods 2006: 147). From 1998, Bradley and Woods added Viewpoints to their repertoire, being amongst the first to teach the technique in Australia (Bradley 2017: 68).

Because Suzuki did not include a warm up or warm down, Woods and Bradley added yoga to Zen Zen Zo's sessions "as a way of increasing strength and flexibility to help prevent soft tissue injuries, to develop breath control, and as a relaxation tool" (Woods 2006: 163–64). They also drew heavily on Lecoq's approach to bouffon clowning (which they had learned with Russell Dykstra at UQ), acrodance (initially taught to them by Christopher Sleight), as well as more piecemeal additions and vocal "extensions" from Western dramatic training, including key concepts from teachers of Naturalistic acting like Lee Strasberg ("sense memory"), Sanford Meisner, and particularly Eric Morris ("emotional release"; Woods 2006: 184; Zen Zen Zo 2008: ix, 97, 120, 137, 149; Everett 2008: 177–8).

4 Zen Zen Zo's Early Work and Brisbane Physical Theatre

Bradley would come to employ a three stage developmental process for the company's fully funded works, consisting of four weeks of creative development at a retreat, generally Montville scout camp near Kondalilla Falls, a bit over 100 kilometres north and inland of Brisbane and the Sunshine Coast (Heddon and Milling 2005: 173–4). As with Dairakudakan or the Body Weather camps of de Quincey and Tanaka, performers shared

---

4 Smith would be a core Zen Zen Zo member, 1993–2010, before seeking further training in Japan and elsewhere, and later moving to Melbourne where she has since worked with Umiumare and Taylor.

accommodation and meals. The morning was spent training. After lunch they worked on the show itself. Nights would often be spent debriefing or sharing resources such as videos, texts, images and so on (Tong 2011: 3). Although Zen Zen Zo were not a Body Weather company, some rehearsals were held outdoors to help stimulate the imagination and to develop corporeal sensitivity. The artists often produced scrapbooks of useful images, inspirations and notes (Tong 2011: 26), which bore some similarity to Hijikata's butoh-fu compilations.

Zen Zen Zo's first productions consisted of butoh sketches developed by Bradley and Barbe. Premiered in *Never the Elephant* (1992), Bradley's honour's year production at the University of Queensland, some of these pieces were retained for the first suite of Zen Zen Zo's butoh programs, variously titled *Butoh: The Way of Mud* (1993, with a cast of ten), *Unleashed* (1996–2000, eight) and the retrospective *Zeitgeist* (2008–10, with a cast of twenty-one). Bradley and Barbe also collaborated on the more thematically coherent production of *Steel Flesh* (Brisbane Festival 1998, four dancers). Bradley's later butoh compilations included *Gaia* (2009) and *Apocalypse* (2011). Pieces within earlier programs were often retained, reworked and sometimes retitled across multiple stagings.[5]

Woods and Bradley employed their variant of SMAT to train the company for its first choreographed spoken drama *The Cult of Dionysus,* which premiered in Kyoto, before returning to Australia, 1994–96 (Zen Zen Zo 2008: x). Zen Zen Zo's *Macbeth As Told By the Weird Sisters* also premiered at Kyoto University, before Brisbane outings, 1995–2002. From 2007, Zen Zen Zo's members regularly developed works at Dairakudakan's Hakuba summer workshops, the Australians appearing in six of Maro's Japanese productions by 2016, while Dairakudakan members Yuyama Daiichiro, Miyamoto Seiya and others had collaborated on three of Zen Zen Zo's Australian works by 2016 (*Gaia,* 2009, *Apocalypse,* 2011, and *Company of Shadows,* 2016; Bradley 2017: 4–5, 109).

Zen Zen Zo's approach to butoh, SMAT and their fusion, was therefore principally the product of a triumvirate led by Bradley as the one with the greatest knowledge of butoh itself, in association with Barbe, as well as Woods, who specialized in SMAT, aided by Christopher Beckey (credited by one reviewer

---

5 The selection of short works in an individual program sometimes changed when programs were remounted. The works identified by Lazaroo (2011) as making up the 2010 staging of *Zeitgeist* differ from those documented by the 2008 video, as does the opening section of the sketch "Unleashed" included in the DVD of *Unleashed* (1996) in comparison with the version of "Unleashed" included in the *Zeitgeist* DVD (2008)

as a co-choreographer for one piece in *The Way of Mud,* 1993; Waller 1993: 1), Helen Smith, and others from UQ. Dykstra's interpretation of bouffon (Everett 2008: 171–180) was also crucial.

Bradley and Woods built on their links with Brisbane tertiary institutions for Zen Zen Zo to become company of residence at UQ from 1996. Becoming highly successful at promoting their work and their image, Zen Zen Zo moved in 1999 to running the annual Stomping Ground training intensive, and later Winter Stomp. From 2002, Zen Zen Zo offered a schools program (Zen Zen Zo New Zealand nd). This has meant that the company often provided the first exposure for young Queenslanders to the Japanese avant-garde (Bradley 2017: 10; Neideck and Kelly 2021: 465–6). From 2003, Zen Zen Zo also hosted youth internships, and in 2004 became company in residence at the Queensland Performing Arts Centre (QPAC), before moving to the old Brisbane museum from 2005 and then later the Brisbane Powerhouse. In the early 2000s, Woods' career in sports health, training and photomedia increased. He worked with the Brisbane Lions Football Club "developing programs in flexibility, core strength and mental skills from 2001–2008" (Lawler 2015), and left Zen Zen Zo in 2005 (Sorensen 2005: 63). The professional relationship of Bradley and Woods essentially ended at this point. By 2012, Bradley had moved on from the position of artistic director of Zen Zen Zo, but remained closely linked to the training (Lazaroo 2012). From 2017, she has led the University of the Sunshine Coast's masters program in the performance (Bradley 2017: 223).

Bradley's and Woods' position as irreverent critics of mainstream institutional theatre was solidified in 1997 when the company collaborated with the Queensland University's Music Conservatorium to stage a production of *The Marriage of Figaro,* in which Woods attired the singers in what Veronica Kelly (1997a: 12) of *The Australian* described as "towering wigs and frocks ... [who] stalk[ed] the balconies like Watteau figurines ... in a musical clock" and who were menaced from below by a "gaggle of red-nosed clowns ... creating mayhem with parodic physical comedy". Although positively reviewed by Veronica Kelly, Patricia Kelly, writing in Brisbane's *Courier Mail* and *Ignite* journal described the production as "cultural trash", insisting that it must "never happen again" (Bradley 2017: 12). It was, Kelly argued:

> not opera but a subversion of the form and an insult to the student participants who had to try to sing some of the most sublime music of the canon .... against constant noisy and irrelevant interruption ... / ... opera ... is .... something to share and enjoy, not ... to be lampooned.
> P. KELLY 1997: 24–25

Patricia Kelly asked in a horrified tone, could "society really accept that anything is fair game?" concluding that, "Art is about creativity, not destruction" (1997: 25–26). One can only imagine how delighted these young rabble-rousing followers of postwar global dance theatre were to solicit such a pearl-clutching response as late as 1997. Recognising the absurdity of it all, Australian First Nations theatre director Wesley Enoch came to Zen Zen Zo's defence (1997: 28), suggesting artists and audiences should "Let the dinosaurs die singing from their pulpits" while the company should go on—as it indeed did. The event helped Zen Zen Zo develop an "almost cult following" with the company celebrating "wanton physicality and flagrant subversion of middle-class aesthetics" (Gilbert and Lo 2009: 163–65).

Like Nobbs and Carroll, Bradley defined her interest in Japanese performance as a reaction to the "very strong hold" which she felt European classicism and "naturalism still had" over Australian theatre (Megarrity 2004: 26). This is not to say Bradley rejected Naturalism altogether, and, while Naturalism served as a key rhetorical and discursive pole around which public debates in Australian theatre were carried out, the practical distinction between 1990s "physical theatre" and "Naturalism" was not always clear (see Marshall 2022a and 2022b). It was in this context that, as former Zen Zen Zo members Jeremy Neideck and Katharine Kelly observe that the regular presentation in Brisbane of butoh and Suzuki workshops, training, and productions during the 1990s and 2000s:

> gave a heady and potent sense of a new way, shaped by the sweaty, sub-tropical nature of late-night rehearsal rooms: we embraced our proud status as grafters, as corporeal, visceral, present, and working. Training in ensemble offered a paradoxical experience ... an instant, communal intensity of ... [apparently] authentic embodied achievement, witnessed and endorsed by the collective, and often led by fierce, charismatic leaders ... inflected by ... transmission through Japanese cultural frames ... with a shadow side of trauma, tension, and disillusion, of knees destroyed by hard floors and artistic spirits broken by a variant of Queensland authoritarianism in our adoption of a more physical theatre.
> NEIDECK AND KELLY 2021: 452

The bootcamp like discipline common to the early work of de Quincey, Frank, the Playbox Suzuki project, and other environments, was therefore enthusiastically embraced in those early years, forging both a community of practice and appreciative audiences. Those who stayed the distance—Bradley, Barbe, Loth, Woods, Carroll, Nobbs, Smith, Beckey, Neideck and others—acquired skills and cultural capital which licenced them to attempt their own original interpretations.[6] As at Melbourne's Dancehouse and Chapel of Change, or with the De Quincey Company at Sydney's Performance Space, a strong if at times fractious, collectivity arose in Brisbane. Neideck and Kelly describe the "impact" of "early butoh and Suzuki training on the artistic life of a generation of artists" as "overwhelming" (2021: 452).

5 Zen Zen Zo, Frank and Reworking Japanese Aesthetics

As we saw in the previous chapter, while Nobbs claimed NSP as a recognisable regional variant on SMAT, he nevertheless identified Suzuki as the author of a fully self-contained, transposable system. Woods and Bradley however perceived "weaknesses" in Suzuki technique from the outset, seeing it in some ways as a "limiting" technique for their performers (Woods 2006: 184; Heywood and Gallasch 2001). Woods was clear that Zen Zen Zo approached SMAT at a distance via SITI, and although Woods and Bradley observed SCOT s training in situ, they did not work directly with Suzuki or his company, a situation which helped them "find our own unique voice" (Woods 2006: 140). After Woods and Bradley trained with SITI in 1998, they enthusiastically drew on Viewpoints to render their process more explicitly "collaborative", so that the pair might act "more as 'facilitators' or 'editors' than auteur-style directors" (Bradley 2017: 67; Heddon and Milling 2005: 173). Indeed, Zen Zen Zo's training sessions often featured two teachers "to provide a [democratic] balance in perspectives" (Woods 2006: 178). This reflected Bradley's and Woods' own experience of SMAT at SITI, where they "received different perspectives … from a range of teachers" (Woods 2006: 147). Woods (2006: 147–150) argued that while Suzuki's intervention as a director for SCOT made up for what the training lacked, he and Bradley felt this was not a suitable model for their peers in Australia, who would not have Suzuki's personal input. In the absence of supplementary training in Viewpoints and other methods, they felt that Suzuki-trained actors

---

6 Neideck has associated himself with what he describes as the "second generation" of butoh artists in Queensland (Neideck & Kelly 2021: 452), working with Bradley and Woods first as a student at QUT, 2004, and training with Dairakudakan in 2008, as well as classes with Umiumare. In addition to his "initial flirtations with butoh" (Neideck 2018: 344) in the form of Zen Zen Zo-esque solos, Neideck was a founding member of butoh trio Red Moon Rising (2008–2010). Neideck led a project to combine elements of butoh with the Korean ritual song and gesture performance form pansori, leading to a final production entitled *Deluge* (2014). Neideck's current work eschews outward butoh signifiers however; see also Bradley 2017; Neideck 2015 & 2016; K. Kelly 2014.

could come across as forced, vocally strained, or lacking in spontaneity. Zen Zen Zo and Frank therefore adopted different methods to release the creativity of the acting ensemble. As Lauren explained, in Suzuki's work, the actor was deeply focussed on personal psychocorporeal challenges: "You're all up there struggling to stay alive" (Coen 1995: 30). Consequently there could be a reduction in sympathetic empathy or attention to fellow performers in the space ("You don't necessarily become your fellow player"; ibid.: 30). The SMAT actor was focussed on playing outward to the eyes of the gods (Waddell 1992: 30), and not to each other. For Woods and Bradley, SMAT came to function as a form of deliberately challenging "crisis training" to be supplemented with more explicitly supportive, collaborative and achievable tasks such as one might derive from Viewpoints or butoh imaging, with Bradley often calling out poetic images for the performers to embody during sessions (Woods 2006: 104; Bradley 2017: 141).

Bradley has claimed that by the 2000s the company "found that more and more we were doing these highly funded co-productions" in diverse genres ranging across drama, music theatre and opera (in McAlister 2008: 87), and so would, as one critic put it, periodically "pull out the G-string and slap on the body paint to dance butoh" (ibid.: 87), tending to alternate butoh style choreographic productions with spoken word productions during the 1990s and 2000s. By 2005, Bradley and Woods described their practice as "butoh-inspired dance theatre" before adopting the term "physical theatre", whilst classifying those works from Zen Zen Zo in which audiences moved with the cast as "promenade theatre" (ibid.: 87; Bradley 2017: 24, 135). Bradley claimed that these acts of *"re-naming"* were part of how they uncoupled the company's practice from its Japanese origins, to render it properly Australian (Bradley 2017: 24). Nobbs (2010: 211) on the other hand, while praising Ellen Lauren as an expert in Suzuki technique, had nothing but scorn for Viewpoints. Although Frank and Zen Zen Zo had much in common, "The fact that the companies don't get on" was "common knowledge" (McLean 2002: 19), and the key creatives rarely referred to each other (see Woods 2006: 99, 141–7, 213).

Zen Zen Zo did not champion the direct adoption of techniques developed in Japan, and Woods and Bradley grew tired of the lingering association of their own work with its source of origin. In 1995 Woods declared that he objected to: "people calling us a Japanese company—that is not our identity" (McLean 2002: 19; Davis 1997: 136). Even so, Christopher Becky, who had worked with Bradley, Woods and Barbe since 1992, characterised Zen Zen Zo as exhibiting a "minimalist Japanese aesthetic" as late as 1999 (Newman 1999: 101). While Bradley did not go so far as the Los Angeles based butoh teacher Tamano Hiroko as to offer "Japanese lifestyle classes" alongside dance technique (Vangeline 2020: 199–204), the Australian did insist that one should:

> go back to the source [and] ... train with the Japanese masters ... Otherwise you are just doing ... a cheap imitation ... I have no problem with people from different countries or cultures teaching and working in butoh but I think it is critical that they go back and understand that ... Japanese culture is very complex; it is not a 10 day trip.
> ROBERTSON 2015: 27

Elsewhere, Woods and Bradley observed that:

> In our search for rich theatres of the body, our first port of call was Asia ... Now I think what we do is an amalgam of something that is ... our own, and something that is influenced by Asian theatre.
> HEDDON AND MILLING 2005: 165

Bradley recognised that the acculturation of butoh was not just a question of practical activities and corporeal sensations, but was also a matter of discursive and linguistic framing—what she called *"re-naming"* and "Cultural Translation" (2017: 24).[7] As an art closely associated with translating words and poetic motifs into corporeal form, butoh can only be transmigrated if one also considers the broader context and language of practice. Nevertheless, these prevarications and inconsistencies in the pronouncements of company members at different times dramatized how politically and culturally challenging it was to render these practices Australian—particularly by a company who membership was described at the time as "predominantly white Australian" (Lazaroo 2013: 382).

The Japanese origins of Zen Zen Zo's training and aesthetic certainly remained part of how it was presented for some time. Bradley and Woods retained a number of Japanese terms for exercises and concepts. Maro's idea of "miburi-teburi" was often invoked, and was glossed in translation as "purposeless movement" or the intention to "carve out miburi (dark unconscious) magic in a teburi (everyday) world" (Lazaroo 2011: 36).[8] Many of Suzuki's Japanese names for exercises were employed (tenteketen, shakuhachi, and so on). As in Japan, students were asked to wipe down the studio floor with a wet cloth prior

---

7   Bradley (2017: 47–57) justifies this construction by reference to semiotics, literary theory and translation studies.
8   See "Maro & Dairakudakan" in chapter five.

to training,[9] which subsequently ended with artists kneeling in a circle before bowing to each other, and pronouncing in Japanese "otsukaresama deshita [thank you for your hard work]" (Woods 2006: 154). When Bradley took the company to Japan to work with Dairakudakan in 2015, male cast members submitted to a "hair shaving ritual", stripping them of their former identities and marking them as members of a collective led by Maro and Bradley (Bradley 2017: 112). In addition to this, Bradley drew on her training in noh aesthetics to place particular stress in butoh on the Japanese concept of "ma", or the potent, charged empty space that exists between things or actions. Bradley argued that it was the "ma", or the interval between acts, rather than the act itself, which generated meaning and affect in butoh and theatre (Bradley 2017: 28).

Bradley also believed it was desirable for performers to understand the aims of exercises. Her peers would "tolerate a certain degree of openness and ambiguity with regards to the instructions", but "if the gap grew too large, they became demotivated and disengaged" (2017: 96). Bradley offered an initial "contextualising talk" of up to ten minutes prior to introducing tasks, departing from the more straightforward requirements of most Japanese teachers to require charges to simply do as instructed (Bradley 2017: 96). Woods characterised the company's practice as "Socratic" (2006: 154). Nevertheless, questions and discussion occurred within circumscribed periods between physical tasking (Lazaroo 2011: 15), and here again Bradley's process recalled that of de Quincey.[10] Bradley also dropped or modified some of Maro's more complex phraseology, such as his idea of embodying "igata (moulds)", and, where possible, used Anglo-European metaphors and images (Bradley 2017: 87, 138–9, 178). Maro generally developed his work in silence, adding music later, whereas Zen Zen Zo routinely employed music and sound to assist performers reach the desired psychocorporeal state.

Overall, Bradley characterised her use of Japanese derived concepts as a form of "translation" and, as implied above, claimed that the success or otherwise of translation depended on the depth of knowledge one had of the source culture (Bradley 2017: 55–58). Innovation came from a position of sympathy and authority rather than ignorance, disrespect, or a desire to exert power through appropriation and mastery. Bradley likened this to acting as an anthropologist. Bradley and Woods observed that when:

> we think through what an exercise [from Japan] means we ask: What are the fundamental principles … and what are we trying to achieve? … We

---

9 This was quite common in Australian butoh; see Anderson (2014: 135); Smith (2013: 44).
10 See accounts of de Quincey's training in chapter three.

do an immediate cross-check and ask ... 'Does this exercise need to ... change for it to be more relevant to us?' ... the answer is usually, 'Yes'.
  HEDDON AND MILLING 2005: 175

Bradley has inflected her translation of butoh by framing it in Jungian terms, relating it to Rabelaisian and Bakhtinian models of carnival as a subversive cultural phenomenon. Bradley conceded that, to some extent, she had "imposed my *own interpretation*" on butoh concepts such as *"Miburi/Teburi* ... in my desire to align" butoh with "Jung's Shadow archetype" (2017: 84). Bradley nevertheless argued that butoh could be interpreted as exploring "the shadow space of the human being which crosses all cultures" (Robertson 2015: 25, 46), noting that Jung defined the shadow self as the "face" of ourselves which "we never show to the world" (Bradley 2017: 30–31). Jung argued that this was a primal or "archetypal" structure within the psyche of all humans, which had become increasingly repressed under modern civilization (Jung 1980: 3–41). Like many other commentators, Bradley considered butoh and Suzuki to be "very grounded" forms, with a "downward focus towards the earth" and a strong emphasis on "the lower body" (in Zen Zen Zo 2008: 149), and the dark, chthonic forces this implied. Butoh in particular helped the performer to, in Bradley's phrasing (2017: 30–31), access the shadow self within the dancer—a denied and defiled version of oneself with which one must become reconciled to be truly whole—enabling one to enact a "stripping back [of] the civilised veneer to find the primal, instinctive self" (in Zen Zen Zo 2008: 149). As Woods put it, in both SMAT and butoh "the actor is asked to conjure up something from their primal self" or "inner unconscious", and exercises in which actors "verbalise a stream of consciousness" were adopted by the company (Wood 2006: 90, 173). Bradley echoed Hijikata's claim that butoh dancer "eat the darkness", in her own words suggesting that performers must "confront and 'devour' or 'eat' their Shadows", incorporating these shadow selves into themselves as fractious beings which agitated body and psyche (Bradley 2017: 30, 119; Hijikata 2000d: 76). Bradley has presented her cast with the "challenge of staging dreams" themselves, in the manner of Surrealist Salvador Dali.[11] Bradley and Woods have therefore characterised butoh and SMAT as practices which encourage psychological reflection and spiritual development (see Bradley 2017: 29–31,

---

11   In following Dali here Bradley departs from Surrealism proper, and hence Hijikata's precedent also. André Breton (1969: 274), founder of the Surrealist movement, insisted that the dream served as a way to access subconscious forces (*"psychic automatism"*), and that precise replication of the dream's superficial imagery itself constituted little more than a degraded "trompe l'oeil" in art.

141, 236, 283; Woods 2006: 19–20), and Nobbs' favoured term of seeing the actor as a "shaman" appears in their discourse too (Heddon and Milling 2006: 161; Lazaroo 2011: 29). As Woods explains (2006: 90), even if the "modem perspective … does not advocate the [literal] channelling of gods", the performer is nevertheless "asked to conjure up something from their primal self, their inner unconscious, and present that as part of their performance".

Bradley (2017: 31–33) further related the dark inversions of Jung and butoh to those clowns and disgraced misfits—beggars, cripples, and so on—who became temporary masters during the Festivals of Misrule inaugurated during early modern European carnivals, mardi-gras, and so on. Bradley (31–33) cites the European carnival traditions described by Renaissance author Francois Rabelais and his critical champion Mikhail Bakhtin. Hijikata and other butoh artists drew on comparable Japanese folk traditions, while Maro himself likened the act of creation to a "festival" which released repressed or forgotten, non-productive movements (ibid.: 87). In terms of technique and content, this meant that Bradley and Woods encouraged a degree of introspection in training and rehearsal, using the prompt of "abandoning" restraint as method to release the performer's fantasies and expressions through what Maro called the "crack" which can open up to allow transmission between daily life and its subterranean counterpart (Umiumare 2014: 12). Also important was the influence of Frenchman Jacques Lecoq (Bradley 2017: 271–9), whose theories of clowning made up UQs curriculum. Continental mime and physical theatre had played a role in the development and export out of Japan of butoh, with Hijikata and Ohno Yoshito learning some elements of Étienne Decroux's approach from director-choreographer Oikawa Hironobu in the 1950s (Vangeline 2020: XXIX–XXX), while Russian physical theatre group Derevo developed a form of butoh-informed "dark clown" (Picon-Vallin 2004: 335–344). Lecoq's concept of "le jeu"—or a light, rhythmic and spatial "playfulness"—was claimed by Zen Zen Zo for a period as a "core principle" underling the company's aesthetics (Lazaroo 2006: 20, 98). As a group largely drawn from Brisbane's undergraduate university drama classes, members were broadly familiar with Lecoq, and the early productions featured butoh clowns (Mr Bean meets Hijikata if you like), epitomised by the double-act of Andrew Cory and Damien Cassidy in *The Way of Mud* (the sketches of "Unwrapped" and "Deflowered", 1993). Bradley strove for what she identified as a "mix of the sacred and the profane" akin to that at Europe's riotous feasts following Lent, an inversion of apparent hierarchies, celebrating the fecund "grotesque body" which gorged and sprouted from itself (2017: 32). As Zen Zen Zo member Scott Wings observed, butoh is "very close to clowning. Because something's moving you, like you're inner clown" (Bradley 2017: 183). Maro identified a ludicrous, carnivalesque quality of "undomesticated movement" in Zen Zen Zo's own performers, especially, "These sort of ridiculous, great big burly men" (Bradley 2017: 191). He described Australian males as:

> so bestial. (*Laughing*). They have a very wild animal kind of energy. They don't think too much about 'what is dance?' ... Even with these big, burly bodies they still do really delicate, sensitive things.
> BRADLEY 2017: 190–191

Bradley expressed similar opinions, claiming that "Australians ... we're very loud and huge in our body language and you really have to learn ... subtlety" (Zen Zen Zo 2008: 139).[12]

While Japanese butoh artists and Body Weather practitioners tend to harness emotion in performance *indirectly*, through the use of poetic images which may or may not have had an emotional tenor, Zen Zen Zo explicitly sought to engage emotion as a foundational element for the generation of performance imagery. Bradley contended that butoh training "helped free up the actors" to enter a state of "abandonment" and impulsiveness, as well as in "expressing emotion through their body" (2017: 149). Zen Zen Zo's approach therefore in a sense inverted that of Hijikata and Body Weather. Tess de Quincey for example saw movement in the first instance as "objective" rather than affectively loaded (de Quincey and Eckersall 2012). By contrast, Bradley's tasks (and some of Barbe's) were often directed at the release of affective memories and sensations. Bradley likened the effects of butoh imaging to the concept of "sense memory" (Zen Zen Zo 2008: 149), a term developed by foundational postwar Naturalistic theatre director Lee Strasberg. In this model from Method acting, the performance of actions and gestures acted as a stimulus for imagination and the development of the actors' responsiveness to other elements on stage (Shirley 2018: 49, 54–60). These diverse influences meant that, unlike for Frank Theatre, the rhetorical and practical distinction between Zen Zen Zo's aesthetic, as opposed to mainstage Naturalism, became less pronounced over time.

Natalie Lazaroo, who trained with Zen Zen Zo for a period, attested to how emotionally powerful their butoh imaging could be, noting that in one exercise, she imagined her repeated death by drowning, as the air was "sucked out" of each of "my organs" to be replaced by water, while she repeatedly rose and fell (2011: 28). By the conclusion, she was "completely in tears", prone on the

---

12 Zen Zen Zo's *Company of Shadows* (2016) included a sketch titled "Boyzzz" which sent up young male energies

floor "exhausted" (103). In follow up exercises, she tried to will a fellow performer to rise up, but unable to do so, an "emotional wave came over me … I felt my insides being ripped out" and began "crying … motionless, with my hand" reaching out for her slumped companion (104). Embodying such poetic images in the manner of butoh was one of several approaches Zen Zen Zo adopted to prevent the physique of SMAT from becoming too rigid. This rendered the actor's expressivity both personal and dynamic. Lazaroo concluded that for Zen Zen Zo, butoh offered a way to explore the "limits" of emotional "expression" (85).

Bradley and her associates had encountered the affective actor training methods of Strasberg at UQ, and although Bradley rarely mentioned the influence of this tradition, it would appear to be one of several which helped transform the often abject affective intensity of butoh into more readable dramatic forms in her work. Where Hijikata tended to transcend emotional legibility itself, rendering the body alternatively hard, tremulous, tetanic and traumatised, expressing a latency of affect beyond language (Marshall 2013: 62–66, 79–81 and 2020c: 66–71)—hence "ankoku butoh"—Zen Zen Zo and many others tended to employ butoh as a tool for expressionistic clarity and potency. Bradley herself concluded that the company "married the hard … martial energy" of SMAT with a "soft, fluid energy and expression of butoh" (Zen Zen Zo 2008: 149), or to put it differently, Zen Zen Zo's works resisted falling too far into the abject hysterically decomposed states which Hijikata often embodied, and so Bradley and her peers tended towards a dramaturgy of emotional legibility consistent with Western models of tragedy, catharsis, identification, and so on.

By around 1997, Zen Zen Zo's butoh had become defined by the frequent use of nakedness, erotic display, burlesque, clown, and an overall style which drew on popular culture as well as art dance, theatre and a heightened version of Naturalistic acting. Bradley had retained from Dairakudakan the use of white body paint and face make-up, the ambiguously erotic body, dancers who performed naked but for a G-string, and facial grimacing—the latter being a focus of several exercises. The combination of stupefied, semientranced performance with nakedness was often seen as productively confusing by audiences, Veronica Kelly observing that "the more flesh is revealed, the less gender seems to matter", rendering the writhing figures more post-human or even "androgenous" than sexually alluring to audiences (Scorch 1993: 2; Kelly 1996: 20).[13] Bradley did not see the use of white body paint as tying

---

13 Another reviewer characterised Zen Zen Zo's work as "naked flames, naked bodies, [and] an orgasm waiting to happen" (Adelaide GT 2000: 39).

Zen Zen Zo to Japanese practice, arguing that it served—as had been said of Sankai Juku (Marshall 1995: 59)—as a "stripping away the individual markers" (Bradley in Robertson 2015: 46) to become a more universalised human subject.

What is so striking about these early butoh works from Zen Zen Zo was how strongly the visual aesthetic recalled that of the whited up dancers from Dairakudakan. Bradley confessed that over the course of her own development and that of the company, "Imitation is a *necessary step* in the innovation process" (2017: 232). Aside from the outward markers already noted, the early choreography was similar to Maro's in many respects, with foetal poses, the rising and collapse of bodies, facial contortions, and at times idiotic, silently gibbering visages, or mouths gaping wide. Zen Zen Zo's work was in this sense comparable to that of many of the first non-Japanese butoh companies becoming established internationally at this time, like the French company Enfin le Jour (1990–2006; Pagès 2017: 202–3). Combined with often epic or atmospheric music, the overall impression was often one of exoticism. While Bradley insisted butoh was an inward state which expressed outwardly, it seems that, at least in the first instance, many company members mastered butoh-like gestures and poses better than they did the fluid, shifting internal dynamics of omnicentral imaging, or of being moved by multiple dispersed forces. Indeed, as Barbe explained, some of Zen Zen Zo's early exercises involved using gesture itself to generate internal sensations:

> We played with taking on huge silent screams, crying masks, big smiles that extended through the whole body or tiny, sinister smiles manifested in the smallest curl of the mouth. They were taken on externally, then we explored how to invest in them internally.
> 2011: 23

In 2014, describing her latest group of performers, Bradley reflected that she while she was "aware" that they lacked "skill" in the specifics of butoh, nevertheless "they make up for in bucket-loads with moxie and a fearless attack on life and art" (Bradley 2017: 232). Much the same could have been said of the first generation Zen Zen Zo artists. Outward markers of the butoh aesthetic persisted in Zen Zen Zo's oeuvre as late as 2010's *Inferno*, with performers in the company's adaptation of Dante's poem exhibiting rolling eyes, clawed hands, arms folding inward towards the body as if in partial paralysis, mouths agape, tongues swollen and protruding (Lazarno 2011: 76), such as has recurred across Japanese butoh productions time and time again.

Even so, Zen Zen Zo's work has never been entirely imitative of Dairakudakan. A curiously recurrent feature was that the intensity of facial contortion combined with the emptying of the dancers' minds frequently caused performers to drool, often copious amounts—a literal instance of the fertile, leaky grotesque body of carnival. This gooey trend would continue through to late productions such as 2009's *The Tempest* (Lazaroo 2011: 102). The addition of clowning in some of the premiere works was a notable innovation on the part of Barbe and Bradley. In the end, the distinctiveness of Zen Zen Zo's aesthetic became externally more visible and clearly articulated as the company moved away from classic butoh signatures to fuse butoh with SMAT, clown, Western acting, Viewpoints, and other elements. Since around 2016, Zen Zen Zo's style remains influenced by butoh and draws on butoh imaging exercises in the training, but exhibits few outward signifiers of Japanese butoh at all.

6 Zen Zen Zo's Early Butoh Productions and Butoh Choruses

Zen Zen Zo staged a number of butoh compilations between 1992 and 2011. In this section, I focus on four individual sketches within these programs. The butoh works of "Unleashed", "Butoh Babies", "Red, Tight and Deadly" and "The Horror" were signature pieces in that they reflected both the Japanese origins of Bradley's and Barbe's aesthetic, whilst subtly departing from these sources. All were performed by dancers adorned with white body paint, most of the men's heads shaved, the women's hair hanging free, dancers attired in G-strings (Figure 16). Musical accompaniment tended to consist of reworked popular styles such as thundering heavy metal or world music electronica, sampling material such as Indian tabla, African thumb harp, jazzy cabaret music, and more (Bradley et al. 2000). Where Frank leapt from one musical source to another during scenes, Zen Zen Zo tended to use consistent musics for each sketch, but like their peers in Frank, the range of styles was broad.

The 1996 version of "Unleashed" began with near naked dancers prone, backs to the audience, faces hidden, curled in upon themselves, gently rocking, before individual dancers switched to hunched over on their knees and then resting upright on their knees (Bradley et al. 2008). Drawing on H.G. Wells' fictional account of racial devolution of future humans into primitive cave dwelling cannibals in *The Time Machine* (1895), one reviewer described the dancers as "foetal Morlocks" which took the form of "slumping, cringing, grimacing butoh dancers ... racked by sudden seizures of movement" (Galloway 1996: 18). Similar motifs appeared at the start of the 1998 full length work *Steel Flesh,* which depicted the "progress through ... the stages of human [technological]

FIGURE 16   Mark Hill (left) and Dale Thorburn (right) in Zen Zen Zo Physical Theatre's *Zeitgeist* (dir. and choreog. Lynne Bradley; Old Museum: 2008).
PHOTO: SIMON WOODS. REPRODUCTION COURTESY OF WOODS

evolution" from the primeval through to "cyberculture", opening with the dancers coming "slowly and painfully to life" like "souls newborn in agony, nuzzling each other for comfort" (Cotes 1998: 15).

Hijikata's early pieces employed the same curled up opening position as part of what he called "a dance of the back" (in Marshall 2018: 163). Many butoh artists have since performed such configurations. Moreover, Amagatsu Ushio of Sankai Juku have framed their work in terms of the recapitulation of primeval evolutionary transitions from "fish to amphibian, then from reptile to mammal" (Baird 2022: 199), and more. Depending on the version, the next sequence in "Unleashed" involved dancers adopting a lizard-like pose, scattering outwards to face the audience, chests to the ground, backs arched, tongues out. Rising to stand, pairs approached each other, bow-legged, to bounce and gesticulate whilst engaging in a series of same-sex and heterosexual couplings, joined at the groin. Manically smiling, they enacted sumo-like sideways stamping movements, becoming more frenetic, and leaping up and down in spirals, ornamenting the movement with their arms and hands in the style of Dairakudakan (Bradley et al. 2000). Pairs bent over each other in a crazed 69 position, the feet of each dancer planted on the ground, and bounced up and down. Post-Surrealist illustrator M C Escher appears to have been an influence here, with pairs of dancers forming two-headed wheel like creatures which rolled about the stage (Escher et al. 2007: 65–66). Choreographic actions like this were well known to those familiar with documentation of Japanese butoh such as Moore's 1991 documentary film. Sketching a series of transformations between different not-quite-human beings, rapid crouching or clawing positions ranged across the stage in ragged waves, before the carrying of spent dancers by their still energised companions, leading to complex lifts producing hybrid bodies. This was followed by the dancers, now standing and challenging the audience, looking over their shoulders with playfully ambiguous expressions, as they moved to the rear wall (Bradley et al. 2008). As with Dairakudakan, the arrangement of dancers sometimes suggested to reviewers images of some greater collective entity: pulsating flowers, "foetal buds", and so on (Van Helten 2008: 90). Even with the direct adoption of gestures from earlier butoh works in Japan, the ambience in Zen Zen Zo's work was more playful and controlled than in pieces by Maro and others. No great enigma was evoked. This was an erotically charged game presented frankly and directly to audiences. Its chaos was contained and its mood largely upbeat, verging on Surrealist comedy.

Companion piece "Butoh Babies"—initially bearing the onomatopoeic title "Bu Bu Bu" (Scorch 1993: 2)—was described as a showcase for creatures whose "curious, innocent delight in their own bodies and each others' … unsettled the audience" (Heddon and Milling 2005: 173). The dancers exhibited a "manic cruelty against", or disinterest in, caring for another's body. Depending on the version, the piece was performed by four (Bradley et al. 2000), to twenty-one dancers (Bradley et al. 2008), the sketch becoming increasingly epic and formalised over time. "Butoh Babies" balanced a sense of energy versus restraint, including protracted periods of facial clowning where figures cast their gaze about with delighted, agonised or stupefied expressions, rolled about in a near spastic manner, kicked their legs up, and clambered around before scooting across their stage on their buttocks. They licked each other's feet, before making messy groupings, coalescing into lines of unison movement. Drooling impressively at several points, "Butoh Babies" was a slow moving piece of abject clowning. It ended with the adult-infants finding eggs, which they cradled in their mouths (a borrow from the yolk sex scene in the Japanese film *Tampopo*, 1987) before threatening to hurl them at audiences. Some commentators found the work "disturbing" (qtd in Heddon and Milling 2005: 173), principally due to the Surrealist, psychoanalytic assumptions which the production dramatized, and which Bradley and her peers shared with Hijikata and Ohno. The eggs were made available to the other dancers by a pair of performers gazing provocatively at the audience, wearing adult women's red high heeled shoes. A second item of red clothing—a headscarf or micro-mini-skirt, depending on the version—completed the fetishistic presentation of these otherwise naked dancers who brought on the concluding erotic toy of the eggs. In short, "Butoh Babies" not only positioned adult-infants as to some degree unstructured and corporeally naïve, but as also explicitly sexualised in terms of desire. Over one hundred years since the 1901 publication of Freud's *Interpretation of Dreams*, the staging of childhood sexuality remains provocative. There were again many precedents for this in butoh's history, notably Hijikata disporting himself amongst children for the film *The Navel and the A-Bomb* (1960).

"Tight, Red and Deadly", choreographed by Barbe, employed a similar style to more explicitly engage with the banality of perverse desire, "perversity" here referring to sexual desire outside of reproductive heterosexual family, and which Surrealism and butoh has long revelled in. "Tight, Red and Deadly" opened with the pair of butoh clowns Cory and Cassidy, attired with red neckties and cuffs at the wrists, carrying onto stage a tray of red high heeled platform shoes akin to those common in pornographic films. Ironically accompanied by quasi-evangelical organ music, male and female cast members then stole from under the front row tight red micro-mini-skirts and processed in slightly awkward lines to form up in a row, holding their hands over their breasts and navels, before shaking about in gay abandon, then lifting up their skirts to reveal the bulge over each of their genital regions. Shoes were tramped along the stage using their hands, and then the principal erotic focus of the shoes was awkwardly transferred to feet, ending with gestures of beatified triumph, playful sexual display. Dancers tottered to the ground to crawl and compare movements. They also shook, slapped and inspected each others' buttocks with classic bouffon expressions. The use of perversely isolated red costume elements and sadomasochistic signifiers as an implicit critique of social conformity and gender roles appeared in many other sketches: giant bows about the waist to later be unwrapped, chains linking a line of ecstatics ("Steel Ribbons", also choreographed by Barbe), red flower-leis bouncing against the dancers' chests (Bradley's "Sloth"), and so on. The genius of "Tight, Red and Deadly" lay in how it revealed an easy proximity between Lecoq's bouffon clowning and butoh itself, an alliance which is not surprising given the influence of pathologically ticcing, hysterical artists of the early twentieth century cabaret on the development of French grotesque clown (Marshall 2013; Gordon 2002; Belvisio 2020). Indeed, if the performers were not mostly bald and whited up (Figure 16), it is debatable whether "Tight, Red and Deadly" would be recognised as butoh at all.

Finally, the short piece "The Horror" by Barbe represented how butoh was nevertheless deployed by the members of Zen Zen Zo to add existential significance to corporeal action. Described by the choreographer as "a harrowing journey into the realm of pure fear" (Barbe 2003), the piece offered slow moving, pained transformations of a group of isolated, standing figures, who reached up, then down, collapsed, to enact a complex set of drumming and weaving arm and finger exercises across their own bodies (Bradley et al. 2000). Standing again, they shuddered, convulsing repeatedly about the diaphragm. Hands moved across the body in pained embraces, accompanied by choral music. Themes and gestures underpinning "The Horror" were extended and reworked in other short works. "Kobe: An Apocalyptic Story" (Bradley et al. 2000), for example, while more lyrical, employed similar devices, adding moments were the cast stood isolated, arms spread in a crucifixion pose akin to that of *Tale of the Sea-Dappled Horse*. The act of reaching up towards the light before falling down, defeated, yet squirming, and ready to try again, was a recurrent feature of much of Zen Zen Zo's work, reflecting a vertical dramaturgy of ascent and descent, upright and fallen, as well as juxtapositions of the collectivity versus isolated figures. Structured around these straightforward affective symbols, the directness of mood evoked by Zen Zen Zo was therefore quite distinct from the more polyvalent, abject aesthetic structures of early Japanese butoh.

A significant development in Zen Zen Zo's aesthetic came with Woods' first production as director, namely Bertolt Brecht's *Galileo* (1993). Suzuki had told the Australian actor playing Macbeth in the 1996 Playbox production that "everything taking place ... on stage is a visualization of your inner world" (Carruthers 1992: 620) and consequently the chorus represented the haunted inner world of the protagonist. For Zen Zen Zo's *Galileo*, Woods stated that, "We explored the psychology of Galileo using butoh dancers to represent the creative energy coming out of his mind and haunting him" (Gold 1994: 4). Variations on these butoh-esque choruses, often performed by actors combining the strong, militant poses of SMAT with elements of spasmodic grotesquery, appeared in numerous Zen Zen Zo productions. *Macbeth As Told By the Weird Sisters* (1995–2002) also featured a chorus of grotesque witches who shepherded a moving audience. The piece was directed by Woods, and co-choreographed by Bradley with Barbe (Barbe 2003). As with Frank's productions, Zen Zen Zo's choice of script was inspired by Japanese productions of the play, with both Suzuki and Kurosawa cited as influences (Zen Zen Zo 2008: xii). Described by Veronica Kelly as "tribal-looking", the witches were dreadlocked, smeared with blood-red makeup and adorned with hides, feathers and leather (Kelly 1998: 32; Roane 1998). They had a definite Bacchic quality and "exude a primitive eroticism" (Broker nd: 103). The score by Colin Webber featured Africanist drumming, vocal ululations and Tuvan throat music. In the chorus' first encounter with Macbeth they presented "a lewd, frenetic come-on, thrusting hips and breasts frantically forward, then suddenly squatting obscenely", serving to "tantalize and appal Macbeth" in equal measure (Brady 1996: 97). Primitive, exotic and cannibal, they later fell upon the defeated Macbeth "like writhing maggots" or a pack of dogs, engaging in a "feeding frenzy" (Kelly 1995b: 15). Lady Macbeth, played by Smith, "squats as if to ditch deliver evil into the world", her "hands become claws" and for "The sleepwalking scene ... Intoning only 'Out, damned spot,'" she "pirouettes into hell ... while the witches mouth fragments of her speech" (Brady 1996: 97). The total effect was to depict what one reviewer described as a "primitive, pan-cultural desire for power" (Brady 1996: 98).

Marginalised butoh primitives continued to appear in Zen Zen Zo's 2009 production of *The Tempest,* with Ariel and Caliban performed by butoh choruses, six actors playing each part. Bradley stated that the production dealt with "every human being's imperative to struggle for freedom—both political and personal", with Prospero's own search for freedom placed on the same level of that of his subjects (Leonard 2009: 42). As Natalie Lazaroo observed, Caliban's grotesque, drooling embodiment served as a "revolt against the oppressive forces that seek to limit him" (2013: 385). At other points "his eyes bulge, his mouth stretches into [the] gaping hole" of many a butoh dancer, and "his ribcage heaves violently" like those of Sankai Juku and others. The presentation of Ariel as butoh-like highlighted the proximity of Ariel to Caliban as the first inhabitants of the island taken from them by Prospero, the magically advanced coloniser. Caliban was presented as a First Nations representative, wearing a Native American mohawk, as well as stringy nativist adornments on his shoulders and wrists. Reviewer Douglas Leonard described these savage "Ur-Indians who are also butoh exponents" as perhaps "a bridge too far" and confessed that at times "I flinched" (Leonard 2009: 42).

At one point, the Ariels and Calibans staged their painful birth from Sycorax, the dark mother figure whom Prospero had driven away. Songs giving voice to their shared oppression were performed by the leading performer playing Ariel, who sang of Prospero's magic at first releasing her from the tree which Sycorax had spitefully imprisoned her within: "suddenly I was free" but:

> I had a new master
> ... and how my heart did ache
> ... the things, Prospero makes me do for him,
> Those wicked things, when will it be through with him?
> When will the day come when I may
> Get to choose to do these things for free?
>   LAZAROO 2013: 43

These passages made clear the political oppression of Caliban and Ariel by the more powerful, learned interloper, but the representation of Caliban as drooling, gibbering, contorted, and near naked still cast the Indigenes as unambiguously primal, uncivilised and violent (Lazaroo 2012: 44–49; Lazaroo 2013: 384–6). Nor did Woods and Bradley so alter the narrative that Prospero no longer emerged as the hero at the conclusion, munificently gifting freedom to the Ariels. The script and the ethnological assumptions underpinning much butoh limited the degree to which these hierarchies of value could be overturned within either the corporeal dramaturgy or the mise en scène. Leonard (2009: 42) nevertheless concluded that, dramaturgically if not politically, it was "the butoh movement adopted wholesale by the Caliban chorus that amounts to a conceptual as well as physical tour de force" of the production.

The success of Zen Zen Zo's adoption of butoh therefore would seem to have arisen from two principal features. The first was the visceral appeal and dynamism of Bradley's and Woods' construction of a butoh chorus. The second, rather more counter-intuitively, lay in how easily the "butoh" elements became all but invisible within a broader comedic fusion, as evidenced in "Tight, Red and Deadly" and the butoh clowns. In this respect, Zen Zen Zo is probably the most representative example of Australian butoh's wider influence.

7 Fusing Butoh with Suzuki: Zen Zen Zo's *Cult of Dionysus* (1994–96)

One of Zen Zen Zo's most successful productions was Woods' staging of Euripides' *The Bacchae* entitled *The Cult of Dionysus*. The script was principally derived from Wole Soyinka's (1974) Nigerian adaptation of *The Bacchae* depicting the conflict between a decadent Yoruba elite versus their restive subaltern subjects. Although often read as a postcolonial parable (Okpewho 1999), Zen Zen Zo omitted reference to slavery except an isolated threat by Pentheus to turn the followers of Dionysus into slaves. Zen Zen Zo's version dramatized a more generalised, primal resistance to civilizational forces. Zen Zen Zo's first version of the play premiered in Kyoto with choreography by Jeannie Donald before being further adapted by Bradley and Woods for an all-Australian cast which would feature at the first Brisbane Festival of the Arts in 1996 (Zen Zen Zo 2008: viii). *Cult* was Helen Smith's first production with Zen Zen Zo, playing one of a chorus of five female Bacchants alongside Bradley, the latter also playing Agave. Afro-Caribbean musical accompaniment was provided by Michael Burke and two other live percussionists.

Characterised as one of the first productions to bring together Suzuki-trained actors with butoh performers, Woods claimed that the company sought "the

FIGURE 17 Zen Zen Zo Physical Theatre's *Cult of Dionysus* (dir. Simon Woods; movement dir. Lynne Bradley; Princess Theatre: 1996). Image at left shows the Chorus of (left to right): Stacey Callaghan, Rebecca Murray, Lynne Bradley, Helen Cassidy. Image at right shows Christopher Beckey as Dionysus (left) and Peter Lamb as Pentheus (right)
STILLS FROM ARCHIVAL VIDEO BY WOODS

halfway point where the emotion of butoh can meet the energy and discipline of Suzuki" (Furst 1994: 3). Judy Pippin and others described the production as "multi-sensory" due to the presence of burning incense, candles, torches, percussive music, striking costumes and make-up (1998: 31), as well as the smell of sweat. The script was in verse, delivered in what one reviewer called the "half-speech, half song-like manner" which Zen Zen Zo shared with Frank, the chorus especially using a rhythmic mode of delivery (Mason 1996: 16). Although led by Beckey as Dionysus and Peter Lamb as Pentheus, reviews consistently focussed on the butoh chorus of Maenads, described as "wild women" who appeared "semi-naked, exotically costumed and spectacularly made-up" (Smith 1996: 14; Broker nd: 103; Figure 17). Helen Gilbert and Jacqueline Lo described the performance as "evok[ing] and sustain[ing] raw, primitive energies" (2009: 163–65). Attired in "ragged skirts of rich reds, oranges and pinks, and strings of beads across their ... bare torsos", chorus members were "smeared" with earth and red make-up, their "faces also streaked with red and hair teased to stand on end, tinted red by dye or lighting", bearing staves or burning torches (Mason 1996: 16; Pippin 1998: 30). Their make up became stained with lines of perspiration as the performance went on. Pippin concluded that the overall effect was "glamorously grotesque" (1998: 30). Unlike in the case of the more overtly political Zen Zen Zo production of *The Tempest*, none of the available reviews characterise the company's depiction of Africanist Bacchants as Ur-primitives to be "a bridge too far"—although this is understandable given that Euripides was explicit that these Bacchants were originally from Persian Lydia in northern Turkey, and had come to the Hellenic city in which the action of the play was set via a journey around the Mediterranean passing through northern Africa and even, in Zen Zen Zo's and Soyinka's telling, "Ethiopia" (Woods et al. 1996; Soyinka 1974: 2; Euripides 1946: 8).

Zen Zen Zo's production opened with Cadmus being rebirthed from the dead, emerging from under a pile of sand on stage, which marked out a path down the centre which would become scuffed and scattered during the performance. Lorne Gerlach, who had performed another narrator figure in Frank's production of *Oedipus* the year before, introduced the story to the audience as something of a burlesque Cadmus, amusingly hunched over and screeching his lines like a cliched crone (Woods et al. 1996). After the Bacchants entered in a stately procession bearing flaming torches, they leapt up and down, their wrists and arms carving out crazed, inconsistent patterns in the style of Dairakudakan, accompanied by Africanist drumming on congas. A variant of this choreography returned at the conclusion, with Dionysus performing a victory dance at the rear of the stage. Quivering with barely contained passion, the chorus crouched, crawled and processed in circles around Pentheus, at times resting low on their haunches as they twisted in a jagged, not quite human rhythm. At times open-mouthed, eyes flaring, sexually confident, shrieking, giggling, and challenging the audience, the thrilling power of performing these roles remains strongly evident in the video documentation (Woods et al. 1996). Using Soyinka's text, the chorus extolled their primitive Nigerian-meets-Northern-Mediterranean-god, chanting "seek him in your blood ... even in the womb ... There is power in his rhythm, in his pulse ... his dance covers you" as the dancer becomes one "with his drum, Dionysus!" (Woods et al. 1996; Soyinka 1974: 21). Echoing Charles Segal's interpretation of the Ancient play, the chorus' offered through "dramatic spectacle" the sensation of being "in the theatre of Dionysus", and so able to share with the performers the "Dionysiac experience" (1982: 157) in which their stomping, butoh-like dance fused themes of violent death, ecstasy, rebirth and suffering.

Dionysus was naked, bar a golden phallus (Woods et al. 1996), akin to that which Hijikata and other butoh dancers had sported (Asbestos-kan 1987; Nakatani 2003; Morishita 2004). Beckey's body was covered in gold, Dairakudakan-style, with a leopard-pattern across his pate. Pentheus' masculinity was announced by a large, upright penis gourd styled after those worn in Papua New Guinea (Figure 17). His head was painted blue with "rivulets of blood" running down from a circle about his neck, announcing his tragic fate in which his head was to be carried as a trophy by his enraptured mother (Pippin 1998: 30). This pairing of Beckey and Lamb produced a striking corporeal and dramaturgical dialectic. Dionysus was tall, lithe, undulating, serpentine and seductive, his sibylline words and homoerotic caressing of Pentheus' body entrancing the at-first-resistant, muscular opponent. Pentheus by contrast stood legs apart, in a deep crouch, his staff firmly held upright by his side or pointed like a rifle against imagined forces before him, his powerful frame very much in evidence. Lamb embodied the hardness of the disciplined warrior and defender of masculine authority (Figure 17); his physique and grounded stance recalled that of Nobbs in several of Frank's productions. Comparing *Cult of Dionysus* to Hijikata's *Nikutai no Hanran* (1968), although Beckey had the exaggerated phallus and thin, feminised form which Hijikata embodied in that work, the hardness of Hijikata's body, its tendency towards tetanic over-extension and muscular density (Asbestos-kan 1987; Nakatani 2003; Morishita 2004), was transferred to the anxious heterosexual warrior Pentheus, whose fear of feminine inversion was all the more obvious because of this reactive tonicity.

Dionysus' visibly contrasting movement, together with his association to the female chorus—who even spoke for him at times, in noh fashion—cast Dionysus as sexually ambivalent or queer; phallically endowed, yet feminine, like many butoh dancers before him. The Bacchants too took on masculine power, at one point pointing their staves aggressively towards the audience in the very same position which Pentheus had used. Beckey claimed that the "lower half" of his body remained solidly positioned so as to ground his movement in a way similar to a Suzuki actor, but the "butoh" component of his gestures produced "continual undulations" in the "upper half of the body", particularly across his chest, torso, side to side, and through languid, curving circuits of the arms, inducing what he described as a "sense of flow within and of the body" (1997: 39–42; Woods et al. 1996). Barbe would offer a similar reading of the combination of SMAT with butoh. Adopting a low but stable, cross-legged pose akin to some of the more advanced walks employed in Suzuki training, Beckey echoed Hijikata's description of butoh dancers who "seem to be performing acrobatic feats on oil paper" finding "their balance on twisted legs" (Hijikata in Viala and Masson-Sékiné 1988: 188). Beckey's embodiment thereby exemplified a middle line between butoh and SMAT.

"Flow" was coded by Woods, Bradley and Beckey as allied to the reproductive fertility and rejuvenation through the primal sacrifice which Soyinka had added to the play, introducing an ending in which Pentheus' blood nurtured a renewal of the fields. Alongside these fluidic factors, Suzuki's militaristic hardness was also present within much of the movement of the otherwise twisting female Bacchants, armed with intimidating wooden staves, and often standing in a crouch, legs apart, arms splayed, as they spat out their words like javelins (Figure 17). Agave too writhed and convulsed up through her lower body like Beckey, spasming from her belly through to her neck and face in divine madness as she bore Pentheus' covered head before her (Woods et al. 1996). After Dionysus had persuaded the enraptured Pentheus to accept the former's suggestion to put on the feminine dress of a Maenad, Lamb returned in a tight, leopard pattern skirt (matching the dappled makeup on Dionysus' head), fringed with pink fur, women's high heeled shoes, a red headscarf and black sunglasses, accompanied by carnivalesque Afro-Caribbean music, whistles and shouts as he processed in a line down the centre of the stage as if on a catwalk (Woods et al. 1996). One critic aptly described the effect as "more *Priscilla, Queen of the Desert* than Thebes ... 405BC" (Postle 1996b: 31), rapidly shifting the mood from "tragedy to burlesque" and back (Pippin 1998: 30). Such a garish, comedic combination of contemporary popular culture with Classical references was very much in the ero guro nansensu style of fellow company Frank. Throughout the production, gender dimorphism, power, race and embodiment were intermingled, shifting, and contradictory.

Cult of Dionysus represented a high point in Zen Zen Zo's fusion of SMAT with butoh, introducing a style echoed in *Macbeth As Told By the Weird Sisters* (1995–2002) and *The Tempest* (2009), but which would become less and less overt within the dramaturgy of the productions over time. After 2016, the butoh choruses employed by both Frank and Zen Zen Zo became a thing of the past. The fusion of SMAT with butoh also produced a gendered body distinct to Hijikata's own celebration of the hyper-masculine, tortured and debilitated bodies of his outcast subjects. In Zen Zen Zo's aesthetic, a "hard", often masculine Suzuki aesthetic was countered by a more "fluid" and arguably feminine or queer butoh corporeality present in the performers' bodies. The oppositional potentialities of butoh and Suzuki, in combination, or singly, structured the corporeal dramaturgy of much of Zen Zen Zo's work—although this visible corporeal opposition declined as the company's approach evolved into the 2010s.

8 Frances Barbe's Tōhoku Australis

Barbe occupied a unique position in Brisbane physical theatre from 1992 onwards, appearing in the first productions of both Frank and Zen Zen Zo. Her choreographies were mounted initially under the aegis of Zen Zen Zo's mixed programs and later were hosted by Frank (*Fine Bone China* and act II of her *Chimaera*, 2008). For Zen Zen Zo, Barbe contributed to both their mixed butoh programs as well as the choreography for early text based works. From 1997, Barbe consolidated her knowledge of butoh, SMAT, NSP, yoga and Viewpoints, principally in the UK and Europe (Barbe 2011 and 2019). She worked at Endo Tadashi's Mamu Butoh Centrum in Germany, 1997–2009, with a spell at SITI in 2002, as well as periods with Kan Katsura (with whom Bradley trained),

Yamada Bishop, Carlotta Ikeda, and others. Endo was a former pupil of Ohno Kazuo, and work at the Centrum shifted Barbe's aesthetic from writhing physical grotesqueries and the bizarre humour of Maro's aesthetic to a more restrained modality, which was "not overly demonstrative", as she put it (2019: 197). Barbe recognised that butoh's pioneers had been seeking "something ancient or pagan", and occasionally she did likewise (2011: 4). Like Bradley, Barbe came to see her work as "butoh-inspired or butoh-based", classifying it in broadly neo-Expressionist terms as exploring "how fully inhabited a movement is" in terms of its psychocorporeal focus, its detailing, and its affective weight (2011: 27, 85). As her peer from Zen Zen Zo, independent dance-maker Helen Smith put it, butoh offered a:

> release of all those pent up emotions and taboos ... things that you are not supposed to feel or express. I ... understood immediately that this was a safe place to explore ... emotions and feelings that are otherwise not allowed.
> ROBERTSON 2015: 75

In combining butoh with Suzuki technique, Barbe also echoed the lead performer from Zen Zen Zo's *Cult of Dionysius*, Christopher Beckey (1997: 42), in claiming that it was SMAT which "planted my feet firmly into the earth so that when I was asked in butoh to 'float like smoke' I had a base on which to build" (Barbe 2011: 113).

While working with Endo, Barbe began "to teach butoh to actors" (in Riccardi 2017), leading to employment at institutions and universities in Kent, then Exeter and London (2001–10), before returning to Australia to take up a position at the Western Australian Academy of Performing Arts, Edith Cowan University (Barbe 2019: 181). Rather than using the metaphor of conceiving the body as an "empty" space to be filled by outside forces, Barbe proposed that it was more accurate to think of oneself as a "container of clear water" into which comes a "drop of coloured dye" which reconfigures the performer's interstitial currents (2011: 136). Fellow Zen Zen Zo member Helen Smith would note around the same time that the student of Hijikata and Ohno, Nakajima Natsu, had tended to describe her own state as one of "filled emptiness" (2013: 11). Smith therefore proposed the rhetorical alternatives of an "awakened", "transparent" or even "dead" body swayed by forces from beyond itself (ibid. 11).

Barbe would continue to choreograph and perform into the 2000s, producing several works outside of Australia. I focus on the solo *Fine Bone China* (2003–08; Figure 3), performed both by Barbe and by dancer Scarlett Perdereau. The piece represented Barbe's only expatriate portrait of Australian identity for non-Australian audiences, being staged in Britain and Europe, before a return season in Brisbane with Frank. *Fine Bone China* attracted the attention of French theatre theorist Patrice Pavis (1998: 217).[14]

Like de Quincey, Barbe drew on classic Australian images, tropes and paintings, notably Sidney Nolan's modernist treatment of the dry, reddened landscape, as well as Frederick McCubbin's iconic narrative triptych *The Pioneer* (1904; National Gallery of Victoria), which depicts a white settler family on an uncleared block of land, the left panel showing the wife lost in thought in the foreground and a carriage serving as a home in the background. The central panel depicts the woman cradling a child over her shoulder while now the man was seated, with a house in the background. The last panel shows a modern citizen discovering the graves of the now deceased pioneers, with the background opening up to reveal a city in the distance. Barbe was struck by the "out-of-place colonial women", depicted by McCubbin and others as enduring a "displacement and friction between figure and landscape", dressed as they were "in their cold climate finery" while "sweltering" in the heat (2011: 40, 55). Barbe drew indirectly on her own "corporeal history" to make the dance, translating in abstract bodily form "memories, such as men crouching in the bush to draw pathways in the sand, or chasing snakes in a car" (41–47).

Pavis summed up the narrative as "a woman dressed strictly, conforming to the etiquette of good society [who] tries to escape social control" on the one hand, and the dangerous forces of nature on the other. She "frees herself ... for a moment but falls back into the surveillance of long ago" (2016). Australia's hot, arid landscapes were evoked by sand on the stage and harsh white light. The dancer entered in a neutral pose, dressed in a white corset, walking forward with a teacup and saucer balanced on her head. Sondra Fraleigh (2010: 162) noted the similarity of Barbe's skin to that of the porcelain, observing that the character's "fussy dress" as well as the "fine China" and "tea" made up the signifiers for a "ritual" which had been "imported to Australia" by British colonists similar to those seated in the London theatre watching Barbe. After offering the cup to the audience, the performer fell to her knees, ran and then shrieked. She lay sideways on the ground, her feet and toes contracted in a characteristic pose of butoh (CTF 2010). She removed items of clothing, the cup now dangling from her mouth as she clawed at the world, dressed only in bloomers and a corset. Pavis (2016) described the choreography as including "Violent contractions of the whole body", open mouthed "grimaces" and "nervous" gestures. With

---

14   All translations from French by the author. Pavis contends that butoh as a whole was, in effect, an "intercultural Grand Guignol", or horror theatre that "turned out badly"; see Pavis 1998; Marshall 2013.

the cup neatly balanced at the base of her spine, the dancer bent over, back horizontal, hands pawing in front of her, evoking first a kangaroo and then a cat (CTF 2010; Barbe 2011: 43). An Australian lyrebird was also corporealized, this animal famous for its tail feathers which colonists likened to a Greek lyre and whose distinctive call was included in the soundtrack. The dancer strove to carry her cup and saucer about the stage, obsessively crouching, pointing and managing the space around her. All but describing butoh as a form, Pavis claimed that in the piece, the body served as the "field of battle for a combat between pain and pleasure, disgust and acceptance". The dramaturgy worked according to oppositional tensions between "sand" versus "porcelain, desert" versus "good society", colonial control versus the untamed bush beyond the house, as well as what Barbe described as a "friction between what is shown (or performed)" and that which was "concealed" or remained implicit within the body (2011: 44). Pavis concluded that ultimately the performance dramatized how the body of the settler woman was itself colonised by masculine, imperial structures and hence cannot become "the true property of the [female colonial] subject". The woman's body was rather moved by forces outside of itself, here cast not simply as those of the domestic ideal and maternity as had been rendered heroic in McCubbin's depiction, but something closer to the fraught haptic energies of Nolan.[15] In this sense, *Fine Bone China* offered a message similar to that of *Hijikata and the Japanese,* where Hijikata gave himself up to national and transnational forces which wracked his form. In Barbe's words, she "wanted to see what my own 'Tōhoku' might be" and so portray the "landscape and history my body comes from" (2011: 59; Figure 3). Nevertheless, the choreography of the piece drew just as heavily on international tanztheater as it did on butoh, being best classified as butoh-esque in its politics, but syncretic in its choreographic dramaturgy.

9 Butoh Diffusions

There were some butoh-like elements within the work of Frank and NSP training, particularly in the more grotesque actions of some of the choruses. Frank however remained a Suzuki-based company. It was Zen Zen Zo's members who systematically explored the fusion of SMAT with butoh and other elements. French grotesque clown and the work of Jacques Lecoq provided a useful entrée for a more dramatic model of butoh which might suit Australian tastes

---

15   See "Body Weather as an Uncanny Project" in chapter three.

and ameliorate shocking qualities. Zen Zen Zo's early productions were visibly proximate to those of Dairakudakan and this remained the case for some time. Nevertheless, Zen Zen Zo's programs tended overall to have a lightness of touch and emotional register or legibility which Dairakudakan lacked. Bradley and Barbe used butoh imagery extensively in their work, but they worked "outwards in" by using physical actions to elicit expressive and psychosomatic responses in the performer. Their approach to butoh was broadly Expressionistic, with butoh judged to provide a way to not only loosen and potentially queer or feminise the body, but also as a means to access and perform affective intensities. This in turn drew Zen Zen Zo's practice close to those Naturalistic artists whose influence on the Australian stage they had elsewhere denounced. Here butoh moved out of dance and into actorly sense memory and a dynamic, at times almost animalistic, version of character-based performance, not altogether unlike Suzuki's use of butoh dancers as actors in some of his own productions.

Today, although SMAT, NSP and Viewpoints are far more common within Australian performance training than butoh itself, there remains a butoh inflection in many cases, most notably at WAAPA, where Barbe and Neideck teach. All of this reflects the paradoxical nature of butoh's highly successful adoption by artists in Queensland, where it became widely sourced in part because its particularities could be dissolved into other practices. It is many years since Zen Zen Zo staged anything which might be recognised as a butoh performance. Bradley's doctoral research project of *Company of Shadows* (2016) is better described as an amusing, episodic promenade performance (Bradley 2017: 172), like a sophisticated ghost train ride. Of those who have passed through Zen Zen Zo, it is Smith who today maintains the strongest filiation to butoh, continuing to teach and to work on Umiumare's ButohOUT! festivals.

Smith's 2011 solo performance of *A Dance For All Seasons* reveals the depth of expertise Australians who persisted with butoh would achieve. *Dance For All Seasons* (MA 2011) was a slow, measured work, the body presented in a sculptural manner, typically slightly off balance, weak yet powerful—close in many ways to the aesthetic of Bradley's sometime teacher Ohno Kazuo. Employing a neo-Romantic string score, the piece evoked a sense of tragic energy, a life force which was bright yet verging on its exhausted extinction. Smith's elegant yet tonically restrained gestures epitomised this tension, alternating between crouched positions with scribbling hands such as are common in butoh, versus tall, tensed, statuesque stances or tableaux. Hijikata's "dance of the back" (Marshall 2018: 163), complex grimacing and mouthing, the dancer rising from her buttocks in a foetal position, and other actions, were deployed as part of a series of abstract portraits or character studies. Smith's little-commented upon work echoed Umiumare's *EnTrance* (2009–12) as a rare production by a mature Australian butoh artist showcasing the diversity and strength of her choreography. *Dance For All Seasons* ended with the very Ohno-esque gesture of the mature, pale-coloured dancer shuffling backwards out of the space, dropping roses as she departed (MA 2011).

Barbe has suggested that taking on some, but not *all*, of the elements of butoh might be one way to avoid direct appropriation in Australia and elsewhere, instead fostering "cross-fertilisation" between what the dancer already knows, and what they learn from butoh (2011: 143). This is what happened in Queensland as the years progressed. Bradley gave up developing a "butoh company" and instead she and her peers took from the style what they needed for each production. The history of Zen Zen Zo reaffirms Ian Maxwell's characterisation of Australian artists as bricoleurs of performance techniques (2017)—or as Yana Taylor put it, artists who conduct "dedicated eclecticism" (Heywood and Gallasch 2001). For a more single-minded focus on butoh processes and aesthetics, one must look to the other artists discussed in this book.

CHAPTER 9

Conclusion: Two Closing Scenes from Australian Adaptations of Butoh and Suzuki

I conclude my survey of butoh and Suzuki in Australia by highlighting two works staged by artists who have previously worked with Australian butoh and/or Suzuki artists, traces of which can be seen in these productions. The influence of Japanese physical theatre is however but one of a number of syncretic elements, visible in the work if one is attentive to them, and to describe the pieces as "butoh" or "Suzuki" style works today is, at best, a simplification. The productions are Not Yet It's Difficult's 2008 staging of *The Dispossessed*, directed by David Pledger, who had acted in the 1992 Playbox Suzuki project and went on to work with Japanese post butoh ensemble Gekidan Kaitaisha. The other is the solo dance theatre work *Copper Promises: Hinemihi Haka* (2012–15), performed by de Quincey's collaborator Victoria Hunt, a work which evolved out of workshops that were supported by Australian intercultural dance company Marrugeku and included some Body Weather training. In these productions, Australian butoh and Suzuki technique is syncretic and mixed, while something very like butoh and Body Weather is now used by both settler-descent and First Nations artists to comment on place, Country, race and other issues in the region. It is above all evidence which arises from bodily sensations and provocations which guides this work. The ethnological assumptions underpinning much butoh and Suzuki continue to inform current practice, even as artists have largely moved beyond simplistic assumptions.

1   NYID's *the Dispossessed* (2008) and Hunt's *Copper Promises* (2016)

Not Yet It's Difficult's production of *The Dispossessed* (2008) was performed in a pit before audiences seated on four sides. It began with a lone figure, smeared with dirt, rotating centre stage, to the accompaniment of a drone score. The space was populated by six isolated figures who appeared to be of both Asian and European descent. Each was located before door panels running along two walls bounding the space. The performers gazed about, before shuddering unevenly, and reflexively twitching through their shoulders and torsos, forearms parallel to the floor. Anxiously exploring the space, they began to spin, bent over, stopping and scrabbling through their hair. They rehearsed

CONCLUSION

FIGURE 18   *The Dispossessed* (Seoul Arts Centre: 2008), presented by Seoul Performing Arts Festival and co-produced by NYID with Wuturi Theatre; concept/direction David Pledger

PHOTOS: GUIMAN SHIN. REPRODUCTION COURTESY OF NYID

beating or slapping each other, their attempts to socialise vexed by the violence inscribed within and between their bodies. Prison-like sirens caused them to smash themselves and each other against the panels. Reduced to shuffling haunted beings, the drone returned, presaging a certain relief, as if the life force of the sun now streamed into each of their cell-like environs. They raised their arms, circled the space, and spun about, each in a private utopia (Figure 18).

In Hunt's solo *Copper Promises: Hinemihi Haka* (2012–15), the audience saw a very different, initially racially ambiguous isolated figure, prone in classic butoh pose. The distorted, electric-like sound of cicadas and flashing lights suggested division and fracture. Crouching, bending, kneeling, hunching, and arching (Figure 19), Hunt folded herself upwards and then onto the ground, arms crossing her body. At times her hands spread and fingers fluttered, suggesting wiriwiri, a characteristic gesture of the Māori haka in which the power of the performer spills into extremities. Hunt executed a deep push from the floor, suggesting a body both drawn into, and forcing itself out of, the earth, like

FIGURE 19 Victoria Hunt in *Copper Promises: Hinemihi Haka* (Sydney: The Performance Space, 2016)
PHOTO: HEIDRUN LÖHR. REPRODUCTION COURTESY OF VICTORIA HUNT

a revenant or memory. Jumping, powerful arms punched and extended. Hunt then pulled this together to walk through a field of splintered light, navigating an invisible structure. A spinning British penny was projected, and Hunt spoke in distorted Te Reo Māori, as if possessed by her ancestors. The final image was of her coming forward, smoke rising in a column from out of her dark hair.

As noted earlier, Pledger performed in *Chronicle of Macbeth* (1992) before developing an idiosyncratic physical training method informed by Australian rules football, biomechanics, SMAT, and critical theory (Hadley 2007: 114; Eckersall 2002: 15–27). Early works were highly physical, including a critique of the tribalism of Australia's often virulently competitive and racist sports world, *Austral-Asian Post Cartoon: Sports Edition* (1998). The company showcased its training in *The Desert Project* (1998), conducted at various locations in the parched inland country of the continent, and *Scenes From the Beginning of the End* (2001–03), featured performers jogging while behind them screened images tracing their journey from desert to the city. Pledger's main link to butoh itself was though a collaboration with Japanese post-butoh company Gekidan Kaitaisha, whose members Hino Hiruko and Shimizu Shinjin had worked with the dancers of Hijikata's studio (A. Broinowski 2017: 131). Gekidan Kaitaisha developed corporeal expressions of "exile", of vexed physical contact, and of ambivalent corporeal self-discipline, all of which were visible in the choreography of *The Dispossessed* (Eckersall et al. 2001: 76–77). *The Dispossessed* was a joint work between NYID and Wuturi theatre, Korea, with three Australian performers (Todd MacDonald, Ingrid Weisfelt, Vincent Crowley) and three Korean performers (Seo Sang Won, Kim Kwang Duk, Sang-A Kong). Pledger described it as representing "an embodied algorithm of 'forever pain' and human suffering" from which the characters strove to free themselves (Pledger et al. nd). They were caught, in Pledger's words, in the attempt to remember "how they should behave as human beings" (Pledger et al. 2008).

Hunt identifies as "an Australian born artist" with "tribal affiliations to Te Arawa, Rongowhaakata, Kahungunu Māori, English and Irish" (Hunt nd). Her career is largely based in Australia, and she was part of all three seasons of Triple Alice (1999–2001). She contributed to many of de Quincey's works, including *Sky Hammer* (2000), *City to City* (2000), *The Stirring* (2007) and *Run: A Performance Engine* (2009; see figures 6 and 7). In addition to training with Tanaka in 2007, and with long-term butoh independent Iwana Masaki, Body Weather artists Oguri, and Van de Ven, she worked with New Zealand based Māori/Pasifika dance theatre company Mau, 2006–2007, led by Lemi Ponifasio (Hunt nd). Hunt has increasingly explored her Māori heritage, reflecting that although she knew her father was "the youngest of seventeen children" who lived in Rotorua on the North Island of Aotearoa, she "did not have much information about them" (Frew 2016). The marae (meeting house) of her father's tribe or iwi had been dismantled and moved to the United Kingdom following its sale in 1893. Named after Hunt's ancestor Hinemihi, her family sheltered in the marae during the deadly Mt Tarawera volcanic eruption of 1886. Hunt reflected, "I would not have existed if not for Hinemihi's shelter and [its] protection" (Frew 2016). In the program, she offered a number of butoh-fu poetic descriptions which helped structure the dance, noting, "I am the house and the house is me. I dance the history of the house and she reveals my history" (Hunt 2019). Hunt's performance was an act of whakapapa, or genealogical remembrance, corporealizing the vexed history of her lineage and the marae that sustained it. Plans are in place to return the marae to Aotearoa. Commentators identified in the piece elements of butoh, Martha Graham's choreography, haka, animal embodiments, and omnicentral imaging (Lancaster 2012).

These two theatrical works, both made by artists principally based in Australia, offer useful snapshots to pause on as one considers the influence of butoh and Suzuki on performance in Australia and the region. *The Dispossessed* looks like a butoh work, and its politics, which dramatizes fraught, divided or haunted not-quite human bodies existing at the margins of life and death, echoes key butoh themes. Even for Hunt, there is a sense of the unheimlich of embodying butoh in Australia and Aotearoa New Zealand.[1] Yet these works are not truly "butoh", if one is to judge by the training of the performers. *Copper Promises* is more recognisably a butoh work than *The Dispossessed*, and although there are no foetal positions or balling of the feet, much of the twisting, grounded choreography reflects the influence of Tanaka and Body Weather (Figure 19). Infused with contemporary dance as a whole and Māori arts, however, it is not necessarily best classified as "butoh", representing instead one of many fusions which have arisen in the region.

Isolating butoh or SMAT within the choreographic language of work staged in Australia today is therefore difficult. There is no doubt that Tanaka's concept of Body Weather, introduced at an early point in the development of Australian butoh, together with the more theatrical heritage established by Maro, his students, and Suzuki, proved decisive in the transmission of Japanese physical performance to Australia. This might be contrasted with the situation in France, where the example of Ohno Kazuo and the teaching of his son played a more significant role (Pagès 2017). Umiumare's work still carries sufficient cultural and national allusions to ground her performance in that form which came out of Japan after World War Two, and Yap's practice overtly stages his transcultural heritage and various manifestations of historical possession. The work of de Quincey and her peers such as Taylor, Van de Ven and Snow still bear the mark of Body Weather and its processes. Yet all of these artists have become so finely tuned in their corporealizations that such Japanese approaches have been uniquely embodied in a novel, arguably decolonising fashion by each. Zen Zen Zo have not staged any recognisably butoh work for some years, though elements of butoh, SMAT and grotesque clown continue to inform their training. Carroll and Nobbs still offer training in NSP, but Frank has not mounted a production since 2015. Neideck and Kelly identified a number of "second wave companies" founded by those who trained or worked with Zen Zen Zo and Frank, but who, as Steven Mitchell Wright of the Danger Ensemble put it, felt there had been "an unhealthy fetishisation of Japan" (2021: 460–64). Developing their own style, they came to stage what Neideck and Kelly characterise as "tableaus of farcical comedy" which alternate with "moments of visceral, destructive beauty". These artists therefore exhibit little visible similarity to either their Australian predecessors' work, or Japanese artists. Butoh and Suzuki technique are still informing work in Australia today, but their influence has receded to become minoritarian, continued by a relatively small selection of active artists.

---

1   See "Body Weather as an Uncanny Project" in chapter three.

CONCLUSION 293

It is however clear that butoh and SMAT, together with Bausch, played a part (though not necessarily a decisive one) in rolling back the suspicion of Expressionist modes which postmodernism had produced within the international dance community, enabling a range of expressive, picaresque and/or affectively loaded forms to reassert themselves within dance and theatre. SMAT and butoh also provided a shot in the arm to New Wave pressures to develop non-Naturalistic, physically based performance in Australia. Some of the work which followed was based on the suggestion that accessing emotional depth or corporeal memories in these ways might release universal, primal or chthonic forces otherwise inaccessible to urbanised Australian subjects. Though the ideology underpinning these concepts remains problematic, and at times spilled into less adept outcomes such as Zen Zen Zo's production of *The Tempest*, the example of Hunt and Marrugeku suggests that, overall, these modalities have contributed to the opening up of Australian performance to First Nations values and histories through collaborations with Big hART, Trevor Jamieson, Marrugeku, Henrietta Baird (who performed in de Quincey's *The Stirring*, 2007), and other artists. Certainly de Quincey's increasing foregrounding of the specific Indigenous histories associated with her sites between Triple Alice and *The Stirring* shows this. Similar aims were vigorously pursued by Umiumare in collaboration with Big hArt and by Taylor in her ongoing collaborative work in "locating" oneself with respect to localised and colonial histories in the landscape (Taylor 2007: 135–142). Members of the Australian intercultural dance company Marrugeku trained at various times in Body Weather, butoh and SMAT, de Quincey taking workshops for the company around 1999 as preparation for Marrugeku's second production *Crying Baby* (2001; Swain 2024). Members of Stalker and Marrugeku have included Adam Broinowski (formerly of Stalker theatre, later with Gekidan Kaitaisha) and Katia Molino (later with NYID; Swain and Eckersall 2012; Gilbert 2021; Ausdance 2013; Swain 2024). Rachael Swain notes that Dalisa Pigram, the co-artistic director of Marrugeku, had developed a series of verbal and kinetic mnemonics around which she created her own performances, producing a "juxtaposition of these strange, unruly and expressive figures" (Swain 2020: 84–86). Developed on Country, Swain argues that:

> a dancer being inhabited by Country, 'daring to be vaguely moved by the radical exteriority of small encounters': with minerals, atmospheres, weather, other species and histories which are 'fully sensed' and 'absolutely real' ... can be seen as a decolonising act.
> 2020: 130

These modalities, developed largely independently of butoh by Pigram and Swain, can be seen as alternative techniques which run parallel to the Body Weather and Hijikata's concept of "butoh-fu". In 2009–11, Marrugeku ran workshops, which included the participation of Māori Body Weather practitioner Charles Koroneho; Hunt, who took part in this series, used these experiences to develop *Copper Promises* (Swain 2015: 509, 520). Despite risks of appropriation and early naïve projects, butoh and Suzuki now have a proven track record of helping to facilitate cross-cultural exchange and cultural critique in the region. Even so, these forms can at the same time reinforce national Australian tropes, notably those of Australian identity as tied to manual exertion, sport, and exchanges of productive capitalism or leisure with the landscape, as was shown in *Doll Seventeen* by Frank. These potentialities exist in tension with those of a more explicitly dialectical approach to Australian cultural identity which butoh and SMAT also foster. The tendency of both forms to hystericize the body, or to stage a gendered confusion, collapse, division, or queering of corporeal mastery, undercuts any triumphalist deployment of butoh or SMAT. Both forms are productive antitheses to the construction of a homogenous or fully capable national subject.

Perhaps the most intriguing aspect of the histories of butoh and SMAT in Australia is the importance of corporeal evidence itself for the ongoing development and critique of Australian performance practice. Be it the experience of being in the desert, the feeling of energy rebounding into one's frame from a sprung floor during stomping, or the high frequency tremors that arise in the bodies of Yap and others, butoh and SMAT utilise concrete manifestations of physical responses to train and disturb body and mind. In Body Weather, this can radically unsettle the dancer's sense of subjectivity. Metaphorically, if not literally, the butoh dancer continues to stand shakily on the grounds it moves across. Trusting the body as source of reliable truth telling—or treating performance and training as "diagnostic" (as Allain puts it; 1998: 73)—can be a disruptive strategy. It has however had considerable success in Australia. Performers serious about interrogating power, ownership, land rights, class, colonialism, race, and national identity through corporeal interventions in dance and theatre would do well to heed the histories of Australian butoh and cross-cultural performance. The ghosts of many beings continue to, in Hijikata's phrasing (in Sas 2003: 24), drop a ladder down into the specifically *Australian* nikutai of not only myself, but of many others inhabiting this Country, forcing us all to eat of the darkness within, and perhaps emerge more aware, if not necessarily healed, following such a process of dark psychocorporeal reconciliation and historiographic musing.

Bibliography

Unless stated otherwise, all URLs consulted May 2023.

ABC. 2009. 'Run: A Performance Engine' ABC Radio National (23 August). On line at: https://www.abc.net.au/radionational/programs/archived/artworks/run-a-performance-engine/3058936

Adelaide GT. 2000. 'Zen Zen Zo Physical Theatre' *Adelaide GT newspaper*, reproduced in Zen Zen Zo. 2008, p. 39.

Akihiko, Senda. 2000. 'Fragments of Glass: A Conversation Between Hijikata Tatsumi and Suzuki Tadashi' *TDR*, Vol. 44, No. 1, pp. 62–70.

Allain, Paul. 1998. 'Suzuki Training' *TDR*, Vol. 42, No. 1, pp. 66–89.

Allain, Paul, and Frances Barbe. 2009. 'On the Shoulders of Tradition From East to West'. *Studies in Theatre & Performance*, Vol. 29, No. 2, pp. 149–159.

Aldred, Debra. 2001. 'Frank Returns'. *Courier Mail* (20 June), p. 21.

Anderson, Mary Elizabeth. 2014. *Meeting Places: Locating Desert Consciousness in Performance*. Leiden: Brill.

Amat, Rohayah Che. 2019. 'Historic Cities of the Straits of Malacca UNESCO World Heritage Site: Threats & Challenges' *Journal of World Heritage Studies*, pp. 9–15.

Amsterdam University of the Arts. 2014. 'Research & Innovation: Artist In Residence'. Amsterdam: University of the Arts, https://www.ahk.nl/en/research/artist-in-residence-air/2012-2013/hisako-horikawa/

Artbank. nd. *Artbank website*. Sydney & other cities: Australian Government, Dept. of Infrastructure & the Arts, https://www.artbank.gov.au/

ArtLark. 2022. 'Australian Icons: Max Dupain's *Sunbaker*' Artlark 27 July, https://artlark.org/2022/07/27/max-dupains-sunbaker-and-the-question-of-australianness/

Ariall, Kate Dobbs. 2008. 'Japanese Mini-Fest at ADF' *CVNC* (*Classical Voice of North Carolina*) (July 16). On line at: https://cvnc.org/article.cfm?articleId=1911

Armstrong, Keith, et al. 2001. *Golden Circle*. Video documentation. Sydney: Embodied Media, https://embodiedmedia.com/homeartworks/golden-circle

Asbestos-kan. 1987. *Body on the Edge of Crisis: Photographs of Butoh Dance Performed & Staged by Tatsumi Hijikata*. Tokyo: Parco.

Aslan, Odette. 2004. 'Tanaka Min' in Aslan & Picon-Vallin (eds), pp. 177–189.

Aslan, Odette, and Béatrice Picon-Vallin (eds). 2004. *Butô(s)*. Paris: CNRS.

Aston, Elaine, and Sue-Ellen Case (eds). 2007. *Staging International Feminisms*. Houndmills: Palgrave.

Ausdance. 2013. *National Dance Forum: Speakers*. Media release. On line at: https://ausdance.org.au/uploads/content/projects/2013-NDF/NDF2013-full-program-v2.pdf

AusStage. nd. *Buddha's Banquet*. 1992. Database entry 17571. On line at: https://www.ausstage.edu.au/

AusStage. nd. *Inland Sea.* 2000. Database entry 28634. On line at: https://www.ausstage.edu.au/

Bailey, Derek. 1993. *Improvisation.* Ashbourne: Da Capo.

Bailey, John. 2006. 'Monstrous Feminine, Japanese-Style' *RealTime,* #71, p. 7.

Bailey, John. 2010. 'See You, See Me' *RealTime,* #97, p. 29.

Baird, Bruce. 2016. *Hijikata Tatsumi & Butoh.* London: Palgrave.

Baird, Bruce. 2022. *A History of Butô.* Oxford: Oxford University Press.

Baird, Bruce, and Rosemary Candelario (eds). 2019. *The Routledge Companion to Butoh Performance.* London: Routledge.

Bandt, Ros. 2020. 'Hearing Australian Identity: Sites as Acoustic Spaces, an Audible Polyphony' *Resonate* (27 August). On line at: https://www.australianmusiccentre.com.au/article/hearing-australian-identity

Barbe, Frances. 2003. Frances Barbe CV. *International Dance Exchange Project website.* Schloss Broellin. On line at: http://www.exit.broellin.de/eX03/Frances-CV.html

Barbe, Frances. 2011. *The Difference Butoh Makes: A Practice-Based Exploration of Butoh in Contemporary Performance,* PhD thesis, University of Kent.

Barbe, Frances. 2019. 'Embodying Imagination: *Butoh* & Performer Training' in Phillip Zarrilli, T. Sasitharan, and Anuradha Kapur (eds). *Intercultural Acting & Performer Training.* London: Routledge, pp. 179–201.

Baxter, Virginia. 1998. 'First Five Minutes' *RealTime Australia,* #24, pp. 3–4.

Baxter, Virginia, and Keith Gallasch. 2003. *In Repertoire.* Sydney/Canberra: RealTime / Australia Council of the Arts.

Baxter, Virginia, and Keith Gallasch. 2012. *In Repertoire.* Sydney/Canberra: RealTime / Australia Council of the Arts.

Beckett, Samuel. 1990. *Complete Dramatic Works.* London: Faber.

Beckey, Christopher. 1997. 'Hom(m)oerotics? or To Queer the Male Body On Stage' *Australasian Drama Studies,* Vol. 31, pp. 33–47.

Beckey, Christopher. 2004. 'The Moment of the Body in the Performance of Immanence: A Reflection on the History of Zen Zen Zo Physical Theatre' reproduced in Zen Zen Zo. 2008, pp. 118–121.

Beddie, Melanie, and Peta Tait. 2021. 'Embodied Exploratory Process in Australian Performance Training & International Influences' *Theatre, Dance & Performance Training,* Vol. 12, No. 1, pp. 5–19.

Beeman, William, with Suzuki Tadashi. 1982. 'The Word is an Act of the Body'. *Performing Arts Journal,* Vol. 6, No. 2, pp. 88–92.

Belviso, Hugo. 2020. *Jekyll's Hide Project.* PhD thesis. WAAPA @ Edith Cowan University.

Bennie, Angela. 2004. 'Looking at Dupain in a Fresh Light' *Sydney Morning Herald* (14 December). On line at: https://www.smh.com.au/entertainment/art-and-design/looking-at-dupain-in-a-fresh-light-20041213-gdkax8.html

Berg, Shelley. 1995. 'Sada Yacco in London & Paris, 1900' *Dance Chronicle*, Vol. 18, No. 3, pp. 343–404.

Bessarab, Dawn, and Bridget Ng'andu. 2010. 'Yarning About Yarning As a Legitimate Method in Indigenous Research' *International Journal of Critical Indigenous Studies*, Vol. 3, No. 1, pp. 37–50.

Birdsall Jones, Christina. 2013. 'The Bronx in Australia: The Metaphoric Stigmatization of Public Housing Tenants in Australian Towns & Cities' *Journal of Urban History*, Vol. 31, No. 2, pp. 315–330.

Blackwood, Michael, dir. 1990. *Butoh: Body on the Edge of Crisis*. AV documentary. New Jersey: Michael Blackwood productions.

Bogdanova-Kummer, Eugenia. 2020. *Bokujinkai: Japanese Calligraphy & the Postwar avant-garde*, Leiden: Brill.

Bollen, Jonathan, and Adrian Kiernander and Bruce Parr. 2008. *Men at Play: Masculinities in Australian Theatre*. Amsterdam: Rodopi.

Bonyhady, Tim. 1997. 'Disturbing the Dead' *Art Monthly*, Vol. 105, pp. 9–12.

Born Dancin'. 2005. 'The Nerve! The Shock!' in *Born Dancin'*. Anonymous dance commentary blog (5 November). On line at: http://atmosphericharmoniesforloners.blogspot.com/2005/11/nerve-shock.html

Boucher, Georgina. 2007. 'Yumi Umiumare' *Peril magazine*, Vol. 3. On line at: http://www.peril.com.au/edition3/yumi-umiumare

Boucher, Georgie. 2009. 'Yumi Umiumare's *DasSHOKU Hora!!* Critique Through "Cross"-Cultural Femininity' *Brolga*, Vol. pp. 39–46.

Bourguignon, Erika. 1995. 'The Relationship of Trance & Dance' paper presented at *Trance, Dance & Ritual: Sacred Movements in the World's Religions*, Harvard University. On line at: https://www.paulbourguignon.com/writing/lectures,%20seminars,%20papers/1995%20-%20The%20Relationship%20of%20Trance%20and%20Dance%20(2).pdf

Brady, Owen. 1996. 'Zen Zen Zo's *Macbeth*' *Theatre Journal*, Vol. 48, No. 1, pp. 97–98.

Bradley, Lynne. 2017. *Found in Translation: Transcultural Performance Practice in the 21st Century*, PhD thesis, Queensland University of Technology.

Bradley, Lynne, et al. 2000. *Unleashed*. DVD video. Melbourne / Brisbane: Contemporary Arts Media / Zen Zen Zo.

Bradley, Lynne, et al. 2008. *Zeitgeist*. DVD video. Melbourne / Brisbane: Contemporary Arts Media / Zen Zen Zo.

Bramwell, Murray. 2002. 'Devilish Toll of Nuclear Testing' *The Australian* (4 March), p. 15.

Brandon, James. 1978. 'Training at the Waseda Little Theatre'. *TDR*, Vol. 22, No. 4, pp. 29–42.

Brannigan, Erin. 2012. 'Transposing Style: Martin del Amo's New Solo Works' *Brolga*, Vol. 36, pp. 25–30.

Braun, Marta. 1994. *Picturing Time: The Work of Étienne-Jules Marey (1830–1904)*. Chicago: Chicago University Press.

Breton, André. 1969. *Manifestoes of Surrealism*. Ann Arbor: Michigan UP.

Brickhill, Eleanor. 2001. '*Nerve 9*: A Body Called Flesh' *RealTime*, #44, p. 35.

Brissenden, Alan, and Keith Glennon. 2010. *Australia Dances*. Adelaide: Wakefield.

Brook, Peter. 1968/1996. *The Empty Space*. NY: Schuster.

Broker, David. nd. 'Sex, Civility & Savagery in the Theatre of Dionysus' *Broadsheet*, Melbourne. Reproduced in Zen Zen Zo. 2008, pp. 102–3.

Broinowski, Adam. 2017. *Cultural Responses to Occupation in Japan*. London: Bloomsbury.

Broinowski, Alison. 1996. *The Yellow Lady: Australian Impressions of Asia*. Melbourne: Oxford University Press.

Brown Steven. 2010. *Tokyo Cyberpunk*. New York: Palgrave Macmillan.

Burridge, Stephanie. 1997. *Impact of Aboriginal Dance on 20th Century Australian Choreography*. Doctor of Philosophy. University of Kent.

Burridge, Stephanie. 2012. 'Connecting Through Dance & Story' in Stephanie Burridge & Julie Dyson (eds). *Shaping the Landscape*. New Delhi: Routledge, pp. 34–51.

Burt, Ramsay. 1998. *Alien Bodies: Representations of Modernity, "Race" & Nation in Early Modern Dance*. London: Routledge.

ButohOUT! 2022. 'Butoh on the Edge: Helen Smith'. Video documentation of Smith's *Lady Macbeth* solo. Melbourne: Vimeo / ButohOUT! On line at: https://vimeo.com/223199245

Buzacott, Martin. 2002. 'Saved By a Classic Cut' *The Australian* (27 September), p. 18.

Byakkosha. 1987. *Byakkosha: The World Dance Caravan Through the Continents*. Program of international tour, Kyoto/Melbourne: Byakkosha/Spoleto.

Cahir, Fred, Dan Tout and Lucinda Horrocks. 2017. 'Reconsidering the Origins of the Australian Legend' *Agora*, Vol. 52, No. 3, pp. 4–12.

Calamoneri, Tanya. 2022. *Butoh America: Butoh Dance in the United States & Mexico From 1970 to the Early 2000s*. London: Routledge.

Cameron, Neil. 1995. *The Running & Stamping Book*. Sydney: Currency.

Cane, Scott. 2013. *First Footprints: The Epic Story of the First Australians*. Sydney: Allen & Unwin.

Candelario, Rosemary. 2019. '"Now we have a passport": Global & Local Butoh', in Baird and Candelario (eds), pp. 245–253.

Card, Amanda. 2014. 'Tess de Quincey: *Nerve 9*' in Erin Brannigan and Virginia Baxter (eds). *Bodies of Thought: Twelve Australian Choreographers*, Sydney: Realtime. pp. 148–159.

Card, Amanda. 1999. *History in Motion: Dance & Australian Culture, 1920 to 1970*. PhD thesis. University of Sydney.

Cardone, Alissa. 2002. 'Killing the Body-Ego: Dance Research With Min Tanaka' *Contact Quarterly*, Vol. 27, No. 1, pp. 15–22.

Carroll, Alison. 2014. *A Journey Through Asian Art*, ABC television. On line at: https://vimeo.com/107790661.

Carroll, Alison. 2017. 'German Artists in the South Seas' *Art Monthly*, Vol. 299, pp. 58–63.

Carroll, Jacqui. 1998. *Changing Lanes: An Exploration of the Journey From Dance.* MA thesis, Queensland University of Technology.

Carroll, Jacqui, dir. 2000. *Rashōmon.* DVD video. Melbourne / Brisbane: Contemporary Arts Media / Frank Theatre.

Carroll, Jacqui, dir. 2003a. *Doll Seventeen.* DVD video. Melbourne / Brisbane: Contemporary Arts Media / Frank Theatre.

Carroll, Jacqui, dir. 2003b. *Oedipus rex.* DVD video. Melbourne / Brisbane: Contemporary Arts Media / Frank Theatre.

Carroll, Jacqui, dir. 2003c. *Midsummer Night's Romeos.* DVD video. Melbourne / Brisbane: Contemporary Arts Media / Frank Theatre.

Carroll, Jacqui, dir. 2006. *Manga Ulysses.* DVD video. Melbourne / Brisbane: Contemporary Arts Media / Frank Theatre.

Carroll, Jacqui, dir. 2007. *Hamlet Stooged!* DVD video. Melbourne / Brisbane: Contemporary Arts Media / Frank Theatre.

Carroll, Jacqui. 2023. Email correspondence with the author, 6 April.

Carruthers, Ian. 1992. 'Traditions in Transformation: Suzuki Tadashi's *Chronicle of Macbeth*'. *Meanjin*, Vol. 51, No. 3, pp. 615–31.

Carruthers, Ian. 1993. 'What Actors & Directors Do to "Legitimate" Shakespeare' in Philip Mead and Marion Campbell (eds). *Shakespeare's Books.* Melbourne: Melbourne University, pp. 175–187.

Carruthers, Ian. 1996. '*Chronicle of Macbeth:* Suzuki Tadashi's Transformation of Shakespeare's *Macbeth*' in Heather Kerr, Robin Eaden, and Madge Mitto (eds). *Shakespeare: World Views.* Newark: Delaware UP, pp. 214–236.

Carruthers, Ian, and Yasunari Takahashi. 2004. *The Theatre of Suzuki Tadashi.* Cambridge: Cambridge UP.

Carty, John. 2021. *Balgo: Creating Country.* Perth: UWA.

Caruth, Cathy. 1991. 'Unclaimed Experience: Trauma & the Possibility of History' *Yale French Studies*, Vol. 79, pp. 181–92.

Casey, Maryrose. 2009. '*Ngapartji Ngapartji*: Telling Aboriginal Australian Stories' in Alison Forsyth and Chris Megson (eds), *Get Real: Documentary Theatre Past & Present.* London: Palgrave, pp. 122–139.

Centonze, Katja. 2009. 'The 'nikutai' in Murobushi Kō' *Danza e ricercar: Laboratorio di studi, scritture, visioni*, no. 1, pp. 163–186.

Cermak, Anton. 1982. Untitled photograph of Tanaka, *Artlink,* Vol. 2, No. 3, cover.

Chan, Margaret. 2015. 'Contemporary Daoist Tangki Practice' in *Oxford Handbooks Online.* New York: Oxford University Press, pp. 1–19.

Chandler, Jan. 2009. '*Burning Daylight*' *Australian Stage Online* (21 November). On line at: https://www.australianstage.com.au/200911203008/reviews/melbourne/burning-daylight-%7C-marrugeku.html

Chapman, David and Carol Hayes (eds). 2020. *Japan in Australia: Culture, Context & Connection.* Oxford: Routledge.

Chapman, Tony. 1993. *One Step On a Journey.* Produced, written and directed by Tony Chapman and Ziyin Wang. Documentary screened on SBS, 1993. Includes interviews with artists, critics and audience. Melbourne: Playbox. Courtesy of Malthouse Theatre.

Cherry, Wal. 1956. '*Summer of the Seventeenth Doll*' *Meanjin,* vol. 15, No. 1, pp. 82–86.

Cho, Hyunjung. 2012. 'Hiroshima Peace Memorial Park & the Making of Japanese Postwar Architecture' *Journal of Architectural Education,* Vol. 66, No. 1, pp. 72–83.

Christofis, Lee. 1997. 'Six New Pieces' *Dance Australia* (February–March), pp. 51–52.

Clifford, James. 1981. 'On Ethnographic Surrealism' *Comparative Studies in Society & History,* Vol. 23, No. 4, pp. 539–564.

Coelho, Abel. 2008. *A Compilation of Butoh Exercises.* Honolulu: University of Honolulu.

Coen, Stephanie. 1995. 'The Body is the Source' *American Theatre,* Vol. 12, No. 1, pp. 30ff, reproduced on ProQuest online.

Cohen, Michael. 1996. 'Seventeen Stories About Interculturalism & Tadashi Suzuki' *About Performance,* pp. 51–58.

Coslovich, Gabriell. 1998. 'Transience Finds Its Feet' *The Age* (5 June). On line at: https://infoweb-newsbank.com

Cotes, Alison. 1998. 'Steel Yourself For Flesh.' *Courier-Mail* (3 September), p. 15.

Crampton, Hilary. 2005. 'De Quincey: *Nerve 9*' *Melbourne Stage online* (3 November), reproduced on De Quincey Co website.

Crampton, Hilary. 2019. 'Dancing Across the Cultural Divide' in *Neon Rising Asialink Japan Dance Exchange.* Sydney: Asialink, pp. 4–7.

Crothers, Chelsea. 2020. *Performer Training Evolutions: NSP, the First Born Son of SMAT.* MA thesis, WAAPA @ Edith Cowan University.

Crombie, Isobel. 2004. *Body Culture: Max Dupain, Photography & Australian Culture, 1919–1939,* Melbourne: Images.

Crotty, Joel. 2010. 'Ballet & the Australian Way of Life' *Acta musicologica,* Vol. 82, No 2, pp. 305–340.

CTF. 2010. 'E45 Napoli Fringe Festival' Promotional video. Naples: Campania Teatro Festival. On line at: https://www.youtube.com/watch?v=ahe4fCzvFRo

Cubby, Ben. 2006. 'The Australian Way' *Griffith Review,* Vol. 13, unpag.

Curran, Georgia. 2017. *Yurntumu-wardingki juju-ngaliya-kurlangu yawulyu.* Book with audiovisual documentation. NT: Batchelor Institute. Video on line at: https://ictv.com.au/video/item/4987?lp=1

Curio Projects. 2017. *Heritage Impact Statement: Locomotive Workshops*. Sydney: Curio.

Curthoys, Ann. 1999. 'Expulsion, Exodus & Exile in White Australian Historical Mythology'. *Journal of Australian Studies,* Vol. 23, No. 61, pp. 1–19, 216–18.

Darnton, Robert. 1999. *The Great Cat Massacre & Other Episodes in French Cultural History*. NY: Basic.

David, Bruno, and Paul Taçon, Jean-Jacques Delannoy, Jean-Michel Geneste. 2017. *Archaeology of Rock Art in Western Arnhem Land*. Canberra: ANU.

Davidson, Jim. 1978. 'Interview: John Romeril' *Meanjin* Vol. 37, No. 3, pp. 300–12.

Davis, Therese. 2017. 'Warning Signals: Indigenous Remembrance & Futurity in Post-Apology Australia: A Reflection From Broome' *Australian Humanities Review,* Vol. 61, pp. 58–73.

Davis, Sue. 1997. 'Interview With Lynne Bradley: Choreographer/Performer With Zen Zen Zo' *Qadie,* reproduced in Zen Zen Zo. 2008, pp. 136–7.

Dawkins, Urszula. 2014. 'The Primordial Present' *RealTime*, #124, p. 12.

D'Cruz, Glenn. 1996. 'From Theatre to Performance: Constituting the Discipline of Performance Studies in the Australian Academy' *Australasian Drama Studies*, Vol. 26, pp. 36–52.

Dean, Beth, and Victor Carell. 1955. *Dust For the Dancers*. Sydney: Ure Smith.

Dean, Beth, and Victor Carell. 1983. *Twin Journey: An Autobiography*. Sydney: Pacific.

Debord, Guy. 1955. 'Introduction to a Critique of Urban Geography' *Situationist International Online*. On line at: https://www.cddc.vt.edu/sionline/presitu/geography.html

Diedrich, Antje and Frances Barbe. 2023. 'Beyond the Stomp: The Nobbs Suzuki Praxis as an Australian Variant of the Suzuki Method of Actor Training' *Theatre, Dance & Performance Training*, Vol. 14, No. 1, pp. 1–18.

Del Amo, Martin. 2005. Email correspondence with author, 19 May.

Del Amo, Martin. 2010. 'Working Solo'. *Brolga,* Vol. 33, pp. 38–40.

Del Amo, Martin. 2019. 'In Response' *Realtime Australia*. On line at: https://www.realtime.org.au/martin-del-amo-in-response/

Deleuze, Gilles, and Félix Guattari. 2008. *A Thousand Plateaus*. London: Continuum.

De Quincey, Tess. 2002. 'How To Stand in Australia' & 'Swarm Bodies'. De Quincey Co website. On line at: https://dequinceyco.net/wp-content/uploads/2010/10/swarmbodies.pdf

De Quincey, Tess. 2003. 'Overview Description of Triple Alice' *About Performance*, Vol. 5, pp. 25–27.

De Quincey, Tess. 2010. 'Thinking Through Dance'. *Brolga,* Vol. 33; adapted from a 2005 workshop presentation. On line at: https://dequinceyco.net/wp-content/uploads/2010/10/thinking1.pdf

De Quincey, Tess. 2021. 'Body Weather Bodies in the Outback'. *Theatre, Dance & Performance Training*, Vol. 12, No. 3, pp. 317–33.

De Quincey, Tess. 2005, 2021, 2022, 2023h and 2023c. Correspondence with the author, 29 September 2005, 29 September 2021, 8 November 2022, July 2023, August 2023.

De Quincey, Tess. 2023a+. De Quincey Company website. Sydney: DQC. On line at: https://dequinceyco.net/

De Quincey, Tess. nd. 'Body Weather Dance in Practice'. De Quincey Co website. On line at: https://dequinceyco.net/wp-content/uploads/2010/10/DanceInPractice.pdf

De Quincey, Tess. circa 2000. *City to City*—Parramatta to Central'. De Quincey Company website. Sydney: DQC. On line at: https://dequinceyco.net/city-to-city-parramatta-to-central-2000/

De Quincey, Tess, et al. 2001a. 'Triple Alice 3: 17 Sept–7 Oct 2001: Samples of Artist's Work' on *Triple Alice 1–3*, website. Sydney: De Quincey Co., https://dequinceyco.net/triple-alice/samplesofartist.htm

De Quincey, Tess, et al. 2001b. *Nerve 9*. DVD video, Melbourne: CAM.

De Quincey, et al. 1999–2001. *Triple Alice 1–3*, website. Sydney: De Quincey Co. On line at: https://dequinceyco.net/triple-alice/infomain.htm.

De Quincey, Tess, and Peter Eckersall. 2012. *Tess de Quincey Interviewed by Peter Eckersall*. National Library of Australia – Oral History Transcript. Canberra: National Library of Australia.

De Quincey, Tess, and Ian Maxwell. 2020. 'A Future Body' in Teresa Brayshaw, Anna Fenemore and Noel Witts (eds). *The Twenty-First Century Performance Reader*. London: Routledge, pp. 166–173.

Desmond, Jane. 1991. 'Dancing Out the Difference: Cultural Imperialism & Ruth St. Denis's *Radha*' *Signs*, Vol. 17, No. 1, pp. 28–49.

Diamond, Elin. 1988. '(In)Visible Bodies in Churchill's Theatre'. *Theatre Journal*, Vol. 40, No. 2, pp. 188–204.

Dithmer, Monna. 1989. '*Dust of Another World*'. *Information* (15 November), reproduced on De Quincey Co's website.

Dolgopolov, Greg. 1991. '*Medea: A Vision of a Void*' *Antithesis*, Vol. 4, No. 2, pp. 164–68.

Duffy, Michelle. 2001. *Music of Place: The Performance of Identity in Contemporary Australian Community Music Festivals*. PhD thesis, University of Melbourne.

Dunlop MacTavish, Shona. 1987. *An Ecstasy of Purpose: The Life & Art of Gertrud Bodenwieser*. Dunedin: Dunlop MacTavish.

Dunn, Sarah. 2003. 'Triple Alice 1: A Participant's Perspective' *About Performance*, Vol. 5, pp. 33–48.

Durland, Steven. 1990. 'Weekend in the Country: A Visit to Min Tanaka's Farm' *High Performance* (Summer), pp. 47–50.

Dussart, Françoise. 2000. 'The Politics of Representation: Kinship & Gender in the Performance of Public Ritual' in Sylvia Kleinert and Margo Neale (eds). *Oxford Companion to Aboriginal Art & Culture*. Oxford: Oxford UP, pp. 75–78.

Dussart, Françoise. 2004. 'Shown But Not Shared, Presented But Not Proffered: Redefining Ritual Identity Among Warlpiri Ritual' *Australian Journal of Anthropology*, Vol. 15, No. 3, pp. 272–287.

Dyson, Julie. 2005. 'Tess de Quincey, *Nerve 9' Dance Forum* (Winter), pp. 9–10.

Eckersall, Peter. 1999. 'Putting the Boot Into Butoh' in Erin Brannigan (ed.). MAP *Symposium*. Canberra: Ausdance, pp. 42–45.

Eckersall, Peter. 2000. 'What Cant' Be Seen: Butoh Politics & (Body) Play?' in Peta Tait (ed.). *Body Show/s: Australian Viewings of Live Performance*. Amsterdam: Rodopi/Brill, pp. 145–153.

Eckersall, Peter. 2002. 'On Physical Theatre: A Roundtable Discussion From Not Yet It's Difficult With Peter Eckersall, Paul Jackson, David Pledger, Greg Ulfan' *Australasian Drama Studies* Vol. 41, pp. 15–27.

Eckersall, Peter. 2004. 'Trendiness or Appropriation? On Australia-Japan Contemporary Theatre Exchange' in Peter Eckersall, Uchino Tadashi and Moriyama Naoto (eds). *Alternatives: Debating Theatre Culture in the Age of Con-Fusion*. Brussels: Peter Lang, pp. 23–54.

Eckersall, Peter. 2006. *Theorizing the Angura Space: Avant-garde Performance & Politics in Japan, 1960–2000*. Leiden: Brill.

Eckersall, Peter (ed.). 2016. *Beyond Contamination: Corporeality, Spirituality, & Pilgrimage in Northern Japan*. Tokyo: Keio University Art Centre.

Eckersall, Peter, and Rachel Fensham, Edward Scheer, Denise Varney. 2001. 'Tokyo Diary'. *Performance Research*, Vol. 6, No. 1, pp. 71–86.

Ellmoos, Laila, et al. 2017. *1917: The Great Strike*. Sydney: Carriageworks.

Elswit, Kate, Miyagawa Mariko, Eiko Otake, and Tara Rodman. 2019. 'What We Know & What We Want to Know: A Roundtable on Butoh & *neuer Tanz*' in Baird & Candelario (eds), pp. 126–136.

Emmerson, Russell, and Gay McAuley and Gary Seabrook. 2003. 'Body Weather at Hamilton Downs' *About Performance*, Vol. 5, pp. 101–121.

Enoch, Wesley. 1997. 'Youth's Reply' *Ignite Theatre Journal*, reproduced in Zen Zen Zo. 2008, pp. 28–29.

Euripides. 1946. *The Bacchae*. Trans. Gilbert Murray. London: Unwin.

Escher, M.C. 1989. *M.C. Escher The Graphic Work*. Koln: Taschen.

Everett, Lynn. 2008. 'Jacques Lecoq's Bouffons in Australia' *Australasian Drama Studies*, Vol. 53, pp. 168–185.

Everingham, Sara. 2009. 'Alice Springs Moves on Public Camping' ABC *News* (5 Oct), https://www.abc.net.au/listen/programs/am/alice-springs-moves-on-public-camping/1091366

Ewers, John. 1947. 'Aboriginal Ballet', *Walkabout*, vol. 1, pp. 31–36.

Fargher, Matthew. 2021. 'Sound & Song: Cultural Collaborations' in Helen Gilbert et al. (eds), pp. 129–143.

Fearn, Nicola. 2013. 'Shaken Out of the Everyday'. *RealTime*, #117, p. 37.

Ferran, Anne. 2013. *Box of Birds*. Catalogue. Sydney: Stills Gallery.

Ferrier, Barry. nd. 'Beach'. Dr Baz. Byron Bay: Ferrier, http://www.barryferrier.com/index.php/barry-ferrier-history/barry-ferrier-paup-rainsford-towner-beach

Fensham, Rachel, and Odette Kelada. 2012. 'Situating the Body: Choreographies of Transmigration' *Journal of Intercultural Studies*, Vol. 33, No. 4, pp. 395–410.

Finnane, Kieran. 1998. 'Performance "Lab" for Alice Artists' *Alice Springs news* (26 August), unpag.

Foley, Kathy. 1984. 'The Dancer & the Danced' *Asian Theatre Journal*, Vol. 2, No. 1, pp. 28–49.

Foster, Michael. 2015. *Book of Yōkai*. LA: California UP.

Fraleigh, Sondra. 2010. *Butoh: Metamorphic Dance & Global Alchemy*. Urbana: Illinois UP.

Fraser, Peter. 2014. *Now & Again: Strategies For Truthful Performance*, MA thesis, Monash University.

Freud, Sigmund. 1973. *The Standard Edition of the Complete Psychological Works of Sigmund Freud* (ed. and trans. James Strachey). London: Hogarth.

Frew, Wendy. 2016. 'Coming Home' *UNSW magazine* (10 March). On line at: https://newsroom.unsw.edu.au/news/students/coming-home

Fuller, Zack. 2018. 'Tanaka Min: The Dance of Life' in Baird & Candelario (eds), pp. 482–90.

Fuller, Zack. 2017. *One Endless Dance: Tanaka Min's Experimental Practice*, CUNY: PhD dissertation.

Fuller, Zack. 2014. 'Seeds of an Anti-Hierarchic Ideal: Summer Training at Body Weather Farm' *Theatre, Dance & Performance Training*, Vol. 5, No. 2, pp. 197–203.

Furst, Dan. 1994. 'The Cult of Dionysus' *Kansai Time Out*, reproduced in Zen Zen Zo. 2008, p. 3.

Gallasch, Keith. 1996. 'Dancing the City' *RealTime Australia*, #11, p. 4.

Gallasch, Keith. 2000. 'Double Vision: Recent Sydney Performance' *RealTime Australia*, #39, pp. 34, 47.

Galloway, Paul. 1996. 'Raw Energy' *Brisbane News*, reproduced in Zen Zen Zo. 2008, p. 18.

Gammage Bill. 2012. *The Biggest Estate on Earth: How Aborigines Made Australia*. Sydney: Allen and Unwin.

Geertz, Clifford. 1973. *Interpretation of Cultures*. NY: Basic.

Gilbert, Helen. 2013. 'Indigeneity, Time & the Cosmopolitics of Postcolonial Belonging' *Interventions*, Vol. 15, No. 2, pp. 195–210.

Gilbert, Helen, and Dalisa Pigram and Rachael Swain (eds). 2021. *Marrugeku: Telling That Story*. Aberystwyth: Centre for Performance Research.

Gilbert, Helen, and Jacqueline Lo. 2001. 'Toil & Traffic: Australian Appropriations of the Suzuki Method'. *Australasian Drama Studies*, Vol. 39, pp. 76–91.

Gilbert, Helen, and Jacqueline Lo. 2007. *Performance & Cosmopolitics: Cross-Cultural Transactions in Australia*. London: Palgrave.

Gold, Hal. 1994. 'Australian Troupe Expanding Intercultural Theatre' *Mainichi Daily News*, in Zen Zen Zo. 2008, p. 4.

Goldberg, Roselee. 2004. *Performances: Live Art Since the 60s*. NY: Thames & Hudson.

Goodall, Jane. 1996. 'Strange Attractors' *RealTime Australia*, #14, p. 35.

Goodall, Jane. 2000. 'Acting Savage' in Peta Tait (ed.) *Body Show/s: Australian Viewings of Live Performance*. Amsterdam: Rodopi/Brill, pp. 14–28.

Goodall, Jane. 2008. 'Haunted Places' in Gay McAuley (ed.) *Unstable Ground: Performance & the Politics of Place*. Brussels: PIE Lang, pp. 111–123.

Goodall, Jane, and Ian Stevenson. 2017. 'Staging de Quincey: Soundscape & Literary Language in Tess de Quincey's *Ghost Quarters*'. *About Performance*. Vols 14–15, pp. 139–153.

Goodman, David. 1988. *Japanese Drama & Culture in the 1960s*. Armonk, NY: Sharpe.

Gordon, Rae Beth. 2002. *Why the French Love Jerry Lewis*. Stanford: Stanford UP.

Gough, Richard. 2021. 'Staging the Process: Rachael Swain & Dalisa Pigram in Conversation With Richard Gough' in Helen Gilbert et al. (eds), pp. pp. 335–67.

Goto, Yukihiro. 1988. *Suzuki Tadashi: Innovator of Contemporary Japanese Theatre*. PhD thesis. Mānoa: University of Hawaii.

Goto, Yukihiro. 1989. 'The Theatrical Fusion of Suzuki Tadashi' *Asian Theatre Journal*, Vol. 6, No. 2, pp. 103–123.

Grove, Robin. 1996. 'Balancing Acts: Ballet in Australia' *Voices*, 1 Jun, pp. 21–34.

Grant, Stuart. 2003. 'How to Say (... Roughly ... Very Roughly ...) What Sort of a Thing a Triple Alice 3 Is' *About Performance*, Vol. 5, pp. 73–81.

Grant, Stuart. nd. 'A Dictionary of Atmospheres'. De Quincey Co website. On line at: https://dequinceyco.net/wp-content/uploads/2010/10/dictionary.pdf

Grant, Stuart, and Tess de Quincey. 2008. 'How to Stand in Australia?' in McAuley (ed.). pp. 247–271.

Greer, Germaine, et al. 2003. 'White Fella Jump Up' and responses *Quarterly Essay* Vol. 11.

Gropius, Walter, and Arthur Wensinger (eds). 1961. *Theater of the Bauhaus*. Middleton, CON: Wesleyan UP.

Hadley, Bree. 2011. 'Re-Constructing Asianness in Australia: Yumi Umiumare, Owen Leong, & the Remobilisation of Monstrosity'. *Liminalities*, Vol. 7, No. 3. On line at: http://liminalities.net/7-3/hadley.pdf

Hadley, Bree. 2007. 'Dis/Identification in Contemporary Physical Performance: NYID's Scenes of the Beginning From the End', *Australasian Drama Studies*, Vol. 50, pp. 111–122.

Hamilton, Margaret. 2011. *Transfigured Stages: Major Practitioners & Theatre Aesthetics in Australia*. Leiden: Brill.

Harris, Amanda. 2022. *Representing Australian Aboriginal Music & Dance 1930–1970*. NY: Bloomsbury.

Harris, Amanda, et al. 2023. 'Performing Aboriginal Rights in 1951: From Australia's Top End to Southeast'. *Australian Journal of Politics & History*, vol. 69, no. 2, pp. 227–247.

Harrison, Kristina. 2003. 'From Observer to Participant: Reflections on the Triple Alice Experience' *About Performance*, Vol. 5, pp. 13–20.

Harrison, Martin. 2000. 'Edge, Desert, Reticulation, Information' *RealTime*, #35, p. 8; also reproduced in *About Performance*, Vol. 5, pp. 29–31.

Haynes, Rosalynn. 1998. *Seeking the Centre: The Australian Desert in Literature, Art & Film*, Cambridge: Cambridge UP.

Hearn, Lafcadio. 2006. *Kwaidan*. NY: Dover.

Heathcote, Christopher. 2013. *Russell Drysdale: Defining the Modern Australia*, Melbourne: Tarra Warra.

Heazlewood, Cheryl. 1996. *Physical Theatre*. Video documentary. Melbourne: Contemporary Arts Media.

Heddon, Deidre, and Jane Milling. 2005. *Devising Performance: A Critical History*. London: Palgrave.

Herbert, Kate. 2000. 'Meat Party' Kate Herbert theatre reviews. On line at: https://kateherberttheatrereviews.blogspot.com/2014/10/meat-party-oct-12-2000.html

Herbert, Kate. 2009. 'EnTrance' Kate Herbert theatre reviews. On line at: https://kateherberttheatrereviews.blogspot.com/2009/09/

Herbert Nungarrayi, Punayi Jeannie. 2002. 'Introduction' in Webb (ed.), pp. 6–9.

Herrington, Joan. 2000. 'Directing With the Viewpoints' *Theatre Topics*, Vol. 10, No. 2, pp. 155–68.

Hess, Liam. 2020. 'The Story Behind Madonna's Iconic Jean Paul Gaultier Cone Bra' *Vogue*, (18 April). On line at: https://www.vogue.com/article/madonna-blonde-ambition-jean-paul-gaultier-cone-bra

Heywood, Nicola (Nikki). 2016. *Undoing Discomfort: Being Real / Becoming Other in an Embodied Performance Practice*, PhD thesis, University of Wollongong. On line at: https://ro.uow.edu.au/theses/4816

Heywood, Nicola (Nikki). 2017. 'Transmitting Embodiment: Grotowski to Body Weather' *Australasian Drama Studies*, Vol. 71, pp. 194–206.

Heywood, Nicola (Nikki), and Keith Gallasch. 2001. 'Body Regimes: Performance Space Forum'. Full archived transcript. *Realtime Australia:* Sydney. On line at: https://www.realtimearts.net/feature/RealTime-Performance_Space_Forums/8448

Hijikata, Tatsumi, et al. 1993. *Hijikata Tatsumi*. Tokyo: Yushi-Sha/Hijikata Archives.

Hijikata, Tatsumi. 2000a. Various essays. *TDR*, Vol. 44, No. 1, pp. 36–81.

Hijikata, Tatsumi. 2000b. 'To Prison.' *TDR*, Vol. 44, No. 1, pp. 60–61.

Hijikata, Tatsumi. 2000c. 'From Being Jealous of a Dog's Vein.' *TDR*, Vol. 44, No. 1, pp. 56–59.
Hijikata, Tatsumi. 2000d. 'Wind Daruma.' *TDR*, Vol. 44, No. 1, pp. 71–81.
Hoff, Frank. 1980. 'Suzuki Tadashi Directs *The Trojan Women*' *Theater*, Vol. 11, No. 3, pp. 43–48.
Hoffman, Ethan, et al. 1987. *Butoh*. New York: Aperture.
Holledge, Julie and Joanne Tompkins. 2000. *Women's Intercultural Performance*. London: Routledge.
Hornblow, Michael. 2009–22. *Michael Hornblow*. Website. Bangkok: Hornblow. On line at: http://www.michaelhornblow.com/
Hornblow, Michael, et al. 2022. 'Of Buffalo.' *Techniques Journal*, Vol. 2. On line at: https://techniquesjournal.com/of-buffalo/
Hosoe, Eikoh, and Mishima Yukio. 1985. *Barakei: Ordeal By Roses*. New York: Aperture.
Hosoe, Eikoh, and Hijikata Tatsumi. 2005. *Kamaitachi*. Numbered 50 facsimile reprint of the 1969 edition with additional English translation. New York: Aperture.
Hunt, Victoria, et al. 2012. *Copper Promises*. Audiovisual documentation. Sydney: TPS. On line at: https://vimeo.com/42674818?embedded=true&source=vimeo_logo&owner=867469
Hunt, Victoria. 2019. *Copper Promises Info Kit & Technical Specifications*. Peterborough, CA: Public Energy. On line at: http://publicenergy.ca/wp-content/uploads/2019/01/Copper-Promises-full-INFO-KIT-121018-compressed.pdf
Hunt, Victoria. nd. *Victoria Hunt*. Website. Sydney: Hunt. On line at: https://victoriahuntperformance.wordpress.com/
Iijima, Yoshiharu. 1987. 'Folk Culture & the Liminality of Children'. *Current Anthropology* Vol. 28, No. 4, pp. 41–8.
Innes, Christopher. 1993. *Avant garde Theatre: 1892–1992*. London: Routledge.
Jackson, Kevin. 2009. 'Run: A Performance Engine' Kevin Jackson's theatre reviews (31 August). Reproduced on De Quincey Co website.
Jackson, Naomi, Rebecca Pappas and Toni Phim. 2021. *The Oxford Handbook of Jewishness & Dance*. Oxford UP.
Jacobs, Jane, and Ken Gelder. 1994. *Uncanny Australia*. Melbourne: MUP.
Jansen, Sara. 2019. 'Returns & Repetitions: Hijikata Tatsumi's Choreographic Practice as a Critical Gesture of Temporalization' in Baird and Candelario (eds), pp. 99–112.
Jillett, Neil. 1987. 'A Clumsy Attempt To Be Outrageous'. *The Age* (14 September), p. 15.
Jillett, Neil. 1991. 'New Clothes Old Hat'. *The Age* (27 September), p. 12.
Johns, Meryn. 2000. 'Sky's the Limit' *Capital Q Weekly* (17 March); reproduced on De Quincey Co website.

Jones, Philip. 2014. *Behind the Doors: An Art History From Yuendumu*. Adelaide: Wakefield / South Australian Museum.

Jung, Carl. 1980. *The Collected Works of C.G. Jung: Vol. 9, Pt 1: Archetypes & the Collective Unconscious*. Princeton: Princeton UP.

Jusoh, Adnan, et al. 2018. 'Megalith Culture in Peninsular of Malaysia' *Jurnal arkeologi Malaysia*, Vol. 31, No. 1, pp. 1–18.

Kanamori, Mayu. 2010. 'Would You Mind If I Settled Here?' *Amerasia Journal*, Vol. 36, No. 2, pp. 62–74.

Kartomi, Margaret. 1973. 'Music & Trance in Central Java' *Ethnomusicology*, Vol. 17, No. 2, pp. 163–208.

Keating, Paul. 1992. 'Launch of the International Year For the World's Indigenous People'. Canberra: Dept. of Prime Minister. On line at: https://pmtranscripts.pmc.gov.au/sites/default/files/original/00008765.pdf

Keating, Paul. 1995. 'Address to the Chinese Chamber of Commerce: Australia & Asia: The Next Steps'. Canberra: Dept. of Prime Minister. On line at: https://pmtranscripts.pmc.gov.au/release/transcript-9481

Kellaway, Nigel. 2016. *Nigel Kellaway: Fourteen Years: A Cautionary Tale: Selected Work Records 1994–2016*. Sydney: Nigel Kellaway / University of Sydney, reproduced on https://ses.library.usyd.edu.au/handle/2123/3943

Kelly, Kathryn. 2014. 'Stories True & Truthy' *RealTime*, #124, p. 6.

Kelly, Patricia. 1997. 'Commentary on *The Marriage of Figaro*' *Ignite Theatre Journal*, reproduced in Zen Zen Zo. 2008, pp. 24–27.

Kelly, Patricia. 2002. 'Aussie Classic Gets Dolled Up' *Courier Mail* (24 July), p. 36.

Kelly, Veronica. 1998. '*Macbeth As Told By the Weird Sisters*' *The Australian*, reproduced in Zen Zen Zo. 2008, p. 32.

Kelly, Veronica. 1997a. 'A Satisfying Romp Across Boundaries' *The Australian* (2 September), p. 12.

Kelly, Veronica. 1997b. '*Salome*' *The Australian* (7 November), p. 21.

Kelly, Veronica. 1996. '*Unleashed*' *The Australian*, reproduced in Zen Zen Zo. 2008, p. 20.

Kelly, Veronica. 1995a. 'Changing Time, The Tragedy of Oedipus'. *The Australian* (7 July), p. 14.

Kelly, Veronica. 1995b. '*Macbeth, Mill Fire*'. *The Australian* (13 April), p. 15.

Khatib, Abdelhafid. 1958. 'Attempt at a Psychogeographical Description of Les Halles' *Situationist International Online*. On line at: www.cddc.vt.edu/sionline/si/leshalles.html

Killoran, Tianna. 2022. 'Sex, Soap & Silk: Japanese Businesswomen in North Queensland', *Lilith*, No. 28, pp. 35–54.

Kingma, Jennifer. 1989. 'Workshop Offers Dance, Theatre Skills'. *Canberra Times* (4 December), p. 21.

Kinsella, Sharon. 2005. 'Black Faces, Witches, & Racism Against Girls' in Lee Miller and Jan Bardsley (eds). *Bad Girls of Japan*. London: Palgrave Macmillan, pp. 143–157.

Kloetzel, Melanie, and Carolyn Pavlik. 2009. *Site Dance: Choreographers & the Lure of Alternative Spaces*. Gainesville: Florida UP.

Koleth, Elsa. 2010–11. *Multiculturalism: A Review of Australian Policy Statements: Research Paper no. 6, 2010–11*. Canberra: Parliament of Australia. On line at: https://www.aph.gov.au/About_Parliament/Parliamentary_Departments/Parliamentary_Library/pubs/rp/rp1011/11rp06#_Toc275248118

Klein, Susan. 1988. *Ankoku Buto: The Premodern & Postmodern Influences on the Dance of Utter Darkness*. Ithaca: Cornell University Press.

Komparu, Kunio. 1983. *The Noh Theater: Principles & Perspectives*. NY: Weatherhill/Tankosha.

Kristeva, Julia. 1980. *Desire in Language* (trans. Thomas Gorz et al). New York: Columbia University Press.

Kristeva, Julia. 2005. 'Motherhood Today' in *Julia Kristeva*. Université Paris 7. On line at: http://www.kristeva.fr/motherhood.html

Lakić Parać, Iva. 2015. 'Social Context of the Fujo'. *Asian Studies*, Vol. 3, No. 19, pp. 145–70.

Lancaster, Lynne. 2009. *'Run:* Carriageworks' *ArtsHub* (31 August), reproduced on De Quincey Co website.

Lancaster, Lynne. 2012. *'Copper Promises' ArtsHub* (8 May). On line at: https://www.artshub.com.au/news/reviews/copper-promises-hinemihi-haka-189162-2299226/

Lazaroo, Natalie. 2011. *Never the Ordinary: Training & Performance in Contemporary Australian Physical Theatre: A Zen Zen Zo Case Study*. MA thesis. University of Queensland.

Lazaroo, Natalie. 2012. 'The Extraordinary Body?' *Axon*, Vol. 3. On line at: http://www.axonjournal.com.au/issue-3/extraordinary-body

Lazaroo, Natalie. 2013. 'These Things of Darkness: A Postcolonial Experiment in Zen Zen Zo's *The Tempest* (2009)' *Contemporary Theatre Review*, Vol. 23, No. 3, pp. 380–89.

Lawler, Ray. 2012. *Summer of the Seventeenth Doll*, Sydney: Currency, ProQuest eBook.

Lawler, Sarah. 2015. 'Zen Zen Zo: Making Theatre Then & Now'. Student slide show. Brisbane: University of Queensland, reproduced at https://www.slideshare.net/sarahlawler/zen-zen-zo-sarah-lawler

Lee, Raymond. 1986. 'Continuity & Change in Chinese Spirit Mediumship' *Bijdragen tot de Taal, Land-en Volkenkunde*, Vol 142, Nos 2–3, pp. 198–214.

Legeza, László. 1975. *Tao Magic*. NY: Pantheon.

Leiser-Moore, Deborah, et al. nd. *Tashmadada*. Company website. Sydney: Tashmada, http://www.tashmadada.com/

Le Moal, Philippe. 1999. *Dictionnaire de la danse*. Paris: Larousse.

Leonard, Douglas. 2002. 'Doll Madness' *RealTime*. #52, p. 35.

Leonard, Douglas. 2009. 'Under a Spell' *RealTime*. #92, p. 42.

Leslie, Michael. 2021. 'This Was Not a Fly-by-night Project' in Gilbert et al (eds), pp. 24–25.

Le Quy, Duong. 2000. *Meat Party*. Sydney: Currency.

Lésoualc'h, Théo. 1978. *Érotique du Japon*, Paris: Veyrier.

Lewis, Robert, and Dominique Sweeney. 2019. 'Perform 'the Space' Not 'in the Space': Incorporating Place, Environment & Imagination in Integrative Practices' *Fusion*, Vol. 5, pp. 85–96.

Lewis Japanangka, Paddy. 2002. 'Indigenous Responses to *Mina Mina* (2001)' in Webb (ed.), p. 22.

Lim, Anne. 1998. 'Master Act for Suzuki Disciples' *The Australian* (31 July), p. 14.

Lo, Jacqueline. 2021. 'Tangled Histories, Haunted Streets: Asian Indigenous Relations in Broome' in Gilbert et al. (eds), pp. 90–101.

Loth, Joanne [Jo], and Rob Pensalfini. 2021. 'Body. Breath. Text. Freedom: An Investigation of Concurrent Training in Linklater Voice & the Suzuki Actor Training Method' *Theatre, Dance & Performance Training*, Vol. 12, No. 1, pp. 80–94.

Loth, Joanne [Jo]. 2001. *Developing a Theatre of the Integrated Actor*. MA thesis, Queensland University of Technology.

MA [Monash Arts]. 2011. *A Dance For All Seasons*. Video documentation. Melbourne: Monash University. On line at: https://vimeo.com/33564915?embedded=false&source=video_title&owner=13123923

Maher, Rachel. 2005. 'Deep in the Desert' *RealTime*, #69, p. 11.

Malaysian Dept. of National Heritage. 2008–11. *Nomination Dossier: Historic Cities of the Straits of Malacca*. UNESCO. On line at: https://whc.unesco.org/en/list/1223/documents/

Maro, Akaji, et al. 1972-present. *Dairakudakan.com*. Dairakudakan company website. Tokyo: Dairakudakan. On line at: http://www.dairakudakan.com/

Maro, Akaji. circa 2008. *Creating Butoh Drama*. Handout provided to workshop participants. Tokyo: Dairakudakan. Courtesy of Bruce Baird.

Marrugeku. 2009. *Burning Daylight*. Booklet & DVD. Broome/Perth: Marrugeku.

Marshall, Jonathan W. 1995. 'Bodies Across the Pacific: The Japanese National Body in the Performance Technique of Suzuki & butoh' *Antithesis*, Vol. 7, No. 2, pp. 50–65. On line at: http://dequinceyco.net/wp-content/uploads/2010/10/j.marshall.pdf

Marshall, Jonathan W. 2001a. '*Mixed Metaphor* [interview with Yap & Umiumare]'. *IN Press magazine*, manuscript copy.

Marshall, Jonathan W. 2001b. '*Mixed Metaphor*'. *RealTime*, #46, p. 27.

Marshall, Jonathan W. 2004. 'Japan Inside Out'. *RealTime*, #63, pp. 4–5, reproduced on https://www.realtime.org.au/japan-inside-out-a-journey/

Marshall, Jonathan W. 2006. 'Dancing the Elemental Body: Jonathan Marshall Talks With Min Tanaka & Yumi Umiumare About the History of butoh & Body Weather

Today' *Performance Paradigm*, Vol. 2, pp. 54–73. On line at: http://www.performanceparadigm.net/wp-content/uploads/2007/06/6marshall.pdf

Marshall, Jonathan W. 2007. 'The Priestesses of Apollo & the Heirs of Aesculapius: Medical Art-Historical Approaches to Ancient Choreography After Charcot' *Forum for Modern Language Studies*, Vol. 43, no. 4, pp. 410–426.

Marshall, Jonathan W. 2008. 'The Theatre of the Athletic Nude: The Teaching & Study of Anatomy at the École des Beaux-Arts, Paris, 1873–1940," *Being There: After—Proceedings of the 2006 Conference of the Australasian Association for Drama, Theatre & Performance Studies* (Jun 2008), http://ses.library.usyd.edu.au/bitstream/2123/2511/1/ADSA2006_Marshall.pdf.

Marshall, Jonathan W. 2011a. 'Kleist's Übermarionetten & Schrenck-Notzing's *Traumtänzerin*: Nervous Mechanics & Hypnotic Performance Under Modernism' in Bernd Fischer and Tim Mehigan (eds). *Heinrich von Kleist & Modernity*. Rochester: Camden, pp. 261–81. On line at: https://www.academia.edu/1489958/_Kleist_s_%C3%9Cbermarionetten_and_Schrenck_Notzing_s_Traumt%C3%A4nzerin_Nervous_Mechanics_and_Hypnotic_Performance_Under_Modernism_

Marshall, Jonathan W. 2013. '"The world of the neurological pavilion": Hauntology & European Modernism '*mal tourné*" *TDR*, Vol. 57, No. 4, pp. 60–85.

Marshall, Jonathan W. 2018. 'Bodies at the Threshold of the Visible: Photographic Butoh' in Baird and Candelario (eds), pp. 158–170.

Marshall, Jonathan W. 2020a. 'Préface', English translation, from Nourit Masson-Sékiné, *De fange en Merveilles: Souffrance/douleur dan la création: Essai sur la danse butoh III*. Strasbourg: Origine, pp. 3–13. On line at: https://ro.ecu.edu.au/ecuworkspost2013/8410/

Marshall, Jonathan W. 2020b. 'Traumatic Dances of the 'non-self': Bodily Incoherence & the Hysterical Archive' in Johanna Braun (ed.). *Performing Hysteria: Images & Imaginations of Hysteria*. Leuven, Belgium: Leuven UP, pp. 61–83. On line at: https://library.oapen.org/bitstream/handle/20.500.12657/42712/9789461663139.pdf?sequence=1&isAllowed=y

Marshall, Jonathan W. 2021. 'Hysterical Aesthetics in Contemporary Performance' in Johanna Braun (ed.). *Hysterical Methodologies in the Arts: Rising in Revolt*. London: Palgrave-Macmillan, pp. 271–95.

Marshall, Jonathan W. 2022a. 'Outside-In or Inside – Out? The Conflicted Discourse of Stanislavsky in Australia & Aotearoa New Zealand (Part 1 of 2)' *Stanislavsky Studies*, Vol. 10, No. 1, pp. 9–20.

Marshall, Jonathan W. 2022b. 'Ragpickers & Radical Naturalism: The Conflicted Discourse of Stanislavsky in Australia & Aotearoa New Zealand (Part 2 of 2)' *Stanislavsky Studies*, Vol. 10, No. 2, pp. 139–150.

Marshall, Jonathan W. forthcoming. 'Intermedial Dance & Acéphalic Butoh: Damien Jalet's & Nawa Kōhei's *Vessel* (2016)' *Dance Research Journal*, forthcoming.

Marshall, Jonathan W., and Emily Duncan. 2018. 'Landscapes as Graveyards: Spectral Return & Performativity in the Contested Landscape' *Australasian Drama Studies*, 72, pp. 66–99. On line at: https://www.academia.edu/37178102/Landscapes_as_GraveyardsMarshallDuncan_pdf

Mason, Francesca. 1996. 'Cult of Intensity' *Performance Studies*. Brisbane: QUT magazine. Reproduced in Zen Zen Zo. 2008, pp. 15–17.

Maufort, Marc. 2000. 'Unsettling Narratives: Subversive Mimicry in Australian Aboriginal Solo Performance Pieces' *Antipodes*, pp. 105–110.

Maxwell, Ian. 2017. 'Theatrical Bowerbirds: Received Stanislavsky & the Tyranny of Distance' in Jonathan Pitches and Stefan Aqualina (eds). *Stanislavsky in the World*, London: Bloomsbury, pp. 325–46.

Maxwell, Ian. 2003. 'Access All Areas: Reflections on Triple Alice 1' *About Performance*, Vol. 5, pp. 65–72.

Maxwell, Ian. 2008. "'All exercise sessions to take place in complete silence': Performance Syndicate & the Rise & Fall of the Grotowskian Ideal' *Australasian Drama Studies*, Vol. 53, pp. 17–41.

Maxwell, Ian. forthcoming. *Jerzy Grotowski in Australia*. Leiden: Brill.

McAlister, Baz. 2008. 'Fusing the Ancient Japanese Dance Art of Butoh With Contemporary Issues [interview with Bradley]' *Time Out*, reproduced in Ze Zen Zo. 2008, p. 87.

McAuley, Gay. 2000. 'Body Weather in the Central Desert of Australia'. De Quincey Co website. On line at: https://dequinceyco.net/wp-content/uploads/2010/10/gm_firt_2000.pdf

McAuley, Gay (ed.). 2008. *Unstable Ground: Performance & the Politics of Place*. Brussels: Peter Lang.

McAuley, Gay, et al. 2003. 'Body Weather at Hamilton Downs' *About Performance*, Vol. 5, pp. 101–21.

McBryde, Isabel. 1994. '"To know the place for the first time": Consideration of Diverse Values for an Australian World Heritage Site' *ICOMOS*, vol. 3, pp. 34–44.

McKechnie, Shirley. 1991. 'Australians Making Dances: The Spatial Imperative' *Dame Peggy van Praagh address*. Canberra: Ausdance. On line at: https://ausdance.org.au/articles/details/australians-making-dances-the-spatial-imperative

McKinnon, Catherine (ed.). 2020. *Adelaide Festival*. Adelaide: Wakefield.

McLean, Sandra. 2002. 'Zen Zen Zo on the Go.' *Courier-Mail* (21 March), p. 19.

McClintock, Anne. 1995. *Imperial Leather: Race, Gender & Sexuality in the Colonial Conquest*. NY: Routledge.

McNeilly, Jodie. 2007. 'A Once & Future Building' *Realtime*, #82, p. 29.

McNeilly, Jodie. 2012. 'Unmoored & Entranced' *Realtime*, #109, p. 5.

Megarrity, David. 2004. 'Immersed: Zen Zen Zo' *Lowdown magazine*, Vol. 26, pp. 8–9.

Meyrick, Julian. 2002. *See How It Runs: Nimrod & the New Wave*. Sydney: Currency.

Mezur, Katherine. 2004. 'Cute Mutant Girls: Sweetness & Deformity in Contemporary Performance by Young Japanese Women' in Peter Eckersall, Uchino Tadashi & Moriyama Naoto (eds). *Alternatives: Debating Theatre Culture in the Age of Con-Fusion.* Brussels: Peter Lang, pp. 73–88.

Mihalopoulos, Bin. 1993. 'The Making of Prostitutes: The Karayuki-san' *Bulletin of Concerned Asian Scholars,* Vol. 25, No. 1, pp. 41–56.

Miller, Sarah. 1995. 'Art'. *Art & Text,* Vol. 36, unpag; reproduced on De Quincey Co website.

Mishima, Yukio. 1961/2019. 'Contemporary Nightmare: An avant-garde Dance Group Dances *Forbidden Colors'* in Baird & Candelario (eds), , pp. 52–53.

Molloy, Susan. 1982. 'An Art Buff Treat at the Gallery'. *Sydney Morning Herald* (14 April), p. 1.

Monaghan, Paul. 2009. 'Greek Tragedy in Australia' in Alena Sarkissian and Pavlína Šípová (eds). *Staging of Classical Drama.* Newcastle: Cambridge Scholars, pp. 38–58.

Moore, Richard, dir. 1991. *Butoh: Piercing the Mask.* AV documentary. New York: Insight Media.

Morant, Alix de. 2004. '*Hôsôtan*, sixième tableau en echo à *L'Après midi d'un faune.*' in Aslan and Picon-Vallin (eds), pp. 268–276.

Morishita Takashi, et al. nd. *Tashiro: Cycle & Memory.* Film documentary. Kyoto: Kei University.

Morphy, Howard, and Margo Boles, eds. 1999. *Art From the Land: Dialogues With the Kluge-Ruhe Collection.* Charlottesville: Virginia UP.

Morelos, Ronaldo. 2004. *Trance Forms: A Theory of Performed States of Consciousness,* PhD thesis, University of Melbourne.

Morris-Suzuki, Tessa. 1994. 'Collective Memory, Collective Forgetting: Indigenous People & the Nation-State in Japan & Australia' *Meanjin,* Vol. 53, No. 4, pp. 597–612.

Mulryne, J.R. 1998. 'The Perils & Profits of Interculturalism & the Theatre Arts of Tadashi Suzuki' in Sasayama Takashi (ed.). *Shakespeare & the Japanese Stage.* Cambridge: Cambridge UP, pp. 71–93.

Mundine, Djon. 2002. 'A Dance Through the Desert' in Webb (ed.), pp. 68–71.

Munn, Nancy. 1973.*Walbiri Iconography: Graphic Representation & Cultural Symbolism in a Central Australian Society.* Ithaca: Cornell University Press.

Munroe, Alexandra. 1994.*Japanese Art After 1945: Scream Against the Sky.* NY: Abrams.

Murphy, Chris. 1996. 'Operation Hypothesis: Tadashi Suzuki's "toil & trouble" Tour'. *About Performance,* Vol. 2, pp. 41–49.

Musa, Helen. 1990a. 'Dramatic Distillation of a Nomadic Exile' *Canberra Times* (21 February), p. 33.

Musa, Helen. 1990b. '*Far From Where* Is Like Caviar to the General' *Canberra Times* (24 February), p. 21.

Nadoya. 1993. *Nadoya.* Edited by Anne Norman and Gordon Thompson at Open Channel. Privately released video. Melbourne: Norman/Nadoya. Courtesy of Norman.

Nadoya. 1994. *Nadoya Nadoya Nadoya.* Promotional video. Melbourne: Norman & Seven S Productions. Courtesy of Norman.

Nadoya. 1996. *Kagome.* CD audio recording and notes. Melbourne: Norman & Absurd Publications.

Nadoya. 1997. *Kagome.* Archival video. Melbourne: Norman & Seven S Productions.

Nakatani, Tadao. 2003. *World of Tatsumi Hijikata the Originator of Butoh: A Collection of Dance Photographs.* Tokyo: Shinsensha.

Nanako, Kurihara. 2000. 'Hijikata Tatsumi: The Words of Butoh: Introduction' *TDR*, Vol. 44, No. 1 (Spring, 2000), pp. 10–28.

Neal, Margo (ed.). 2021. *Songlines.* Canberra: National Museum of Australia.

Needham, Tessa. 2007. *'The Stirring' Australian Stage* (9 November). On line at: http://www.australianstage.com.au/reviews/sydney/the-stirring--de-quincey-co.-864.html

Neideck, Jeremy, et al. 2015. *Deluge.* Vimeo video. On line at: https://vimeo.com/131725555?embedded=true&source=vimeo_logo&owner=4965329

Neideck Jeremy. 2016. *The Fabric of Transcultural Collaboration: Interweaving the Traditional Korean Vocal Form of p'ansori & the Contemporary Japanese Dance Form of butoh in a Transculturally Australian Context.* PhD thesis, Queensland University of Technology.

Neideck, Jeremy. 2018. '"We need to keep one eye open": Approaching butoh at Sites of Personal & Cultural Resistance' in Baird & Candelario (eds). pp. 343–357.

Neideck, Jeremy and Kathryn Kelly. 2021. 'A Special Relationship: A Broad Survey of Japanese Performance Training Methodologies' Influence on Brisbane Actor Training Since the 1990s'. *Theatre, Dance & Performance Training,* Vol. 12, No. 3, pp. 450–469.

Neill, Rosemary. 1992. 'Suzuki Guts *Macbeth* of Drama' *The Australian* (2 March), p. 10.

Newman, Geoffrey. 1999. 'Wizards of Oz' *Weekend Australian,* reproduced in Zen Zen Zo. 2008, p. 101.

Nicholls, Christine. 2002. 'Grounded Abstraction: The Work of Dorothy Napangardi' in Webb (ed.), pp. 60–67.

NMA. nd. 'White Australia Policy'. Canberra: National Museum of Australia. On line at: https://www.nma.gov.au/defining-moments/resources/white-australia-policy

Nobbs, John. 2006. *Frankly Acting.* Brisbane: Frank Theatre.

Nobbs, John. 2010. *A Devil Pokes the Actor.* Brisbane: Frank Theatre.

Nobbs, John. 2019. *Every Little Bit: The Nobbs Suzuki Primer.* Brisbane: Frank Theatre.

Nobbs, John. 2020. *36 Nobbs Jung Cantos For the Actor.* Brisbane: Frank Theatre.

Nobbs, John and Jon Brokering. 2016. *Insights We Got From Tadashi Suzuki, the Shogun of Toga.* Brisbane: Frank Theatre.

Nobbs, John, and Jacqui Carroll. nd.1. *Oz Frank Theatre Matrix.* Website. Brisbane: Frank Theatre. On line at: http://www.ozfrank.com/

Nobbs, John, and Jacqui Carroll. nd.2. *NSP: The Nobbs Suzuki Praxis.* Website. Brisbane: Frank Theatre. On line at: https://www.nobbssuzukipraxis.com/

Nobbs, John, and Jacqui Carroll. 2015. *Self-Discovery in a Silver Room: The Frank Suzuki Actor Knowhow Package.* DVD and booklet. Melbourne: Contemporary Arts Media. On line at: http://www.ozfrank.com/Silver%20Room%20Text.pdf

Norman, Anne. nd. *Anne Norman.* Website. Melbourne: Norman. On line at: https://annenorman.com/

NSW NPWS. nd. *Mungo.* Sydney: NSW National Parks & Wildlife Service. On line at: http://www.visitmungo.com.au/downloads/mungo-book-1788-1901.pdf

O'Brien, Sean. 2005a. *Yumi Umiumare: Butoh Dance.* Video documentary. Sydney: ABC / O'Brien.

O'Brien, Sean. 2005b. *Tony Yap: Full Moon Trance.* Video documentary. Sydney: ABC / O'Brien.

O'Brien, Sean. 2001a. *Sunrise at Midnight.* Video. Sydney: Sophie Jackson and Sean O'Brien.

O'Brien, Sean. 2001b. *Sunrise at Midnight.* Media release. On line at: https://www.yumi.com.au/content/2017/12/29/sunrise-at-midnight

Odom, Maggie. 1980. 'Mary Wigman: The Early Years 1913–1925' *TDR*, Vol. 24, No. 4, pp. 81–92.

Okamoto, Tarō. 2009. 'On Jōmon Ceramics' *Art in Translation*, Vol. 1, No. 1, pp. 49–60.

Okpewho, Isidore. 1999. 'Soyinka, Euripides, & the Anxiety of Empire'. *Research in African Literatures*, Vol. 30, No. 4, pp. 32–55.

O'Regan, Tom. 1988. 'The Historical Relations Between Theatre & Film' *Continuum*, Vol. 1, No. 1, pp. 116–120.

Orr, Marnie, and Rachel Sweeney. 2011. 'Surface Tensions' *Double Dialogues*, Vol. 14. On line at: http://www.doubledialogues.com/article/surface-tensions-land-and-body-relations-through-live-research-inquiry-rockface/

Palao, Alec. 2002. *Board Boogie: Surf & Twang Downunder.* Audio CD and booklet. London: Big Beat.

Papas, Kath. nd. *Kath Papas Productions.* Melbourne: Papas. On line at: https://kathpapas.net/zero-zero/

Parsons, Jonathan, and Angharad Wynne-Jones. 1996. 'Interview: Tess de Quincey & Stuart Lynch' *TPS Quarterly*, Vol. 9, pp. 14–17 and 27–30.

Pascoe, Bruce. 2014. *Dark Emu*, Broome: Magabala.

Pavis, Patrice. 1998. 'Du Butō considéré come du grand-guignol qui a mal tourné'. *Europe: Revue littéraire mensuelle*, 76, pp. 200–19; also reproduced in 2007, *Vers une théorie de la pratique théâtrale.* Villeneuve d'Ascq: Presses universitaires du Septentrion, pp. 251–266. On line at: https://books.openedition.org/septentrion/13738?lang=en#access

Pavis, Patrice. 2016. 'Pour une analyse des spectacles: A 'femme ôtée''. *Critical Stages*, Vol. 2. On line at: http://www.critical-stages.org/2/pour-une-analyse-des-spectacles-la-femme-otee-lexemple-de-fine-bone-china-de-et-par-franbaibe/

Phillips, Ruth. 2015. 'Aesthetic Primitivism Revisited'. *Journal of Art Historiography*, pp. 1–25.

Picon-Vallin, Béatrice. 2004. 'Derevo: Quand le butô contamine la clownerie'. in Aslan and Picon-Vallin (eds), pp. 335–344.

Picott, Karla. 1995. 'Blurring the Barriers' *Townsville Bulletin* (6 May), unpag; reproduced on De Quincey Co website.

Pippen, Judy. 1998. 'Ranged Between Heaven & Hades: Actors' Bodies in Cross Cultural Theatre Forms'. *Australasian Drama Studies*, Vol. 32, pp. 23–34.

Playbox. 1992. *Chronicle of Macbeth*. Program. Melbourne: Playbox.

Pledger, David. 2017. *Wall of Noise, Web of Silence*. PhD thesis. Melbourne: RMIT.

Pledger, David, et al. 2008. *The Dispossessed*. Audiovisual documentation and interview. Melbourne: NYID.

Pledger, David, et al. nd. *Not Yet It's Difficult*. Melbourne: NYID, https://notyet.com.au/

Porter, Roy (ed.). 1996. *Rewriting the Self*. London: Routledge.

Postle, Julia. 1996a. 'Occupying Positive Space'. *Realtime*, #11 (February-March), p. 6.

Postle, Julia. 1996b. 'Integration & Excess'. *Realtime*, #14 (August-September), p. 31.

Potter, Michelle. 1996. 'Making Australian Dance'. *Voices*. Jun, pp. 10–20.

Potter, Michelle. 2011. 'Australians Abroad'. *NLA magazine*. Dec, pp. 21–23.

Powell, Brian. 1991. 'Taishū Engeki'. *Japan Forum*, Vol. 3, No. 1, pp. 107–13.

Power, Liza. 2010. 'His Steps Shaped by the Shamans' *Sydney Morning Herald* (20 April). On line at: https://www.smh.com.au/entertainment/dance/his-steps-shaped-by-the-shamans-20100419-spcm.html

Price, Norman. 1987. Video record and notes of Byakkosha photography session conducted at Hanging Rock, Victoria, 1987. Possession of Norman Price.

Priest, Gail (ed.). 1996. *Compression 100*. Sydney: TPS / RealTime Australia. Archival copy. Courtesy of Jonathan Bollen.

Premont, Roslyn. 2020. *Dorothy Napangardi*. Alice Springs: Gallery Gondwana.

Premont, Roslyn, et al. 2023. *Gallery Gondwana website*. Alice Springs: Gallery Gondwana, https://www.gallerygondwana.com.au/

Pronko, Leonard. 1993. 'Chronicle of Macbeth'. *Theatre Journal*, Vol. 45, No. 1, pp. 110–112.

Pryce, Larissa. 2012. *Embodying Places: Making Meaning in Performance*, PhD thesis, Murdoch University.

Purdon, Noel. 1992. 'Macnoodles' *Adelaide Review* (March), pp. 33–34.

Radic, Leonard. 1992. 'Suzuki's Meditation on the Mind of Macbeth' *The Age* (2 March), p. 12.

Rainsford (Paul Towner). nd. *Chapel of Change*. Melbourne: Rainsford. Website now defunct; author's archival copy; http://www.chapelofchange.com/ (consulted June 2022).

Rankin, Scott. 2012. *Two Plays*. Sydney: Currency.

Reid, Robert. 2022. 'Suzuki Method & *The Chronicle of Macbeth' Stories of M.* Melbourne: Malthouse Theatre. On line at: https://stories.malthousetheatre.com.au/stories/suzuki-method-and-the-chronicle-of-macbeth/

Reid, Robert. 2023. Email correspondence with the author, 17 February.

Rentell, Anne-Louise. 2000. 'Into the Dreamland' *Total Theatre,* Vol. 12, No. 1, http://www.totaltheatre.org.uk/archive/features/dreamland

Reynolds, Henry. 2003. *Law of the Land.* Melbourne: Penguin.

Riccardi, Valentina. 2017. 'Intercultural Theatre Practices: Interview With Frances Barbe'. *Theatre Times* (December). On line at: https://thetheatretimes.com/intercultural-theatre-practices-interview-frances-barbe/

Roads, Curtis. 1988. 'Introduction to Granular Synthesis' *Computer Music Journal,* Vol. 12, No. 2, pp. 11–13.

Roane, Tim, dir. and writer. 1998. *Toil: The Making of "Macbeth As Told By the Weird Sisters"* DVD. Brisbane: Zen Zen Zo / Contemporary Arts Media.

Robertson, Jo. 2015. *Drawing Us In: The Australian Experience of Butoh & Body Weather,* MA thesis, University of Sydney.

Robertson, Jo. 2017. "This is what I had been looking for': Australian Practitioners on Finding butoh & Body Weather' *About Performance,* Vols 14–15, pp. 121–137.

Romeril, John. 1994. 'Chrome, Stretch, Stalk Those Market Niches'. *Meanjin,* Vol. 53, No. 3, pp. 531–536.

Romeril, John. 1997. *Love Suicides.* Sydney: Currency.

Romeril, John. 2001. *Miss Tanaka.* Sydney: Currency.

Romeril, John, et al. 2001. *Miss Tanaka.* Prompt pack / education resource. Melbourne: Malthouse.

Rose, Deborah Bird. 1992. *Dingo Makes Us Human: Life & Land in Australian Aboriginal Culture.* Cambridge: Cambridge University Press.

Rose, Deborah Bird. 1996. *Nourishing Terrains: Australian Aboriginal Views of Landscape & Wilderness.* Canberra: Australian Heritage Commission.

Ross, Stephen, and Allana Lindgren, eds. 2017. *The Modernist World.* London: Routledge.

Rothfield, Philippa. 1998. 'A Question of Visions' *RealTime,* #27, p. 4.

RT. 1996. 'Kagome Kagome' *Realtime,* #12, p. 34.

Sachs, Curt. 1933. *Eine Weltgeschichte des Tanzes* [*World History of the Dance*]. Berlin: Notenbeispielen und 32 Bildertafeln.

Sakamoto, Michael. 2018. 'Michael Sakamoto & the Breaks: Revolt of the Head (MuNK Remix)' in Baird and Candelario (eds), pp. 525–532.

Sakamoto, Michael. 2022. *An Empty Room: Imaging Butoh & the Social Body.* Middletown, CON: Wesleyan UP.

Sant, Toni. 2003. 'Suzuki Tadashi & the Shizuoka Theatre Company'. *TDR,* Vol. 47, No. 3, pp. 147–158.

Sas, Miryam. 2003. 'Hands, Lines, Acts: Butoh & Surrealism' *Qui parle*, Vol. 13, No. 2, pp. 19–51.

Sasamori, Takefusa. 1997. 'Therapeutic Rituals Performed by Itako'. *World of Music*, Vol. 39, No. 1, pp. 85–96.

Savage, Paula, and Lara Strongman. 2002. *Tracy Moffatt*. Wellington: City Gallery.

Segal, Charles. 1987. *Dionysiac Poetics & Euripides*. Princeton: Princeton UP.

Schacher, Alan. 2000. *Done by Gravity Feed: Relationships Between Body & Site in the Performance & Installation Works*. MFA thesis, UNSW.

Schacher, Alan. 2021. *Alan Schacher: Biography & CV & other documents*. NSW: Alan Schacher website. On line at: https://alanschacher.net/

Schaefer, Kerri. 2009. 'Place, Identity, Belonging, & Performance' in Marrugeku, *Burning Daylight*. Pamphlet & DVD. Broome/Perth: Marrugeku, pp. 56–71.

Scheyer, Ernst. 1970. *The Art of Mary Wigman & Oskar Schlemmer*, NY: Dance Perspectives.

Schneider, Robert, and Nathan Schneider. 2020. 'Taishū Engeki' *NTQ: New Theatre Quarterly*, Vol. 36, No. 3, pp. 256–271.

Scorch. 1993. *'The Way of Mud' Scorch Magazine*, reproduced in Zen Zen Zo. 2008, p. 2.

Sheer, Edward. 2000. 'Liminality & Corporeality: Tess de Quincey's butoh' in Peta Tait (ed.). 2000. *Body Show/s: Australian Viewings of Live Performance*. Amsterdam: Rodopi/Brill, pp. 136–144.

Shepherd, Tory. 2022. 'Two Sides of the Wire'. *The Guardian* (21 August). On line at: https://www.theguardian.com/australia-news/2022/aug/21/two-sides-of-the-wire-how-the-overland-telegraph-brought-colonial-triumph-and-aboriginal-devastation

Shirley, David. 2018. 'His Dream of Passion: Reflections on the Work of Lee Strasberg & His Influence on British Actor Training' *Stanislavski Studies*, Vol. 6, No. 2, pp. 165–182.

Shoubridge, William. 1994. 'Is' *The Australian* (8 April), unpag; reproduced on De Quincey Co website.

Shiarz, Samad, and Alice Palmer. 2021. *Yumi & the Art of Butoh*. Documentary video. Melbourne: Media factory. On line at: http://www.mediafactory.org.au/2021-real-to-reel/2021/06/01/yumi-and-the-art-of-butoh/

Silverberg, Miriam. 2006. *Erotic Grotesque Nonsense: The Mass Culture of Japanese Modern Times*. LA: California UP.

Smith, Heather, Garth Day, Brian Thomas and Luke Yeaman. 2005. 'The Changing Pattern of East Asia's Growth' *Economic Roundup*. Canberra: Dept. of Treasury, Summer 1 March, https://treasury.gov.au/publication/economic-roundup-summer-2004-05/the-changing-pattern-of-east-asias-growth#P8_143

Smith, Helen. 2013. *Being Moved: The Transformative Power of butoh*, MA thesis, Monash University, Melbourne.

Smith, Helen, with Yumi Umiumare et al. 2017. *Evocation of Butoh: Forum Q&A.* Melbourne: La Mama. On line at: https://vimeo.com/214496124

Smith, Naomi. 2000. 'Dance & the Ancestral Landscape'. *Writings on Dance*, Vol. 20, pp. 57–73.

Smith, Sue. 1996. 'Hypnotic Tale of Madness' *Courier Mail,* reproduced in Zen Zen Zo. 2008, p. 14.

Snow, Peter. 2002. *Imaging the In-Between: Training Becomes Performance in Body Weather Practice in Australia,* PhD thesis, University of Sydney.

Snow, Peter. 2003. 'P4: Performance Making in Alice' *About Performance,* Vol. 5, pp. 49–63.

Soyinka, Wole. 1974. *The Bacchae of Euripides: A Communion Rite.* London: Norton.

Sorensen, Rosemary. 'Original Sin [interview with Bradley & Wright]' *The Courier Mail.* Reproduced in Zen Zen Zo. 2008, p. 63.

Sorensen, Rosemary. 2021. 'Revelation Found in Broad Daylight' in Gilbert et al. (eds), pp. 86–89.

Splinter Orchestra. 2016. *Mungo.* Audio recording. Sydney: Splinter Orchestra. On line at: https://splitrec.bandcamp.com/album/mungo

Spunde, Nikki. 2012. '*DasSHOKU shake!!*' *Australian Stage* (29 September). On line at: https://www.australianstage.com.au/201209295849/reviews/melbourne/dasshoku-shake-%7C-yumi-umiumare-and-theatre-gumbo.html

Spunner, Suzanne. 1998. 'Brilliant Bunraku Business'. *Realtime* #23, p. 11.

Spunner, Suzanne. 2005. 'Corroboree Moderne' in Julie Wells, Mickey Dewar and Suzanne Parry (eds). *Modern Frontier: Aspects of the 1950s in Australia's Northern Territory.* Darwin: Darwin UP, pp. 143–164.

Stanner, W.H. 1991. *White Man Got No Dreaming,* Canberra: ANU.

Stein, Bonnie Sue. 1986. 'Min Tanaka: Farmer/Dancer or Dancer/Farmer: An Interview'. *TDR: The Drama Review,* Vol. 30, No. 2, pp. 142–151.

Stephenson, Peta. 2007. *Outsiders Within: Telling Australia's Indigenous-Asian Story.* Sydney: UNSW Press.

Stevens, Rachel. 2012. 'Political Debates on Asylum Seekers During the Fraser Government' *Australian Journal of Politics & History,* Vol. 58, No. 4, pp. 526–541.

Stock, Cheryl. 2012. 'Different Inflections' in Stephanie Burridge and Julie Dyson (eds). *Shaping the Landscape.* New Delhi: Routledge, pp. 84–102.

Stock, Cheryl. 2015. 'From Urban Cities & the Tropics to Site-Dance in the World Heritage Setting of Melaka' in Victoria Hunter (ed.). *Moving Sites.* London: Routledge, pp. 387–406.

Strehlow, Theodor George. 1971. *Songs of Central Australia.* Sydney: Angus & Robertson

Suzuki, Tadashi. 1984. 'Culture Is the Body!' *PAJ,* Vol. 8, No. 2 (1984), pp. 28–35.

Suzuki, Tadashi. 1986. *The Way of Acting* (trans. by J. Thomas Rimer) NY: Theatre Communications.

Suzuki, Tadashi, et al. 1984–2009. *Suzuki Company of Toga*. Website. Toga: SCOT. On line at: https://www.scot-suzukicompany.com/en/

Sykes, Jill. 1989. 'The Strange Intensity of butoh' *Sydney Morning Herald* (27 March), unpag.; reproduced on De Quincey Co website.

Sykes, Jill. 1990. 'Serenity From Savagery' *Sydney Morning Herald* (2 February), p. 10.

Sykes, Jill. 1992. 'Quest For Meaning in a Desert Sunset' *Sydney Morning Herald* (26 October), unpag; reproduced on De Quincey Co's website.

Sykes, Jill. 1993. 'Butoh in Mungo' *Dance Australia*, pp. 22–24.

Sykes, Jill. 1994a. 'Walking Instinctively' *Sydney Morning Herald* (2 April), unpag; reproduced on De Quincey Co website.

Sykes, Jill. 1994b. 'Japanese Footprint on the Dusty Australian Outback' *Sydney Morning Herald* (4 April), p. 19.

Sykes, Jill. 1997. 'Visions of the Nether World' *Sydney Morning Herald* (6 May), unpag; reproduced on De Quincey Co website.

Sykes, Jill. 1998. 'Pungent Images' *Dance Australia* (August-September), pp. 58–59.

Sykes, Jill. 2005. 'Nerve 9' *Sydney Morning Herald* (21 October), unpag; reproduced on De Quincey Co website.

Swain, Rachael. 2015. 'A Meeting of Nations: Trans-Indigenous & Intercultural Interventions in Contemporary Indigenous Dance' *Theatre Journal*, Vol. 67, No. 3, pp. 503–21.

Swain, Rachael. 2024. Online interview with the author, 1 April 2021, Perth.

Swain, Rachael. 2020. *Dance in Contested Land*. London: Palgrave.

Swain, Rachael. 2012. 'Making *Mimi*' in Gilbert et al. (eds), pp. 26–41.

Swain, Rachael, and Peter Eckersall. 2012. *Rachael Swain Interviewed by Peter Eckersall*. National Library of Australia – Oral History. Canberra: National Library of Australia.

Swain, Rachael, and Dalisa Pigram. 2021. 'Trans-Indigenous & Intercultural Dance Praxis' in Gilbert et al. (eds), pp. 144–161.

Tracey, Caroline. 2022. 'The Ephemeral Forever' *Shenandoah*, Vol. 72, No. 1, https://shenandoahliterary.org/721/the-ephemeral-forever/

Taha, Adi Haji, and Abdul Jalil Osman. 1982. 'The Excavation of the Megalithic Alignment at Kampong Ipoh, Tampin, Negeri Sembilan' *Journal of the Malaysian Branch of the Royal Asiatic Society*, Vol. 55, No. 1, pp. 78–81.

Tait, Peta (ed.). 2000. *Body Show/s: Australian Viewings of Live Performance*. Amsterdam: Rodopi/Brill.

Tamisari, Franca. 2000. 'Dancing the Land, the Land Dances Through Us'. *Writings on Dance*, Vol. 20, pp. 31–43.

Tanaka, Min. 1981. 'Min Tanaka & the Body Weather Laboratory' *Contact Quarterly*, Vols 3–4, No. 6, pp. 5–9.

Tanaka, Min. 1986. 'I Am An Avant-Garde Who Crawls the Earth: Homage to Tatsumi Hijikata' *TDR*, Vol. 30, No. 2, pp. 153–55.

Tanaka, Min, and Derek Bailey, et al. 1993. *Mountain Stage,* video and booklet. UK: Incus.

Tanaka, Min, and Okada, Masato, et al. 2019. *Between the Mountains & the Sea,* Tokyo: Kosakusha.

Tanaka, Stefan. 1993. *Japan's Orient: Rendering Pasts Into History.* Berkeley: University of California Press.

Tano, Hideko. 2010. *Body Culture Centre,* website. Tokyo: Body Culture Centre. On line at: https://hidekotano.jimdofree.com/

Taylor, Gretel. 2007. 'Perceiving & Expressing Place: Site-Specific Performance By a White Sheila' *Local-Global: Identity, Security, Community,* Vol. 3, pp. 135–142.

Taylor, Gretel. 2008. *Locating: Place & the Moving Body,* PhD thesis, Victoria University.

Taylor, Gretel. 2010. 'Empty? A Critique of the Notion of "Emptiness" in butoh & Body Weather Training' *Theatre, Dance & Performance Training,* Vol. 1, No. 1, pp. 72–87.

Taylor, Gretel. 2012. 'Dancing Country Two Ways'. *Writings on Dance,* Vol. 25. On line at: https://www.academia.edu/8291459/Dancing_Country_Two_Ways

Taylor, Gretel. 2017. 'Dancing Into Belonging: Towards a Copresences in Place'. *Brolga,* Vol. 41. On line at: https://ausdance.org.au/articles/details/dancing-into-belonging-towards-co-presence-in-place

Taylor, Gretel. 2020. 'Porous & Present Bodies: Site-Response Performance in an Era of Environmental Crisis'. *Dancehouse Diaries,* Vol. 12, No. 2. On line at: https://www.dancehousediary.com.au/?p=4637

Taylor, Gretel. circa 2022a. *Gretel Taylor.* Website. Melbourne: Taylor, https://www.greteltaylor.com/

Taylor, Gretel. 2022b. Email correspondence with author, 9 January.

Taylor, Yana. 1996. 'Empty Spaces & Bodies'. *Postwest,* Vol. 12, pp. 15–18.

Taylor, Yana. 2007. *Doctors of Presence: Tadashi Suzuki's Training Method in Sydney Contemporary Performance,* PhD thesis, University of Sydney.

Taylor, Yana. 2010. 'Slow Dance or Fast Sculpture: Suzuki Training in Sydney's Contemporary Performance'. *Australasian Drama Studies,* Vol. 56, pp. 182–202.

Thomson, Helen. 2001. 'Meat Party'. *Australasian Drama Studies,* Vol. 39, pp. 162–64.

Thompson, Helen. 1987. 'Dancing Demons on a Descent Into Hell'. *The Australian* (15 September), p. 10.

Tilly, Christopher. 2017. *Landscape in the longue durée.* London: UCL Press.

Toepfer, Karl. 1997. *Empire of Ecstasy: Nudity & Movement in German Body Culture, 1910–1935.* LA: California UP.

Tong, Merlynn. 2011. *Teacher's Notes: 'Cabaret'* Brisbane: Zen Zen Zo.

Tonkin, Maggie. 2017. *Fifty: Half a Century of ADT.* Adelaide: Wakefield.

Torgovnick, Marianna. 1990. *Gone Primitive: Savage Intellects, Modern Lives.* Chicago: Chicago UP.

Treyvaud, Stefan. 2003. 'Kitsch Makes Up For Glitches' *Courier Mail* (22 September), p. 13.

TRU. 2021. 'Butoh Diaspora' online symposium. Tokyo: Tokyo Real Underground. On line at: http://www.tokyorealunderground.net/ (consulted August 2021).

Tucker, Albert. 1946. 'Exit Modernism'. *Angry Penguins*. No. 1, pp. 9–12.

Uchida, Takahiro, et al. nd. *The-Noh.com*. Caliber Cast. On line at: https://www.the-noh.com/

Ulzen, Karen van. 1994a. 'Butoh Blend' *Dance Australia* (June-July), pp. 68–69.

Ulzen, Karen van. 1994b. 'Foetal Attraction' *Dance Australia* (October-November), p. 20.

Ulzen, Karen van. 1992. 'A Feat of Endurance' *Dance Australia* (December 1991–January 1992), p. 42.

Umiumare, Yumi. 1999. 'Butoh: A Journey Towards the Light' in Erin Brannigan (ed.). MAP *Symposium*. Canberra: Ausdance, pp. 41–42.

Umiumare, Yumi. 2009. Notes for *EnTrance*. On line at: https://www.naomiota.com/entrance.html

Umiumare, Yumi. 2014. 'On Rituals'. *Dancehouse Diary*. Vol. 7. p. 12.

Umiumare, Yumi. 2020. 'Tea Politics'. *Dancehouse Diary*, Vol. 11. On line at: https://www.dancehousediary.com.au/?cat=1134

Umiumare, Yumi. nd. *Yumi Umiumare* website & videos. Melbourne. On line at: https://www.yumi.com.au/

Umiumare, Yumi. 2023. Correspondence with the author, 2023.

Umiumare, Yumi, and Peter Eckersall. 2012. *Yumi Umiumare Interviewed by Peter Eckersall*. National Library of Australia – Oral History Transcript. Canberra: National Library of Australia.

Umiumare, Yumi, and Takeshi Kondo. 2020. *The Art of Butoh: From Japan to Australia*. AV documentary. Sydney: Japan Foundation.

Umiumare, Yumi, with Helen Smith et al. 2017. *ButohOUT!* Melbourne: ButohOUT! On line at: https://www.butohout.com/

Van Helten, Seanna. 2008. 'Now & Zen' *Rave*, reproduced in Zen Zen Zo. 2008, p. 90.

Vangeline. 2020. *Butoh*. NY: NY Butoh Institute.

Van Hout, Vicki. 2021. 'Strategic Obfuscations in Marrugeku's *Burning Daylight*' in Gilbert et al. (eds), pp. 102–117.

Varney, Denise. 2011. *Radical Visions 1968–2008*. Leiden: Brill.

Vedel, Karen. 2007. 'Silica Tales & Other Moves in Lhere Mparntwe' *Journal for the Anthropology of Human Movement*. On line at: http://www.helsinki.fi/collegium/english/staff/vedel/

Vernon, Coralie. 1997. 'Butoh' *Journal of the Asian Arts Association of Australia*, Vol. 6, No. 1, p. 2.

Viala, Jean, and Nourit Masson-Sékiné. 1991. *Butoh: Shades of Darkness*. Tokyo: Shufunotomo.

VC. nd. 'Tokyo Shock Boys (comedy)', notes and entry for theatre flyer. Athenaeum, 1995. Melbourne: Victoria Collections of Museums Victoria. On line at: https://victoriancollections.net.au/items/55d6b37b2162f12260c9e05c

Vincent, Jordan. 2010. '*Rasa Sayang*' Sydney Morning Herald (24 April). On line at: https://www.smh.com.au/entertainment/theatre/rasa-sayang-20100423-tjdw.html
Waddell, Terri. 1992. 'Shifting Language of Theatre' *Melbourne Report* (March), pp. 29–30.
Waites, James. 1999. 'Potato Country' *Realtime Australia*, #30, p. 7.
Waller, Richard. 1993. 'Zen & the Art of Butoh a Bold & Lively Brew' *Courier Mail*, reproduced in Zen Zen Zo. 2008, p. 1.
Ward, Russell. 1958. *The Australian Legend*. Melbourne: Oxford UP.
Ward, Charlie. 2009. 'A Tale of Two Legends' *Meanjin* Vol. 68, No. 4, pp. 93–99.
Watanabe, Tamotsu. 2013. 'Dialogue Between Sankai Juku Artistic Director Ushio Amagatsu & Theater Critic Tamotsu Watanabe' *Wochi Kochi*. https://www.wochikochi.jp/english/special/2013/11/sankaijuku.php
Webb, T.D. 1987. "*Road to the Stamping Ground* [review]' *Pacific Studies*, Vol. 11, No. 1, pp. 178–180.
Webb, Vivienne. 2002. 'Form & Content' in Webb (ed.), pp. 72–77.
Webb, Vivienne, editor and curator. 2002. *Dancing Up Country: The Art of Dorothy Napangardi*. Sydney: MCA.
Williams, Margaret. 1972. 'Mask & Cage: Stereotype in Recent Drama' *Meanjin* Vol. 31, No. 3, pp. 308–313.
Winnicott, D.W. 1971. *Playing & Reality*. London: Routledge.
Winther-Tamaki, Bert. 2011. 'The Globalist Stance of Okamoto Tarō's Tower of the Sun'. *Review of Japanese Culture & Society*, Vol. 23, pp. 81–101.
Wischusin, Robin, and Tony Chapman and Ziyin Wang. 1993. *Chronicle of Macbeth*. Edited video of performance screened on ABC, 1993. Melbourne: Playbox. Copy of author.
Wittenberg, Nicole, film dir. 1994. *The Romance of Orpheus*. DVD video. Melbourne / Brisbane: Contemporary Arts Media / Frank / Live Theatrefilm.
White, Julia. 2003. 'Drawings & Texts' *About Performance*, Vol. 5, pp. 83–98.
Wolf, Patrick. 1991. 'On Being Woken Up: The Dreamtime in Anthropology & in Australian Settler Culture' *Comparative Studies in Society & History*, Vol. 33, No. 2, pp. 197–224.
Woods, Simon, dir. 1996. *Cult of Dionysus*. DVD video. Melbourne / Brisbane: Contemporary Arts Media / Zen Zen Zo.
Woods, Simon. 2006. *Suzuki & Beyond: Adapting the Suzuki Actor Training Method*. MA thesis. University of Queensland.
Yano, Christine. 2013. *Hello Kitty's Trek Across the Pacific*. Durham: Duke UP.
Yap, Tony. 1999. 'A Mixture of Influences' in Erin Brannigan (ed.). *MAP Symposium*. Canberra: Ausdance, pp. 40–41.
Yap, Tony. 2007. Draft of Australia Council of the Arts Application for the 2008 Fellowship; manuscript courtesy of Yap.
Yap, Tony. 2017. *Strife of Light Bearer*. Video trailer. Melbourne· La Mama Theatre / Tony Yap Co. On line at: https://vimeo.com/217051804

Yap, Tony. circa 2020. CV. On line at: http://www.tonyyapcompany.com/

Yap, Tony. 2021. *Trance-Forming Dance: The Practice of Trance From Traditional Communities to Contemporary Dance.* PhD thesis, University of Melbourne.

Yap, Tony. 2022–23. Email correspondence with author, May 2022 – May 2023.

Yap, Tony, et al. 2023. *PAN-oramic Pavilion & MAP Pavilion Mini-Fest.* Program brochure, Melbourne: Tony Yap Co et al.

Yap, Tony, et al. 2011. *Tony Yap Company Annual Report.* Melbourne: Tony Yap Co et al.

Yap, Tony, et al. 1984. *Transition & Change.* Archival video documentation of live performance. Horsham/Melbourne. Courtesy of Yap.

Yap, Tony, et al. 1998. *Saint Sebastian.* Video documentation produced by Dancehouse as part of the *Mixed Metaphor* season, Melbourne. Personal copy.

Yap, Tony, et al. nd. *TYC: Tony Yap Co.* Website. Melbourne. On line at: http://www.tonyyapcompany.com/

Yap, Tony, and Peter Eckersall. 2012. *Tony Yap Interviewed by Peter Eckersall.* National Library of Australia – Oral History Transcript. Canberra: National Library of Australia. On line at: https://catalogue.nla.gov.au/Record/5981739

Zacharias, Gerhard. 1964. *Ballet, symboliek en mysterie.* Bussum: Dishoeck.

Zamorska, Magdalena. 2018. *Intense Bodily Presence: Practices of Polish Butō Dancers.* Berlin: Peter Lang.

Zen Zen Zo. 2008. *The Zen Files: A History of Zen Zen Zo Through Reviews, Articles & Interviews, 1992–2008.* Brisbane: Zen Zen Zo.

Zen Zen Zo New Zealand. nd. *Zen Zen Zo New Zealand.* Website. Christchurch. On line at: https://www.zenzenzonz.com/

Zurbrugg, Nicholas. 1989. 'Sound Art, Radio Art, & Post-Radio Performance in Australia' *Continuum,* Vol. 2, No. 2, pp. 26–49.

Index

Aboriginal: *see* First Nations Australian
Admiring La Argentina   5, 8, 20, 48, 119, 154, 189
Alice Springs   78–82, 84–86, 97–104, 127, 193–194, 198
altered states: *see* possession
Animal/God: The Great Square   177, 207–209
animality in butoh and Suzuki   10, 22, 43, 54–55, 76, 87–88, 96, 113, 117, 120–21, 148, 159, 162–165, 176–177, 182, 187–188, 192, 194–195, 199–202, 204, 207–208, 216, 269, 284–285, 291
Another Dust   62, 150
Ashikawa Yoko   31, 50–52, 55, 57, 58–59, 71, 119, 126, 143, 211, 215, 228
ausdruckstanz (dance of expression, German)   5, 7–8, 12, 16–17, 20, 37, 49, 62, 121, 189, 192, 213, 217
Australian Legend, the   29–31, 39–43, 49, 70–72, 119, 212, 236, 242, 253

Bacchae, The (including adaptations)   151–153, 223–224, 228–229, 235–236, 278–282
Baird, Bruce   4, 8–10, 13–16, 48, 52, 58, 121, 136–139, 155, 202, 213, 226, 246, 273
ballet   8, 13, 16–18, 36–37, 49, 56, 60, 81, 132, 136, 142, 189, 213, 225, 227, 233–234, 257–258
Barbe, Frances   X, 1, 27–28, 38, 141, 210, 227, 235–237, 245, 254–264, 269–272, 275–276, 281–287
Bausch, Pina   5, 22, 38, 121, 293
Big hArt   176, 188, 193–198, 293
bisoku   55, 69–70, 76, 87
Body Weather   2, 4, 6, 9, 11, 14, 18, 23–29, 43, 50–130, 133, 145, 166, 189, 195, 198, 205, 215, 248, 254, 259–60, 269, 285, 288, 291–294
Body Weather farms (Hakushu, etc)   27, 53–55, 59–61, 72, 77, 121, 124, 215, 222
Body and the Double Bass, The   154, 159, 208
Bogart, Anne   224, 239, 253, 259, 263–264
Bradley, Lynne   V, XI, 1–2, 27–29, 133, 135–141, 145, 214, 216, 246, 255–283, 286–70
Broome   36, 44, 156, 188–193, 198

Buddha's Banquet   144–145, 185
bull trance   176, 199–202
butoh
    butoh cabaret   23, 28, 58–59, 122, 136–144, 171, 177–186, 275
    butoh, early Australian criticism of   21–23
    butoh: definition & history   8–16, 20, 31–33
    butoh-fu   9, 260, 291, 294
    butoh in France   13–16, 20–21, 31–33, 38, 52–53, 58, 118–9, 121, 136, 271
    butoh in Poland   19, 33
    butoh and photography / photomedia   1, 6–9, 11, 15, 32–33, 48, 53, 58, 74, 93, 99–101, 103, 111–113, 118, 125, 134, 138–139, 159–163, 174, 179–180, 190, 203
ButohOUT!   28, 134–135, 177, 210, 286
Butoh: Piercing the Mask   13, 32, 121, 150, 223, 274
Byakkosha   18, 22, 27, 48, 147, 246, 257, 282, 298, 317

Carroll, Jacqui   XI, 1–2, 27–28, 41, 44, 211–255, 258, 262, 292–294
Chinese in Australia   32, 41–44, 46, 49, 64, 69, 71, 162–165, 190–191
chorus, choric   2, 12, 29, 141, 153, 204, 212–213, 216, 221, 228–231, 236–237, 240–241, 249, 251, 255, 272–282, 285
Chronicle of Macbeth   XI, 2, 12, 27–28, 46, 48, 153, 158, 172, 189, 211–213, 221–223, 228–238, 242, 251, 262, 276, 288–290
City to City   105–8, 122–3, 291
clown   42, 177, 186, 189, 223, 255, 259–261, 268–275, 278, 285, 292
Compression 100   105–108, 122–123
Copper Promises: Hinemihi Haka   288–294
copying and mimeticism   10, 271
Corroboree   17–19, 37, 64, 81
Crosby, Matthew   XI, 134, 153, 158, 180, 183–185, 214
Cult of Dionysus   29, 236–237, 255, 260, 278–283
Curtin, Peter   12, 225, 230–231, 251

Cuocolo, Renato 150–153
Cuocolo, Renato: *see also* IRAA

Dairakudakan V, 1–4, 11, 13, 22, 24, 27–28, 31–32, 48, 52, 58, 61, 122–124, 131–145, 155, 168–188, 202, 211–214, 221, 240, 246, 255–274, 280, 283, 286, 292
Dali, Salvador: *see* Surrealism
dancing Country 30, 34, 92–94, 127, 165, 198
dancing the landscape/site 2, 5, 14, 27–31, 34, 37–38, 41, 47, 50–57, 63–80, 83–114, 118, 120, 124–130, 162–165, 175–176, 188, 203–205, 209–210, 236, 242, 284–285, 290, 293–294
DasSHOKU series (*Tokyo DasSHOKU Girl, DasSHOKU Hora!!, DasSHOKU Cultivation!!, DasSHOKU Shake!!*) IV, 28, 140–145, 159, 177–186
Dante, Alighieri 106, 271
Dean, Beth 17, 37, 64, 81
Decay of the Angel 131, 145, 172–174, 177, 204–206
Del Amo, Martin XI, 119–124
Denley, Jim XI, 73, 84–85, 100–101, 112, 115, 158
De Quincey, Tess XI, 1–2, 5, 9, 17–19, 21, 23, 26–28, 34, 43–44, 47–131, 139–140, 143–145, 150, 158, 162–166, 189, 195, 198, 205, 210, 224, 226–227, 248, 259, 262–263, 266, 269, 284, 288, 291–293
Dictionary of Atmospheres 55, 90, 92, 94, 98–104, 110, 205, 227
Digging-Stick-Possessing Women Dreaming (Kanakurlangu Jukurrpa) 82, 93
Digging-Stick-Possessing Women Dreaming: *see also* Minamina
Dionysian performance 28–29, 118, 148, 151–154, 199, 217, 221–224, 228–230, 235–237, 255, 260, 278–283
Dispossessed, The 288–292
Doll Seventeen 29, 41, 44, 212, 235, 248–254
Dreamings 33–34, 67–68, 81–83, 86, 89, 92–95, 103, 110
Drysdale, Russel 63–64, 68, 72, 84
Dunphy, Caroline 235, 250, 252

Eckersall, Peter XI, 2, 11, 22–23, 46, 48–53, 56–66, 88, 90, 99, 103, 109–111, 131–133, 136–137, 141–151, 157–159, 166–172, 176, 179–180, 189, 198, 203–204, 240, 269, 290–293

EnTrance 142, 149, 186–188, 198, 203, 206, 287
emptiness 24–25, 30, 34–36, 55, 71, 90, 124–126, 134, 139, 165–167, 195, 200, 247–248, 266, 272, 283
Eulogy For the Living 177, 204–205, 209
ero guro nansensu (erotic grotesque nonsense) 131, 136, 140, 143, 176, 211–212, 240, 282
Expressionism 2, 5–8, 12, 16–17, 20–21, 36–38, 49, 56, 62, 74, 88, 114, 119, 123, 143, 174, 189, 192, 211–213, 217, 222, 250, 253, 283, 286, 293

Farewell Cult 172, 221, 229–231
Fine Bone China 38, 210, 255, 282–285
First Nations Australian 2–4, 13–14, 17–19, 27–30, 33–37, 43–47, 50, 63–69, 72–73, 78–106, 109–110, 124–128, 151, 155–157, 164–165, 176, 188–198, 223, 243, 248–249, 262, 277, 288, 293
flamenco 11, 13, 75, 154
Fleeting Moments 131, 142, 170–172, 178, 187
Frank Theatre 1–2, 12, 23, 28–29, 38–41, 44, 131, 136, 174, 211–214, 221, 224–227, 232–254, 258, 262–264, 268–269, 272, 276, 279–282, 284, 285–286, 292–294
Fraser, Peter 61, 69, 72, 83, 89, 100–103, 113, 119, 124
Freud, Sigmund 5, 65, 129, 140–141, 184, 244, 275
Freud: *see also* Uncanny

ganguro girl 176, 179–186
Gilbert, Helen 21–23, 63, 193, 197, 262, 279, 293
Greek theatre, Classical 148, 151, 166, 215, 218, 236, 249, 270
Grant, Stuart 27, 50, 65, 69, 80–89, 92–94, 97, 103–104, 124, 145
Gravity Feed 110, 180, 189
Greer, Germaine 90–92, 101
Grotowski, Jerzy 2, 42–43, 61, 71, 120, 132–133, 145, 150–153, 218, 239

Hakutōbō 27, 31, 46–50, 59, 74, 141, 143
haunting 3, 6, 12, 19, 25–28, 50, 64–65, 70–71, 78–79, 89–90, 103, 110, 118, 126–131, 156–158, 164–165, 174–175, 182, 191, 208, 216–217, 228, 231–232, 235, 238, 240, 276, 286, 289–294

INDEX 327

haunting: *see also* Uncanny
Heazlewood, Cheryl   133, 145
Hello Kitty   182–183, 186
Heywood, Nicola (Nikki)   38, 43, 60–61, 66–74, 78, 105, 119–124, 222, 225, 235, 263, 287
Hijikata Tatsumi   1–16, 19–25, 31–33, 48–55, 58–61, 64, 68, 71, 74, 80, 87, 90, 107, 110, 117, 119, 121, 131, 134–145, 148, 153–155, 160–165, 168, 172–173, 179–180, 185, 192, 209–211, 215, 217, 227–228, 246, 259–260, 267–270, 273–275, 280–286, 290, 294
Hijikata Tatsumi: one thousand embodied states bequeathed to Tanaka   52, 54–55, 227
Hiroshima   20–21, 62, 193–197, 256
history of the senses   63–64, 109
Horrors of Malformed Men   137, 180
Hosoe, Eikoh   6, 8, 15, 32–33, 74, 134, 138–139, 160–163, 179–180
hostess club   58–61, 135–137, 144, 178, 183
How Could You Even Begin to Understand?   28, 131, 166–175, 203
"How to Stand in Australia" (Grant & de Quincey 2008)   27, 50, 65, 69, 80, 124, 145
Hunt, Victoria   81–83, 96–103, 112–123, 119, 129, 288–294
hysterical, butoh & Suzuki as   2, 10, 24, 28, 41, 56, 62, 74, 105, 114–125, 130, 137–138, 144, 174–186, 200, 212, 220, 246–247, 251–253, 257, 270, 274–276, 294

Indigenous Australian: *see* First Nations Australians
inland sea   67–68, 81, 95, 120–122
IRAA   2, 132, 150–153, 157, 166, 199, 220
In-Compatibility   166, 169
Is/Is.2   69, 73–79
itako   55, 168, 203

Jamieson, Trevor   188–198, 293
Japanese rituals & pedagogic conventions in training   21, 59–60, 68, 78, 87, 213–214, 225–227, 239, 240–243, 262–267
Jōmon culture   15–16, 51
Jujutsu (all art is magic)   24, 134, 199–204
Jung, Carl, & Jungian perspectives   18, 147–148, 218, 227, 242–244, 258, 267–268

kabuki   7, 13, 57, 141, 155–156, 188, 216, 229–232, 238–240, 245–248, 258
Kagome   131, 158–164, 168, 171, 196, 203
Kaiin no Uma (Tale of the Sea-Dappled Horse)   2, 131–133, 137–140, 143–144, 153, 255–257, 276
kamaitachi   8, 15, 32–33, 74, 134, 138–139, 160–164, 179–180
Kasai Akira   246
Kellaway, Nigel   51, 69, 133, 189, 221–222, 226–227
Kinjiki   4–8, 48, 53
Kurosawa Akira   139, 232, 240–241, 276

Lake Mungo   18–19, 33, 44, 51, 58, 63–79, 83–89, 97, 100–103, 106, 120, 127, 131, 145, 162–165, 189, 205, 222, 226
landscape as body or bones   33–34, 37, 50, 64–67, 76–77, 158, 195, 206
Lauren, Ellen   224–232, 253, 259, 264
Lawler, Ray: *see Doll Seventeen*
Lecoq, Jacques: *see* clown
Liminal City   108, 205
Lo, Jacqueline   21–23, 44, 63, 190, 262, 279
Loth, Joanne (Jo)   213, 219, 227, 232, 235–236, 241–242, 246, 254, 258, 262–263
Love Suicides   131, 142–144, 154–158, 174, 188, 193
Lovric, Melissa   58, 61, 136–137, 141, 144–145
Lynch, Stuart   51, 57–58, 69, 75–79, 83, 105–108, 122–123

Macbeth (including adaptations)   2, 12, 27–28, 48, 54, 139, 153, 158, 172, 189, 211–213, 217, 220–223, 228–238, 242, 251–253, 258–260, 276–277, 282, 290
Maijuku   51–53, 57–63, 77, 122, 137, 222
Māori dance & culture   81, 289–294
Maro Akaji   v, 1–4, 6, 11–13, 22–24, 27–28, 31–32, 48, 52, 58, 61, 122–124, 131–145, 153–155, 168–188, 202–203, 211–214, 221, 240, 246, 255–257, 259–274, 280, 283, 286, 292
Marrugeku   5, 79, 176, 188–193, 288, 293–294
Maxwell, Ian   XI, 14, 23, 42–43, 80, 83, 96, 116, 287
MB (muscle/bones or mind/body exercise)   54, 60, 69, 86, 225
Meat Party   131, 157–158

Melaka Art & Performance Festival (MAPFest) 28, 134–135, 177, 204–205, 209–210
miburi-teburi 139–141, 168–169, 184, 265–268
mime, French 7, 223, 268
mime, French: *see also* clown
mimih 78–79, 188–189
Minamina 67–68, 81–83, 88, 92–95
Mishima Yukio XI, 1, 6–8, 134, 138–139, 145, 148, 172–174, 228
Miss Tanaka 131, 142, 154–157, 174, 188, 191, 193
Mixed Company 131, 136, 152–154, 176, 180, 199
mnemonic returns in the body, incidents of 88, 128–130, 269–270, 288, 294
Molino, Katia 189, 223, 228, 231, 293
Monday 140, 180
Moore, Richard 13, 32, 150, 223, 235, 274
Movement on the Edge 61–62

Nadoya Music and Dance Company 131, 158–164, 168, 171, 179, 196, 203
Napangardi, Dorothy, & her kin 17, 67–68, 81–83, 88, 90–95, 126–127
Naturalism 2, 27, 42, 49, 155, 158, 211, 214, 223, 231, 253, 259, 262, 269–270, 286, 293
Ngapartji Ngapartji 176, 188, 193–198
Neideck, Jeremy XI, 140, 226–227, 234, 241–242, 254, 257–258, 261–263, 286, 292
Nerve 9 26–28, 62, 105, 114–123, 130
Neville, Peter 156–163
nikutai (carnal body) 4–8, 12–15, 24, 58–59, 122–123, 217, 294
Nikutai no Hanran, or *Hijikata and the Japanese: Rebellion of the Body* 4–8, 11, 14–15, 52, 135, 215, 281
Nobbs, John XI, 1–2, 12, 18, 24, 27–28, 41, 44, 54, 211–255, 258–259, 262–264, 268, 281, 292–294
noh 16, 57, 61–62, 134, 139, 151, 157, 165, 171, 179, 200–201, 214–220, 224, 231, 245–250
Norman, Anne: *see* Nadoya
NSP (Nobbs Suzuki Practice) 1–2, 12, 28, 41, 211–214, 221, 224–225, 227, 232, 235, 239, 241–248, 253–254, 258, 263, 268, 282, 286, 292–294
NYID (Not Yet It's Difficult) 23, 189, 242, 288–292
NYID: *see also* Pledger

O'Brien, Simon 140–142, 147, 162–165, 187, 200–202
Odamura Satsuki 73, 156–165, 170–173
Odamura Satsuki: *see also* Nadoya
Oedipus, adaptations, etc 235, 238, 280
Ohno Kazuo 5–12, 20, 31–32, 48, 58, 68, 116, 119–120, 135, 143–145, 154, 173, 189, 208–209, 221–222, 246, 257–259, 274, 283, 286–287, 292
Ohno Yoshito 119–120, 124, 257–259, 268, 292
Okamoto Tarō 203
omnicentral imaging 24, 53, 69, 87–88, 113, 117, 123, 128, 259, 271, 291,
O'Neill, Lisa 235–239, 248–253
Ooldea 193–195
Orpheus: *see Romance of Orpheus*
Osorezan (Mount Osore) 168, 203
Ōsuka Isamu 18
Ōsuka Isamu: *see also* Byakkosha
OzFrank: *see* Frank

Pavis, Patrice 20, 284–285
Pigram, Dalisa 188–192, 293–294
Pigram, Dalisa: *see also* Marrugeku
phallic prostheses 179, 183–185, 280–281
physical theatre 23, 28–30, 39–43, 133, 136, 150–153, 158, 211, 221–223, 255–264, 268, 282, 288
Pledger, David XI, 23, 41, 158, 189, 219, 223, 231, 242, 288–292
possession 1–6, 16–18, 24–25, 28, 34, 55–57, 63, 77, 118, 120–121, 131, 134, 140–142, 146–151, 154–161, 168–169, 175–176, 186–188, 199–211, 219–220, 228, 232, 239–240, 244–246, 268, 290, 292
prehistoric monuments in Europe 15, 66, 109–110, 114, 121
primal 4–6, 15–19, 34, 40, 75, 86, 98, 147, 180, 202, 218–219, 227, 240–244, 249, 255, 267–268, 272, 276–282, 293
Public Image Limited (PIL) 221, 240

Quincey: *see* De Quincey, Tess

Rainsford (aka Paul Towner) 133, 145, 172–174
Rasa Sayang 177, 204–206
Rite of Spring (*Le sacre du printemps*) 16–19, 64, 77

Robertson, Jo   6, 23–26, 61, 78, 90, 121, 125, 213, 257–258, 265–267, 271, 283
Rogan, Ben   IV, XI, 134, 153, 179–185, 204
Romance of Orpheus   235–237, 258
Romeril, John   39, 142–144, 154–158, 174, 188, 239
Run: A Performance Engine   108–114, 291

Sakamoto, Michael   XI, 5, 8, 15, 33, 80, 145
Sankai Juku   4–8, 15, 26–27, 31, 48, 61, 121, 132, 135, 143–145, 257, 271–273, 277
Santos, Lynne   47, 69, 83, 89, 134, 145, 151–154, 158–162, 171, 222
Schacher, Alan   32, 51, 58, 108–110, 180
SCOT (Suzuki Company Of Toga)   27, 48, 54, 211, 215–216, 221–224, 228, 235, 238, 246, 256–259, 263
Sebastian, Saint   138–139, 153
Segments From an Inferno   105–106
shamanism: *see* possession
site-specific   28, 47, 52–55, 90–94, 98–114, 118, 124–130, 204–205, 236
site-specific: *see also Dictionary of Atmospheres*
SITI (Saratoga International Theatre Institute)   224, 253–254, 259, 263–264, 272, 282, 286
Sky Hammer   75, 95, 98, 291
SMAT (Suzuki Method of Actor Training)   1–8, 11–14, 18–20, 24–33, 41–42, 49, 60, 133, 174, 189, 211–214, 221–228, 232–235, 241–248, 253–254, 258–264, 267, 270–272, 276, 280–294
SMAT: as authoritarian: *see* Japanese pedagogic conventions in training
SMAT: vocal strain in performance   214, 231–232, 259, 263–264
SMAT: *see also* stomping
Smith, Helen   134, 139–140, 185, 255–263, 266, 276–280, 283, 286–287
Stirring, The   108–114, 210, 291–293
Snow, Peter   5, 14, 18–19, 34, 51–54, 58, 61, 67–74, 78, 83, 86–90, 95–98, 129, 189, 292
Soyinka, Wole   274, 278–281
spirit medium: *see* possession
sports culture   39–42, 52, 57, 136, 143, 223–227, 242–243, 261, 290, 294
Square of Infinity   69–70, 73–75, 87

Stalker   42, 188–189, 293
stamping: *see* stomping
Stewart, Amanda   XI, 73, 114–116, 122, 158, 222
Strangeland: *see The Dispossessed*
stomping   4, 11–14, 18, 41, 222–227, 248, 261, 280, 294
Summer of the Seventeenth Doll: see *Doll Seventeen*
Sunrise at Midnight   36, 44, 74, 131, 162–165, 174–175, 179, 207
Surrealism   7, 15, 56–58, 64, 74, 88, 107–108, 111–114, 117–118, 121, 137–141, 145, 202, 205, 256, 267, 273–275
Suzuki Tadashi   XI, 1–8, 11–14, 18–33, 36–49, 54–56, 60, 133, 153, 158, 169, 172, 174, 189–190, 211–249, 253–267, 270–272, 276–294
Suzuki Tadashi & montage, bricolage or collage   211, 220
Swain, Rachael: *see* Marrugeku
Sydney Front   42, 133, 189, 221–222
Sydney Front: *see also* Kellaway

taishū engeki   141–143, 155–157, 177–178, 185
Tanaka Min   1–6, 9–11, 14, 19, 27, 30–34, 43, 48, 51–61, 68, 70–79, 88, 99, 105–107, 110, 119–124, 128–129, 135–136, 139, 143, 174, 180, 189, 211, 215, 221–222, 225–228, 259–260, 291–292
Tanaka Min: Australian premiere   32, 48
Tanaka Min: *see also* under Hijikata & Body Weather
Tankard, Meryl   5, 38
tanztheater (German dance theatre; *see also* Ausdruckstanz)   7–8, 12, 16, 20, 37–38, 49, 121–124, 189, 192, 213, 285
Tasmanian rain dance (alleged)   218, 243
Taylor, Gretel   XI, 5, 17–18, 24–25, 30, 34–37, 51, 54–56, 61, 64, 69, 74, 81–83, 87, 95–98, 104–105, 119–121, 124–128, 134, 153, 259, 292–293
Tempest, The   272, 277–282, 293
terra nullius   30, 34–36, 47, 195
Theatre Gumbo   142, 176–180, 185–186
Toga: *see* SCOT
Tōhoku   8–9, 15, 18, 25, 32–33, 38, 51, 55, 74, 134, 138–139, 142, 159–164, 168, 179–180, 203, 210, 282–285
Tōhoku australis   38, 282–285

Tokyo DasSHOKU Girl: see DasSHOKU series
Tokyo Shock Boys 178, 240
Tony Yap Company: *see* Mixed Company
trance: *see* possession
Transition and Change 149–150, 174
Triple Alice 23, 47, 51, 54, 55, 63, 67, 71–72, 75, 78–104, 109–110, 117, 124, 127–128, 145, 291–293
Tucker, Albert 64

Umiumare, Yumi Tsuchiya IV, 1–2, 5, 23–29, 34–36, 43–44, 69, 73–74, 122–124, 131–145, 150, 153–199, 203–206, 209–211, 214, 240, 257–259, 263, 268, 286–287, 292–293
Uncanny 3, 6–7, 27–28, 65, 70–71, 89–90, 129, 196–198, 291–292
unheimlich: *see* Uncanny

Van de Ven, Frank 51, 57, 60, 83, 96–98, 119–121, 124, 189, 198, 291–292
Nijinsky, Vaslav 16–19
Viewpoints 29, 254, 259, 263–264, 272, 282, 286

Ward, Russell 29–31, 39–43, 49, 70–72, 119, 212, 236, 242, 253

Warlpiri & their dance 64, 80–83, 87–95, 102, 126–127
whakapapa 81, 291
whirling dervish 151, 236
white butoh 4
Woods, Simon XI, 1–3, 27–28, 41, 214–216, 221, 232, 255–268, 276–282
Wuturi Theatre, Korea: *see The Dispossessed*

Yap, Tony Ding Chai XI, 1–2, 11, 24–28, 43–44, 48, 69, 73–74, 108, 124, 131–136, 142, 145–180, 186–188, 198–210, 219–220, 247, 292–294
yamamba 159, 179–187
yarning 86, 90–94, 100–103, 110, 194–195, 198
yōkai 8, 15, 32–33, 74, 131, 137–9, 158–164, 176–187
Yuendumu 17, 64, 81–84, 126–127

Zeitgeist 258–260, 270–276
Zero Zero 145, 166–170, 203
Zen Zen Zo Physical Theatre 2, 10, 21–23, 28–29, 34, 39, 131, 136, 139, 174, 177, 185, 214–216, 221, 227, 232, 235–237, 241, 255–287, 292–293

Printed in the United States
by Baker & Taylor Publisher Services